Renn Butler has performed a great s[...] readers who are seriously involved in [...] and who have become convinced that there are more things in heaven and earth than are dreamt of in the conventional philosophies of the modern world view and mainstream psychology. Based on research that has been taught and studied during the past thirty years in graduate school seminars and public lectures, this is the first book to set forth the basic outline of that research for a larger public. Describing systematic correlations between experiences in non-ordinary states of consciousness and planetary cycles, Butler has also included his own insights and impressions after decades of work in this field. The writing is clear and accessible. The spirit of the book is modest and compassionate. The resulting work is an invaluable guide for all those courageous individuals and therapists who are engaged in exploring the unfolding mystery of the psyche and its relationship with the greater cosmos.

Richard Tarnas, professor of psychology and cultural history, California Institute of Integral Studies, author of *The Passion of the Western Mind and Cosmos and Psyche.*

Pathways to Wholeness

Pathways to Wholeness

Archetypal Astrology and
the Transpersonal Journey

Renn Butler

muswell hill press

London • New York

First published by Muswell Hill Press, London, 2014

© 2014 Renn Butler

www.muswellhillpress.co.uk.

British Library CIP Data available

ISBN: 978-1-908995-04-9

Printed in the United Kingdom

To Rick,
in gratitude and appreciation.

Contents

Acknowledgments..xiii

Chapter 1: The Birth of a New World View 1
Breakthrough in Europe 1
An Unexpected Rosetta Stone.. 3

**Chapter 2: Transpersonal Psychology and Archetypal
     Astrology: The Research of Stanislav Grof and
     Richard Tarnas** 7
Stanislav Grof's Expanded Cartography of the Human Psyche 7
The Perinatal Matrices 9
Richard Tarnas' Archetypal Astrology 15
Tarnas' Correlations with the Perinatal Sequence 19
Several Further Distinctions.. 26

**Chapter 3: Issues in Psychedelic Therapy and
     Self-Exploration** 29
Non-specific Amplifiers of Mental Processes 30
The Level of Trust and Support... 30
Set and Setting... 31
The Dosage, Quality, and Purity of Psychoactive Substances 33
Medical and Psychiatric Contraindications for Holotropic States 35

Chapter 4: The Astrological Archetypes 37
Sun.. 37
Moon 38
Mercury 39
Venus 41
Mars.. 42
Jupiter 44
Saturn 46
Uranus 49
Neptune 51
Pluto 54

Chapter 5: The Transit Cycles of Neptune-Neptune,
    Saturn-Saturn, Pluto-Pluto, and Uranus-Uranus............57
  Transits of Neptune-Neptune 58
  Transits of Saturn-Saturn.. 61
  Transits of Pluto-Pluto.. 66
  Transits of Uranus-Uranus 71

Chapter 6: The Archetypal Pairs... 77
  Transits of Neptune 77
  Sun-Neptune.. 77
  Moon-Neptune 81
  Mercury-Neptune 86
  Venus-Neptune 90
  Mars-Neptune.. 93
  Jupiter-Neptune 95
  Transits of Saturn 100
  Sun-Saturn.. 100
  Moon-Saturn.. 105
  Mercury-Saturn 111
  Venus-Saturn 114
  Mars-Saturn... 118
  Jupiter-Saturn 124
  Transits of Pluto 127
  Sun-Pluto... 128
  Moon-Pluto.. 132
  Mercury-Pluto 137
  Venus-Pluto 140
  Mars-Pluto... 143
  Jupiter-Pluto 149
  Transits of Uranus 156
  Sun-Uranus.. 156
  Moon-Uranus 161
  Mercury-Uranus 164
  Venus-Uranus 167
  Mars-Uranus.. 171
  Jupiter-Uranus 175
  The Fundamental Alignments 179
  Saturn-Neptune.. 180
  Saturn-Pluto... 184
  Saturn-Uranus.. 193
  Uranus-Pluto.. 201
  Neptune-Pluto.. 208

Uranus-Neptune 215
The Modifying Alignments 223
Sun-Sun 223
Sun-Moon 224
Sun-Mercury 226
Sun-Venus 227
Sun-Mars 229
Sun-Jupiter 230
Moon-Moon 233
Moon-Mercury 234
Moon-Venus 235
Moon-Mars 236
Moon-Jupiter 237
Mercury-Mercury 239
Mercury-Venus 240
Mercury-Mars 241
Mercury-Jupiter 242
Venus-Venus 244
Venus-Mars 245
Venus-Jupiter 247
Mars-Mars 249
Mars-Jupiter 251
Jupiter-Jupiter 254

Chapter 7: Putting It All Together: Scenarios in

        Self-Exploration **257**
1. A Grieving Elderly Lady Needs Emotional Comfort and Relief.... 257
2. An Organizer of Intentional Dance Events Wants to
   Add an Increased Level of Safety for His Participants 259
3. Three Spiritual Friends Support Each Other in
   Healing Sessions with Psilocybin Mushrooms 261
4. A Member of the Clergy Seeks a Direct Experience
   of the Numinous Principle 262
5. A Team of Therapists Conducting Psychedelic Sessions
   in a Healthcare-Funded Program Consults the Transits
   of Their Patients 265
6. A Breathwork Practitioner Looks at the World
   Transits Before Scheduling a Workshop 265
7. A Married Couple Considers Sitting for Each Other
   in Internalized Psychedelic Sessions 266
8. A Graduate Student Organizes a Psychedelic Healing
   Session for Himself 267

9. A Military Veteran Suffering from PTSD Begins a
   Course of MDMA Psychotherapy 271
10. A Young Meditator Experiences Kundalini and
   Spiritual Emergency 272
11. A Young Woman Diagnosed with Bipolar Disorder
   Wants to Stop Taking Lithium 275

Epilogue..277
Endnotes..281
Bibliography and Suggested Reading..293
Index..305

Acknowledgments

When I was nineteen years old, I had the opportunity to live as a work-scholar at the Esalen Institute in Big Sur, California, at a time when both Stanislav Grof and Richard Tarnas were on the staff, Grof as an honored Scholar-in-Residence and Tarnas as Director of Programs. Through many fascinating discussions with Tarnas, I immersed myself in their research together. This profound year eventually culminated in a month-long seminar in transpersonal psychology with Stan and Christina Grof and many prominent guests from the emerging new field.

I left Esalen encouraged to pursue my own study and exploration, while maintaining a student relationship with Tarnas and some intensive training in Holotropic Breathwork. Along with conceptual understanding, I am deeply grateful to Tarnas for decades of intellectual mentoring and emotional support, and to both Tarnas and the Grofs for their far-reaching spiritual vision. I hope that this book is able to convey some of the same spirit of responsible inner exploration and grounded optimism that has inspired me for so many years.

Thank you to the many people who participated in our workshops in Victoria over the past two decades and my colleagues in the Holotropic Breathwork community around the world. Thanks also to the artists and family members who gave me permission to use their beautiful and evocative mandalas, which are presented in color in the e-book format.

I owe so much to the exceptional people—residents, managers, and staff—of the group homes where I had the privilege of working for over twenty years as a health care worker during the research and writing phases of this book. The nurturing family atmosphere of these homes provided a precious real-world complement to the decades of intense mental focus. Much appreciation also to my astrology colleagues and world-music dance friends in Victoria for many great years of fun and companionship.

I am indebted to my editor Keiron Le Grice for countless invaluable suggestions and improvements, one of a handful of scholars with the background in archetypal astrology to give this book the care it needed. I am also grateful to John Lankford and Rick Tarnas for reading large sections of the manuscript. Finally, many thanks to my publishers at Muswell Hill

Press, Tim Read and Mark Chaloner, for their constructive suggestions and patience during the long rewrites and completion of this project.

For brief feedback, technical support, or helpful comments on specific sections, my appreciation goes to Anna Lundeen, Grant Smith, Jean Ure, Derril Butler, Janet Smith, Chad Harris, Geraldine Pluyms, Nadine Plotnikoff, Adelia MacWilliam, Karen Lawrence, Melanie Lichtinger, Dhyani Jo Sinclair, Donna Dorsey, Jason Youngman, Felix Reuben, Robert Gamble, Forrest Boden, Sarah Butler, Kayt Mills, Renee Storey-Lucier, Carole Neeves, Diana Inouye, Silvia Guersenzvaig, Tom Mattson, Kelly Kerr, and Tammy Nielsen. A warm thank you to Deborah Hayden for helping me to complete the Holotropic Breathwork training. I also received important personal support and illumination on key issues in archetypal and holotropic astrology from discussions with Matthew Stelzner.

The generous-hearted people and mystical natural setting of Esalen and Big Sur during my formative twenties played a deeply inspiring and healing role in my life. A special appreciation to John Soper, Carolyn Soper, Gayle Silverman, Gaye Wessel, Brian Lyke, Dick and Christine Price, Claire Carter, and Rita Rohen. I am also grateful to my parents for the courageous steps they took in finding their own life paths and for setting positive examples of self-exploration.

Finally, this book would not have been possible without the emotional encouragement of my friends and colleagues Carol Trescott, Patrick Johnson, Janat Dundas, Ariel Sun, John Lankford, Lorna Kohler, Christy Fisher, Pat Amos, William Van Gastel, Mima Djordjevic, Jeremy Walsh, and Pamela Hedley. I am very grateful for their support over many years.

R.B.
December 2013
Victoria

CHAPTER 1

The Birth of a New World View

Breakthrough in Europe

In the mid-1960s, Stanislav Grof, a young Czechoslovakian psychiatrist working at the Psychiatric Research Institute in Prague, made some extraordinary discoveries concerning the fundamental structures of the human psyche. Conducting sessions with a wide range of individuals in a program of systematic LSD psychotherapy, Grof and his clients encountered experiences that gradually and then irrevocably challenged the orthodox Freudian model in which he and his colleagues were working.

The experiences that emerged during these sessions suggested a far deeper understanding of the human psyche and the cosmos itself than had been previously imagined in any existing psychological theory. After supervising over 3000 sessions and studying the records of another 2000 from colleagues around the world, Grof eventually introduced a far-reaching new model that accounted for the observations of his clients' sessions, integrated a number of other psychological theories, and reached into areas of human spirituality described by the great mystical traditions of the world.

Grof's research, although representing a dramatic breakthrough in Western psychiatry and psychology, is supported by many precedents in non-Western and preindustrial societies. Since the dawn of history, guided *non-ordinary states of consciousness* have played a central role in the spiritual and ritual life of humanity. Stretching back more than 30,000 years, the shamans of ancient cultures began their healing professions through a spontaneous or induced experience of death and rebirth. In a firsthand way, they explored territories of the psyche that transcend the boundaries of normal individual awareness. Similarly, in the rites of passage, initiates were guided into non-ordinary—or what Grof has termed *holotropic* (from *holos*, meaning "wholeness"; and *trepein*, meaning "moving toward")—states of consciousness and had a personal experience of higher realms that transcend the physical world.

In the ancient mystery religions of the Mediterranean, neophytes participated in various mind-expanding processes in order to move beyond the limits of individual awareness and experience directly the sacred or *numinous* dimensions of existence. The celebrated Mother Goddess mysteries of Eleusis, for example, which were held near Athens for almost two-thousand years, we are now virtually certain used *ergot*, a naturally occurring form of LSD.[1] Many of the creative and intellectual giants of Western culture, including figures such as Pythagoras, Plato, Aristotle, Epictetus, Euripedes, Sophocles, Plutarch, Pindar, Marcus Aurelius, and Cicero, all attest to the life-changing power of their experiences at Eleusis or one of the other mystery sites.

As well as the ritual use of psychedelic substances, many cultures have used methods such as trance dancing, rhythmic drumming, sensory overload and sensory deprivation, sleep deprivation, breathing maneuvers, fasting, meditation, and other techniques to enter holotropic states. Preindustrial cultures around the world understood an important fact of human nature that we in the modern West have forgotten—that exploring the psyche can mediate a profound reconnection with the cosmic creative principle, helping people to heal a range of emotional and physical problems, transcend their fear of death, and reach a more integrated level of functioning in everyday life. Modern consciousness research, such as that conducted by Grof, has found that individuals who undergo these transformative processes automatically develop an interest in spirituality of a universal, non-sectarian, and all-encompassing nature. They also discover within themselves a sense of planetary citizenship, a high importance given to warm human relationships, and the desire to live a more simple and satisfying life in harmony with nature and ecological values.

The considerable time and resources that other cultures devoted to finding effective techniques for exploring the inner terrains of the psyche is in marked contrast to the values in our modern industrial society. The dominant world view in Western civilization is concerned primarily with the external and physical layers of reality. In many ways it denies the existence of the human psyche altogether, and especially of higher spiritual or transpersonal states.

Grof's research thus provides an unexpected gateway to a deeper knowledge of the long neglected inner world. As we will see, the systematic exploration of the unconscious in holotropic states can initiate a profound transformation of awareness—a transformation that many now believe is urgently needed if we are to face and successfully overcome the great problems of our time. However, the journey into the heart of the psyche can be an immensely challenging process, exposing individuals to the depths and heights of human emotional experience. A map of the inner terrain, a way of understanding and predicting what might take place during holotropic-exploration sessions, would therefore be of invaluable benefit.

An Unexpected Rosetta Stone

For years, Grof and his colleagues had looked unsuccessfully for some kind of diagnostic system—such as the *Minnesota Multiphasic Personality Inventory* test (MMPI), Shostrom's *Personal Orientation Inventory* (POI), the *Rorschach Inkblot Test*, and others—to predict the experiences of their clients in deep self-exploration. Decades later, when the cultural historian Richard Tarnas discovered and systematically applied what Grof would later call the "Rosetta Stone" of archetypal astrology to this problem, Grof had to ironically concede that the one successful predictive technique turned out to be a system that was even more controversial and beyond the range of conventional science than his research in psychedelic therapy. Despite their deep initial skepticism toward astrology, however, the correlations that he and Tarnas observed were striking and consistent over time. Whether the catalyst was Holotropic Breathwork, a psychoactive substance, or a spontaneous eruption of unconscious contents during a psychospiritual crisis, archetypal astrology provides, in Grof's words, "the only system that can successfully predict both the content and timing of experiences encountered in non-ordinary states of consciousness in experiential psychotherapy."[2]

Given the widespread misunderstanding of and skepticism toward astrology in the modern era, a brief preface is required before we proceed. Although many of the founders of modern science—notably Johannes Kepler and Galileo Galilei—retained a deep belief in the principles as well as the practice of astrology, and of a higher cosmic intelligence or God, subsequent generations would later discard this understanding as the relic an older time. Although the astrological vision became deeply discredited in the modern scientific West, the world view underlying it maintained credibility and continued to flourish in the philosophical movements of late Neoplatonism, Idealism, and Romanticism, in a direct lineage from Socrates and Plato.

This situation began to change in the mid-twentieth century, however, with the work of the pioneering psychiatrist C. G. Jung. Jung's discovery of the archetypes of the collective unconscious, his formulation of synchronicity ("an acausal connecting principle"), and his speculations concerning the *anima mundi* (world soul) provided a conceptual framework for the mature rebirth of a more psychologically oriented and nuanced form of astrology. Brought to fruition through the writing of figures such as Dane Rudhyar, Robert Hand, and Liz Greene, this new approach drew on the insights of Jungian depth psychology while leaving behind many of the fatalistic dogmas of the old astrological tradition. Hand's work also set the stage for a much more rigorously self-critical and self-questioning discipline.[3]

Then Grof's friendship and collaboration with Tarnas was to initiate another major leap in the field. A highly respected philosopher and psychologist, as well as historian, Tarnas gained international acclaim with his best-selling *The Passion of the Western Mind* (1991), which went on to become required reading in a number of university courses around the world. He followed this in 2006 with *Cosmos and Psyche,* in which he presented over five-hundred pages of systematic and compelling evidence to support his groundbreaking theory.

Tarnas begins by introducing the concept of archetypes that has played such an important role in the Western philosophical tradition. For now, we can describe the archetypes simply as primordial patterns of experience, which influence all people and cultures in the form of basic habit patterns, instincts and emotions. In *Cosmos and Psyche's* bold hypothesis, Tarnas suggests that the dynamic interplay of these timeless universals that have shaped our history occurs in coincidence with geometric alignments between the planets and the Earth, intelligible through an emerging epistemology and method of analysis which he calls *archetypal astrology.*

In contrast with traditional astrological belief and practice, the archetypal approach that Tarnas introduces is non-fatalistic and non-deterministic. The archetypes are recognized at all times as being complexly multivalent and multidimensional—taking different forms in different situations and at different times in people's lives. Each archetypal complex can manifest in a wide range of possible expressions, while still being true to its basic thematic character. Tarnas carefully demonstrates that the methodology he presents is *archetypally* predictive rather than *concretely* predictive. Although planetary alignments can illuminate many essential characteristics of an historical epoch or individual life experience, and even suggest basic expected characteristics of an upcoming period, he emphasizes that the specific concrete expression the archetypes will take at any time remains indeterminate—contingent on additional factors such as cultural context, free will, co-creative participation, and perhaps unmeasurables such as karma, grace, and chance.[4]

It should be acknowledged that many of the fundamental tenets of the emerging archetypal world view concerning the nature of the human psyche and of the universe itself are compatible with the most recent branches of modern science, including quantum-relativistic physics,

Pribram's holographic model of the brain, Sheldrake's study of morphogenetic fields and morphic resonance in biology, Prigogine's study of dissipative structures, systems theory, chaos theory, cybernetics and information theory, the anthropic principle in astrophysics, and others.[5] Grof also mentions the pioneering attempts of Ken Wilber and the successful accomplishment of Ervin Laszlo in integrating transpersonal psychology into a new comprehensive paradigm.[6] I would further note Keiron Le Grice's work in *The Archetypal Cosmos*, which draws on the implications of Tarnas' research and integrates many of the new scientific theories in direct support of an archetypal or holotropic world view.[7] Perhaps the most concise way to describe this emerging paradigm in science is the realization that consciousness, rather than being an accidental by-product of neurophysiological and biochemical processes in the brain, is an integral component of the universe itself.[8]

The most well-known area of Tarnas' study to most readers has been his exploration of cyclically unfolding archetypal dynamics in human history and culture, deeply informed by the principles of Jungian and transpersonal depth psychology. A less widely known aspect of his inquiry, and the area on which this book concentrates, is based on his research with Grof into holotropic states of consciousness. In 1990, I proposed the term *holotropic astrology* to describe this facet of Tarnas' research that is specifically concerned with holotropic states.[9]

Tarnas refers to astrology as a kind of "archetypal telescope" directed on the psyche, a way of understanding and contextualizing the material that emerges in deep self-exploration. Grof similarly concludes that the role of holotropic and psychedelic states of consciousness in psychology is comparable to that of the microscope in biology and the telescope in astronomy. When responsibly combined, the therapeutic effectiveness of these powerful magnifying processes of the psyche cannot be overstated. During my own three decades of research with workshops, consultations and personal experience, I have come to believe that archetypal astrology and holotropic exploration have the potential to revolutionize humanity's relationship with its deeper nature and help us to rediscover a more harmonious relationship with each other, the natural world, and the larger cosmos.

CHAPTER 2

Transpersonal Psychology and Archetypal Astrology: The Research of Stanislav Grof and Richard Tarnas

Stanislav Grof's Expanded Cartography of the Human Psyche

In 1976, following the ban on medical research using psychedelic substances, Grof and his partner, Christina Grof, developed a comparable non-drug technique for entering holotropic states, which they called Holotropic Breathwork. During fifty-five years of research using powerful drug and non-drug catalysts, Grof discovered that individuals who enter holotropic states of consciousness have access to three broad layers of experience.

The first layer is referred to as the *biographical*. This layer contains most of the emotional material known in conventional forms of psychotherapy. Individuals who access the biographical layer of their psyches in holotropic states confront traumas and conflicts left over from physical and sexual abuse, a hostile family atmosphere, sibling rivalry, or severe toilet training. They may work through memories of emotional deprivation and unmet needs in infancy, such as isolation in an incubator or lack of bonding. They can also discharge leftover emotional traces from serious illnesses, operations, and accidents, an important category of experiences missed by most of the major psychological schools. Especially significant are those that involve a threat to breathing such as partial suffocation, near-drowning, diphtheria, or whooping cough.

The next layer of experiences that people encounter in deep self-exploration Grof termed the *perinatal* layer (from *peri*, meaning "surrounding" and *natalis*, meaning "birth"). Perinatal experiences are based around the memories of birth labor and delivery, combined with dramatic encounters with dying and impermanence in human life. As Grof's patients worked through these experiences, their awareness automatically opened out into ecstatic spiritual dimensions in the universe at large. Consciously reliving the stages of biological birth coincided with a profound spiritual rebirth and transcendence of the fear of death.

Beyond the perinatal layer is a broad category of experiences that Grof termed the *transpersonal* or *Jungian* layer of the psyche, because Jung was one of the first major Western psychiatrists to integrate transpersonal themes in his understanding of the psyche. During transpersonal experiences, people have access to material normally considered beyond the range of individual awareness. The most common of these are embryonic, ancestral, racial, or collective memories; identification with other people, groups of people, or all of humanity; past life experiences; identification with the consciousness of specific animals, plants, or inorganic materials; archetypes and mythological sequences; and encounters with the Universal Mind, Absolute Consciousness, or the Supracosmic Void.

Transpersonal experiences, by their very nature, represent a serious conceptual challenge to certain basic tenets of the Newtonian-Cartesian model that has dominated Western science since the seventeenth century, a model focused almost exclusively on the external, physical layers of reality. As well as resulting in profound emotional transformations, transpersonal experiences often include detailed information about aspects of the universe that were previously unknown to the individual. Many of these insights can then later be independently verified. Grof concludes that transpersonal phenomena as well as observations in other fields, such as the systematic study of near-death experiences (NDEs), out-of-body experiences (OOBEs), and highly improbable meaningful coincidences (synchronicities), fall in the category of what science refers to as "anomalous phenomena."[1] In the history of science, when enough of these kinds of anomalous observations have accumulated, there is usually a period of tension during which proponents of the older paradigm actively resist any integration of the unexplainable data and observations. However, eventually, a new and more inclusive scientific model emerges to successfully replace the previous one. Many researchers believe we are currently in this kind of transition period.[2]

Transpersonal experiences suggest not only that consciousness itself is a fundamental aspect of every part of the universe, but that the human psyche seems to possess a dual nature. In the everyday or *hylotropic* mode of awareness, meaning literally "matter-oriented consciousness" (from the Greek *hyle*="matter" and *trepein*="oriented toward" or "moving toward" something), the human mind functions much as conventional science describes, essentially oriented toward a specific time and place in the material world. However, under certain conditions, the psyche seems to have access to experiences involving a wide range of other times and places, essentially to the entire field of universal consciousness.

Grof compares the confusion and disorientation created by the new observations in modern consciousness research with the conceptual cataclysm that occurred in physics in the first three decades of the twentieth century with the advent of Einstein's relativity theories and quantum mechanics. He further suggests that the radical revisions that will be needed in our scientific world view to integrate the anomalous phenomena from consciousness research represent a logical completion of the changes that have already occurred in our understanding of the world of matter. Like many other researchers in these converging fields, he is cautious but clearly excited about the possibility of this paradigm shift occurring in the near future and believes that it is well underway.

The Perinatal Matrices

Grof's discovery and systematic mapping of the perinatal layer of the human psyche is one of his most important contributions to Western psychotherapy and psychiatry, and we can now consider this research in more depth. He found that perinatal sequences tend to emerge in four broad, overlapping clusters of experience, which he termed the *Basic Perinatal Matrices*.

Basic Perinatal Matrix I—The Amniotic Universe, Union with the Mother

Grof's Basic Perinatal Matrix I (or *BPM* I) is based around the intrauterine unity between mother and fetus. In a healthy womb, the conditions for the fetus are close to ideal. Oxygen and nourishment are supplied and waste products are taken away through the umbilical cord and holotropic research suggests that in such conditions the fetus enjoys a profound emotional and spiritual connection with the mother.

People who access these experiences can relive specific biological details of fetal existence such as hearing the mother's heartbeat or the peristaltic action of the intestines, as well as specific emotional states from her everyday life. These memories are overlaid with themes from nature that share with the intrauterine state a free-flowing lack of boundaries, such as an identification with serene aquatic life forms, with the consciousness of the ocean, or with interstellar space. Journeyers may also access states of blissful cosmic union depicted in various cultural forms, including existence in heaven or paradise, *atman-Brahman* union, the Tao, *samadhi*, or *Tat Tvam Asi* ("Thou art that"). Grof refers to this category of unitive states as the *oceanic* or *Apollonian* type of ecstasy. Related archetypally to the planet *Neptune*, these oceanic states are among the most profound experiences that human beings can have and satisfy our greatest yearning to reconnect with the cosmic creative principle.[3]

The first perinatal matrix also has a difficult side, based on situations where the mother was under stress or ill, using drugs or alcohol, or had ambivalent feelings toward the pregnancy. Individuals accessing these *disturbances of intrauterine life* can relive the specific chemical and emotional conditions in the womb. These are often accompanied by transpersonal elements of a similar thematic type such as identification with fish in polluted waters, contaminated nature, negative astral influences, or experiments by insidious demons. Grof observed that full experience of this material leads to unusually deep healing and a sense of having consumed the toxic energies. When unhealed, it can be an important source of hypochondria and psychotic distortions of reality in later life. In milder forms, people with unresolved amniotic memories may have a deep fear of rejection and problems bonding emotionally with other human beings.

Basic Perinatal Matrix II—Cosmic Engulfment and "No Exit"

Grof's second perinatal matrix (BPM II) is based around the onset of labor. The situation in the womb deteriorates radically as first noxious chemicals and then claustrophobic pressures interrupt what is often a blissful and ecstatic connection with the mother. The cervix is not yet dilated and the fetus is pressed from all sides by the contracting uterine walls.

Individuals who access these memories experience overwhelming feelings of entrapment, encagement, hopelessness, helplessness, and guilt that extend outward into their perception of the entire universe. They identify deeply with the victims from many times and places, including populations devastated by famine and plagues, those who died in all the wars and concentration camps of history, or with mothers and infants who have died in labor. Themes from nature include insects trapped in a spider's web, fish ensnared by an octopus, or animals slaughtered by predators.

People influenced by BPM II may also experience various archetypal sequences such as encounters with the Devouring Mother or Judging God, loss of paradise, existence in hell, or cosmic engulfment. These themes are depicted in many cultural forms, relatively independent of the person's culture of origin or beliefs. Full experience of the "no exit" material in holotropic states automatically consumes its negative effect in the psyche and allows the process to move to the next stage.[4]

Basic Perinatal Matrix III—The Death-Rebirth Struggle

Grof's third perinatal matrix (BPM III) is based around the dynamic stage of labor with a corresponding activation of powerful biological energies. The cervix is now open and the infant is slowly forced down the birth canal by uterine contractions that range between fifty and one hundred pounds of force. This leads to a synergistic struggle of both mother and fetus to end the often intense suffering that they are inadvertently inflicting on each other.

Subjects working through this material experience crushing mechanical pressures, an activation of aggression, and a sense of *titanic fight*. Grof notes that aggression is a natural response of any organism subject to life-threatening situations or extreme pain. In the process of working through these leftover emotions, people can have images of active attacks in wars and revolutions, volcanic explosions, or mythological battle scenes. A distinguishing feature of BPM III is that subjects tend to identify experientially with both victims and perpetrators—as well as watching as an observer—reflecting the fact that in the dynamic stage of labor the situation is not hopeless, and the individual begins to simultaneously identify with the driving forces of the mother's contracting body.

Grof discovered that people working through this material can also experience *sadomasochistic feelings*, based on the suffocation during labor. The blood and oxygen supply to the fetus is supplied through the umbilical cord, which is fed by arteries wound through the uterine walls. During each contraction, the flow of blood through these arteries is cut or diminished and this is experienced as suffocation. It is a documented biological phenomenon that choking creates a strange form of sexual arousal, and that intense pain or torture can also lead to an extreme type of ecstasy that transcends pain and pleasure. These phenomena are observed in men hanged on the gallows, who frequently get erections or ejaculate, in the reports of concentration camp surivors, and in the files of Amnesty International. Other manifestations are the practices of *autoerotic asphyxiation* and the *self-flagellation* of certain religious sects.[5] The close connection between choking and suffering, sexual arousal, and spiritual ecstasy seems to offer a kind of built-in escape valve for human consciousness. When the intensity of suffering reaches beyond a certain point, our psyche is somehow able to transcend the limits of the ego and reconnect with its cosmic identity.

Many births involve this kind of prolonged suffocation, suffering, and sexual arousal. As Grof documents, the fact that our first sexual experience occurs in the context of the life-threatening pain, suffocation, and activation of aggression during delivery provides a logical psychodynamic basis for many types of sexual variations and dysfunctions in later life.[6] Some mothers also report that giving birth resembles the ultimate sexual orgasm. Ideally, people have an opportunity to do their deep inner work before pregnancy, so that undigested perinatal material in their own psyches does not complicate their ability to surrender to the powerful natural forces of delivery.

Subjects working through material from the dynamic stage of labor also face another set of experiences which Grof termed *scatological*. These are based on the fetus' encounter with blood, mucus, fetal liquid, and sometimes feces or urine, although episodes in holotropic states clearly exceed what the infant could have actually experienced. During the process of confronting the mandatory waste products of biological life, subjects can have images of wallowing in excrement or wading through all the sewage lines on the planet. Similarly, while facing the inevitable decay of the physical body, they can see piles of rotting and putrefied corpses.

Journeyers in holotropic states can also encounter *demonic* sequences. These often begin with issues around the nature of evil and the relationship between good and evil, and eventually deepen into a full confrontation with demonic archetypes. In his clinical work, Grof observed that facing this material has unusually deep healing effects, especially on conditions of chronic physical pain.[7]

Finally, subjects pass through experiences of purifying fire, described by Grof as *pyrocatharsis*. This can take the form of vast conflagrations and burning cities, nuclear explosions, or of fire in a more symbolic form. As this happens, they have a sense the fire is purifying everything that is rotten and corrupt in their souls and preparing them for rebirth.

Perinatal experiences are often accompanied by dramatic physical manifestations, including nausea and projectile vomiting, frantic motor phenomena, explosive discharges of aggression, profuse sweating, and hypersalivation. Subjects may also release enormous amounts of tension in tremors, twitches, jerks, and complex twisting movements that closely resemble the infant's positions during labor. Many of these obstetric details, such as breech birth or use of forceps, can later be independently verified. As the Grofs write:

> Memories of various stages of the birth trauma—Basic Perinatal Matrices or BPMs—belong to the most common experiences in Holotropic Breathwork sessions. They accurately portray various aspects of the birth process, often with photographic details, even in individuals who have no intellectual knowledge of the circumstances of their birth (Grof 2006). This can be accompanied by various physical manifestations indicating that the memory

of birth reaches to the cellular level. We have seen individuals reliving birth develop bruises in places where forceps was applied, without knowing this was part of their early history; the accuracy of this fact was later confirmed by parents or birth records. We have also witnessed changes of skin color and *petechiae* (tiny purplish red spots caused by seeping of small amounts of capillary blood into the skin) appearing in people who were born with the umbilical cord twisted around their neck.[8]

The transpersonal side of BPM III may include experiences of temptation, sacrifice, purgatory, or judgment. Subjects can also identify with dying-and-reborn deities such as Christ, Persephone, Dionysus, or Osiris, with mythological heroes such as Hercules performing his labors, or with primal cosmic deities such as Shiva or Kali. The experiences in this matrix culminate in a kind of driving arousal that transcends pain and pleasure, which Grof refers to as the *volcanic* or *Dionysian* type of ecstasy. Facing this material in supportive contexts is followed by dramatic psychological and emotional breakthroughs and the disappearance of symptoms that had been resistant to all previous approaches.

Some of the most fundamental problems in a human lifetime can be seen as a replay of birth, an attempt by the psyche to complete and integrate the experience—as if, Grof observes, we have been born biologically but not yet emotionally. The psyche has a relentless tendency to create and draw toward itself experiences that match the thematic quality of people's inner material. Thus, an individual with leftover trauma from choking in the birth canal will unconsciously tend to create situations of high stress, in which there is "no room to breathe" or with "the world closing in." These patterns can persist indefinitely until the material is faced on the level from which it originates, as powerful emotions within the unconscious.[9]

Although the universal presence of perinatal material in the psyche may seem new or unusual to some readers, Grof points out that each of the major BPM III themes being discussed, for example, has clear manifestations in the outer world. The aggressive side of BPM III can be seen in the Earth's long history of war, conflict, and terrorism. The sexual element is taking both positive and negative forms, in erotic emancipation as well as in sexual violence and exploitation. Demonic themes are evident in acts of insatiable greed and cruelty around the world, and the scatological dimension in the ongoing degradation of our environment, and in a more symbolic way as economic and political corruption.

And finally, though I am not sure if Grof mentions this in his writing, I would add that unfaced *pyrocathartic* elements of BPM III could be seen as manifesting in the dual threats of nuclear holocaust and global warming, driven by our destructive and self-destructive addiction to fossil fuels. There are clear counterparts of each of these external problems, in the psyche, and holotropic research suggests that confronting them internally will help lead to a dramatic reduction of their effects in the outer world.[10]

Basic Perinatal Matrix IV—Rebirth and Separation from the Mother

Grof's BPM IV is based around the completed delivery and birth, as the infant leaves the life-threatening confinement of the birth canal and begins separate biological existence. Although in many ways the variable conditions in the early days of life, such as hunger, thirst, heat and cold, are less ideal than the intrauterine state, in comparison with the challenges in the birth canal, the post-natal situation is experienced as a dramatic liberation from danger and reconnection with the nourishing Feminine principle. These ecstatic episodes will then be further enhanced by tender bonding and breastfeeding between mother and newborn.

Individuals engaged in deep self-exploration under the influence of BPM IV experience a cluster of themes centered around breakthrough and transcendence. The volcanic arousal and suffering of the previous stage of BPM III eventually reach the extreme limit, then culminate in a sense of total failure on every imaginable level—physically, emotionally, intellectually, morally, and spiritually. Individuals feel that they have hit the absolute "rock bottom" of existence, an experience usually referred to as *ego death.*

Grof observed that this is almost immediately followed by visions of blinding white or golden light, peacock feathers and spectra patterns, and the inside of great halls and cathedrals—representing the enormous expansion of space as the infant exits the birth canal. Subjects also participate in inner sequences depicting the end of wars or revolutions, the discovery of medicines or technology that benefit all humanity, and global liberation. Related mythological themes include the successful feats of heroes slaying the dragon, capturing the Golden Fleece, or drinking ambrosia with the gods and goddesses on Mount Olympus. They may also feel an ecstatic reunion with divine consciousness personified as Isis, Demeter, Lakshmi, Mary, or Parvati, as God, or in a more abstract form as a loving and compassionate presence. People can also experience what Grof and Tarnas refer to as the *Promethean* type of ecstasy, as electrifying cosmic insights burst into their awareness.

In a blessed atmosphere of salvation and redemption, individuals who reach these states of rebirth have a profound sense of heightened vitality, awakening, and the disappearance of physical and emotional symptoms.

These are accompanied by feelings of deep forgiveness and brotherly and sisterly feelings toward all humanity. Grof found that people who work through the leftover emotions from birth automatically discover within themselves what he calls "intrinsic human values."[11] These include a sense of higher responsibility, ecological sensitivity, ideological tolerance, and utmost respect for life. People develop an interest in living a more meaningful and less complicated way of life with a basic philosophy of "minimum consumption, maximum satisfaction." They also feel a natural urge to act in cooperation and synergy with others to solve shared problems. At the same time, they become more self-assured about expressing their own unique personalities and develop critical attitudes toward the abuse of power.[12]

Richard Tarnas' Archetypal Astrology

Grof's research into the deeper realms of the human psyche thus significantly expanded our understanding of psychopathology and psychotherapy, as well as shedding new light on many aspects of sexuality, spirituality, and culture. But a fundamental element of this new consciousness paradigm was yet to be discovered. In 1976, as we saw, Richard Tarnas, working closely with Grof at the Esalen Institute in California, made some dramatic and unexpected correlations between Grof's clinical work and the principles of archetypal astrology. Tarnas discovered remarkably precise and detailed correlations between Grof's perinatal matrices and the archetypal meanings observed to correspond to the planets Neptune, Saturn, Pluto, and Uranus.[13] He found that the experiences of Grof's clients under the influence of the four perinatal matrices closely reflected the classic descriptions of these four planetary archetypes, found in the astrological literature.

Furthermore, Tarnas discovered that the unfolding of the birth chart over time revealed *when* a specific perinatal matrix was more likely to be activated in people's experience. Thus, individuals who enter holotropic states during powerful geometric alignments of *Saturn*—representing the archetype of boundaries, separation, constriction, and challenges—are more likely to experience elements of Grof's BPM II: Cosmic Engulfment and No Exit. When *Uranus* is activated—related to experiences of freedom, breakthroughs, and awakening—people will tend to encounter themes from BPM IV: Rebirth.

These discoveries represented a kind of unexpected cosmic validation of both Grof's work and the foundations of archetypal astrology, two independent streams of research that corroborated what increasingly seemed to be universally preexisting, or a priori, patterns of consciousness. Tarnas' research validated the universality of the perinatal matrices, and connected their unfolding with the empirically measurable movement of the planets.

It may be helpful now to introduce several key principles in the field of archetypal astrology. These include the concept of archetypes, the issues of synchronicity and free will, and the formation of geometric alignments between the planets, referred to as aspects and transits.

The Archetypal Cosmos

One of the most fundamental ideas in the Western philosophical tradition is that the universe is permeated with timeless patterns of consciousness and experience, which later, in their psychological forms, Jung would call archetypes. Although the manifestations of these universal forms in human experience are highly complex, multivalent, and multileveled, Tarnas summarizes in *Prometheus the Awakener* three broad ways that the archetypes have been understood in Western civilization: as mythic deities, as metaphysical principles, and as inner psychological structures.

The ancient Greeks perceived the archetypes as living gods and goddesses—Zeus, Aphrodite, Apollo, and so forth—in the great Homeric epics at the dawn of Western culture. Later, Plato reconceived these figures as timeless Ideas or Forms that both transcend and create the phenomenal world; for example, something has beauty to the extent that the archetype of the Beautiful exists within it. In the twentieth century, Jung rediscovered the archetypes as ordering principles that exist primarily within the human psyche itself: the anima and animus, the shadow, the great mother, the wise old man, the hero, the self, and others.

Over hundreds of centuries, astrologers have observed that the activation of these universal forms in human life occur in systematic and meaningful coincidence with geometrically formed alignments between the Sun, Moon, and planets in the solar system. For example, the way in which the impulses toward freedom, breakthroughs, and rebirth manifest in people's life experience is consistently related to alignments of the planet Uranus; awakenings of spirituality, imagination, and compassion to alignments of Neptune, and so forth.

The archetypes combine their meanings in complex ways, creating the rich tapestry of both people's subjective inner experience and the actual physical world. People's birth charts record the "cosmic state" of the archetypes at the moment of their birth, reflecting patterns of experience that will unfold and express themselves in many different forms throughout their lifetimes.

Synchronicity and Free Will

The relationship between planetary alignments and the activation of archetypal fields in human life does not take a simple cause-and-effect form, but one based on what Jung called synchronicity or "an acausal connecting principle." In order to illustrate this concept, Tarnas uses the metaphor of the hands on a clock in relationship with the ringing of a dinner bell. When the hand points to six, we can be reasonably certain that the dinner bell will ring, because we have observed that same sequence of events many times in the past. However, this does not imply that the clock's hands *cause* the bell to ring. In a similar way, astrologers recognize that the planets do not cause events—rather, they are only physical reflections or mirrors of higher cosmic principles that inform both the physical universe and our experience of it.[14]

Every archetypal energy also has a wide range of possible expressions, each true to its basic thematic nature, and it is not possible using astrology alone to predict which of the many potential expressions will manifest at a given time. Because of the multivalent and multidimensional nature of the archetypes—their basic formal patterning that manifests in a diverse range of concrete expressions—archetypal astrology is recognized as being non-fatalistic and non-deterministic. With sufficient training, we can determine the basic thematic character associated with a given planetary alignment, but usually not its exact outcomes. The specific concrete expression the archetypes will take in human life at any time remains indeterminate, contingent on additional factors such as human free will, the capacity for co-creative participation in the positive enactment of each archetypal field, and the cultural context. Said another way, we can never know exactly how the Universal Mind, transformed down into human free will and subject to an apparent need for variety and surprise, will finally express those energies.

Every planetary alignment represents experiences that are happening or trying to happen. The more people understand the emotional-archetypal impulses that are operating in their psyches, the more consciously and responsibly they can work with those tendencies, helping them to manifest in the most constructive and life-supporting ways possible. The study of astrology helps people to move in the direction that their deepest inner wisdom or inner healer is already trying to take them.

Aspects and Transits

The birth chart is a map of the solar system at the moment of a person's birth, the beginning of separate biological existence. It reflects many of the dominant emotional and archetypal themes that people will explore and embody in their lifetimes. In order to perceive archetypal patterns in human experience, astrologers look at alignments between the Sun, Moon and planets, measured around a great circle, known as the *ecliptic*, relative to the Earth. These alignments are referred to as *aspects*.

The most important aspects are based on divisions of the 360° circle by the whole numbers 1, 2, 3, 4, and 6—to form the conjunction (two planets 0° apart in the sky), the opposition (180° apart), the trine (120°), square (90°), and sextile (60°) aspects respectively. The conjunctions, squares, and oppositions are sometimes referred to as *dynamic* aspects, while the trines and sextiles as *flowing* aspects.[15]

When two planets are in aspect, the archetypal energies associated with them have a tendency to combine and interact in people's life experience. For example, an individual born with Venus and Mars in aspect will experience in various ways the friendly, fun-loving, and aesthetic qualities associated with Venus in ongoing interplay with the dynamic, energetic, and assertive impulses associated with Mars. Some of the ways that Venus-Mars combinations can manifest include a passionate and enthusiastic social nature, an appreciation of active forms of fun and entertainment, an ardent pursuit of aesthetic experience, and, sometimes, issues around balancing the yin and yang impulses in their emotional lives.

Another type of aspect is referred to as a *midpoint*. Midpoints occur when one planet falls midway between two other planets, bisecting the distance between them. For example, Mars appearing at the midpoint of Jupiter and Uranus is written as MA=JU/UR. In this situation, the archetypal qualities associated with all three planets will be dynamically combined in people's life experience.

Transits are based on a similar principle. Transits occur when the position of a planet in the sky at the present time activates or "lights up" the position of a natal planet. The movement of the luminaries and planets, all at different speeds, resembles a ten-handed clock—with each hand symbolizing a different facet of the universal or divine consciousness. We could say that the universe's impulse toward love is reflected by the movements of Venus, its urge to amplify and expand by Jupiter, its tendency toward change and variety by Uranus, and so forth.

Transits do not have to be exact alignments to be in effect. Through systematic examples from the lives of cultural figures, Tarnas demonstrates that the influence of personal transits often begins 3–5° before the exact alignment of the two planets and continues until 3–5° after exactitude, with the archetypal intensity gradually increasing up to exact and then decreasing in a bell-like curve. He found that they tend to be felt most strongly within 3° of exact on either side, with a further *penumbral* range of 5° before and after exact. This observed operative range is referred to as the *orb*.

However, Tarnas notes that Mars and Saturn transits can be exceptions to this tendency. The dynamic transits of Mars (i.e., Mars activating a natal planet by conjunction, square or opposition) can come into effect up to 6–7° before the exact alignment—which seems to correlate with Mars' archetypal nature to jump ahead. By contrast, transits of Saturn—thematically related to inhibition or slow beginnings—often delay their full effects, prolonging them through the final months of a transit cycle.

As well as personal aspects and transits, a third category of alignment is referred to as *world transits*. World transits occur when two or more planets align with each other in the sky, representing an activation of their corresponding archetypal impulses in the entire collective psyche of humanity and in historical events.[16]

Although there are additional factors in astrological analysis—including signs, houses, progressions, and many others—the information conveyed by aspects, transits, and world transits tends to be by far the most comprehensive and in-depth in practice. These alignments, properly interpreted, provide consistently accurate insights into the underlying dynamics in people's psyches as a whole, and as they change over time.

Tarnas' Correlations with the Perinatal Sequence

We can now explore more deeply Tarnas' correlations between the four perinatal matrices and the archetypal principles associated with the planets Neptune, Saturn, Pluto, and Uranus.

Neptune and the Basic Perinatal Matrix I: The Amniotic Universe, Union with the Mother

In review, Grof's first perinatal matrix (BPM I) is based around the emotional and biological unity between mother and fetus in the womb, with accompanying transpersonal themes of existence in heaven or paradise, union with divine consciousness, and oceanic ecstasy. Tarnas recognized that these profound experiences correspond in precise thematic ways with the archetypal meaning traditionally associated with the planet *Neptune*. The common denominator of both the Neptune archetype and BPM I is states in which the usual boundaries between self and other, self and nature, or self and divine have been transcended, or are in the process of being transcended.

Tarnas observed that individuals with a strongly activated Neptune will tend to experience the world through the stencil of the fetus' oceanic unity with the mother. At best, this may include feelings of basic safety and belonging, a stimulated inner life and dream life, fundamental openness to spirituality, and sense of cosmic unity. Of course, these correlations will be more pronounced in holotropic states as opposed to everyday life. Grof's research further suggests that the difficult experiences associated with Neptune may be related to emerging *toxic womb* memories, in which the lack of boundaries is perceived as confusing, deluding, weakening, or noxious. These distortions may persist indefinitely until the traumatic memories are worked through.

The Neptune-BPM I impulse toward oceanic unity will then find expression through the other archetypes interacting with Neptune as indicated by transits. Neptune-*Sun* transits can manifest as mystical feelings toward the creativity, purpose, and self-expression associated with the Sun archetype. During Neptune-Sun transits, the numinous principle may also seem to grant easier access to its masculine embodiments and personas, for example, in the form of the archetypes Apollo, Buddha, Christ, the

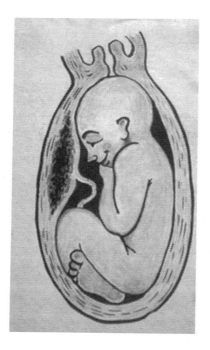

Figure 1. The Amniotic Universe (*Neptune*). Neptune corresponds to the seamless field of awareness that underlies the phenomenal universe and All There Is. Tarnas recognized that an important manifestation of the Neptune principle in human life is the biological and emotional union between mother and fetus in utero, the basis of Grof's *BPM I*. If events in childhood then reinforce the blissful security of the womb, individuals will carry peaceful and mystical overtones through their entire lifetimes.

Heavenly Father, or the Cosmic Sun. By comparison, Neptune-*Moon* transits tend to enhance feelings of higher connection through the Moon's tender emotional bonding, nurture, and community. Here, the divine principle seems more likely to reveal its compassionate *feminine* faces such as Isis, Demeter, Parvati, Mary, or Kwan Yin.[17]

In general, when Neptune's archetypal energies are flowing in a healthy way, the blissful union between mother and baby becomes a prototype for happy and satisfying relationships in everyday life.

Saturn and the Basic Perinatal Matrix II: Cosmic Engulfment and "No Exit"

Grof's BPM II is based around the early stage of labor where the womb unity has been interrupted but the cervix is not yet open, enclosing the vulnerable fetus in a "no exit" situation. The accompanying transpersonal themes include existence in hell, expulsion from paradise, and cosmic engulfment. Tarnas was able to recognize that BPM II experiences correspond precisely with the archetypal character of the planet *Saturn*. Thus, individuals strongly influenced by the Saturn archetype during a given period, and especially in holotropic states, will tend to perceive the world through the stencil of the contracted no-exit stage of birth. Saturnian experiences often include a feeling of challenge and difficulty that require much hard work to overcome, but when resolved also lead to a deep maturation and sense of accomplishment.[18]

Planets aligning with Saturn by transit will then reveal the general areas of life in which the Saturn-BPM II impulses will tend to manifest. Saturn strongly transiting the *Sun* can manifest as constrictions in the solar archetype's vitality, creativity, and self-expression. Saturn-Sun transits can also mediate confrontations with the divine principle in its contracting, judging, or negating *Terrible Father* expressions such as Yahweh, Ouranos, or Cronos.

By contrast, Saturn transiting the *Moon* may at times represent a constriction in the sense of nurture and belonging associated with the Moon. An engaged Moon-Saturn archetype may also reveal the repressive or demanding faces of the divine principle in its *feminine* embodiments, such as Mother Death, the Crone, or the Sphinx. When activated by Saturn, it is as if the other archetype will be in a kind of birth labor in the psyche, held and compressed in a challenging no-exit state until its energies are liberated.

Ultimately, Saturn is associated with the force of *involution* in the universe—what Grof refers to as the *hylotropic* or "moving toward matter" principle. From a transpersonal persepective, we could say that the early

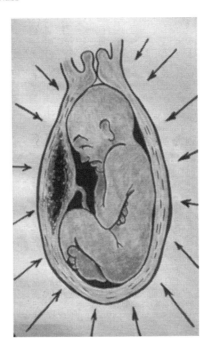

Figure 2. "No Exit" (*Saturn*). Saturn represents the archetype of boundaries, constriction, contraction, challenges, and time in the universe. Tarnas realized that, in the perinatal unfolding, Saturn manifests most intensely through the no-exit stage of birth, a key element in Grof's *BPM II*. These experiences are based on the early stage of labor where the womb unity has been interrupted, but the cervix is still closed and the fetus is pressed within the contracting uterine walls.

stage of labor is an important "transform station" of consciousness, where a piece of the eternal and infinite Universal Consciousness becomes tied to physical matter—compressed into the boundaries of a finite human body in time and space.

Pluto and the Basic Perinatal Matrix III: The Death-Rebirth Struggle

Grof's third perinatal matrix (BPM III) is based around the dynamic stage of labor, where the cervix is now open and the frail head of the fetus is jammed into the narrow pelvic opening by powerful uterine contractions. Accompanying themes include a sense of titanic fight, sadomasochistic arousal, confrontation with demonic energies, scatological materials, and pyrocatharsis—all in the context of a determined death-rebirth struggle.

Tarnas recognized that these various elements correspond in remarkable detail with the archetypal qualities associated with *Pluto*. The classic Plutonic themes which are described in the astrological literature include encounters with the shadow side of human nature, issues around power, aggression, the problem of evil, emotional baggage and garbage, sadomasochistic feelings, and confrontations with purifying fire, often then followed by experiences of rebirth, renewal, and regeneration. Astrologers such as Liz Greene, Robert Hand, Caroline W. Casey, and many others have written about the healing and transformation that can occur when Pluto's shadow energies are faced internally. Holotropic states significantly increase the safety and effectiveness of this process.

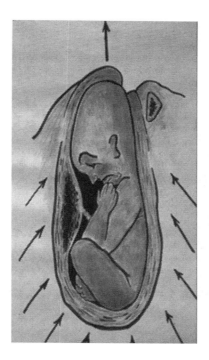

Figure 3. The Death-Rebirth Struggle (*Pluto*). Pluto represents the powerful processes of evolution, transformation, and primal life force in the world, the active side of the divine principle. Tarnas recognized that in the perinatal unfolding, Pluto manifests most fully through the dynamic stage of labor, the basis of Grof's *BPM III*. Journeyers accessing this material experience a relatively standard set of themes—a sense of titanic fight, sadomasochistic feelings, confrontation with biological materials, issues around the problem of evil, and passing through purifying fire or pyrocatharsis.

Tarnas found that the Pluto-BPM III energies will then find channels of expression through the other planetary archetypes interacting with Pluto during a transit. Pluto combined with *Mercury* can manifest as confrontations with Pluto's primal shadow energies, with a specific Mercurial emphasis on dark or obsessive thoughts, intellectual power struggles, or intensely challenged belief systems. An activated Pluto-*Venus* can take the form of encounters with Plutonic-BPM III themes in the Venusian realm of friendships and relationships, enjoyment, and sexuality. In any alignment that involves Pluto, the second archetype will be in a kind of death-rebirth struggle in the person's psyche, affecting their consciousness in powerful, often irrational ways until the associated energies and emotions left over from birth have been worked through.

Uranus and the Basic Perinatal Matrix IV: Rebirth and Separation from the Mother

As we saw, Grof's fourth perinatal matrix is based around the final intensification of pressure in the birth canal, the completed delivery, and the beginning of separate biological existence. Related transpersonal themes include feelings of spiritual rebirth, transcendence of the fear of death, and reconnection with the cosmic creative principle. Tarnas recognized that these breakthrough sequences correspond in precise thematic ways with the archetypal character of *Uranus*, and that they have the potential to manifest in some form whenever the Uranus archetype is activated in a person's psyche.

The range of positive experiences associated with Uranus transits includes feelings of electrifying vitality and inspiration, an unexpected resolution of difficult situations, and spiritual or numinous awakenings. On some level, people will be in touch with, or have a strong craving for, experiences of birth and rebirth.[19] They may also display Uranus' archetypal impulses in more problematic ways such as manic hyperactivity, chronic problems with authority and structure, or unreliability in relationships. Uranus represents the impulse toward freedom. Its shadow side is rebelling against the wrong things without adequately facing one's own inner material.[20]

The Uranus-BPM IV principles will then find expression and inflection through the other archetypes interacting with Uranus by transit. Combined with *Mars*, their liberating direction can take the form of explosive releases of leftover energy and aggression from the birth process, with accompanying themes of heroic rebellion, slaying the dragon, or liberation through active effort. Influenced by *Neptune*, Uranus' urge for transcendence can manifest as awakenings of compassion, imagination, and reconnection with Absolute Consciousness.

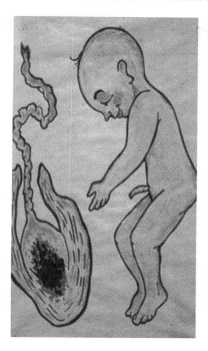

Figure 4. Rebirth and Separation from the Mother (*Uranus*). Uranus represents the impulses toward liberation, awakening, and change in the world, the archetypal forces that seek to break consciousness out of limiting patterns and reunite it with the divine source. Tarnas found that in the perinatal layer of the psyche, Uranus corresponds closely to the fourth perinatal matrix, or *BPM IV*—the sequences of ego death, birth, and rebirth that occur during systematic self-exploration.

     Tarnas' correspondence between the perinatal matrices and the archetypal meanings associated with the four outer planets thus had the effect of deepening the theory and practice of astrology. He succeeded in bridging the credible core of the old astrological traditions with the most recent advances in consciousness research, depth psychology, and psychiatry. Grof's expanded cartography of psyche not only integrates the entire range of biographical, perinatal, and transpersonal domains that routinely emerge in deep self-exploration, but shows how they are connected. Most importantly, his clinical research confirms that there is a *finite* amount of negative material in the individual psyche.

     Techniques of therapy and self-exploration, as well as astrological counselling styles, which focus solely on the post-natal, *biographical* layer of the psyche—i.e., events from infancy to the present—are overlooking important sources of human problems in the perinatal and transpersonal domains of the psyche. They are also missing the powerful healing mechanisms that exist on those levels.

On the other hand, counsellors who are familiar with the entire range of material that might emerge in their clients' inner lives are able to offer deeper levels of support. By recognizing the timing of specific thematic passages in the emotional death-rebirth cycle, they can remind their clients that, however challenging their experiences, "this too shall pass." Whatever someone is going through in the transformational journey, the key is to trust the process. Surrendering deeply to the feelings of depression and encagement associated with Saturn and BPM II, for example, automatically consumes their effect in the psyche and allows the material to move in a more liberating direction. Actively facing and giving expression to the dynamic energies of Pluto and BPM III clears the pathway to rebirth and transcendence.

At the same time, therapists and sitters conducting powerful experiential sessions such as breathwork or psychedelic therapy will find that they can benefit from the insights of archetypal astrology. Planetary transits provide a wealth of information about the basic timing, intensity, and direction of psychological dynamics, and since the time of Jung himself this knowledge has been used by professionals around the world to better understand their clients' emotional unfolding. I hope this book helps to advance the accessibility of holotropic exploration and archetypal astrology for both practicing therapists and the educated, dedicated public.

Several Further Distinctions

Serious students of archetypal astrology may also appreciate the following further distinctions and clarifications. Most of these have been either emphasized or suggested by Tarnas in *Cosmos and Psyche* or in personal communications.

Holotropic States Versus Everyday Life

Tarnas' correlations between the perinatal matrices and the outer planets apply, primarily, to the experiences of people who have entered powerful holotropic states, rather than in their experience of everyday life. Individuals who enter holotropic states under dynamic Saturn transits have a higher likelihood of accessing elements of BPM II ("no exit"), but they may or may not experience BPM II themes from day to day. Of course, what usually happens is that the intense perinatal emotions that would ideally be faced in a condensed form during a single holotropic session will, in everyday life, be spread out and experienced in a diluted way over the course of weeks, months, or years. Instead of experiencing the BPM II feelings of compression, entrapment, and meaninglessness in a powerful healing session, a person might experience a vague sense of ongoing pressure, encroaching threat, or dissatisfying routine that essentially passes as normal life.

Transits Versus Aspects

The planet-BPM correlations refer to transits rather than aspects. That is, the emergence of a given perinatal matrix in a person's emotional experience is based on passing *transit* alignments, rather than on lifetime *aspect* alignments. The spiritual rationale behind people's natal aspects can only be described as an unfathomable mystery, perhaps reflecting the craving for variety of experience of the Universal Mind itself.

Interpenetrating Waveforms Rather Than Discrete Entities

Tarnas demonstrates through historical examples, in *Cosmos and Psyche*, that the activation of archetypal forces in human experience resembles complexly interpenetrating waveforms rather than discrete, separate entities that turn on and off like light switches. All the archetypes exist in some degree of manifest or latent form within every perinatal matrix and every inner experience, as well as in every part of the universe:

> The basic BPM correspondence is an important and striking one, but many other nuances and complexities are involved that make it misleading to focus only on a simple one-to-one correlation between the four matrices and the four planets. After all, the entire process is Plutonic from beginning to end. It is also entirely Neptunian. The perinatal is the convergence point of the biological-instinctual-Freudian with the archetypal-spiritual-Jungian, and every matrix reflects that convergence—i.e., of Pluto and Neptune. Also the entire process is shaped by Saturn (as separation, incarnation, form, suffering, differentiation, etc.) and by Uranus (the unpredictable, the creative trickster, the introduction of change and the new into the timeless unity, etc.). Saturn is present even in positive BPM I experiences as the safe, bounded container.[21]

Other Factors That Underlie the Variability of Experience

And finally, although the correlations in archetypal astrology are profound, there are many additional factors that seem to determine the content and depth of people's holotropic experiences. These include the number of previous sessions they have undergone; the level of trust they have with their sitters; the set and setting they employ; and, as suggested above, the apparent need for variety of experience of the cosmic creative principle.

CHAPTER 3

Issues in Psychedelic Therapy and Self-Exploration

Before exploring the intersection of transpersonal psychology and archetypal astrology in more depth, there are a number of important issues in psychedelic therapy and self-exploration that we should also address. Of all the techniques for entering holotropic states of consciousness, the ingestion of psychoactive substances is undoubtedly the most powerful and controversial. Much of the debate around their use began in the late 1960s during the period of what became known as the "drug hysteria," when many young people were experimenting with psychedelics for the first time in an atmosphere of grandiose expectations and lack of experienced supervision. Sensationalist reporting of some tragic suicides and the exaggerated response of the authorities led to a blanket prohibition against not only the recreational use by young people, but the legitimate clinical programs as well. In retrospect, Grof suggests, to evaluate these powerful substances under the chaotic conditions of the 1960s was like determining that matches are inherently dangerous because children might play with them.

For many decades the opportunities for clinical research have been very poor. Fortunately, this situation has shown some dramatic improvements in the past few years. The work of the *Multidisciplinary Association for Psychedelic Studies* and other professional groups and churches has helped to create a more favorable atmosphere in the academic world, and a growing number of universities in Europe and North America have resumed their therapeutic research projects. This includes some promising work in the treatment of military veterans suffering from post-traumatic stress disorder (PTSD). As well, the almost universal experimentation with psychedelics among young people has over time evolved a somewhat more mature ethic around their use.

It is in this climate of renewed openness that I hope this book can make a contribution. Psychedelics are very powerful substances that need to be approached with utmost care and responsibility. In many ways, the ideal situation would be healthcare-funded healing centers open and available to the public, staffed by dedicated nurses, counselors, and therapists.

In the absence of such programs, I am not encouraging or condoning people to rush out and take illegal drugs, especially those with a history of severe emotional problems or mental illness, or who have serious medical conditions.

The purpose of this book is to help those who have already chosen to use psychedelic substances to do so in the safest way possible, by taking care of themselves, preparing ahead, and minimizing the risks. There is a great need for more informed debate around these issues. Like many observers in this field, I also hope that legislators and administrators will inform themselves by reading the professional and scientific journals rather than the doubtful reports of sensation-hunting journalists.

What follows is a brief review of some of the most important issues and misunderstandings in this field.

Non-specific Amplifiers of Mental Processes

According to Grof, psychedelic substances can be properly understood as *non-specific amplifiers* of psychological processes. They actively complete chemical and neural circuits in the brain that are usually interrupted—filling in the antenna, so that emotional material which is normally inaccessible can now flood into consciousness. Thus the content of people's experiences does not come from the drug, per se, but from the psyches of the experiencers themselves. [1]

Thus, ten people ingesting LSD or psilocybin mushrooms on the same day will have ten different, sometimes even diametrically opposite, experiences. As well, one person undertaking a series of ten sessions spread out on different days might have ten different experiences. These properties of individuality and variability of experience is why it became imporant to find an effective predictive technique. Before Tarnas and Grof explored the diagnostic capacity of archetypal astrology, therapists had no way to predict when someone might, for example, suddenly encounter deeper and more difficult material that could require special levels of support.

The Level of Trust and Support

Whether the ingestion of a psychedelic substance ultimately becomes a positive or a negative experience depends on several major factors. The most important of these is the *level of trust* between journeyers and the people around them—their friends, guides, and sitters. As difficult material begins to surface, the journeyers' assessment of the overall safety of the situation, and the possible reactions of the people nearby, will determine whether they fully let go and face the material or desperately hold on and try to repress it. Unfortunately, the act of repressing emotional material that is trying to surface can keep it stuck in a halfway, undigested position in the psyche for days, weeks, or even years afterward.

This is the situation that many young people find themselves in, as they are being admitted to the emergency rooms of hospitals, and why psychedelic substances have acquired such a generally poor reputation in the medical community. At this critical moment in someone's life, the availability of encouraging, non-repressive support from the on-duty staff could, in many cases, quickly resolve the emerging material, change the individual's life for the better, and send him or her in a positive direction.

Similarly, patients admitted with sudden-onset emotional symptoms, such as those undergoing a psychospiritual crisis or *spiritual emergency*, if given an opportunity to simply lie down and do some deep breathing under the care of trained therapists, could have significant emotional break-throughs and be, as one researcher put it, laughing about their experiences over dinner as opposed to entering a lifetime of damaging stigma and suppressive medication.[2]

Set and Setting

The *setting* is the physical space where people undergo their sessions. Individuals who have adopted an internalized, therapeutic approach do their sessions in a soundproof space, ideally with beautiful scenery nearby. Those participating in the deep-indigenous traditions often perform their ceremonies in a sacred lodge or out in nature. Spiritually minded adults tend to seek out a beautiful natural setting, an intentional dance event, or an outdoor music festival; whereas many young people have their first psychedelic experience at a concert or a party, surrounded by friends, acquaintances, and sometimes by large groups of people they don't know.

Grof also discusses the various kinds of intention or *set* that partici-pants adopt before going into their sessions and the agreements they make with other people involved in the experience. Seekers with an *internalized set* undergo sessions in order to safely activate the energies and emotions in their unconscious and face whatever comes up. The goal is to surrender deeply to the material regardless of the content and give it full verbal and physical expression. Working through leftover material is observed to be healing in two ways: by reducing the amount of emotional and energetic charge in the psyche, and by widening the pathway to unitive transpersonal states which have a meta-healing value.

People undergoing internalized sessions of this type are supported by at least one experienced sitter who is not under the influence of any substance. However, a male-female *dyad* is optimum.[3] The participant agrees to remain in the reclining position with eyeshades and headphones on for the duration of the experience. During LSD sessions, this would be at least five to six hours, and for psilocybin mushroom sessions, at least three hours. Grof makes a further distinction between a *psychedelic set*, in which individuals do a single overwhelming dose of LSD or other psychedelic substance in order to reach transcendent experiences, and a *psycholytic set*, in which they do smaller doses in a series, as an adjunct to traditional psychotherapy.

Explorers approaching sessions with a *mystical set* have an intention to enter mystical states of awareness, emotionally and spiritually bond with their friends, and connect more deeply with nature. Challenging emotional material is seen as being an occasional by-product of the process, but it is not sought out, and there are generally unspoken limits on the range of emotions that a person would be supported in facing.

The term *recreational set* applies to the act of ingesting psychedelics at a concert, a party, or other social event where the goal is to have a fun and interesting experience, essentially something out of the ordinary. Obviously, this kind of set is not conducive for facing deep emotional material and some unfortunate young people may find themselves in a situation where the intensity of their emotional process falls outside the range of acceptability for that environment. And finally, anyone familiar with the powerful effects of psychedelic substances would not hesitate to use the term *criminal set* to describe the administration of any substance to someone without his or her knowledge.

In practice, sessions undergone with internalized, mystical, or recreational sets can, under certain conditions, have degrees of overlap. Some young people experimenting with psychedelics at a concert or party do manage to have a genuine transcendent experience, which then persuades them to seek out a more conducive place for their next encounter. More reliably, the widespread *intentional dance venues* featuring world-music DJs create a fairly supportive setting for journeyers approaching sessions with both recreational and mystical sets in mind. (However, as always, people with a history of severe emotional problems should be careful before doing any kind of psychedelic outside of an inpatient setting.) Intentional dance events tend to attract many experienced and mature explorers. Along with healthy snacks, fresh fruit and herbal teas, the best of these events also offer a *safe room* or *chill room* with designated guides on hand to support people who are struggling and need a comforting presence.

A simple addition to this format, a *process room*, would offer an even higher degree of support. This would be a separate, enclosed space staffed by two or three experienced sitters comfortable with the full range of perinatal and transpersonal material. At least one of these sitters should be female. Anyone who felt the need would be free to come in, lie down, and give full expression to whatever was emerging in their process. For some participants, this might take hours, while for others just a few minutes. As soon as they felt good again, they could then rejoin their friends on the dance floor or in the relaxation spaces.

As the powerful evolutionary wave corresponding to our current Uranus-square-Pluto world transit moves through 2020 and beyond— which we will explore later—it is highly probable that many people will have intensified levels of emotional experience, making these kinds of processing spaces more and more crucial. The addition of a supportive sanctuary within an already safe event-space would be a small step toward recreating the miracle of the Eleusinian Mysteries in ancient Greece. As Grof writes, the role that these deeply established spiritual psychedelic rituals played in the formation of Greek culture, and thus the entire Western civilization, is yet to be fully acknowledged.[4]

Ceremonies in the *deep indigenous tradition*, especially those originating in the Amazon areas of Brazil and Peru, represent another wave of exploration opportunities that are now available to people in many parts of the world. The number of journeyers in these powerful rituals ranges from one or two up to several dozen and thus have various degrees of mystical and internalized sets. In general, the higher the ratio of shaman and assistants to journeyers, and the more permission there is for full verbal expression, the more safe and conducive the event will be for deep processing.

The Dosage, Quality, and Purity of Psychoactive Substances

Inexperienced journeyers tend to attribute the character of their experiences to the quality of the drug or plant that they have ingested. If they have a good experience, they attribute it to the "good stuff" and if they have a bad experience, to "bad stuff." However, the *quality* of a psychedelic substance, and even the type of substance used, is much less important than most people realize. Significantly more important factors that determine the content of people's sessions include the set and setting they employ, the level of trust they have with their friends and guides, and their astrological transits.

Similarly, certain highly motivated individuals, believing that the greater the *dosage* they take, the more intense and liberating their experience will be, may ingest large doses of psychedelics under less-than-ideal circumstances. It is not uncommon to see young people who have already encountered more perinatal material than they could digest. Although, in principle, more intense journeys are likely with higher dosages, it is again people's sense of safety, their level of inner resistance, and their transits that will ultimately determine the depth of their experiences.

For example, Grof and his colleagues observed that patients with extreme obsessive-compulsive symptomatology could, for a number of initial sessions, ingest high doses of LSD without demonstrating any change in consciousness. In one example, they administered 1000 micrograms of LSD intramuscularly to one of their severely obsessive-compulsive patients in the psychedelic program who had felt no effect from the LSD in a number of previous instances. After several hours, the young man yawned, sat up and was considered sufficiently lucid to go into the kitchen and cut bread for a snack.[5] Conversely, people with a basic openness to their emotional process and under the influence of powerful Uranus, Neptune, or Pluto transits can enter deep holotropic states after inhaling only a small amount of marijuana, after a few minutes of deep breathing, or even spontaneously—as in the case of those undergoing a spiritual emergency. It should be noted that the *threshold dosage* of LSD for human beings is between 300–500 micrograms. Beyond this level, there are no further chemical effects on the brain or changes in consciousness.[6]

And finally, the *purity* of psychoactive compounds is obviously very important. Most LSD that is available in the West at the present time is apparently chemically pure and seems to be rarely handled by the more unscrupulous criminal elements. Psilocybin mushrooms are either the real thing or completely fake, although there is always the possibility that an unknown source could add something foreign to them. Similarly, it is very unlikely that individuals ingesting ayahuasca, ibogaine, or other natural plant medicines will encounter anything less than pure versions of these compounds. It is MDMA, or ecstasy, that has the highest potential for batches adulterated with other substances. This is for two main reasons: first, because its typical powdered form is easy to tamper with, and second, because it is one of the most desirable party drugs for naive and unquestioning young people.

Another important issue is the possible side effects of the *pure* form of psychoactive substances themselves. Clinical researchers after more than five decades of *in vitro* and *in vivo* testing have been unable to find biological side effects of pure LSD. Effective in incredibly minute quantities—millionths of a gram—the lysergic acid molecules are broken down into their constituent parts and secreted into the urine stream within two hours after ingestion. What are known as "flashback" effects are not caused by chemical residues left in the body, but from unprocessed emotions from the unconscious that were activated but not fully worked through. Psilocybin mushrooms and ayahuasca also have no significant toxic elements.

It is with ecstasy, again, because of its amphetamine content that due care and diligence needs to be observed. All amphetamine-based drugs can cause problems for people with pre-existing heart conditions or hypertension. Ecstasy can also lead to dehydration, or hyperthermia, in warm environments if people do not drink enough water—or to low blood sodium levels, or hyponatremia, from drinking too much water, a problem which can be easily corrected by ingesting salt or electrolytes during the evening. Research into other effects from prolonged high-dose exposure to ecstasy, such as possible change in the neurons that make serotonin in the brain, has yielded mixed results and at this point seems inconclusive, with the effects almost certainly less serious or permanent than originally believed. It should be noted that most of the fatalities associated with ecstasy have occurred when it was combined with medicinal drugs such as monoamine oxidase inhibitors (MAO Inhibitors).[7]

Medical and Psychiatric Contraindications for Holotropic States

Holotropic states can, at times, involve highly strenuous emotional and energetically charged material, and therefore people approaching them need to be aware of certain medical and psychiatric contraindications. The most important contraindications of a medical nature include cardiovascular disease and high blood pressure, brain hemorrhage, aneurysms, myocarditis, or atrial fibrillation—and the risks increase exponentially with fast-acting psychedelics such as 5-MeO-DMT. Other concerns include serious diabetes, glaucoma, retinal detachment, osteoporosis, a history of dislocations and fractures, and severe epilepsy. Not all the conditions in this second category are absolute contraindications, but people need to discuss them fully with their sitters and physicians beforehand. Individuals who have recently undergone surgery or suffered a recent injury should also be aware of the possibility of reinjuring themselves in the strenuous phases of breathwork or psychedelic therapy sessions.

Bronchial asthma is not a contraindication, but people should have their inhaler on hand and sitters need to be aware of the possibility of suffocation material from birth emerging, which, as always, can be very healing if supported. And finally, pregnant women should not ingest powerful psychedelics for obvious reasons. Even Holotropic Breathwork can pose a risk in the later trimesters because an activation of the mother's own perinatal material could potentially induce labor. However, Grof notes that, because of the openness of the mother's psyche, the weeks and months after delivery provide opportunities for unusually deep inner work. Avenues for emotional processing should, ideally, be considered a standard option available to post-partum mothers. Health care providers including nurses, midwives and doulas trained in nurturing and releasing forms of breathwork could offer an invaluable additional service to the women in their care.

With regard to *psychiatric contraindications*, people with a history of severe emotional problems, especially those who have been hospitalized or diagnosed with mental illness, need to be very careful before considering doing any kind of psychedelic or intense breathwork. Under ideal conditions, the holotropic approach has been proven to benefit many categories of mental illness of psychogenic origin, i.e., problems that do not have a clear biological basis such as those caused by brain tumors or fevers.[8] However, patients with a history of serious psychological problems often need extra care that extends beyond the time frame of a breathwork seminar—backup care which can only be provided by an inpatient facility. There is an urgent need for responsible therapists to begin pilot projects and create these kinds of programs.

The other psychiatric concern is that a tendency toward dangerous acting out that characterizes bipolar disorder, in particular, can present special safety and legal issues for deep work with manic individuals. The possibility that anything the person does for the rest of his or her life might be attributed to the emotional processing is, in our present philosophical climate, a serious obstacle to working with some of the people who need it most. An inpatient facility with twenty-four-hour supervision for the periods between sessions would, again, offer an opportunity for manic individuals to work through their driving emotional material and reach states of genuine rebirth.

CHAPTER 4

The Astrological Archetypes

With these various backgrounds, we can now explore the archetypal meanings represented by the Sun, the Moon, and the planets as they align with each other over time.

Sun ☉

Ye are the light of the world.

The archetype of the Sun manifests as the center of the individual psyche, the experience of basic selfhood or "I am." It symbolizes our sense of personal autonomy, our warmth and enthusiasm for life, the light of vitality inspiring us to shine before the world. At one level, the Sun represents the center of individual awareness, the self-referencing aspects of the ego—while on a deeper level, the center of the larger psyche, the Self.

The Sun is thus embodied in the Hindu concept of the *Atman*, the individual self that is, at root, essentially commensurate with the higher Universal Self or *Brahman*. It represents the divine fire of individual consciousness, borrowed from and reflecting the great flame of universal consciousness—the Universal Mind transformed down into the physical dimension as individual ego and biological life force. The Sun is the eternal "I" within us, the creative spark at the center of our beings that is ultimately the cosmic creative principle incarnated into the biological realm, as us.

This "light of the conscious ego" can manifest in many different forms, depending on the quality of modeling behavior by the father or breadwinner, experiences during birth and childhood, and the other archetypes interacting with the Sun. The Sun's energy flowing in a healthy way fills people with creative spirit, zest, and exuberance. Like authors of their own life journeys, they will feel confident in expressing their true nature and contributing to the larger social world. When the Sun's vitality is suppressed, people may feel a basic lack of energy and self-assurance, while in excess, they might be overly yang, domineering, or self-centered.

In industrial cultures such as ours, the purposeful and achievement-oriented qualities associated with the Sun tend to be over-valued, which has created serious and damaging imbalances in the modern world. The outpouring radiance of the Sun archetype can shrivel and scorch gentle earthly life if the Moon's reflective soul does not have equal time to cool and moisten the landscape of awareness. Intellect without feelings, will-power without conscience, and high achievement without inner satisfaction are signs that the archetypal Sun is dominating the archetypal Moon, and this is a problem that can surface in both men and women. The solar principle has flourished in the modern West's celebration of individuality and the stupendously creative as well as the destructive qualities of our culture—as if the brighter the sun, the darker the shadow.

In the birth chart, alignments of the Sun indicate, in broad thematic ways, how people's essential life-force and vitality are embodied and expressed in the world. Other archetypes interacting with the Sun will play a heightened role in their basic life experience.

Moon ☽

Earth the mother of all life.

The Moon symbolizes the nurturing ground of our mothers, homes and families, the unconditional human love that softens our emotional boundaries and unites us with the greater community of life. It represents feelings of intimacy and tenderness, our needs to bond and live with others as a family group: as "we" rather than "I". Like the melting radiance of moonlight that blends contours in its encompassing glow, the Moon represents the generous Feminine, the bonds of compassion and kinship that make true civilization possible.

The Moon is tied to earthly life, "Mother Earth," and astronomers believe that it was formed from the leftovers of an impact between a planet Theia and the Earth that occurred four-billion years ago. Perhaps true to the lunar archetype's nurturing role, this event gave the Earth the right amount of mass needed for its gravity to hold in a life-supporting atmosphere. The Moon's gravity also stabilized the Earth's fluctuating axis of rotation which helped to create the conditions for biological life.

In the birth chart, alignments of the Moon suggest the basic ways in which people meet their needs to be safe, nurtured, and accepted, both authentically and in substitute forms such as materialism and consumption. The Moon also reveals how they reach out emotionally and respond to feedback from the world. It represents their merely human side, their vulnerability and dependence, their basic emotional openness to others. These qualities emerge most fully when people are under stress or tired, needing just to be themselves in the familiar and soothing security of their private home space.

As newborns and in the womb, we are completely submerged inside the lunar archetype, personified through the nurturing feelings of our mothers and care-givers. The mother's physical and emotional states are translated directly to the fetus through chemicals in their shared blood supply, as well as through intimate psychological links—archetypally related to both the Moon and Neptune. The fetus essentially lives in the mother's subconscious. When a baby is wanted and the mother is happy and in good health, the resulting *good-womb* experiences foster feelings of security and belonging for their entire lifetimes.

The Moon also represents the maternal nurture that acts as a buffer or *encapsulation* around the painful energies and emotions of labor. When a child is cared for, he or she can largely forget about the trauma of birth—things were bad for awhile but now they are back to normal, i.e., similar to the security of the womb rather than the threatening pressures of the birth canal. These early experiences are recorded in the psyche in clusters of memories that determine people's deepest feelings about life on earth, about how safe it is to be dependent on other human beings, and about whether they really belong in the human community.[1]

The Moon's energy flowing in a healthy way helps to create in people feelings of rootedness, connection, and trust. Planets aligning with the Moon reveal how their emotional and family lives will be supported, stimulated, or challenged by other influences.

Mercury   ☿

Hermes the winger messenger of the gods.

Mercury represents the impulse toward thought and communication in human life, mental energies transmitted through our thinking, speaking, reading, writing, and learning. It governs the combination of sensory perceptions, unconscious memories, and archetypal fields creating the basic climate in our minds and what we convey to others. Mercury is also associated with movement and travel. Finally, it suggests our capacity to analyze, conceptualize, and interpret.

Robert Hand writes that the Mercury archetype acts as a kind of *modulator*, decoding order out of coded or condensed wave forms, for example, converting sound waves into music or speech.[2] This supports the modern theory that the brain functions as a kind of mental receiver, rather than the actual source of consciousness. To use Grof's analogy, although by cutting wires in a television set we can distort the picture, this does not demonstrate that the program itself originates inside the television. Similarly, by stimulating parts of the brain, scientists can effect specific changes in consciousness, but this does not demonstrate that consciousness originates inside the brain. As Grof explains:

> Very few people, including most scientists, realize that we have absolutely no proof that consciousness is actually produced in the brain and by the brain. There is no doubt that there exists vast clinical and experimental evidence showing significant interconnections and correlations between the anatomy, physiology, and biochemistry of the brain, on the one hand, and states of consciousness, on the other. However, it represents a major logical jump to infer from the available data that these correlations represent a proof that the brain is actually the source of consciousness. Such a deduction would be tantamount to the conclusion that the TV program is generated in the TV set, because there is a close correlation between functioning or malfunctioning of its components and the quality of the sound and picture. It should be obvious from this example that the close connection between cerebral activity and consciousness does not exclude the possibility that the brain mediates consciousness, but does not actually generate it. The research of holotropic states has amassed ample evidence for this alternative.[3]

In Greco-Roman mythology, Hermes-Mercury was said to be the messenger of the gods, a recognition by the ancients that our thoughts ultimately come to us from the archetypal realm, "the gods." Mercury is the archetypal messenger who translates these meanings into our own symbolic mental language—this is done so perfectly that we may believe we are creating the thoughts ourselves. Learning to see beyond this illusion is one of the goals of meditation. With loving attention, people observe their minds as a space of pure awareness, through which flows an endless series of thoughts and images—mental patterns arising and subsiding like clouds moving through an open sky. Over time, people learn to notice and let go of their thoughts without harboring or fearing them, and as they experience the emotions that underly these passing thoughts, the emotions are released.

The psychologist James Hillman also refers to the process of "seeing through" the literal surface of our thoughts to their basis in universal archetypes. The archetypes penetrate to the last corner of what we think of as our personal minds. As these timeless patterns emerge in the psyche, our perceptions about the smallest things and even how we think about our perceptions change accordingly.[4]

When Mercury's mental channels are open, people will be interested in and curious about the world. They will be able to effectively express their point of view, while also hearing what others say. Hyperactivated Mercury energies can manifest as lack of concentration, nervous restlessness, or inability to sleep.

Other archetypes combining with Mercury suggest basic ways that people receive and communicate information. They also shed light on the general subjects, themes, and issues in which they may be most interested. Combined with Venus, people will tend to speak in more graceful, harmonious, and considerate ways, showing an interest in topics of love, friendship, fun, and the arts. When aligned with Pluto, their communication style may be more forceful and intense, with a possible emphasis on mental persuasion, deep human motivations, and the shadow side of the psyche.

Venus   ♀

Pleasure is the beginning and the end of living happily.
Epicurus

Love is perfect kindness.
Joseph Campbell

Venus rules experiences of love, beauty, and harmony in human life, magnetic emotional attractions that draw people into higher unions of intimacy, friendship, and cooperation. Venus corresponds to Eros, our impulses toward love and affection. When we fall in love, it is said in archetypal psychology that Venus has entered our awareness, filling us with tender and elated feelings. The goddess of love becomes a stencil through which we perceive the beloved and the world around us. Venus is the spice of life, the sweetness and color in creation that refine our senses and awaken our souls to see the real, deeper beauty in all things.

The Venus-Aphrodite principle has been ardently celebrated in the West's three great creative watersheds: classical Greece, the Renaissance, and our own twentieth and twenty-first centuries. In the first two periods, the beauty of the human body was glorified in art and sculpture while, in our own time, Venus has returned in the fame culture, the blossoming of world cinema, and the mass obsession with pop stars. Aphrodite can be seen on the cover of every supermarket magazine and it is her face that is entrancing consumers as they hungrily pore over the provocative imagery inside them. Yet as Caroline W. Casey writes in her classic *Making the Gods Work for You*:

A mythology invites us to be active participants. Celebrity culture is really an oxymoron, because it engenders passivity and cultivates nothing but envy and teenage yearning. Instead of participating in Uranus's real revolution, we settle for "a revolution in hair care products."[5]

Venus allures humanity toward the social graces, inviting us to live beyond the bland and the everyday, but like all sweetened food this archetypal goddess is best enjoyed in balance. If people are willing to register only their pleasant feelings, the depth and richness of their emotional worlds will gradually recede, as Venus' exalted potentials are buried in obsessions over manners, prestige, and appearance.

The Venus complex can be disappointing, at times, a beautiful mirage that offers passing emotional and sensory pleasure and then entices us on toward the next plateau of self-discovery. Rather than embracing youth and sexual attractiveness forever, which are transitory, the mystics tell us that we can experience the Aphrodite archetype directly through our own psyches—*Higher Beauty*. At this level, Venus enhances a more gentle and loving way of being with the larger world. Enchanted by a deeper feminine grace, people may enjoy an aesthetically satisfying relationship with all around them. In its most sublime form, Venus reminds us of the divine harmony permeating the creation, panoramas of supernatural beauty that mediate access to a higher spiritual presence.

When Venus' archetypal impulses are flowing in a healthy way, people can relax, have fun, and feel emotionally connected with others. They will value warm, trusting friendships and relationships. When damaged or suppressed, they may feel unlovable, unattractive, or unable to enjoy any aspect of life. Venus can also manifest in distorted forms such as vanity, conceit, or snobbish feelings toward what might seem to be the coarse or the plain. Individuals may also be prone to self-indulgence.

The other archetypes combining with Venus will tend to color people's basic experiences of love, friendship, and pleasure, their styles of relating, and their responses to beauty. When combined with Uranus, Neptune, or Pluto, Venus' love and sexuality can be pathways to transcendent ecstasy.

Mars ♂

Glorious Hector held out his
arms to his baby,
who shrank back to his fair-girdled nurse's
bosom
screaming, and frightened at the aspect of his own
father,

*terrified as he saw the bronze and the crest with
   its horsehair,
nodding dreadfully, as he thought, from the peak
   of the helmet.*
Iliad VI, trans. R. Lattimare
(The son of Hector, the Trojan champion, is terrified by his father's armor).

Mars represents the emotional impulses toward action, assertion, and gratification of desire, the dynamic energy propelling every organism to assert itself and satisfy its biological and emotional needs. A pure expression of Mars' drives is an infant crying out angrily when it wants food or attention. Mars is related to the urge to define ourselves through interaction, to confront and overcome challenges, to press onward. It also symbolizes our instincts to fight real or perceived threats, and in traditional astrology was considered a malefic influence because of the many problems caused by human aggression. While every organism needs Mars' dynamic energy to protect itself and pursue its valid needs, our capacity to direct violence at each other, at other life forms, and at the planet's ecosystems has become a threat to our species' survival.

Holotropic research suggests that one of the major sources of this unnecessary or *malignant* pool of aggression is in the perinatal layer of the psyche, based on the life-and-death struggle during labor—archetypally related to both Mars and Pluto. As Grof notes, aggression is a natural response of any organism subjected to life-threatening suffocation and extreme pain, but because the infant cannot fight back, scream, or leave the situation, rage is pent up in the musculature and held indefinitely for belated discharge.[6] The fetus also introjects into its body and psyche the driving forces of the contracting uterine walls themselves. Many individuals and entire cultures are then driven to create conflicts in the external world that can seem to justify and validate these emotions of aggression and fear, rather than facing the true origin of this material, in their own psyches. People who access perinatal experiences have no trouble accepting the idea that humanity's long history of war, genocide, and destruction of nature are the result of these aggressive energies being projected and acted out in the world.

When Mars' archetypal impulses are operating in balance, people will enjoy a steady flow of vitality, strength, and courage in their lives, expressing them in cooperative and synergistic forms with others. They will fight only when there is something real and serious at stake, yet will always seek peaceful alternatives to conflict, win-win solutions that can benefit everyone involved. Sexual feelings will be pursued with both passion and sensitivity to the needs of the partner. When Mars' energies are constricted or repressed, people may feel chronically tired, weak, or unable to stand up for themselves. When its urges are overcompensated, on the other hand, they may act in rash, aggressive, and competitive ways, hurting others and undermining their own best interests.

Other archetypes combined with Mars will function as adverbs, affecting how its drives are expressed and in what directions. When aligned with Jupiter, people might display their martial impulses in bold, adventurous, or grandiose ways. Combined with Saturn, Mars' energies will tend to take more focused, sustained, and careful expressions.

The highest form of the Mars archetype, as in Taoist philosophy, is "to act but not to compete."

Jupiter ♃

Jupiter says, "I will give you an abundance of opportunities. Half of them will be really good ideas and half will be illusory seductions, tailor-made to fool you."
   Caroline W. Casey, *Making the Gods Work for You*, 1998

There is no calamity greater than lavish desires.
There is no greater guilt than discontentment.
And there is no greater disaster than greed.
   Lao Tzu, *Tao Te Ching*

Jupiter corresponds to feelings of growth, optimism, and abundance in human life. Elevating and uplifting, opening and expanding, it symbolizes our yearning to reach out and broaden our range of experience, to stretch higher, go beyond, and integrate more of life's available opportunities. While the challenging transits of Saturn and Pluto are more powerful and will outweigh those of Jupiter, Jupiter's buoyant energies can, at the very least, help to provide a welcome relief from the more challenging and painful experiences in life.

Robert Hand writes that the archetypal Jupiter acts in two primary ways: by physical expansion of an entity (a growth in size) or by integration of an entity into the larger world (a growth in connection).[7] Jupiter's *impulse toward expansion* can manifest as opportunities to expand projects or businesses, attain promotions or recognition, and other kinds of material success. People often have inflated expectations of this side of Jupiter, and its transits do not usually manifest in the material forms that people are expecting. Even when it does correspond to worldly achievement, the activated Jupiter does not always invoke the self-knowledge to use that success wisely or even to enjoy it. We can see this in ambitious public figures who become famous, and then undermine themselves when their unexplored emotions come forth as unwise sexual behavior or greed. And in more common forms, Jupiter's materialistic urges can lead to a high-consumption, yet ultimately boring and dissatisfying way of life—almost the norm in Western industrial societies.

By contrast, Jupiter's *impulse toward integration* draws people to explore the greater cosmos through study, travel, or adventures in consciousness, seeing how various things fit together. Both of these drives—expansion and integration—entail growth out into the world, but in different ways. Expansion makes something bigger by incorporating the surrounding area into itself. The process of integration, on the other hand, consists of recognizing a commonality with the surrounding area and adopting a new identity that includes both it and oneself as a higher unity.

Genuine growth often involves an interplay of these two forces. An activated Jupiter archetype can begin by giving people an inflated sense of their importance, and then, through humbling feedback from the world, they adopt a more healthy and inclusive perception of who they really are. Jupiter's influence can manifest in a range of ways: from striving toward material goals, putting on weight, or overspending money, to attending classes, enjoying other cultures, or exploring the psyche. To use a metaphor from nature: a leaf can expand in physical size, or we can recognize that it is already part of a larger whole—the tree—just as the tree is part of a larger forest, and so on.

Jupiter tends to amplify and enlarge whatever archetypes it combines with, often unconsciously, and its ever-present shadow qualities are excess and grandiosity. Without introspection, Jupiter may only inflate what is already there, rather than leading to actual growth or improvement. It helps people to fulfill their desires and attain what they think they want, but does not guarantee that they will be happy with their choices in the long run. Joseph Campbell talks about this problem—of climbing rung by rung to the top of the ladder and then realizing later that it is against the wrong wall. In the realm of philosophy, Jupiter also represents the quest for higher truth, and its shadow side is believing that we have *The Truth*, when human beings only ever have a partial vision. Jupiter's overall effect can be seen as beneficial, leading to psychological and spiritual growth through people's broadened life experiences, and helping things to turn out in a positive way. It gives us the opportunity to make mistakes and learn from them, and even our biggest mistakes help others to learn by seeing what doesn't work.

When the Jupiter archetype is operating in balance, people will have optimistic, positive, and tolerant feelings toward the world, respecting others' points of view and granting them the same freedom and opportunities that they expect for themselves. They will enjoy reaching out and broadening their horizons. When Jupiter's urges are overcompensated, people may display attitudes of arrogance, hypocrisy, or greed until they are willing to face the emotional material underlying them. Wilber writes that our deepest inner yearnings are to reconnect with divine consciousness, and if we do not have access to genuine transcendent states, we will have an automatic tendency to fill the void with material and social substitutes. He calls this drive for wholeness the *Atman project*.[8]

Other archetypes combining with Jupiter suggest where people have special opportunities for expansion and expression—what comes easily. They also indicate where they may have tendencies toward inflation, excess, or taking things for granted. Under the right conditions, Jupiter combined with the transcendent impulses of Uranus, Neptune, or Pluto can bring life-changing expansions of consciousness.

Saturn ♄

In order to create the phenomenal worlds, the Divine has to abandon its original state of pristine undifferentiated unity. Considering how fantastic the experience of identification with Absolute Consciousness is from the human perspective, it seems strange that the creative principle should seek an alternative, or at least a complement, to a simple experience of itself. . . . What could possibly motivate the Divine to seek separation, pain, struggle, incompleteness, and impermanence, in short, precisely the states from which we are trying to escape when we embark on the spiritual journey? . . .

[According to the experience of subjects in holotropic states] Spirit has a profound desire to experience what is opposite and contrary to its own nature. It wants to explore all the qualities that in its pristine nature it does not have and to become everything that it is not. Being eternal, infinite, unlimited, and ethereal, it longs for the ephemeral, impermanent, limited by time and space, solid, and corporeal.
  Stanislav Grof, *The Cosmic Game*, 1998

I have seen the moment of my greatness flicker,
And I have seen the eternal Footman hold my coat, and snicker,
And in short, I was afraid.
  T. S. Eliot, "The Love Song of J. Alfred Prufrock"

Saturn represents the elements of form, structure, and boundaries in the universe, the contracted energies that give the world its solidness and concreteness, its material substance. Without the Saturn archetype, there would be no physical definition or boundaries. Everything in the universe would exist simultaneously and overlap in a kind of unified, flowing blend of amorphous consciousness.

Saturn also corresponds to *necessity*, our need to work, fulfill our obligations, and take the world seriously, where we have important lessons to learn over time. It manifests through the authority figures and role models who convey to us the world's limits and expectations, and the potential for living a rewarding life within those limits. Saturn can feel like a harsh taskmaster, at times, but it is the faithful and constant ally of our highest Spirit, teaching us firmly what we ourselves have ultimately chosen to learn. Because in our partial awareness, we may forget these choices, we can react defensively to Saturn's challenges. Overcautious and fearful attitudes are a common response to the trials of living, although the defensive ego does not succeed in stopping painful episodes from happening, and its rigid boundaries only impoverish the overall quality of our lives. Saturn seems to demand that we take its worldly limitations seriously, while also discerning between authentic limits and those projections which are simply based on unconscious fear.

In the realm of perception, Saturn manifests through the *hylotropic* or "moving toward matter" mode of awareness—the natural complement to the *holotropic* or "moving toward wholeness" principle. As Grof describes, the hylotropic mode is the state of mind that most people experience in everyday life and that Western psychiatry considers to be the only one that accurately reflects objective reality. This everyday or hylotropic mode of perception is an important part of life in the material world, and to understand it more fully, we will need to look at the world from a transpersonal, philosophical point of view.

In *The Cosmic Game*, Grof outlines the agreement between modern consciousness research and the essential insights of the world's great mystical traditions. These traditions refer to a seamless field of awareness that underlies all of existence, sometimes referred to as the Universal Mind, Absolute Consciousness, Goddess, or God. This timeless consciousness seems to have, for various reasons, a deep yearning to create beings and worlds different from itself, to which it can relate. Some of the motivations attributed to Absolute Consciousness for creating the world are described as the unbridled creativity of an artist, the insatiable curiosity of a scientist, the boundless passion of a lover, neverending boredom or, simply, cosmic loneliness.

In order to create the physical universe, the Absolute Consciousness splits off parts of itself into separate, distinct entities in time and space. Through a complex process, it erects screenworks and boundaries within its own nature, giving birth to autonomous beings that can interact with each other and with the Absolute Consciousness itself. As the Absolute incarnates and subdivides into more and more diverse entities, a process of separation and self-forgetting occurs. At each level—from the primal, undifferentiated wholeness of Absolute Consciousness, to pairs of opposites, to archetypes, and on down to material objects and biological organisms—there is a greater and greater loss of freedom and wholeness.

Saturn represents this dividing and separating principle. It is the force of contraction that causes the many separate units of awareness in the material world to forget who they really are. Every form in the universe, whether an archetype, an inanimate object, or a living being was once, and still is, a part of this greater cosmic field—which is why the spiritual journey is often referred to as *awakening* or Self-*realization*. And thus, write the mystics, although our descent into separation was originally voluntary or even enthusiastic, there is inherent suffering for the individual egos that become aware of themselves as mortal, finite beings. The process of incarnation is so painful that we forget where we came from, and the highest yearning of our soul is to regain this lost wholeness and remember who we really are. This awakening process is symbolized in different ways by the archetypes Uranus, Neptune, and Pluto.[9]

As Grof and Tarnas suggest, the process of Absolute Consciousness' incarnation into matter is reflected in the stages of biological birth. The trauma of delivery is one of the thresholds where the Absolute buries itself into physical form and obscures its true nature. The birth process is where the Universal Consciousness becomes an individual consciousness, the spiritual is made physical, the divine "is made flesh." In a healthy womb, the fetus' awareness is still undifferentiated from that of the entire universe. As the uterine walls begin to contract, its awareness is compressed into the boundaries of its own body. The nourishing womb that was the prototype of the entire universe becomes a torture chamber, as the infant loses all sense of meaningful contact with the mother and the divine for what feels like an eternity. Its consciousness becomes stamped onto the fate of the physical body, tied to a specific time and place in the material world. These traumatic memories, then compounded by wounding experiences in childhood, form the basis for feelings of helplessness, inadequacy, guilt, loss, and depression in later life.

The trauma of delivery also creates a tremendous fear of death and it is during Saturn transits that people tend to feel this fear most strongly. Biological birth and the consequent fear of death are the deepest source of many human problems—the division between self and other, humanity and nature, and humanity and divine. Saturn represents the primal wound of incarnation, the thousand arrows of trial and failure that remind us of our fragile mortality and the inexorable encroaching passage toward death. Deeply facing these fears on an emotional level is the crucial threshold to overcoming Saturn's negative imprints and reconnecting with our lost wholeness.

A well-integrated Saturn principle confers in people feelings of responsibility, humility, and patience. They will live comfortably within nature's material boundaries while recognizing that consciousness itself is without boundaries. In its negative form, Saturn can manifest as religious and scientific fundamentalism, slavish identification with one's job and social role, or chronically narrowed horizons. In contrast, people who have not integrated Saturn's imperatives—the "reality principle"—will have trouble accepting any kind of discipline or structure. They may lack strength and focus.

The archetypes combining with Saturn suggest where there may be a certain degree of necessary painful experience in the lifetime. They reveal important tests and challenges, and where people may value routine and structure more than freedom, variety or excitement. Although often perceived as difficult, the experiences associated with Saturn are a necessary part of a larger cycle. Its lessons help people to cultivate the discipline, endurance, and fortitude that can ultimately liberate them from Saturn's unconscious oppression over the human mind.

Uranus   ♅

What another would have done as well as you, do not do it. What another would have said as well as you, do not say it; written as well, do not write it. Be faithful to that which exists nowhere but in yourself—and thus make yourself indispensable.
André Gide

Improvement makes straight roads; but the crooked roads without improvement are roads of genius.
William Blake

Uranus represents the archetype of freedom, breakthroughs, and rebirth, the lightning bursts of illumination and providence that resolve old problems and open our minds to unseen new horizons and opportunities. Gracing humanity with many original gifts, inspired talents, and outpourings of creativity, it ultimately symbolizes the moment of reawakening to our true cosmic identity, not a onetime event but a series of breakthrough epiphanies along the evolutionary cycle.

The Uranus archetype manifests through the inner and outer catalysts that encourage us to take risks, reach beyond boundaries, and follow what inspires us. It is our impulses toward youth and vitality, liberation and change, the quest for untold new possibilities. Uranus accelerates awareness, breaking up patterns of repression and control in order to liberate our emotional energies into more vibrant and exciting forms.

Tarnas argued that the planet Uranus was in some way incompletely and misleadingly designated by its given name:

> Although the astrological archetypal principle associated with Uranus is clearly connected with the heavens and the cosmic, the sky, the air, the starry cosmos, astronomy and astrology, space travel and the like (all of which do suggest a connection with Ouranos, the Greek sky god), the larger principle is more fully and multivalently suggested by the mythic figure of Prometheus in all the ways we know (the impulse towards the new, the unexpected, the trickster, the creative breakthrough, awakening, liberation, rebellion, technology, scientific knowledge, cultural innovation, the restless quest for innovation and new horizons, impulsive anti-authoritarianism, etc.).[10]

Prometheus was famous for stealing fire—i.e., science and culture—from the gods and giving it to humanity. For this altruistic rebellion he was chained upon a mountaintop where a vulture devoured his liver day after day, while each night the liver regenerated itself. The Promethean impulse associated with Uranus governs the unique contributions and qualities that people bring into this world from beyond. It also conveys the dual nature of human beings: we are both emanations of divine consciousness (Prometheus the renewing god) and biological creatures (his earthly suffering).

Our nature as biological organisms means that we cannot escape from suffering, old age, and death, but we are much more than finite beings. For every limitation imposed by Saturn, there is a channel for reconnection with our true identity and the overcoming of those limits and separations. Prometheus must endure his earthly karma but he is aware of a bigger picture. His principled defiance and refusal to give in to the static attachments and power structures of Zeus represent the human soul, which is ultimately incorruptible and transcendent.

The emancipating qualities associated with Uranus can take different forms at different times in people's lives. As Tarnas realized, they correspond to the release of the infant from the suffocating birth canal and the miracle of new existence. They support the emergence of gifts and talents, opportunities and insight, and the successful outcome of risks and experiments. Ultimately, this archetype represents the rebirth into transcendent awareness that occurs at the moment of biological death or spiritual ego death. Uranus' effect is unsettling, stimulating, electrifying. It shakes up old structures so that new and better possibilities can emerge, new life can be reborn.

A well-integrated Uranus or Prometheus archetype confers in people the confidence to pursue their own life path, trusting their inner creative and spiritual instincts above the example of the majority. At the same time, they will show respect for the rights and freedoms of others and find avenues to express their talents in ways that benefit the larger world. They will feel a zest and enthusiasm for life, a sense of eternal freshness and renewal in each moment.

Uranus' shadow qualities emerge when people have not explored their own deeper emotions and lack the balance and maturity to integrate its liberating effect. Distorted Promethean impulses can take the form of a freedom-at-all-costs approach to relationships, extremist political viewpoints, impractical eccentricity, or chaotic anarchism. On the other side, a repressed Uranus may show up as hostility to change and resistance toward those one perceives as different or unusual. As Tarnas demonstrates, Uranus is the archetype of awakening. To fear its energies indicates that people are holding on too tightly, and probably to the wrong things.

Planets aligning with Uranus suggest the areas in people's lives that may be most subject to sudden unexpected breakthroughs, rebellion against limitations, and experiences of rebirth.

Neptune ♆

The experience of cosmic unity is characterized by transcendence of the usual subject-object dichotomy. The individual in this state becomes deeply aware of his or her unity with other people, nature, and the entire universe, and with the ultimate creative principle, or God. This is accompanied by an overwhelming positive affect that can range from peace, serenity and bliss to an ecstatic rapture. . . . This state of mind is referred to as "contentless yet all containing," "formless but pregnant with form," one of "cosmic grandeur yet utmost humility," or characterized by loss of ego while at the same time the ego has expanded and become the whole universe. Different subjects experience and describe this event within different symbolic frameworks. Most frequent references are to Paradise, The Garden of Eden, Heaven, Elysian Fields, unio mystica, the Tao, Atman-Brahman union, or Tat Tvam Asi (Thou art That).
    Stanislav Grof

Heaven, earth and human are one body.
    Tenet of Confucianism

Look within, you are the Buddha.
    Buddhist scriptures

The kingdom of God is within you.
Jesus

God dwells within you as you.
Tenet of Siddha Yoga

Neptune represents the highest impulses toward unity and no-boundaries in consciousness, revealing in its ultimate nature the seamless web of connection between all things in the universe. It helps us overcome the illusions of separateness between ourselves and other people, the natural world, and the divine principle, unveiling the sacred energy flows permeating every part of the physical realm. Transcending apparent boundaries and divisions, Neptune can awaken experiences of blissful union and higher meaning in our perceptions of the world.

Ultimately, Neptune symbolizes the field of pure observing awareness or Absolute Consciousness that underlies the physical world, and of which we are an inseparable part. Beneath and within Absolute Consciousness, the mystics also refer to the *Supracosmic Void*, the mysterious primordial emptiness and nothingness that is conscious of itself and contains all of existence in a potential form. At this level, Neptune is more than an archetype—it represents the totality of all the archetypes and All There Is.

As we have seen, in order for the divine play of incarnation to take place, the Absolute Consciousness must differentiate and split off parts of its own nature into separate, autonomous entities. We are the Neptunian divine having a human experience. Neptune symbolizes the deepest ground of being, the source and resting place of all things, where we come from and where we are going to. Like drops of water that are evaporated from the sea and then carried through many cycles of experience, only to flow back inexorably into the sea again, our deepest yearning is to reconnect with our lost wholeness.

The Neptune archetype reminds us of our higher nature in dreams, inspiration, and imagination, as ideas and connections from beyond the veil of everyday reality emerge into the world of form. It softens the edges of our being, drawing awareness down into the realm of soul where it can be re-enchanted and renewed. There are many levels of the Neptunian feeling, from soaking in warm water, walking in nature, or emotionally merging with a partner—to the serenity of the infant at the mother's breast, life in the amniotic womb, or spiritual oneness with all of creation. Feelings of unity and commonality inspire a natural desire to be of service and help others. As the Buddhists observe, when the arrow of ego-based suffering is removed, kindness follows automatically. An integrated Neptune opens channels of spirituality, empathy, and intuition. People will feel a basic trust in the direction of their own inner lives, what Joseph Campbell called following one's bliss.

The shadow side of the Neptune complex emerges when its boundary-dissolving nature is experienced as confusing, deluding, or inflating. Grof's research suggests that these problems are more likely to surface when people are being influenced by toxic-womb memories from their earliest development. These memories can lead to blurred boundaries between the everyday world and various transpersonal realms later in life, for example, projecting wholly divine or demonic qualities on oneself or others. The solution to Neptunian distortions is not to harden the boundaries of the ego but to surrender to the painful material in holotropic states, allowing it to cleanse itself from the system. This releasing process opens pathways to transcendence.

Grof refers to Neptunian states as the *oceanic* or *Apollonian* type of ecstasy, experiences demonstrated to have a meta-healing outcome in psychotherapy and self-exploration.[11] These oceanic Neptunian states are also an antidote to the problems of alcoholism and drug addiction. From the perspective of transpersonal psychology, substance abuse, codependence and other forms of escapism are recognized as being understandable but mistaken attempts to return to the womb and reorient toward Higher Power. Addicts who reach melted ecstasy in self-exploration report that this was the experience they were craving all along. The intoxicated state is then seen to be just a crude approximation and caricature of real oceanic experiences. C. G. Jung, who had a significant influence on Bill Wilson, the founder of Alcoholics Anonymous, describes this nourishing healing process simply as: *spiritus contra spiritum*: "spirituality is the antidote to spirits."[12]

By fixating on the surface of reality and reducing the great range and depth of the psyche to mere biology, many therapists in the West are not supporting, and in many ways are actively suppressing, this essential spiritual quest. People who adhere to the old materialistic, Newtonian understanding of the world may be pragmatic in their everyday lives, but their inner experience will over time become dry, barren and dissatisfying, and without higher meaning. In order to be truly healthy—embodying what Grof calls "higher sanity"—people need to learn to be comfortable in both worlds. We can be responsible and productive in the real world, while also periodically entering holotropic states of consciousness that can offer to human life a deeper sense of meaning and connection.

Neptune enhances the spiritual potential in any archetype it combines with. Planets aligning with Neptune suggest how its impulses toward mystical union, imagination, and compassion are likely to manifest in people's life experience. Neptune alignments also reveal the potential for spiritual confusion, delusion, or inflation—personally identifying with an archetype in a diluted form over months or years, rather than fully experiencing its emotional content in one or two powerful inner sessions.

Pluto ♇

The moral constrictions of Saturn's judgmental and defensive view of Nature, sexuality, and the elemental instincts is transformed into the full Plutonic awareness of all instincts and all of Nature being a sacramental expression of the Divine Shiva. . . . The Grim Reaper, the weight of the world, the Old Testament god Yahweh, is suddenly recognized at a more profound level as Shiva, pressing his foot relentlessly on the baby to bring liberation.
  Richard Tarnas

Pluto as an image of the dark maternal roots of the psyche is forever pulling us out of life and back into the womb of the Mother, either for renewal or death.
  Liz Greene

Only the man who goes through this darkness can hope to make any further progress.
  C. G. Jung

Pluto represents the forces of evolution and transformation in the world, the inexorable cosmic processes that wear down old structures in the psyche, in nature, and in society to bring forth regeneration and new life. The Pluto archetype drives the revitalizing experiences of birth, sex and death in the world, decaying outmoded forms—egos, bodies, worlds, and universes—and creating new ones in a ceaseless flow of changing manifestation.

Tarnas suggests that while Saturn represents death in astrology, Pluto is tied to death and rebirth, the relentless universal forces overseeing the entire process. Pluto symbolizes the active side of divine consciousness, the restless creative impulses that birth all things out of the Macrocosmic Void, symbolized by Neptune, only to sooner or later break them down again, recycling their essential consciousness into new forms. Without this higher dynamic principle represented by Pluto the universe would remain breathlessly serene and unchanging, without change or movement.

The Pluto archetype embodies itself through the Hindu deities Shiva, Shakti and Kali, the Greek Dionysus and others. From the ego's point of view, there is a dark side to Shiva's action. In the continuous flow of universal change, all things must inevitably die while their essential energies are reborn. The mystics tell us that these transmutations are only Absolute Consciousness taking on new shapes and forms but, as we have seen, there is suffering inherent for the many beings who are aware of themselves as finite and temporary, subject to aging and dying. Looking back across the solar system from Pluto, our Sun, the symbol of individual selfhood, is just another twinkling star in the sky—and to some this suggests the uncaring and impersonal attitude of Shiva's actions toward individual life. People unconsciously influenced by Pluto's energies can act in a similarly ruthless way toward other human beings and the earth's vulnerable living things in general. This archetype can evoke the brutal side of human nature or even the demonic. Individuals driven by obsessive inner emotions may feel that they embody the forces of evolution in the universe, rather than being the very person who needs deep healing and transformation.

The effects of the Pluto complex can be seen in the titanic energies unleashed in earthquakes, volcanoes, and nuclear explosions; in the body's shudders and convulsions during orgasm and childbirth; in seizures, emesis, and the peristaltic action of the intestines; and in the inexorable natural processes of dying, decay, and bursts of new life in springtime. As Tarnas recognized, many of these Plutonic forces manifest during the dynamic stage of childbirth through a cluster of themes—titanic fight, the sadomasochistic, scatological, demonic, and pyrocathartic—that Grof observed in his thousands of clinical sessions. Later, in adulthood, Pluto also governs the process that pushes this unresolved material up into awareness where it can be finally worked through and completed. Pluto's driving energies must be faced on an emotional level to be released. When left buried inside, the ego must consume enormous amounts of energy to suppress them, squandering the body's vitality and leaving people chronically tired and worn out.

At the same time, if Pluto's archetypal forces are acted out in the world, they can take the form of dominating, aggressive, or destructive tendencies or fanatical religious and political ideals. These are the result of Plutonic material pressing upward from deep within the psyche, warping people's natural balance and equilibrium. The many forms of "power trip" can be seen as attempts to get on top of and control Pluto's emerging emotions, rather than facing them internally. The entire range of Plutonic themes can be experienced safely in holotropic states without any negative effects in the outer world.

A well-integrated Pluto complex indicates a fundamental ability to adapt to long-term change. People will feel a harmonious relationship with sexual and natural energies, including their own deeper inner nature. They will see the value in actively cooperating with the ongoing processes of death and rebirth in the psyche. Planets aligning with Pluto reveal where issues around shadow, power, and aggression are most likely to surface in people's everyday lives. They also suggest how and where the potential for profound renewal and regeneration are likely to manifest.

CHAPTER 5

The Transit Cycles of Neptune-Neptune, Saturn-Saturn, Pluto-Pluto, and Uranus-Uranus

One of the priorities that Tarnas established in this field is in recognizing a clear distinction between the planets on one hand and the archetypal principles with which they correspond. In archetypal astrology, we thus refer to "archetypal causation" rather than "planetary causation." The planets themselves are not seen as causing our experiences—they are only symbols or representations of timeless archetypal forces that ultimately transcend the physical realm.

With the introductions now complete, we can proceed with the main body of our research. The transit cycles of Neptune to Neptune, Saturn to Saturn, Pluto to Pluto, and Uranus to Uranus, because they happen at approximately the same ages for all people, correspond to fundamental archetypal patterning in every human lifetime. They are blueprints for deep emotional processes that are universal in the human experience. From the individual point of view, the ongoing transit cycles represent the unfolding of what could be described as a profound love affair with the divine principle. The deepest yearning of our psyches is to reconnect with this cosmic ground. At the same time, the mystics tell us that the divine needs relationships with beings different from itself—with us— in order to be fulfilled. We could say then that the major astrological cycles in human life represent key watersheds in this ongoing romance. Every transit represents an invitation from the ultimate Beloved—for awakenings of magic and mystery, of consolidating routine and growth-promoting pain, of pressing intensity and promising excitement, and unexpected rekindling surprises—a partnership that is never static, never boring.

From the transpersonal side, the major transit cycles in a human lifetime represent the divine consciousness' interplay with the incarnated aspects of its own being—the divine now loosening, now pulling up the slack, offering degrees of autonomy to the separated parts of itself, then inevitably drawing their awareness home again. In the future, as in all non-Western and preindustrial cultures before us, I hope that due attention will be given to these important thresholds in a human lifespan and opportunities carefully presented to realize their full awakening potential.

Transits of Neptune-Neptune

The Numinous is a category which exists totally outside of conventional science's comprehension. Yet it is the one category of experience which is dearer to the human soul than any other, for the Numinous is the repositor of all meaning, the reason for our existence, the Logos. . . .

This most unsubstantial and blithe of realities is in truth the most absolute controller of consciousness, the true creative dictator of the psyche's conditions. Even the most finite and unimaginative hard-as-nails perception is a visionary play of the infinite Imagination.
   Richard Tarnas, *Prometheus the Awakener*, original unpublished
   version, 1980

We are not human beings trying to have a spiritual experience. We are a part of one spiritual Being having all the experiences.
   The perennial philosophy

Neptune-Neptune Transits in Everyday Life

During transits of Neptune, people often feel a heightened yearning to connect with the divine source. The current position of Neptune in alignment with the position of Neptune in a person's birth chart is referred to as a *Neptune-Neptune* transit. The most important of these are the sextile (in the mid-twenties), the square (early forties), the trine (early to mid-fifties), and the opposition (late seventies through mid-eighties). These are periods when the numinous layers of reality—the idealistic, the imaginal, the mythic, and the spiritual—will tend to be closer to the surface of awareness. During these times, people may have an easier access to feelings of mystical union with other human beings, with the natural world, and with the cosmic creative principle itself. Neptune re-enchants people's consciousness, enabling them to see the cosmic patterning and meaning in the universe within and around them.

The shadow side of the Neptune archetype emerges when individuals are for various emotional reasons unable to connect with positive

Neptunian states. The hunger of the psyche for these experiences will then have an automatic tendency to impel them toward unhealthy substitutes, such as drug and alcohol abuse, narcissistic fantasy, or other forms of escapism. Neptune-to-Neptune transits represent periods when the numinous principle is actively trying to dissolve the outmoded boundaries in the psyche and holotropic research suggests that people will find deeper satisfaction in their lives by allowing these openings to occur.

Neptune-Neptune Transits in Deep Self-Exploration

All Neptune-to-Neptune transits are magical periods for self-exploration. The spiritual realms are more accessible than at other times, the veils between worlds more transparent and permeable. The Neptunian principle opens and re-enchants consciousness, making it easier for people to surrender to the full range of their psyche's emerging material. It pours up and out in an unimpeded series of living emotional images, like flowing vignettes in a cosmic movie. Participants also have a greater capacity to see through the surface of emerging problems to their deeper archetypal source, helping them through any difficult spots in the process.

Perinatal Experiences

As self-discovery reaches the perinatal realm, the archetypal Neptune acts as a homing beacon, pulling journeyers' awareness back toward the numinous ground of being. As Tarnas recognized, they will have special access to the feelings of oceanic connection that Grof refers to as the Basic Perinatal Matrix I—*The Amniotic Universe* and *Union With the Mother*.

Participants may also pass through leftover disturbances from the intrauterine stage of development. Toxic-womb memories can include feelings of being poisoned, tormented by negative astral influences, or experimented on by demonic entities. Subjects may also believe that their psyches have become completely transparent, convinced that other people can read their minds, that their experiences are being broadcast to the world, or that everything they have ever done is accessible to others. These perceptions reflect the lack of physical, emotional, and spiritual boundaries between mother and fetus in utero. When people work through this material, their experiential field clears dramatically as they reach states of blissful unity with the entire universe, with the Great Mother archetype, or God.

Figure 5. Holotropic Breathwork experience. "Pilgrimmage to My Inner Buddha" Alejandra Scigliano (Sun-Neptune in square with natal Neptune). "I felt immediately inspired to paint the mandala, which was surprising because I had faced a major creative block for two years with almost no output. But as soon as I started to paint, I was taken right back into the session and transported into another dimension. I was able to understand my whole life journey and the glow I feel when I connect with that source of inner wisdom or Buddha nature that is at the heart of everyone."

Transpersonal Experiences

Neptune-Neptune transits also support far-ranging exploration in the transpersonal layers of being. Every aspect of the material world has a spiritual corollary—the Platonic Forms behind the forms—and Grof's research suggests that in holotropic states people can access every part of this inner universe. It is not uncommon to experience a direct identification with other people or groups of people, with specific animal or plant species, and even with inorganic materials and processes.

Subjects may also access experiences from Jung's *historical uncon-scious*, including episodes from the lives of their parents, their ancestors, or humanity at large; from species in the evolutionary pedigree; or even from events in the history of the universe that predate the development of the brain and the nervous system. People can also on occasion face what are perceived as episodes from other lifetimes, including obscure historical details which can sometimes be verified later. Additional sequences, from Jung's *archetypal unconscious*, appear to transcend the realm of time and space altogether. The most common are an identification with archetypal figures and mythological patterns, with the Universal Mind, Absolute Consciousness, or the Macrocosmic Void—the profoundly empty yet all-containing, conscious space that underlies all things.

Transits of Saturn-Saturn

Here, on both the individual and the collective levels can be seen the source of the profound dualism of the modern mind: between man and nature, between mind and matter, between self and other, between experience and reality—that pervading sense of a separate ego irrevocably divided from the encompassing world. Here is the painful separation from the timeless all-encompassing womb of nature, the development of human self-consciousness, the loss of connection with the matrix of being, the expulsion from the Garden, the entrance into time and history and materiality, the disenchantment of the cosmos, the sense of total immersion in an antithetical world of impersonal forces.
Richard Tarnas, *The Passion of the Western Mind*, 1991
(Referring to the Saturnian stage of the birth process, Grof's BPM II).

This rite of initiation, with its revelation of father first as ogre and persecutor, its requirement of acceptance of the 'rules' and conditions of the world, and its ultimate vision of a merciful Father and an immortal soul, seems to be the archetypal Saturnian path. . . . Each thing that is worth having must be approached by the route that winds past the throne of the Father.
Liz Greene, *Saturn: A New Look at an Old Devil*, 1976

Saturn-Saturn Transits in Everyday Life

Saturn-to-Saturn transits represent the classic coming-of-age experiences, as people pass through the end of one phase of life followed by the birth of another. Often during these transits, people feel as if they are turning a major corner or being pressed in by circumstances. Saturn transits usually correspond to some degree of stress and pressure; time seems to slow down as people turn their attention to serious long-term issues and problems. With the flashlight of consciousness shining on the empty half of life's glass, they have a keen awareness of what is not working, and of challenges yet to be overcome.

The observed operative range or *orb* on either side of exact for Saturn-Saturn transits tends to be fairly wide—approximately ten degrees for the squares and ten–fourteen degrees for the oppositions, which thus last from eighteen to twenty-four months. However, the orb for the powerful Saturn-conjunct-Saturn or *Saturn-return* transits is even larger—twenty degrees before and after exact, and thus they can be in effect for up to thirty-six months.

Aligning just over every seven years, the dynamic transits of Saturn to Saturn represent the critical maturation periods of ages six to seven (Saturn square Saturn), fourteen to fifteen (opposition), twenty-one to twenty-two (square), twenty-eight to thirty (conjunction), and so forth. During these watershed transitions, people often feel a need to integrate deeper levels of responsibility, duty, and expectation. Typically, they become more grounded and centered, more realistic.

Although Saturn's challenges can be painful, at times, they play a fundamental role in the development of the mature and autonomous individual. Life's inevitable ups and downs also help people to cultivate qualities of patience, self-reliance, and staying power. Often the Saturn archetype can feel like a deflating influence, reminding people of their limitations, the material boundaries and time constraints within which all life must exist. Humbly facing their human shortcomings, people are reminded of the inescapable consequences of their actions and the ways they need to take the world seriously, often awakening remorse for past mistakes and an urgent resolve to do better.

Yet along with these painful lessons of fallibility comes an understanding that the greatest oppressor of humanity is fear itself and that the root of all fear is the fear of death. Every form in this world, including everything that we know and love, will ultimately pass away. On these shifting sands, people come to realize that, in the end, the only secure resting place is the soul's reconnection with the timeless ground of being.

The flowing Saturn-to-Saturn transits (the trines and sextiles) also contribute serious themes, and when combined with other Saturn influences they can increase the Saturnian flavor of everyday life. During these times, people can be successful at patterning and structuring their worlds, in both positive and ultimately confining ways.

Saturn-Saturn Transits in Deep Self-Exploration

Saturn-Saturn transits tend to have a cooling and containing, yet also focusing effect in emotional work. They help people to face and clear out the most dense and challenging layers in their psyches, especially material centered around emotional separation, physical pressure, and existential suffering. Experiences associated with Saturn can also foster qualities of spiritual endurance, fortitude, and forbearance.

The *trine and sextile* transits correspond to moderately strong, mildly supportive influences for deep work. Their sobering effect helps journeyers recognize the need to set up a proper space ahead of time—trustworthy sitters, a soundproof room, evocative music, and backup support for later—that will enable them to fully let go and face their deeper material. These transits also remind people of the importance of maintaining clear professional boundaries between sitters and clients. Saturn helps to create an atmosphere of responsibility and integrity, with everyone knowing their role and doing their part in the healing experience.

The extremely powerful *dynamic* transits of Saturn to Saturn have a similar effect, but with an additional cooling and sobering quality. Journeyers can have very rewarding experiences but, as always, it is important to take care of logistical details ahead of time and not leave essential elements to chance, in order to ensure that their emotional needs are met. A safe space on the outer level helps people to work through the trauma-based structures on the inner level, leading to opening and releasing.

In the early stages of exploration, journeyers can work through episodes in their lives involving situations of painful loss, separation, or victimization. They may also process leftover traces from serious accidents, illnesses, and operations, especially those that posed a threat to life or bodily integrity. As mentioned, during any Saturn transit, journeyers undergo strict, unrelenting reviews of their ethical behavior in the world, and make urgent commitments to live in more responsible and compassionate ways. Although the relationship of personal ethics to the opening of spiritual doors might be seen as complex and paradoxical—with so much of this work about facing one's own corruptibility, letting go of past mistakes, and reaching states of forgiveness—journeyers in holotropic states receive serious, ongoing ethical lessons from within their own being and develop a strong desire, above all, not to hurt anyone.

Perinatal Experiences

As exploration reaches the perinatal realm, Saturn transits will, similarly, tend to direct the flashlight of people's awareness toward the more dense and constricted material in their psyches. This can happen in two ways: first, by focusing their attention on the BPM II, no-exit matrix, as Tarnas recognized. These experiences are based on the early stage of labor where the contracting walls of the uterus have ended the fetus' blissful existence and turned it into a torture chamber, but the cervix is still closed and there is no way out. These experiences are an important source of feelings of entrapment, hopelessness, depression, and guilt in later life until they are faced and worked through.

Tarnas notes that the full activation of the no-exit matrix is most likely when Saturn-to-Saturn transits are accompanied by powerful transits of Saturn-Pluto or Saturn-Neptune. These intensely challenging alignments

(Saturn-to-Saturn combined with Neptune or with Pluto) can evoke the most extreme forms of BPM II, but also thereby effect its full emergence and release. Journeyers facing these very severe archetypes should be given every support that is humanly possible.

The second way that Saturn transits focus people's attention is by helping them to face the challenging aspects of material activated by their Uranus, Neptune, and Pluto transits. These might include delivery-room complications in Uranus' rebirth matrix (BPM IV), intrauterine toxicity in Neptune's amniotic matrix (BPM I), or inhuman pressures in Pluto's hard-labor matrix (BPM III). While the Saturn principle can delay the emergence of positive states or deflate their more exuberant forms, it also provides the staying power to remain with the process to the end of the line. This archetype seems to grant rewards for patience and persistence.

As always, people with heavy Saturn transits may benefit from nourishing physical contact if they request it. Ideally, healing sessions should take place in a comfortable studio filled with the finest expressions of nature and the human spirit, such as beautiful flowers, tasteful art, soft fabrics, and picture books of interesting and exotic landscapes. A positive, structured event at the end of the day which is centered around the participant, such as a special shared dinner and walks in nature, will help to support the healing and integrating process. Because Saturn sometimes delays the completion of material, people may need some extra time in the evening to lie down and face remaining pockets of material.

Transpersonal Experiences

Experiences in the transpersonal realms under Saturn transits may also embody the qualities of constriction, division, maturation, endurance, and rewards over time. These can include traumatic episodes in the lives of people's ancestors or the suffering of various human groups through history. Subjects may identify with vulnerable ecosystems or entire species decimated in the name of short-term profit, or with the entire human race facing multiple threats to its continued survival.

Journeyers can explore long-term processes in evolutionary history, such as the formation of granite or the development of bone structures in vertebrates. The following composite report from a series of internalized marijuana sessions, undertaken with transiting Saturn opposition the subject's natal Saturn, and transiting Neptune opposition natal Uranus, illustrates a number of Saturnian themes:

Although the overall flavor of this series was an expression of the Neptune opposition Uranus transit, the Saturn opposition Saturn seemed to play an important inflecting and focusing role. For one thing, I felt an agonizing sense of physical anxiety and deflation of vanity issues in my everyday life triggered by crowding of my teeth, which were important factors spurring me to do the regular work. I also did not have access to a proper processing space or experienced sitters and had to do many bite-size mini-sessions rather than a smaller number of more intense major sessions. And, in retrospect, although the process took me over an incredibly wide inner ground—exploring the basic patterning of many transpersonal territories—there was a certain quality of darkness and compression in my experiential field that only lightened up years later with a whole new cycle of transits.

In terms of content, several mini-sessions of this series stand out as expressions of the Saturn opposition Saturn alignment. After experiencing at length the consciousness of a particular species of flower, the process suddenly took my awareness down through the flower's stem into the Earth itself. I was somehow directly identifying with the consciousness of solid rock and perceived that rock is made from conscious and timeless divine energy that has been compressed into solid form. Its basic character is infinite patience and forbearance. Rock or granite is not a glamorous position to have in the world but it does make up the necessary stage upon which the countless interesting dramas of earthly life can unfold. Rock can be buried for aeons but maintains, wherever it exists, an open identification with the divine and knows that sooner or later its energy will be freed. This experience went a long way toward releasing my feelings of pressure.

The above experiences were based on contracting forces in the realm of *matter*. In contrast, the following internalized marijuana session, undertaken with Saturn square natal Saturn, and a world transit T-square of Saturn-Uranus-Pluto—formed by two planets in 180° opposition, with a third planet at 90° angles to both—focused on pressures in *time*:

> For many years now, I have been increasingly worried that I might be getting too old to keep doing sessions and have the breakthroughs that I still know are possible. Along with the usual trust issues, I have been terrified of developing some kind of health problem that would prevent me from continuing on this path, that time is running out. With these fears coming to a head and feeling generally washed up, I decided on the date in question to do a milder internalized marijuana session of five inhalations, though I still maintained two sitters and a soundproof space.
>
> I went through some horrible feelings of being stuck, as a kind of rigid demonic energy took over my consciousness and plunged me into ultimate darkness. This gradually intensified to cosmic dimensions and then suddenly shifted to a long sequence of explosive breakthroughs that lasted for many hours. My body was determinedly twisting from side to side on the mat. All

of a sudden, I felt that I was identifying with the consciousness of a grandfather clock, with my side-to-side movements the periodic swings of its hand. The experience was so real that I was sure it was apparent to the sitters.

I then had a powerful feeling that I was transcending the dimension of time altogether and gaining access to experiences from another time and place. I became the consciousness of humanity along the southern tip of South Africa around 50,000 years ago, the few who survived the catastrophic drought of 70,000–50,000 B.C. that wiped out all archaic *Homo sapiens* in Africa except along the southern tip. I experienced both their tenuous grip on life, but also the evolution occurring in the survivors' technology and consciousness that gave birth to modern *Homo sapiens*. I felt a sense of vast empowerment and new beginnings as the drought receded and the world was left open to settle.

After a while, this shifted to an emotionally opposite kind of scene. I felt the consciousness of archaic *Homo sapiens* in Africa, several millennia earlier, during the same epochal drought that killed almost every human on the continent. Finally, I identified with some aquatic organism floating off land in warm waters in the Paleozoic Era, about 300 million years ago.

These collective memories have changed my perception. I feel less time pressure, more centered on living in the moment. I now feel that the universe has its own schedule and that everything happens in its own good time. In some small way, my consciousness has reached the other side.

Journeyers undergoing the dynamic Saturn-to-Saturn transits may also explore various archetypal principles, both by themselves and in the context of the perinatal unfolding, such as the Fall from Paradise, the Harsh Taskmaster, the Grim Reaper, Thantos, Maya, or the Senex. They will also continue to review the effects of higher principles of education, cause and effect, and balancing in human life.

Finally, subjects can explore the process of what the mystics refer to as *incarnation* or *involution*—as the cosmic creative principle gives birth to the physical universe and the dimension of time out of its own substance, with the resulting loss of freedom and connection engendered for all the separate beings created in the process.

Transits of Pluto-Pluto

A deep experiential encounter with birth and death is regularly associated with an existential crisis of extraordinary proportions, during which the individual seriously questions the meaning of existence, as well as his or her basic values and life strategies. This crisis can be resolved only by connecting with deep, intrinsic spiritual dimensions of the psyche and elements of the collective unconscious. The resulting personality transformation seems to be

comparable to the changes that have been described as having come about from participation in ancient temple mysteries, initiation rites, or aboriginal rites of passage.
 Stanislav Grof, *Beyond the Brain*, 1985

Pluto-Pluto Transits in Everyday Life

Pluto-to-Pluto transits represent an intensification of the processes of deep self-discovery, emotional death and rebirth, transformation, and regeneration in human life. The Pluto-sextile-Pluto transit of the mid-twenties, and the Pluto-trine-Pluto of the late-forties to early-fifties, represent tremendous opportunities for deep and sustained exploration of the unconscious. During these times, the universe seems to be unusually supportive of any efforts toward emotional uncovering work, often providing the resources necessary for this rewarding activity. The flowing Pluto-to-Pluto transits are also helpful for upgrading, cleaning up, or clearing out situations in people's everyday worlds.

The alignment of Pluto *square* Pluto of the late thirties to early forties (moving to the mid-to-late forties as the century progresses) is one of the most important transits in a human lifetime. The double-activated Pluto—involving Pluto both as a transiting influence and as the planet being transited—can symbolize important confrontations with the shadow side of human nature. This might take the form of aggressive control issues, power struggles, emotional obsessions, or disturbing encounters with the shadow side of others. People who have acted in a habitually ruthless way in their lives may experience these same energies coming toward them from the external world. Robert Hand describes this balancing process as "diamond cuts diamond." However, even normally peaceful individuals can find themselves engaged in heavy emotional situations that seem to draw out their own latent forceful or aggressive tendencies. Whatever the apparent source of the outer problem—unless it involves an actual threat to life or limb—the most helpful response is to turn inward and unilaterally face the emerging material in one's own psyche.

If holotropic sessions are not available, some of Pluto's energies can be worked through in an incremental way by yelling into pillows, in a safely parked car, or somewhere deep in nature. It may be helpful to engage in the process of *active imagination*, a method enhanced during the midlife period by the concurrent transit of Neptune square Neptune. People can start by envisioning an encounter with the person with whom they are having trouble, and then let the imagined scene progress without judgment in whatever direction it wants to go, deeply feeling the emotions on all sides. These inner scenarios typically move in the direction of peri-natal material. For example, a sense of ridiculing or humiliating insults from a smug housemate can transform into images of Shiva's giant foot ruthlessly squashing the psyche down toward ego death and rebirth, or of the mother's contracting body forcefully pressing the baby out through the birth canal. During all Pluto transits, it is valuable to allow oneself to feel both the emotions of victimized helplessness and the perpetrating inner forces.

As people face the emotional material underlying their conflicts, they gradually become more comfortable with the pressure generated by these conflicts, and will withdraw their projections from the external situation. At this point, they may even quietly appreciate the offending person as a catalyst to self-discovery. Access to proper holotropic sessions can expedite this process.

Pluto-Pluto Transits in Deep Self-Exploration

All Pluto-to-Pluto transits are powerful indicators for emotional work, greatly intensifying the level of people's charic experiences. The Pluto complex breaks loose repressed contents from the psyche, pushing them into consciousness with enormous force. Like a volcano in its effects, sub-terranean emotional forces are driven upward, building pressure until the upper structures are finally exploded away, releasing the tension. Holo-tropic states provide a safe and effective way to free these energies, allow-ing the process to take place internally, rather than in a more messy and prolonged form in people's outer lives.

In the initial stages of exploration, the double-activated Pluto will go a long way toward breaking down people's resistance to entering holo-tropic states. Various interpersonal and intrapersonal encounters, espe-cially during the Pluto-square-Pluto transit of the midlife, eventually lead many to make the correct interpretation that the true source of these encounters is emerging material from their own psyches. As they begin to surrender and face these contents directly, Pluto provides a tremendous boost to full cathartic experience.

Perinatal Experiences

When self-exploration reaches the perinatal layer, Tarnas found that Pluto-to-Pluto transits will have a tendency to engage material centered on the dynamic stage of labor, which Grof terms BPM III—the *Death-Rebirth Struggle*. Reflecting the fetus' experience of being forced down the narrow birth canal by powerful uterine contractions, people may face any of the classic BPM III themes: titanic aggression, sadomasochistic feelings, demonic energies, scatological materials, or confrontations with purifying fire.

The atmosphere in perinatal sessions during Pluto transits in general can feel, for periods of time, like an unfolding catastrophe. However, these experiences also have a strangely liberating, rebellious, and at times sexual quality. Journeyers experience feelings of overwhelming scandal, disaster, betrayal, and judgment, and simultaneously, a strange sense of identifying with the perpetrating forces. They may become absolutely convinced that their process has, once and for all, gone over the line—imagining that their session is destroying the whole world or even the entire universe. These scenes are then followed by sequences of dramatic rebirth and renewal of the world, resulting in tremendous physical and emotional healing and release of inner pressure. Observations in holotropic states suggest that the projections of catastrophe reflect the fetus' experience of being pushed further and further away from the lost womb. Its entire experience is happening inside the mother's body, which for the fetus represents the entire universe, and thus, in the adult's later consciousness, reliving the loss of the womb is experienced as destruction of the world or of the universe. Grof observed repeatedly that full surrender to these sequences of death and rebirth leads to unusually deep healing.

The following excerpt from a supervised and internalized psychedelic session, undergone with transiting Pluto square the subject's natal Pluto, illustrates this classic pattern of death and rebirth:

> The non-verbal love, gratitude, and shared credit that I was sure were being perceived by my sitters, now began to sour in the most inexorable and uncanny way. I was convinced that they were becoming gradually concerned and then deeply alarmed by my signals, as a bad side of my being came forward and revealed itself, setting in motion an unstoppable cascade of planetary-scale destruction. My moral failure would now set in motion a chain-reaction of failures and disasters. All the evolutionary yearning of billions of years on this planet, culminating in the great hopes of a peaceful interconnected global village, spiritual ecology, and transpersonal psychology were now at that moment being irrevocably wiped out.
>
> A while later, I suddenly realized that I was now in a totally different place—I was a newborn, craving nourishing contact with mom and dad. The uncanny feelings of destruction had all just been happening inside my psyche, with my mind filling in the gaps to try and make sense of the experience. I can still only marvel at the incredible authenticity and convincing nature of this experience.

As subjects face this material, they release enormous amounts of tension in aggressive motor discharges, shaking and tremors, projectile vomiting, episodes of choking and determined coughing—in an atmosphere of what Grof calls *Dionysian* or *volcanic* type of ecstasy. At certain points, they can also become convinced that they are dying. As people surrender and allow these experiences to happen, death and birth appear to be indistinguishable, as the agonizing death of the old ego structures gives way to the ecstatic rebirth of a new, more-integrated wholeness in the psyche. The following holotropic session of a graduate student was conducted with transiting Pluto square natal Pluto:

> My legs were shaking and vibrating for hour after hour, as my body consumed huge amounts of tension by holding me in the place between contraction and release. I was emotionally dying. Intense energies were flowing through me with images of destruction, and I perceived that there was going to be destruction one way or another—either of structures in my internal psyche or in the external world. I just lay back and let my consciousness flow into the music. There were many dramatic releases of energy, and by the end of the evening I felt quietly and peacefully ecstatic.

As this material resolves, journeyers see that the inordinate pursuit of wealth, power, and prestige are just an attempted defense against the overwhelming energies and emotions left over from birth and consequent fear of death. As the feelings of inner threat disappear, they are freed of the need to be in control, leading to far greater options for actual positive contributions in the world. The following holotropic session was conducted with Pluto trine the subject's natal Pluto:

> At one point, I arrived at a kind of archetypal INTERSECTION where the old, outmoded structures of the material world are consumed by fire. I could feel a massive healing wave emerging from deep inside me and beginning to regenerate my entire life.

Transpersonal Experiences

Material from Jung's historical and archetypal unconscious during Pluto transits will also tend to have an aggressive, destructive, evolutionary, and transformative character. Journeyers can work through leftover emotions from traumatic events in world history. They may encounter archetypal figures who embody themes of death, descent into the underworld, and spiritual rebirth such as Christ, Osiris, Persephone, or Dionysus. Finally, they may identify with the consciousness of various animals, plants, or inorganic materials or processes. The following is from a holotropic session undertaken with Pluto square the subject's natal Pluto:

> I experienced the violent consciousness of highly toxic chemicals being dumped systematically into the world's oceans. I felt that in some way they are an acted-out expression of disowned aggressive feelings in the psyche of

humanity. Connecting with specific life forms in the ocean in real time, I could not turn away as they pleaded: "Help us . . . we're dying . . ." It is clear that life in the oceans is vanishing, and that no amount of positive thinking or rationalization can change this terrible fact. It was a deeply sobering experience and one that will stay with me for the rest of my life.

Figure 6. Holotropic Breathwork session of a European participant. "Dream Man" Heike Daniel (Pluto square natal Pluto, and Neptune square natal Neptune). Part of a several-year process in which she worked through powerful emotions from the collective psyche around the genocide of indigenous people in the new world.

Transits of Uranus-Uranus

After the subject has experienced the limits of total annihilation and "hit the cosmic bottom," he or she is struck by visions of blinding white or golden light. The claustrophobia and compressed world of the birth struggle suddenly opens up and expands into infinity. The general atmosphere is one of liberation, salvation . . . and love.

Stanislav Grof, *LSD Psychotherapy*, 1980 (On the experience of ego death and rebirth in deep, systematic self-exploration).

Uranus-Uranus Transits in Everyday Life

Transits of Uranus to Uranus represent some of the most emancipating archetypal influences that human beings can experience, although their strength may be offset or accentuated by other transits. Very often they correspond to periods of dramatic awakening, opening of horizons, and healing resolutions in people's lives, and thus every effort should be made to cooperate with their liberating effects. The light of cosmic consciousness seems to shine more brightly through these periodic fold lines in the tapestry of the human lifespan.

The transits of this breakthrough cycle include the Uranus-Uranus conjunction (at birth), the sextile (ages 11–13), square (17–20), trine (24–26), opposition (38–41), trine (54–56), square (61–63), sextile (68–70), and conjunction (81–84). However, as Tarnas discovered through his research into the creative trajectories and biographical events of hundreds of cultural figures, the most powerful of these are the conjunctions, oppositions, and squares, referred to as the *quadrature* alignments.

The first transit in this cycle, the Uranus square Uranus of the late teens (until approximately 20½) represents the first period of relative independence in many young people's lives, as they leave the security of their parents' sphere and gain access to many new kinds of opportunities and experiences. Of course, few transits occur in isolation, and the Saturn-square-Saturn that begins during the end of the Uranus-Uranus— around age twenty—can represent, during the same period, a challenging encounter with the material demands of adult life for some unprepared youngsters.

The Uranus-opposition-Uranus alignment of the early forties is the classic midlife transit, an experience Tarnas describes as the "full moon of the Prometheus archetype." People often feel a determined impulse to regain their youth and youthful freedoms, sometimes manifesting in cliched forms such as taking on a younger lover or buying a sports car, to more enduring changes such as shedding layers of character armor and finding more direct, inner sources of satisfaction. As well as emotional and spiritual openings, people often experience bursts of creative illumination.[1] For some, it is also a time of stress as the double-activated Prometheus archetype is not gentle in its determination to free people from dissatisfying routines of external conformity and inner repression.

The second Uranus-square-Uranus transit, of the late fifties, climaxes the "golden decade" of the fifties and offers more opportunities for emotional liberation and renewal, as well as for some a contemplation of retirement. And, finally, the Uranus return of the early eighties can be for hardy souls a time of spiritual crowning, when the healing journeys and experiences of an entire lifetime deeply register, the burdens of incarnation further lift, and the eternal soul burns brightly within the weakening frame.[2]

The Uranus-Uranus trines of the mid-twenties, and early-to-mid-fifties, and to a lesser extent the sextiles, represent further chances for creative awakening and self-discovery. The trines, especially, are very supportive for exploration of the unconscious.

Uranus transits can also, at any time, evoke the considerable shadow qualities of the Prometheus archetype. Problems such as manic hyperactivity, erratic lack of focus, unconstrained acting out, and nervous tension can be seen as the result of driving inner material pressing upward into awareness.

Uranus-Uranus Transits in Deep Self-Exploration

The archetypal field engaged during Uranus-to-Uranus transits offers dramatic avenues for deep inner work, adding to sessions the character of sudden unexpected opening, healing resolutions, and self-realization. The Prometheus archetype rebels against the static structures of the tyrant ego, liberating people's awareness back into more exciting, stimulating, and life-supporting forms.

In general, the curiosity and restlessness for new experience that many people feel during Uranus-Uranus transits will tend to make adventures in self-discovery more appealing. These are fantastic transits for a first session, for the first session in a new series, or for moving into completely new layers of experience. When Uranus is also aligned in the sky with Pluto, Neptune, or Jupiter, its liberating power will be exponentially increased.

Perinatal Experiences

When self-exploration reaches the perinatal region of the psyche, Uranus transits can help people to successfully face the full range of material engaged by their ongoing Saturn, Neptune, and Pluto transits. Tarnas found that the Uranus complex can also help to constellate the overall experiences of rebirth and transcendence that Grof terms BPM IV. The following is from an internalized psychedelic session of a subject with obsessive-compulsive symptoms from severe toilet training in childhood. It was conducted during his Uranus-opposition-Uranus midlife transit, and transiting Pluto square natal Pluto:

> After many surges of aggressive energy, suddenly, at the three-and-a-half hour threshold, I felt a pressure in my abdomen and had to go to the bathroom. During other sessions, I had been obsessive about wearing an adult brief because I was terrified that I might accidentally pee on the foamy and upset the sitters. I tried to go where I was lying, but then just suddenly sat up on my knees and tore off the brief. I asked my sitters if I could pee where I was.

I don't know if they said yes or no but they didn't object, and my male sitter held a plastic urinal under me. As a few drops came slowly out, I felt my inner field lifting in feelings of dramatic rebirth, with bursts of cosmic electricity shooting through my entire being. Finally, at last! Hallelujah!! . . . Hallelujah!! This turned out to be a permanent threshold in my process and I never had serious issues about making a mess in a session again. I also felt more peaceful and resolved that night than during any session up to that point.

When people come out the other end of the death-rebirth experiences of BPM III and reach the rebirth states of BPM IV, they feel a tremendous relief from danger and threat. Although they may still register some less-than-perfect biological memories from the first hours of life—such as hunger, wetness, variations in temperature, or medical interventions—for most people these are absolutely minor compared with the life-threatening suffering in the birth canal. The following is from a holotropic session undertaken with Uranus opposition natal Uranus:

> I finally broke through and realized that I was in the rebirth state of BPM IV. I noticed that there were still some minor problems, but they were nothing, nothing at all compared to the unimaginable agony of the previous stage.

The depth and scope of people's rebirth experiences in a given session will depend of course on many factors, including how much perinatal material they have already worked through, their level of trauma, the quality of trust they have with their sitters, and their transits. With powerful transits of Pluto also engaged, Uranus-to-Uranus transits are some of the many influences that could support people in accessing the full experience of BPM IV. Grof observed that subjects undergoing systematic sessions eventually pass through states of unbearable tension and a fusion of ecstasy and agony, finally culminating in a sense of total failure on every imaginable level. This is followed by visions of blinding white or golden light, peacock feathers and spectra patterns, and the inside of giant halls and cathedrals.

In an atmosphere of redemption and salvation, journeyers experience feelings of blessed rebirth, forgiveness, and kinship with humanity. They often have the sense that they have cleared out an enormous amount of personal baggage. Grof found that reaching experiences of BPM IV, as well as BPM I and nourishing transpersonal states, leads to a dramatic healing of physical and emotional symptoms, a positive restructuring of the personality, and higher functioning in everyday life. People also discover within themselves natural, positive human values. As we have seen, these include an urge for meaningful work, ecological sensitivity, ideological tolerance, and a high priority placed on warm human relationships.

Transpersonal Experiences

Transpersonal material under Uranus-to-Uranus transits tends to share with perinatal sessions the themes of unexpected breakthrough and resolution of problems. Journeyers may experience a release from the effects of traumatic episodes in the lives of their ancestors, their racial group, or the human species in general. They can also reach feelings of forgiveness and liberation from karmic burdens leftover from a painful past life. During these experiences, people often have the profound realization, confirmed in the Eastern traditions, that not forgiving others may create just as much karma as hurting them.

Mythological sequences under Uranus transits center around the successful completion of superhuman tasks, the miraculous returning home, or rebirth from the underworld of various archetypal heroes. Even stories of mythological ruin turn out to portray emancipating processes, as in this holotropic session of a graduate student undergone with Uranus opposition his natal Uranus, and Jupiter trine Uranus in the sky:

> I suddenly became the mythological figure Icarus, defying the limits of his father Daedalus and flying too close to the sun. The wax on my wings began to melt and soon I was plunging down into the ocean. Rather than leading to a disaster in the session, however, I experienced my two female sitters as the cooling oceanic divine into which all human mistakes are eventually received, forgiven and dissolved.
>
> I remember that the Icarus story had a shocking and frightening impact on me as a child. In retrospect, I feel that I have reached a point in my unfolding where the potential for impulsive excesses or big errors in judgment has hopefully decreased. Many of the high-flying rebellious energies of the Uranus-Icarus archetype have played themselves out through my inner life.
>
> Writing about this now, I am excited to have made the Icarus archetype conscious. I have been deeply afraid of overdoing things in my life—what an incredible liberation! During this awakening process, I have appreciated so much the kind support of my female sitters.

At this level of exploration, mythological images meet Joseph Campbell's important criteria of being "transparent to the transcendent." Journeyers see that the deities of all cultures are just doorways, faces of the one cosmic consciousness—the universal field of pure awareness that embodies all cultures and forms.

The guiding atmosphere in Uranus-Uranus sessions tends to be one of unexpected awakening, relieved excitement, and shared credit for the breakthroughs of the day. Journeyers with strong Uranus transits, in general, have a greater chance of reaching a positive state by the end of their sessions and finishing it in a good place. Grof notes that what is most important from a therapeutic point of view is not how much material people work through, but how good they feel at the end. The Uranus archetype acts as a cosmic midwife, drawing people's awareness through whatever material is blocking its free flow and out into the liberating space of the Universal Mind. At best, they will feel a sense of ecstatic reentry, bonding with their friends and family and laughing about the difficulties they have overcome.

CHAPTER 6

The Archetypal Pairs

We can now introduce the combinations of archetypal principles which astrologers refer to as *archetypal* or *planetary pairs*. As the planets form alignments with each other, their corresponding archetypal fields are activated in human experience. The following chapters will explore the range of these expressions, in both everyday life and in deep self-exploration.

In contrast with traditional astrological practice, the approach set forth by Tarnas and outlined in this book is archetypally predictive rather than concretely predictive. Every transit represents a range of experiences that could happen or are trying to happen, but the specific forms they take will also depend on the level of awareness and understanding that people bring to their inner lives. This is why inner work is so beneficial. Self-knowledge is the missing element, the unplayed trump card that can help to tip our experience in positive directions. The more we know about the archetypal impulses operating in our psyches at a given time, the more consciously we can work with those energies and help their most positive forms to manifest.

Readers will notice a high degree of overlap and repetition of content in the following sections. This is because every transit that includes one of the archetypes Neptune, Saturn, Pluto, or Uranus, for example, will tend to share many of the same basic qualities and characteristics. Most transits of Neptune will embody certain fundamental Neptunian themes—including a yearning for higher meaning, opening to spirituality, dissolution of boundaries, and so forth. The same degree of overlap is true for all alignments that involve one of the planets Saturn, Uranus, or Pluto.

Transits of Neptune

Sun-Neptune

It speaks out [of] . . . a million eyes, it expresses itself in countless gestures, and there is no village or country road where that broad-branched tree

cannot be found in whose shade the ego struggles for its own abolition, drowning the world of multiplicity in the All and All-Oneness of Universal Being.
    C. G. Jung (Sun square Neptune 0°16′)
    Psychology and Religion (Referring to India).[1]

We are spirits in the material world.
    Sting (Sun conjunct Neptune 10°50′) "Spirits in the Material World"

Sun-Neptune Transits in Everyday Life

Sun-Neptune transits combine the archetypal Sun's enthusiastic, expressive, and vital nature with Neptune's mystical, imaginative, and compassionate character. These archetypes often have a warming effect on people's spiritual lives. Neptune softens the boundaries of awareness, making people more sensitive to the world within and around them. Feeling more in touch with their natural idealism, they often yearn to connect with some kind of higher meaning or purpose beyond their usual ego boundaries. At best, they can perceive the sacred energy permeating every molecule of creation.[2]

The effect of the Sun archetype is to channel Neptune's spiritual feelings through the lens of the archetypal yang or masculine principle. People are more likely to perceive the refined mystical qualities in their own masculine side or in the males around them. They may also experience heightened creative feelings or a fascination with the rich archetypal expressions of world culture in cinema, art, and music.

As well as these experiences, the *dynamic transits* may also symbolize feelings of weakness and vulnerability, as the Neptune archetype works to draw people's consciousness inward toward itself. By surrendering to the play of dreams and imagination within their inner lives and deeply feeling the emotions associated with it, their awareness will over time smooth out and transform into feelings of cosmic unity. During this process, it is important that they also keep their feet on the ground of everyday routines and warm human connection, in order to balance Neptune's proneness toward wishful imagination and fantasy. In holotropic workshops, the supportive contact with sitters and other breathers at the end of the day provides this grounding connection with the real world.

Under the less-than-ideal conditions that many young explorers find themselves in, Neptune's yearning for spirituality can also lead to imbalances in judgment or esoteric forms of egotism. As Hand describes, to say, "I am God" may be the expression of a high philosophical truth. To say, "I am God and you're not" is a sign of inner work yet to be done. Under Neptune-Sun transits, it is probably best to avoid extreme world-denying and ascetic practices that draw people too far from ordinary reality for extended periods of time. A yearning for the divine, especially in its masculine personas, may also lead them to overidealize certain types of guru figures, experiences which could range from a helpful transmission of spiritual knowledge to cultish brainwashing and exploitation. The most any teacher can do is to help people get in touch with their own emotional process and rediscover a connection with the divine through their own psyche.

Sun-Neptune Transits in Deep Self-Exploration

Sun-Neptune transits are very strong, highly supportive indicators for holotropic states. Journeyers will be more attuned to the numinous layers of reality and have less resistance to letting go. The Sun-Neptune field helps to create a magical and hallowed atmosphere around healing work, adding a rich, warm, and mythic quality to the experience. These archetypes also enable people to de-literalize their process, seeing through the surface layer of emotional and physical symptoms to their perinatal and transpersonal roots.

In holotropic states, journeyers allow the emerging material to fill their awareness, surrounding the universe around them without judgment or reserve. There is always a part of the psyche that remains simply watching. This inner witness or observer does not have to be maintained by force of will—it is an expression of the Absolute Consciousness itself, the numinous ground of being or sacred space that remains when every other structure has been consumed.

Perinatal Experiences

The themes that emerge during Sun-Neptune transits include an outpouring of golden imagination, rediscovery of the spiritual side of the masculine principle, and transcendence of the separate ego consciousness—self awakening to Self. As exploration reaches the perinatal layer, Tarnas found that an activated Sun-Neptune can help to smooth out disturbances from people's amniotic history and open up fresh channels for healing transpersonal energies to flow in.

As toxic-womb memories begin to surface, journeyers can briefly feel their wills are being weakened or paralyzed, or that they are on the edge of falling asleep. As the material then begins to deepen, they may identify with contaminated and spoiled nature, or feel negative astral energies or influences. Facing this material automatically consumes it from the system. Sun-Neptune transits also help journeyers to connect with supportive-father and healing-male energy through their sitters as well as feelings of universal brotherhood.

Transpersonal Experiences

As the inner womb sweetens and transcends into the Universal Womb, people recognize that their individual self or *atman*, represented by the Sun, is essentially commensurate with the higher universal Self or *Brahman*, symbolized by Neptune. In Hindu philosophy, this is described in shorthand simply as *atman-Brahman*. They may also experience various masculine faces of the divine, personified in archetypal forms such as Apollo, Buddha, Christ, the Heavenly Father, or the Cosmic Sun. The full experience of any archetype in holotropic states has an integrating effect, reducing the ongoing problem in the spiritual path of "psychic inflation"— personally identifying with an archetype in a partial form, spread out over months or years, rather than surrendering to its full emotional content in supported non-ordinary states.

At the most rarefied layers of discovery, people may apprehend the principle of higher meaning or *Logos* in the universe, or connect with the divine in a more abstract form such as radiant light or a loving presence. They may also experience life in heaven or paradise, especially warm and sunny paradises such as the Greek Elysian Fields or Islands of the Blessed, a realm of eternal sunshine at the ends of the world. On occasion, Neptunian sessions can be overseen by an oceanic emcee such as a specific aquatic life form.

The following report from a supervised and internalized psychedelic session of a male graduate student with Neptune square his natal Sun, and Sun conjunct natal Neptune, illustrates many of the unique features of this archetypal complex:

> On the long drive to the session space, I felt completely drained of energy and enthusiasm. The whole experience seemed utterly pointless and hopeless. After about an hour, these perceptions began to lift as I tapped into a transcendent archetypal sequence: God's love for His son. On a deep level I identified with both of these inner figures, as my heart chakra opened wide.
>
> Later, in the session, for a long time I felt completely out of contact with my female sitter as I projected *Judging Birth Canal* onto her. I turned to my male sitter, whom I perceived in that moment as "Daddy," for support. He was completely and fully there, lying diagonally with his chest against mine.
>
> After a long period of bonding with this plentiful fatherly energy, I had a sense that I had fallen through a false floor in my psyche and landed in the palm of a nourishing karmic pattern with roots in other lifetimes. I was grateful that my challenges with the archetypal feminine had allowed me to fall deeply enough through the cracks in my being to discover this positive inner pattern. As I accepted the nourishment, I was determinedly transcending and finding the right relationship with God.

Sun-Neptune transits also help people in the resolution phase of the day, enhancing a sense of oceanic or Apollonian type of ecstasy. Feeling more attuned to the spiritual vitality in nature, long walks outside can be unusually satisfying. People may perceive sunlight, especially, as having special mythic or numinous qualities. In holotropic sessions, Sun-Neptune represents the inner equivalent of a magical sunny day on a pristine seashore.

Moon-Neptune

Late on the third day, at the very moment, when, at sunset, we were making our way through a herd of hippopotamuses, there flashed upon my mind, unforeseen and unsought, the phrase, "Reverence for Life."
  Albert Schweitzer (Moon conjunct Neptune 2°29′)
  Out of My Life and Thought, 1949

My religion is kindness.
  The Dalai Lama (Moon conjunct Neptune 0°51′)

Moon-Neptune Transits in Everyday Life

During Moon-Neptune alignments, people often feel more sensitive and connected with their surroundings. At the same time, the Neptune principle softens their emotional boundaries, helping them to feel their own process more deeply and smoothly. Awakening channels of sympathy and compassion, they may also empathically relate to others' experiences. People often feel deeper bonds with their family and crave the quiet peace and serenity of a loving home life.

The Moon-Neptune archetypal field awakens a connection with *soul,* the heart of the psyche that acts as a fertile interface between the feminine emotional world, the body, and the spiritual realms. People may access deeper layers of creative inspiration and imagination as the veils between inner and outer worlds recede. At best, they can feel a sense of union with all of humanity or with aspects of nature.

When people's yearning for mystical union is unmet, however, they may find themselves drawn to unhealthy substitutes such as drug and alcohol abuse. Feelings of weakness, dependence, confusion, or toxicity might also reflect the influence of unhealed material from their intrauterine history. At times, they can express their compassionate feelings in indiscriminate ways, taking care of chronic victims or addicts who are unwilling to take any responsibility for their problems, or do their own inner work.

Moon-Neptune Transits in Deep Self-Exploration

These archetypes help to bring mystical, soulful, and compassionate elements to deep inner exploration, enhancing a sense of higher meaning and feelings of loving connection. They open and soften people's awareness, allowing them to enter holotropic states in a more fluid and seamless way. People's process emerges in an unimpeded stream of flowing emotion.

At the biographical layer of exploration, they may remember happy and peaceful times in their families, satisfying emotional relationships, or nourishing experiences in nature. After rebirth sequences, it is not uncommon to relive bonding with the parents or nursing at the mother's breast, as in this holotropic session undertaken with Neptune conjunct natal Moon:

> I was a newborn needing a lot of quiet time with Mom and Dad. Feeling loved and nourished, I was taking in non-verbal support from their physical presence. I bonded with my female sitter, especially, for what seemed like many peaceful hours. We had a special mother-son talk where she told me that it was okay to take in nurture in my life. In this deeply regressed state, I idealized her and felt that she embodied the kindness of the ages.
>
> After a long time in this blissful state, suddenly my lips began to purse in a sucking position and I could feel moisture in my mouth, as I relived my breastfeeding as an infant.

In psychedelic sessions during any transit, journeyers can pass through states of utter vulnerability. It is almost impossible for them to maintain any kind of emotional boundaries with the people around them for the entire day of the session, so sitters need to act with utmost care and responsibility.

Perinatal Experiences

Tarnas discovered that perinatal experiences under Moon-Neptune transits have an increased chance of including memories of the oceanic union between mother and fetus in utero. Journeyers can experience amniotic elements such as hearing the heartbeat of the mother, perceiving her thoughts, or sharing her emotional state, details which can sometimes be verified later. These are typically overlaid with feelings of melted or oceanic ecstasy and images of heaven or paradise from various cultures. Related natural scenes include the serene ocean after a storm, untouched tropical islands, pastoral utopias and the magical night sky—all positive elements of *Mother Nature*.

If there were stresses in the intrauterine life, Moon-Neptune alignments can help people to work through the resulting problems. When

Figure 7. Holotropic Breathwork session of an Argentinean participant. "In the Lap of the Goddess" Silvina Heath (Neptune conjunct natal Moon). "I am a spirit not yet born—sitting in the lap of the Goddess, cozily wrapped in her arms. I feel so good there! We are both looking toward a bright, white star which sends us rays of light. I am thinking this is where I have to go, but not yet . . ."

requested, supportive physical bonding with the sitters can enhance this process and lead to healing miracles. In general, journeyers will feel more emotionally connected with their sitters, perceiving them as warm, patient and loving. The following supervised and internalized LSD session, with Moon conjunct natal Neptune, illustrates toxic-womb material opening out into an identification with the subject's biological mother, and then into a nourishing transpersonal realm:

> I was back in the toxic womb, with both sitters lying supportively beside me. After a period of contentless suffering, I began to feel how difficult it was for my mom to have my disharmonious energies inside her when she was carrying me. Then I identified with her as a young woman and the karmic enormity of what she had to bear, with three children in a row on top of a fairly demanding husband. I felt deeply impressed by her strength of character and how she has thrived so well in the second half of her life. Later in the session, I was crying, feeling the loneliness of the cosmic creative principle itself. I felt that, as an awakening being, I would now be able to cultivate a mutually nourishing, loving, and even entertaining relationship with the divine principle for the rest of my life.

An awakened Moon-Neptune field can go a long way toward undoing feelings of being unloved or of not belonging in this world. The overall direction of the perinatal unfolding is toward the release of traumatic leftovers from birth, facing the problem of death, and reconnecting with the Great Mother archetype or the divine in other forms. During these sequences, journeyers can feel themselves in the hands of the delivering feminine and may project divine female energy coming through their sitters. Other perinatal themes include the blissful reunion of souls in the underworld and death as the ultimate going home.

Transpersonal Experiences

The tendency of the Moon-Neptune field to dissolve emotional boundaries enables journeyers to relate to the experiences of other people or groups of people, other life forms, or all of creation. The following account from a holotropic session, undertaken with Moon conjunct natal Neptune and a Moon-square-Neptune world transit, illustrates this quality of universal compassion:

> I felt the emotions of shock, fear, pain, and humbling of the events of September 11, 2001. As I cried and felt the pressures around this crisis, I had a sense that expressing the feelings was somehow helping to consume them from a pool of repressed emotion in the collective psyche. It seemed plausible that my experiences could help to soften the traumatic reactions around the events of 9-11 more than any amount of concerned activism could hope to accomplish.
>
> Next I was crying and feeling the grief, pain, and humiliation of the Palestinians for the loss of their land and livelihoods. From the Israeli's side, I felt a determined impulse to protect myself from threatening and maddening constant attack. Then I was the consciousness of the Jewish people in Europe being tortured and killed in the concentration camps of World War II. Wailing aloud, I felt a deep and consuming fear. I felt deeply connected with all the protagonists of humanity and saw the harmfulness and shallowness of any kind of separate identification. We are all in this together.
>
> Later, I relived episodes from the Mongol invasions of the Arabian peninsula and the burning and massacre of Baghdad in 1258. I could understand how what many in the West see as the closed and static cultures of the Arab world are the result of extremely shocking and traumatic events in their history that were never fully digested. I also relived ancient fears in the Western psyche of the "East," stemming from centuries when the military power of the Mongol Khans was unstoppable. As I sensed old karmas lifting, I could feel a direct channel of energy and consciousness moving from the West through the Middle East, and on to China and back, an unbroken stream of cultural awareness flowing both ways—as if ancient boundaries and fears were finally being lifted. For the first time in human

history, the entire human race is directly communicating and interacting with itself.

As well as working through traumas and conflicts in the collective psyche, journeyers can explore special bonds of friendship and family ties between countries.

The compassion that people in holotropic states feel for all humanity eventually extends to the entire universe. They can empathically identify with various animals, feeling a special resonance with serene aquatic species such as jellyfish, whales, or plankton. They may also identify with the nurturing instincts in all of nature embodied in something like a *Protectress* archetype, as in this holotropic session with Neptune conjunct the subject's natal Moon:

> I was experiencing what I recognized as the Great Mother or Cancer-Protectress archetype in nature and could see, superimposed over the natural world, the figure of an astrological Crab. Within the infinite struggles and dramas of nature, with their endless life and death of individual organisms, there is a cosmic regulating principle that maintains overall balance and harmony.

At the archetypal level, journeyers may encounter deities who embody qualities of loving maternal compassion such as Isis, Demeter, Mary, Parvati, or Kwan Yin. The birth of the physical universe can be perceived as the Divine Mother pouring herself into her creation. Profound experiences of God in its feminine forms can soften people's outlook and improve their relationship with female energies in general, regardless of their gender. Subjects may also experience kind and caring masculine figures such as Buddha or Jesus.

The following composite account from two ayahuasca sessions of a female graduate student, undergone with Neptune conjunct her natal Moon, illustrates the spiritual and unitive nature of the Moon-Neptune field:

> I was inundated with a flood of feminine archetypes: Sorceress, Fairy, Dancing Tantric Deva, Mediterranean Fertility Goddess, Nun, Princess, Queen and High Priestess. Each of these archetypes wove their way through my deepest being, and I experienced and saw visions of myself as each one. It was joy and bliss and Divine Play. . . . When we are put directly in touch with the love that is our core—true Self Love—we are healed and made whole in ways that completely transcend human understanding . . .
>
> In the aftermath of this miracle healing, I began to feel a deep sense of love for the female body, for *my* female body and all of its unique feminine parts, and especially its capacity to participate in the creative process through the gift of child-bearing. I encountered myself not only as a child of the Great

Mother but also as a potential Mother herself—one who could also participate in the child-bearing and mothering-nurturing process. I felt that I had become disconnected from this aspect of the Divine Feminine because of many previous lifetimes in which I had foregone this aspect of womanhood due to religious commitments, sexual trauma, and early death. My sense was that it is time now to rectify this disconnection.

Then I was swept into a series of the most exquisitely beautiful visions whose essence was the sacred nature of marriage and sexuality, the union between man and woman, and the holiness of family—and how all of these sacraments participate in and embody a Holy Mystery. What we have done as human beings is not merely to have created social institutions around marriage and family, but to have attempted to capture, in human form and to the best of our limited abilities, great spiritual impulses which have their origin in the higher dimensions and are seeded out of the greater impulses of the Cosmos. I not only saw the visions but I also participated in them in a way that felt so real that, in the days after the ceremony, I almost felt that I should be wearing a wedding ring to symbolize that I had participated in a *hieros gamos* and been wedded in spirit!

In the evening, quality time shared with family and friends in a beautiful natural setting will help to integrate the experience. People may feel sweetly immersed in the soul of nature, perceiving soft moonlight as having special numinous attributes. Soaking or swimming in clear bodies of water can also have a profoundly nourishing effect. Journeyers may understand the mystical importance of water in Taoism: it does not seek to elevate itself but always takes the lowest position. Despite this, water can overcome the hardest structures.

By the end of the day, journeyers have an increased chance of reaching peaceful states, as their feelings smooth out into serene consciousness. With proper support, sessions approached during Moon-Neptune transits can have a meta-healing effect and lead to a sacralization of everyday life.

Mercury-Neptune

I've dreamt in my life dreams that have stayed with me ever after, and changed my ideas: they've gone through and through me, like wine through water, and altered the color of my mind.
    Emily Brontë (Mercury trine Neptune 3°28')
    Wuthering Heights, 1847

Human existence is girt round with mystery; the narrow region of our experiences is a small island in the midst of a boundless sea.
    William James (Mercury semisextile Neptune, date only, calc. for noon: 1°40') *Utility of Religion*, 1874

Mercury-Neptune Transits in Everyday Life

Mercury-Neptune transits combine the thought processes and communication associated with Mercury with the vision, imagination, and spirituality of Neptune. These archetypes open up parts of the mind that tend to be less developed by many people, the right-brain or pattern-perceiving aspects of awareness. Musing, reflecting, and daydreaming, they may see streams of meaningful images flowing through their minds, nourishing their souls just by closing their eyes or looking softly into the distance. They may also find satisfaction submerging themselves in the ocean of entrancing novels, serene music, or meditative states. People often have more rich and vivid dreams. And finally, with a tendency to think about and express their highest idealism, these transits support more compassionate forms of listening and speaking.

The shadow side of the Mercury-Neptune field includes various forms of mental distortion and projection. Under the influence of emerging emotional material, people may confuse inner and outer realms, believing that their subjective perceptions are an accurate picture of external reality. Their thought and speech might also be more wishful, emotional, or disorganized and they could be prone to missing appointments. In order to avoid problems and misunderstandings, people should make an extra effort to be concrete and explicit in their communications.

Individuals with Mercury-Neptune transits can also sometimes encounter issues around honesty, unconsciously blurring important boundaries or ethical distinctions. Idealistically wanting to believe, they might also become purposely or inadvertently misled by others. Finally, some individuals can become carried away by their yearning for cosmic unity, projecting higher meaning on the most trivial numbers, symbols, or events in everyday life. The perception of synchronicities in the world requires that people maintain their critical faculties.

Mercury-Neptune Transits in Deep Self-Exploration

Mercury-Neptune transits are highly positive in self-exploration. Alone, they are not the most therapeutic of influences, but by opening people's minds to other layers of reality, they also support the process of emotional surrender. These archetypes offer the glimpses of transpersonal perception that can allure people beyond their everyday barriers and inertias.

Imagery in holotropic sessions tends to be unusually rich and vivid. The material can emerge in dramatic imaginal flows, like a montage of seemingly unrelated snapshots that seem to carry the message that all things in the universe are interconnected, a cosmic slide show representing the great hologram of life. People may also be able to de-literalize the surface layer of any challenging moments that emerge in their sessions, seeing through apparent problems to their perinatal and archetypal roots.

The inner terrains that journeyers encounter under any transit can at times transcend their ability to conceptualize. They might feel that their experiences are impossible to relate to within any imaginable mental framework. It is important for both journeyers and sitters to let go of judgments and preconceptions about what is happening, and simply trust the flow of emerging experience as the process resolves itself. In psychedelic sessions during the dynamic Mercury-Neptune transits, people may feel that they are unable to adequately convey the depths of what they are going through, separated by a yawning mental chasm which cannot be bridged by words of any kind. By taking all the time needed to make verbal agreements and develop trust beforehand, breathers and sitters can allow these moments of disjunction to arise without feeling a need to change them during the session.

Under any transit, people in holotropic states can perceive even the most well-intentioned comments as temporarily alarming or confusing. Ideally, sitters keep their comments clear, short and supportive so as not to present any hooks that journeyers might fixate on as they work through difficult memories and the trust issues associated with them. The general rule is for sitters not to initiate communication but to respond to the breathers' own requests. Unambiguous positive statements such as "You're doing great," "You've got lots of time" and "We're totally here for you" are preferable to "Are you okay?" or "Are you all right?"—questions which can be impossible to adequately answer, or even relate to, at certain points in the process.

Perinatal Experiences

When individuals encounter the perinatal layer of the psyche, their mental distortions and projections can become extreme. For periods in a session, they may entertain dramatically mistaken conceptions such as believing that they are choosing life or death for someone, for example, their fathers or mothers, or that the outcome of their therapy will determine the fate of the world. They may also feel temporary disorientation as they identify with the elderly suffering from senility or Alzheimer's. This loosening of the ego's hold over consciousness is typically followed by healing flows of images and insights, culminating in experiences of contentless bliss. Journeyers may also perceive the world of matter turning into an ecstatic flow of divine thoughts.

Mercury-Neptune transits also sometimes correspond to interesting synchronicities, as in this holotropic session during a world transit of Mercury sextile Neptune, and Pluto square the subject's natal Pluto:

As the destructive energies within me came forward and revealed themselves, I perceived that all around the planet a great hush fell on the people, as global jubilation turned to disbelieving shock and then growing panic.

Synchronistically, at that exact moment, there was complete silence in the session room for several minutes. Later, when I asked the sitters what had happened, they said that for some reason during those minutes, inexplicably, they could not get the CD player to work. And there was obviously no worldwide panic. It had all been in my psyche.

Transpersonal Experiences

As self-exploration reaches the transpersonal realms, journeyers may directly identify with other people, other life forms, or elements of nature. They can emit startlingly real animal sounds, assume the voice intonations of other people, or even occasionally speak in languages they are unfamiliar with, the authenticity of which can sometimes be verified later.

At the archetypal level, they may further resolve issues around honesty, dishonesty, and the reconciling of contradictory truths in human life by experiencing the consciousness of snakes, as in this holotropic session undergone with Mercury conjunct the subject's natal Neptune:

I explored issues around lying and deceit in human life. These scenes were overlaid with a sense of the primitive ego consciousness of snakes—embodied in their hard structured vertebrate design, which seemed to be the prototype of the both defining and limiting human spinal column—as well as with the temptations of the archetypal Serpent. I encountered the awareness of a snake and then all snakes, with forked tongues that cannot be trusted. I perceived the snake's tongue as a representation of duality, the pairs of opposites in the material plane that can only be resolved by again reaching states of cosmic unity.

On occasion, participants can directly perceive or identify with the Universal Mind or Absolute Consciousness. They may also experience the essentially empty yet all-containing nature of the Macrocosmic Void, known in Indian philosophy as *sunyata*. Subjects who access these most rarefied layers of awareness often report that words are inadequate to describe their profoundly paradoxical and transcendent quality, sometimes referred to as "the peace that passeth all understanding."

In the integration phase of sessions, journeyers can feel a deep resonance with ancient languages such as Sanskrit, Greek, Mandarin or Hebrew, with sacred chants from the world's spiritual traditions, or with mystic syllables such as OM or AUM. Although at this point in the day, they may begin to share their experiences, they might still be in a highly subjective state and unable to digest much outside input. Communication in the session room needs to stay focused around the participant and his or her needs.

As always, it is advisable not to make important life decisions for at least a week after any major session.

Venus-Neptune

How do I love thee? Let me count the ways.
I love thee to the depth and breadth and height
My soul can reach.
>   Elizabeth Barrett Browning (Venus trine Neptune 1°57') *Sonnets from the* *Portuguese*, 1850

By learning the language of heavenly patterns, we begin to see that every- *thing is married to everything.*
>   Caroline W. Casey (ME=VE/NE 1°10') *Making the Gods Work for* *You*, 1998

Venus-Neptune Transits in Everyday Life

During these sweet transits, Neptune awakens the mystical and devotional nature of the Venus archetype, while Venus brings elements of beauty, grace and harmony to Neptune's spiritual quest. At best, these can be some of the most deeply satisfying influences that human beings may experience.

With love and sex enjoyed as pathways to a deeper mystical union, people's relationships can be magically renewed as old emotional boundaries between partners are blissfully melted away. The Neptunian impulse toward purity may also lead some toward platonic relationships, seemingly unsullied by the messes of biological and emotional involvement. People's friendships can also embody mystical and compassionate qualities and they may feel a spiritual kinship with all of humanity. Finally, they may discover a new appreciation for serene new-age music, refined art, and beautiful natural scenes.

The shadow side of Venus-Neptune emerges when people's yearning for the divine is repressed or unmet. Impelled by spiritual desire, they may long for a soul-mate, an ideal love who can open doorways to states of exotic bliss and enchantment. This sometimes translates into a sense of disappointment with the merely human, flesh-and-blood side of their current partners and relationships. People's feelings of dissatisfaction are ultimately based on resistance in their own psyches; in order to experience the divine through another, we first have to discover it within our own beings. With judgment clouded by infatuation, some people might also be prone to romantic illusions, projections, or being projected on by others. At other times, they may indulge in sentimental fantasies, sensory escapism, or drug and alcohol abuse. Reflecting a deep yearning for melted oceanic states, some individuals may also become extremely yin and passive.

Venus-Neptune Transits in Deep Self-Exploration

Venus-Neptune transits are moderately strong yet highly desirable influences in self-exploration. These exquisite yin archetypes help to create a gentle, soothing, and mystical atmosphere around healing sessions. People's experiences can be permeated with a feeling of divine grace, a sense of higher love and kindness welcoming them into the transpersonal realms and softening their reentry back into the social world.

Perinatal Experiences

In the early stage of exploration, journeyers can remember harmonious periods in their family life, happy romantic relationships, and moments of aesthetic inspiration. As the process deepens into the perinatal realm, Grof and Tarnas found that the Venus-Neptune field will help to awaken experiences from the intrauterine stage of development. People often have easier access to states of melted or oceanic ecstasy, an experience of their souls blissfully absorbed into the loving Universal Womb. Intrauterine experiences may also open out into images of beautiful and ideal nature— Mother Nature at her best. Venus-Neptune transits can help people to clear out leftover toxic-womb material and the relationship problems it creates, sweetening the inner womb and their ability to trust and bond with other human beings.

Transpersonal Experiences

Transpersonal themes emerging under Venus-Neptune transits tend to include the loving and devoted nature of divine consciousness and the tantric merging of various archetypal principles. Journeyers can experience love and sex as cosmic forces permeating the creation, the divine as friend or beloved, or the Absolute Consciousness' love for his/her children. In a state of deep devotion, they can participate in humanity's reunion with the divine Feminine at this special moment in history.

The following is a composite report from three Holotropic Breath-work sessions of a female social worker who had transiting Neptune con-junct her natal Venus:

My first experience of Holotropic Breathwork was in Houston, Texas when Stan Grof came to town to conduct a weekend workshop. I was vaguely familiar with his work and decided to at least attend the evening talk to become more familiar with this interesting modality. I enrolled and the next day to my great surprise, I experienced a deep and total spiritual communion with the Divine. During this process, I had so much energy in my body that I thought my arms were going to burn off. My hands were in the air for hours as I felt like I was touching and talking to God. I did not want the experience to ever end. I remember tears streaming down my face at the end of the ses-sion because I did not want to let go of this beautiful energy that had embraced me. Later when I talked to Stan, he suggested that I had experienced some-thing truly transpersonal. I have been on a committed transpersonal path for many years but now consider Holotropic Breathwork to be the missing link in my spiritual growth.

After having such a powerful first experience during a weekend workshop, I decided to do a week-long module in Taos, New Mexico. This time I also experienced a deeply spiritual and sensual union with the divine. Like a beautiful endless rapture, I would compare it to lovemaking in its most inti-mate form. There was never any climax but a continuous exchange of energy—archetypal energies merging together. From the literature I have read about *Sri Yantra*—the union of Shiva and Shakti—I would have to say that that mythological depiction is the closest to describing my experience. The union of Shiva and Shakti is the most powerful cosmic creative principle that I know of and consider this the most profound transpersonal experience that I have ever had. Before it happened, I did not even know if it was even possible to experience Sri Yantra but this is the name that I gave that experience.

My second Taos breathwork experience involved the same beautiful union but this time it included an anthropomorphic form, my first real visual experi-ence in a holotropic state. The previous two sessions were of just pure energy with no visual component but in this one, I somehow recognized the face in the experience and considered him something like a soul mate. He would be what I consider the perfect male energy. I felt this experience to be a gift from the divine to let me know that what I have been searching for in this life does indeed exist.

Journeyers may also encounter beautiful goddesses such as Ishtar, Parvati or Saraswati, Plato's Higher Beauty, or Narcissus' self-absorption. They might also experience virgin goddesses such as Mary or Persephone, symbolizing the eternally transcendent layers of the Feminine that remain undisturbed by biological cycles of birth and death. Sometimes they come to see the value in what the Grofs have termed *oceanic sex*. In this approach to lovemaking, the most important part of sexuality is the loving spiritual contact and merging after the orgasm.

At the end of sessions, journeyers may be unusually open to nurturing and bonding experiences with their partners, friends, and family. They may resonate with soothing new-age or oceanic music and art of a high aesthetic value. They can also feel deeply moved or even experience rapture in the presence of nature's most refined expressions, such as radiant pastel sunsets, pristine rainbows, adorable songbirds, or gentle flowers. During any Neptune transit, journeyers can perceive water as being imbued with mystical Taoist properties.

Mars-Neptune

Sexuality is a sacrament.
   Starhawk (Mars trine Neptune 2°09′) *The Spiral Dance: A Rebirth of the Ancient Religion of the Great Goddess,* 1979

There is no way to peace. Peace is the way.
   Mohandas Gandhi (Mars quincunx Neptune 0°02′)

Mars-Neptune Transits in Everyday Life

The meeting of the archetypal Mars' assertive and dynamic qualities with Neptune's passive, flowing nature has some unusual and some very helpful characteristics. On the positive side, Neptune can weaken the sometimes selfish and headstrong dynamicism of people's martial drives, helping them to slow down and be more aware of the effects of their actions in the world. They may also be drawn to service work with those less fortunate. Finally, Mars-Neptune transits support the active pursuit of mystical states of consciousness.

As well as these positive effects, people with the *dynamic* transits may feel a kind of toxic, blah malaise, a sense of inner paralysis and uncomfortableness that can make it more difficult to get things going or make a strong impression. Feelings of uncertainty, discouragement or disorientation are possible, as Mars' archetypal heat smoulders away inside, unable to find an outlet within Neptune's dampening field. Robert Hand notes that individuals may also face the unpleasant results of past actions. As always, it is important that people do not act in deceptive or underhanded ways. Mars-Neptune transits are also not especially good times for confrontations with others—which might be unusually discouraging—but better for confronting oneself.

The dynamic transits resemble a kind of time-out on assertive activity. They correspond to two-week intervals (Mars-to-Neptune alignments) or four-year spans (Neptune-to-Mars) when people may need to learn more how to coast and go with the flow.

Mars-Neptune Transits in Deep Self-Exploration

The flowing transits of Mars-Neptune represent moderately strong but supportive influences in self-exploration. The natural impulse of these archetypes to pursue holotropic states can enhance a sacred yet purposeful atmosphere around sessions. A feeling of higher service to the process of healing and letting go will tend to permeate the day. These influences also help to create a give-and-take, energetic play with the divine principle. Although even the trines may symbolize a brief sense of low energy or pointlessness, these feelings tend to open out into specific psychological content that consumes the disillusioning forces and transmutes them into more inspiring forms.

The *dynamic transits* also share these helpful features as well as some possible challenging ones. Whether their more difficult or positive qualities predominate will depend, in part, on other transits that journeyers are experiencing. On the more challenging side, the dynamic transits can for periods of time take the wind out of people's sails, undermining the very sense that the experience is worthwhile. Vague feelings of toxic malaise generated by these archetypes sometimes extend to attitudes toward the healing modality itself—people may feel confused about whether to try and cathartically express the material or just do nothing and accept the situation. With a ghoulish sense of dynamic energies spoiling within their beings, they can feel uncertain where to place their assertive impulses, but be unable to turn them off. Trying to let go seems to be another form of personal desire, efforts to surrender as just another futile, egoic act. Rather than being harmful, however, these transits seem to be an important cooling-off period for the Mars archetype, a forced reflection about not taking the slightest worldly action for granted.

In terms of content, people with Mars-Neptune transits can undergo urgent evaluations of their ethical conduct in the world. They examine their basic strategies for pursuing their emotional and material desires, as well as focus on specific incidents in which they were not kind or aboveboard in their actions. At times, they may also recall moments in which other people did not act in a straightforward way with them. By feeling the emotions on both sides of these issues and the consequences of their human mistakes, journeyers can reach states of forgiveness and willingness to be forgiven. They realize that forgiveness is not something we can actively will into being. Like divine grace, it happens to us, when we allow ourselves to feel, deeply, the human emotions and consequences on all sides of an issue.

Perinatal Experiences

In the perinatal and transpersonal realms of discovery, people often continue their process of ethical self-evaluation. They may have the sinking awareness that every action they have ever taken sticks with them over lifetimes, like a pool of amniotic fluid around their psyches. Generalized feelings of being a cosmic scoundrel can deepen into disturbances of intra-uterine life, in which questionable motivations are strangely indistinguishable from toxic biology, and somehow one's very existence feels like the problem. People facing toxic-womb sequences can have a sense of anguish, torment, debilitation, and wasting away. Full surrender to these states consumes them from the system and opens the pathway to refreshing experiences of the universal womb and reunion with the cosmic creative principle.

Transpersonal Experiences

As exploration continues, journeyers may encounter various sly, wily, or oily modes of being. They may also confront subtly strange, bizarre or uncanny energies, or the archetype of Deception itself. Direct identification with the mournful consciousness of predators in nature such as wolves is also possible. On the pleasant side, they can develop an interest in mystical or oceanic forms of lovemaking, or participate in internal tantric scenes centered on sexual deities such as Shiva and Shakti, or Ares and Aphrodite.

In the integration phase, journeyers may enjoy gentle physical activities such as yoga, dancing, swimming, or tai chi. Long soaks in warm water can also have a deeply soothing and renewing effect. These archetypes can help people to discover the divine stillpoint behind the biological rhythms of breath, thought, and impulse. At the ultimate level, Mars-Neptune represents *Nirvana*: the blissful extinction of desire.

Jupiter-Neptune

There are many paths up the mountain.
Ramakrishna (Jupiter quincunx Neptune 1°43′)

The Universe writes its metaphors in the most sweeping and majestic terms, in the night's diamond sky, "deeper than day can comprehend."
Richard Tarnas (Jupiter trine Neptune 1°35′) *Prometheus the Awakener*, original unpublished version, 1980

Jupiter-Neptune Transits in Everyday Life

Jupiter-Neptune transits represent some of the most positive and uplifting archetypal influences that human beings can experience. Jupiter expands Neptune's impulses toward mystical union, softening people's boundaries and allowing them to access new and unseen layers of meaning. Opening deeply to the divine soul or anima mundi that permeates the phenomenal realm, people may become aware of rich symbolism and metaphor spread through the entire creation. They can experience waves of imagery welling up through their psyches like a kind of cosmic cornucopia or divine spring, often including unusually rich dreams. Some individuals may become interested in the mystical branches of the world's religions or esoteric schools of thought. Finally, their soaring optimism and grand ideals can lead to outpourings of generosity, compassion, and caring in everyday life.

At the same time, the Neptune archetype can help to enhance the sense of broadened experience, benefic goodness, and abundant plenitude associated with Jupiter. People may have a sense of ultimate safety and well-being, seeing that the world resembles a kind of cosmic ashram, school, or festival and all that is really happening is adventures in consciousness. Neptune can also refine and spiritualize Jupiter's ideals of success and prosperity. People come to realize that, beyond a basic level of security, what they value most in life are warm human connections and feelings of meaningful service. As Tarnas documents, Jupiter-Neptune *world transits* similarly correspond to periods of heightened idealism and spiritual reenchantment across the entire world culture.[3]

The shadow side of the Jupiter-Neptune field is pronounced, and one of the most recognizable of any archetypal influence. The inflated Neptune principle can manifest as wildly impractical or spaced-out plans without a hope of realization. A perception of complex synchronicities in the most minute details of everyday life, far-flung speculations about extra-terrestrial encounters, and the blurring of important mental distinctions suggest a confusion between the holotropic and hylotropic modes of reality.

The imaginatively engaged Jupiter can also lead to the most grandiose kind of economic fantasies. People may envision huge creative projects with endless franchise spinoffs that create a multiplier effect of prosperity, benefitting thousands. Confusing inner and outer realms, they may believe that the abundant imagery in their psyches can and should be translated into material reality. It is always advisable for individuals with major Neptune-to-Jupiter transits (conjunctions, oppositions, squares, trines, or sextiles) to get a sober second opinion before investing money on faith, because of the very real possibility of over-optimism and overextension. Some people may also succumb to spiritual materialism or being taken advantage of by cultish philosophies that promise increasing levels of attainment with every expensive new seminar.

The archetypal field associated with Jupiter-Neptune alignments offers a major opportunity to open or widen the pathway to the inner divine principle. In order to transmute the distortions in judgment that often accompany these transits, some people may need to work through toxic-womb leftovers from their intrauterine history.

Jupiter-Neptune Transits in Deep Self-Exploration

Jupiter-Neptune transits correspond to fantastic, extremely positive influences in holotropic work and their healing potential will be dramatically enhanced if Uranus or Pluto is involved in any way. These archetypes unveil landscapes of grand mystique, inspiring in people magic feelings of connection with their inner lives, with others, and with the larger ocean of consciousness. They symbolize the most expanded vision of reality that human beings can apprehend, Absolute Consciousness revealing its true nature.

Jupiter broadens Neptune's spiritual perspective, allowing people to experience their emotions as a flow of archetypal or mythological energies, like vignettes in a cosmic movie. They will be more able to submerge themselves in the inner worlds, consuming the emerging material with less resistance. These may be the safest of all influences for undergoing journeys into the psyche and the spiritual universe at large. As long as people ensure a basic level of preparation—a comfortable space with no time limit and at least one sober, experienced sitter or friend—these archetypes present a *via regia*, a "royal road" into higher transpersonal states. Opportunities for spiritual opening can feel as bountiful as drops of water in a vast sea. A sense of divine magic and sacredness will tend to permeate sessions, helping to ensure positive resolutions and integration of any difficult material that emerges.

In the early stage of exploration, journeyers may work through conflicts between the Jupiter archetype's proneness toward worldly materialism and Neptunian impulses toward transcendence. These seemingly competing directions gradually integrate as people gain access to the numinous field of awareness permeating every part of the material world.

Perinatal Experiences

When people's exploration reaches the perinatal realm of the psyche, the Jupiter-Neptune field can help them to work through material at any stage in the process. Their capacity to deeply trust and surrender will be a

Figure 8. "No Fear" Alejandra Scigliano. A deep feeling of protection and transcendence of fear in a Holotropic Breathwork session of an Argentinean participant, during a world transit of Jupiter conjunct Neptune.

tremendous asset. These archetypes also have a special resonance with BPM I, as Tarnas recognized, presenting a valuable opportunity to work through toxic-womb memories.

As the process unfolds, amniotic elements tend to open out into transpersonal themes that share with the womb the quality of free-flowing lack of boundaries. This may include an identification with whales, jellyfish or plankton, the consciousness of the ocean, or of interstellar space. As the unhelpful trauma-based boundaries in awareness are dissolved, journeyers gain access to states of blissful union with the entire universe, existence in heaven or paradise, and oceanic ecstasy.

Transpersonal Experiences

As exploration continues in the transpersonal realms, people may take experiential journeys through the various components of mystical symbol systems such as astrology, tarot, or the Kabbalah. Compassionately identifying with the experience of other people and other life forms, they may also discover a new problem-solving capacity, finding natural synergy and positive solutions that benefit everyone.

Jupiter-Neptune can also mediate access to the archetypes of Providence, the Great Benefic, Cornucopia, the World Soul, the Mythic Round, or the Tree of Life. The heart of these scenes evokes feelings of magical abundance, overflowing generosity, and cosmic grandeur. The following ayahuasca session of a female artist, conducted during a world transit of Jupiter conjunct Neptune, reveals her experience of an immanent, universal and all-encompassing divinity:

> Again and again, the angelic beings stressed the preciousness of matter and the human body. We here on earth stand in awe of the light beings and the beauty of heaven, but they themselves stand in awe of the miracle that is matter. Great effort and tremendous supercosmic intelligence contributed to the design of this planet and our physical bodies. The light beings said that we must do absolutely everything possible to honor and take care of these special, special vehicles of light. We are not here because we cannot make it in the higher realms, because we are tainted or spiritually inept, because we have been cast out of heaven, or because we cannot get off the wheel of samsara. We are here to participate in a great experiment and we are here to allow GOD-GODDESS-ALL THAT IS to express itself through the unique cosmic substance that is matter. Perhaps it is a way of demonstrating that God can be actualized absolutely everywhere and in absolutely anything. The pure consciousness of God—realizing itself with full consciousness—can be realized in and through all forms and manifestations of the multicosmos.

Figure 9. Katia Soliani (Neptune conjunct natal Jupiter). In this dream inspired by a Holotropic Breathwork session of an Italian artist, we can see elements of paradisean and aquatic serenity related to Neptune, and a sense of grand spaciousness and abundance, associated with Jupiter.

The highest impulse of these archetypes is toward mystical union with the universe at every level, blissful reabsorption into the eternal divine field. Deeply immersed in a grand cosmic panorama, people explore the macro-creative projects of Absolute Consciousness, the multi-levelled flows of divine energy into and out of incarnation that offer essentially unlimited adventures in consciousness.

At the end of sessions, journeyers may enjoy exceptionally rich bonding and loving resolutions with their friends and family, continuing the healing process. These archetypes support a deep and thorough integration of spirituality into every area of people's lives. In an atmosphere of overflowing abundance and plenitude, they will also have a sense of shared credit for the breakthroughs of the day.

They may feel a special resonance with water, from relaxing in warm baths to refreshing swims in clear rivers and lakes which can be experienced as floating inside the being of Mother Earth herself. Journeyers will be highly tuned in to the aesthetic abundance of nature, including expansive panoramas of sea and sky or the majesty of the moonlit evening. Lying beneath the Milky Way, they can feel their beings floating in the eternal and unchanging divine womb, tucked in by a cosmic blanket of stars.

*   *   *

Transits of Saturn

Sun-Saturn

You gain strength, courage and confidence by every experience in which you really stop to look fear in the face. You are able to say to yourself, "I lived through this horror. I can take the next thing that comes along."
Eleanor Roosevelt (Sun trine Saturn 5°28′) *You Learn by Living*, 1960

It is not the end of the physical body that should worry us. Rather, our concern must be to live while we're alive—to release our inner selves from the spiritual death that comes with living behind a façade designed to conform to external definitions of who and what we are.
Elisabeth Kübler-Ross (Sun trine Saturn, date only, calc. for noon: 4°07′) *On Death and Dying*, 1969

Sun-Saturn Transits in Everyday Life

During Sun-Saturn transits, the natural exuberance, enthusiasm, and vitality of the archetypal Sun tends to be somewhat more tempered, contained, or constricted by the archetypal Saturn. These alignments help people to ground and center themselves. They provide opportunities to express creative energies within defined avenues and channels. People can apply themselves toward difficult and disciplined challenges in a steady and incremental way, often with successful results.

The *dynamic* transits may also represent more severe meetings of the solar and Saturnian principles. People can feel deeply the pain and sorrows of the world. All dynamic Saturn transits are a reminder of our human mortality, and it is normal to feel held back or limited in some way. The quickest route through these feelings, however, is not to fight against them but to consciously register them. It can be helpful to set aside some time every day to lie down and just surrender into any emerging feelings of fear, loss or pressure. As Casey writes, when people feel themselves being pulled downward by Saturnian depression, the most helpful response is to turn toward it and dive. By falling through the cracks in our ego's protective structures, we open the door for healing transpersonal energies to lift us from within.

Feelings of hindered vitality are also possible during these transits, so it is important that individuals take care of their health and get enough rest. Finally, bosses and authority figures can be less sympathetic to people's creative suggestions and initiatives. These archetypes test our ability to fit into concrete reality, to live in the real world. Saturn frequently overdoes itself, however, as we slavishly submit to self-imposed demands that are not ultimately life-supporting or satisfying. The challenge with Saturn is to distinguish between those demands that are really necessary and those that are based on past traumatic events.

Sun-Saturn Transits in Deep Self-Exploration

Sun-Saturn transits are associated with sobering and grounding influences in inner work. They help to focus people's attention on important personal problems and issues that need to be addressed, ensuring that their sessions will be deep, real, and meaningful. These archetypes also impart a sense of serious responsibility and the determination to stay with the releasing process until the end of the line.

The *dynamic* transits of Saturn to natal Sun may also correspond to passing feelings of discouragement or lower energy. They do not pose a problem for any kind of breathwork. Similarly, they are not a contraindication for systematic psychedelic sessions planned in a series and should be welcomed as a grounding anchor. However, these are not the ideal transits for a first psychedelic session, especially for clients suffering from severe depression or trust issues, unless there are very positive Uranus, Neptune, or Pluto transits also in effect. With experienced sitters, however, people can have good results under any Saturn transit.

In general, when the Sun-Saturn field is activated, journeyers may need some extra encouragement going into their sessions, to counteract the stoic and self-repressive tendency of these archetypes. One of the important challenges in holotropic exploration is in learning to let go of control, to set aside the persona of being a "together" person and let oneself become the needy participant. In the safe, structured space of a workshop or session room, people surrender into their emerging material while letting the sitters take care of external reality.

Grof observed that, in holotropic states, the psyche tends to present for processing clusters of memories that are bound together by the same emotional or sensory quality. The common thread can be a negative feeling or sensation, such as suffocation, failure, inadequacy, or abandonment or a positive one such as love, happiness, success, or satisfaction. He called these memory clusters *systems of condensed experience*, or *COEX systems*.[4]

The first layer of the psyche that tends to surface under Sun-Saturn transits includes COEX systems based around unresolved issues with the father or dominant parent. These might involve memories of punishment, judgment, or unmet needs for loving contact. Other biographical memories include scenarios that evoked feelings of ridicule, humiliation, or shame. The sitters' role is to offer unconditional support for as long as breathers need while these memory fragments purge themselves from their psyches. Male sitters, especially, have an important responsibility during their clients' heavy Sun-Saturn transits. They need to exercise great care and understanding in order not to corroborate the client's emerging material and be perceived as cold or judging. If projections on the male sitter become intense, the steady comforting presence of a female sitter will act as a supportive stabilizing anchor.

Perinatal Experiences

Tarnas found that when self-exploration reaches the perinatal region of the psyche, Saturn-to-Sun transits will tend to engage experiences from Grof's Basic Perinatal Matrix II—*No Exit* and *Cosmic Engulfment*. When journeyers' process is dominated by BPM II, any activation of Saturn, even by flowing transit, can help to focus their attention on the no-exit material and effect its resolution.

As we have seen, BPM II is based around the early stage of labor, in which the fetus has lost the oceanic paradise of the womb and is now pressed in from all sides by the contracting uterine walls. At this point, the cervix is still closed and there is no way out. When people access this leftover material, they have overwhelming feelings of entrapment, engagement, hopelessness, helplessness, and depression and can identify with the

Figure 10. A BPM II sequence from an internalized psychedelic session, undertaken with probable Saturn opposition natal Sun, and Pluto conjunct Neptune ("late 1950s"). "The incipient uterine contractions are experienced as an attack by a monstrous octopus."

Figure 11. An experience of BPM II. "Landscape of Everlasting Pain" Taino Leinonen (Saturn square natal Sun, and a world transit of Sun opposition Saturn). Holotropic Breathwork session of a Finnish participant in which he identified with an old woman wandering in a landscape of everlasting pain and loneliness.

victims from many different times and places. They may perceive the world as a meaningless cardboard facade in which pain, suffering, and death are all that really exist. Grof observed that full surrender to these hellish experiences, including the sense that they will never end, automatically consumes their negative effects from the psyche and allows the material to move in a more cathartic direction.

When journeyers' emerging material centers on the dynamic stage of labor, or *BPM III*, Sun-Saturn transits will guide the process toward specific important edges, thresholds, and challenges in the perinatal sequence that need to be faced.

Transpersonal Experiences

As self-exploration reaches the transpersonal realms, the Sun-Saturn complex will help to focus journeyers' attention on various states of isolation or compression within the universal field of consciousness. This can include challenging episodes in the lives of their ancestors, their racial background, or of humanity in general. Archetypal figures that emerge include jealous and judging patriarchal deities such as Yahweh, Cronos, or Zeus in his controlling persona. People can also explore the imbalance of the archetypal Sun's yang energy in our modern industrial culture. On the positive side, they can tap into the archetype of the Wise Old Man, a personification of distilled and seasoned life experience, honestly faced and deeply integrated.

The following holotropic session of a graduate student undertaken with Saturn square natal Sun, and a world transit of Mars square Saturn, illustrates a number of important features of this archetypal complex:

Before the session, I was consumed with an irrational paranoia that the house was not soundproof and that if I made any noise the police would come and take me away. We delayed starting for several hours while I went around to every neighbor in possible earshot to introduce myself and tell them we were doing emotional release work and not to worry if they heard anything. Still not satisfied, I insisted that we do the session in a dingy basement room where we could put pillows up against the small windows.

We finally started three hours late. After a long period of nondescript suffering and expression of aggressive energies, during which I held a pillow over my face to muffle the sound, I began to feel like I was experiencing another time and place. I was a young black man in the southern United States being taken away to the woods by townspeople, including several uniformed police officers, to be lynched. My inordinate fear of police suddenly seemed to be completely justified in light of this emerging experience.

Next the scene shifted to a World War I battle where I identified with a mortally wounded soldier, bleeding alone in the mud and crying out in agony before being carried away on a wagon. I perceived that the dying cries of a young English soldier had been trapped in some kind of time bubble that was now being opened and freed in the holotropic session of a Canadian student eighty years later. I felt that his pain was finally being heard and released.

After these sequences, I lost most of my fear of making sounds in holotropic work and it never came up again as a serious issue.

Near the end of the session I interpreted something the male sitter said as a judgment, and felt for a long time that a positive outcome of the day was in jeopardy. However, the female sitter comforted me in a maternal way, lying next to me and touching my shoulder. As I took in this needed support, the experience deepened into a COEX of being almost constantly criticized and dominated by my father when I was a child. After a long hot bath, I began to feel a bit better and we all shared a warm meal together.

While the experiences associated with Saturn-to-Sun transits are not always pleasant, they have a helpful humbling and deflating effect on the ego, opening it to the waves of healing energies symbolized by transits of Uranus, Neptune, and Pluto.

Moon-Saturn

You cannot make yourself feel something you do not feel, but you can make yourself do right in spite of your feelings.
    Pearl Buck (Moon sextile Saturn 2°11′)
    To My Daughters, With Love, 1967

We are healed of a suffering only by experiencing it to the full.
    Marcel Proust (Moon trine Saturn 1°25′) "The Sweet Cheat Gone,"
    Remembrance of Things Past

Moon-Saturn Transits in Everyday Life

The meeting of the Moon and Saturn archetypes presents some major challenges and some valuable opportunities. The Moon represents our human needs for acceptance, belonging and support, while Saturn signifies the universe's tendency to create states of painful limitation and testing in biological life. Moon-Saturn transits correspond to twelve-to-twenty-hour interludes, or ten-to-twelve-month periods when people's basic sense of well-being and access to nurture may feel somewhat more structured, qualified, or repressed by the Saturn principle.

The catalyzing influences may seem to come from external areas such as issues with a partner, pressures in the family, or excessive demands at work, or they can arise directly from the inside in the form of coolings of affection, pangs of conscience, or self-doubt. Whatever the source, these are supportive transits for serious, focused introspection. Every dynamic Saturn alignment corresponds to some degree of pain, but also the objective distance to allow that pain to fully emerge and be released. When people feel depressed or an impulse to be alone, it is often best to trust these urges, taking some time every day to lie down, feel the emotions deeply, and let them register. The awakenings of soul that often emerge during Moon-Saturn transits will more than compensate for their difficulty. The *flowing* transits provide similar avenues for introspection, but usually without the same feelings of pressure or severity. Saturn seeks quality over quantity, making these good times to structure a satisfying balance between work, relationships, and alone time.

At best, the Moon-Saturn field will help to foster the incisive self-honesty that can stop or reduce the process of projecting on the outer world. People often see the source of their dissatisfaction to be in their external circumstances. They imagine what they need to be happy is a certain number of digits in their bank account, a rise in social status, or a promotion—however, if these are attained, their psyches quickly adjust to the new situation and it fails to deliver the promised satisfaction. Often then, people adopt a new goal that they hope, this time, will bring them the peace of mind they crave. This problem can continue indefinitely because the real source of human well-being comes from the inside, from the quality of connection with the inner divine.

Moon-Saturn Transits in Deep Self-Exploration

Moon-Saturn transits, especially the dynamic transits of Saturn to natal Moon, represent very important influences in self-exploration. The Saturn archetype focuses people's attention on the real, serious emotional material they need to look at, ensuring that healing sessions will be deep and meaningful. The *flowing* transits represent moderately strong, mildly supportive energies for emotional work. They create an attitude of seriousness and responsibility, helping people to recognize the importance of structuring a proper support system ahead of time, one that combines both the safety required by the Saturn archetype and the emotional support and nourishment needed by the Moon.

The *dynamic* transits symbolize extremely strong and somewhat more challenging indicators in holotropic states. In general, they will not pose any problem for breathwork sessions. Similarly, Moon-Saturn transits falling on dates that are already part of a pre-planned series of individual sessions should be welcomed as a grounding and anchoring influence. These archetypes are in no way a contraindication for deep work, but every support needs to be given to clients before, during, and after their sessions to compensate for the Moon-Saturn archetype's emotionally severe and self-punishing tendency.

It is important that people's first experience is as nourishing as possible; a good first session will instill the courage and trust necessary to face more difficult material later on. Finally, individuals with limited access to either experienced sitters or a proper session space may prefer to avoid the dynamic Saturn-to-Moon transits for major sessions planned in advance. With adequate support, individuals can have positive healing experiences under any Saturn transit. However, these are not conducive archetypes for high-dose sessions undertaken without proper support and supervision. If experienced sitters are not available, it might be better to do a series of shorter, bite-size sessions with a milder catalyst during these periods.

The first layer of material that tends to surface in self-exploration contains biographical memories around parental punishment or judgment, a hostile family atmosphere, sibling rivalry, or severe toilet training. COEX systems, or systems of condensed experience, related to Moon-Saturn include feelings of humiliation, worthlessness, self-hate, or being controlled or abandoned by the mother. Participants can also work through condensed leftover traces from serious accidents, operations, or illnesses. Most of these are problems of what Grof calls the *commission* type: traumatic foreign energies lodged in the psyche that can be released through a process of catharsis.

Saturn-Moon transits are also associated with the emergence of problems of the *omission* type, based on situations where people's legitimate needs for warm bonding in infancy were not met. As we have seen, these unfilled needs leave a permanent vacuum in the psyche which can only be resolved by returning to the original state of emotional vulnerability and then receiving the supportive nurture that people missed as infants. It needs, of course, to be offered in a sensitive and appropriate way, preferably under the peer supervision of a workshop setting or male-female dyad.

In general, journeyers with heavy Saturn-to-Moon transits may be more susceptible to issues around abandonment. As this material emerges in psychedelic sessions, they can project and imagine that the sitters are making judging and ridiculing comments or are about to leave the room in disgust and frustration. They may experience deeply ambivalent emotions toward the feminine source of nurture, with alternating feelings of wanting to push away the female sitter, yet also desperately needing her to stay for the healing process. It is important that sitters offer unconditional support to journeyers for as long as they need, without an arbitrary time limit. Their human understanding and care can be a magical healing antidote to past experiences of deprivation and rejection.

The following supervised and internalized LSD session, conducted during a world transit of Moon trine Saturn, illustrates experiences emerging from the biographical layer of the psyche:

> I was reliving heartbreaking feelings from my childhood of being less lovable than my brother. My parents, encouraged by our ambitious and materialistic church, had set up routine musical and other types of competitions between

us, supposedly to motivate us on to higher achievement. I was almost always the loser in the important ways. The feeling of provisional, conditional love never ended and I never felt good enough. As I worked through these feelings, my sitters sat down close on both sides of me in a parental way. I wept deeply in gratitude and thankfulness.

Overall, people explore the convergence of both facing their inner material, or "karma," symbolized by Saturn, while also getting their needs for emotional support finally met, represented by the Moon. Both are possible at the same time, with a sense of something like spiritual "penance" and emotional healing often coming from the same experience.

Perinatal Experiences

Tarnas found that when self-exploration reaches the perinatal realm during Saturn-to-Moon transits, explorers have a greatest likelihood of accessing material from Grof's Basic Perinatal Matrix II—*Cosmic Engulfment* and *No Exit*. BPM II is, as we have seen, centered around the early stage of labor where the uterine walls have begun to contract around the vulnerable fetus but the cervix is not yet dilated. Subject to alarming mechanical pressures, the fetus has lost all meaningful connection with its mother but there is not yet any way out of the situation.

As people work through this leftover material, they have overwhelming feelings of loss, isolation, depression, failure, and guilt. These are often accompanied by images of hell from various cultures, with an emphasis on the unbearable separation from the divine source. Grof notes that the literal, fundamentalist interpretation of hell as lasting for an eternity is based on a confusion between real time and subjective time. While the BPM II sequences are certainly perceived as being unending and inescapable, they may take only minutes or hours in real time. When journeyers are influenced by BPM II, they also tend to feel lack of satisfaction in all the Freudian erogenous zones, including complete disinterest in sex, extreme oral frustration, and oppressive feelings of constipation.

When people's emotional material is dominated by *Pluto and BPM III*, Moon-Saturn transits will help them to face and complete specific important edges, conflicts, and thresholds in the process.

Transpersonal Experiences

Transpersonal sequences during any transit can appear by themselves or as overlying layers of biographical and perinatal material. Some of the rich variety of experiences that emerge under Moon-Saturn transits include an identification with animals that are highly enduring and self-reliant, such as cacti; that are isolated, such as bottom-feeding fish; or that are armored, such as crabs or snails. The following is from an internalized marijuana session of a graduate student undertaken with Jupiter trine his natal Moon-Saturn conjunction:

> I was finally able to hold a steady balance between the wounded karma of my feminine side and the driving energy of my masculine side. I experienced these parts of my consciousness as being two boundaries of ego on both sides of my psyche. Then suddenly, both lines began to twist outward, peeling endlessly down for hour after hour as I let go of control. After a long, long period of this opening, the process finally resolved as I experienced the consciousness of a Nautilus shell. I perceived the Nautilus as being an ultimate expression of inward-drawing, Moon-Saturn energy. This experience turned out to be a permanent threshold in my spiritual opening.

Journeyers can explore the relationship in nature between solids and liquids, for example, the antibacterial effect of the enzymes contained in saliva on our teeth. An interesting astronomical phenomena correlated with Saturn is the consciousness of black holes, perceived as an infinitely collapsing, centripedal, and inwardly drawing state of being.

Archetypal experiences include confrontations with the Terrible Mother in various cultural forms, including the Pre-Columbian serpent-headed Coatlicue, the Egyptian lion-headed Sekhmet, or the Indian Kali. Subjects may also face the archetype of the Vicious Spoiler or the Harpies—in Greek mythology, mean-spirited birds with the heads of women who enjoyed soiling outdoor picnics. Some of these same negative lunar archetypes can also occur in sessions dominated by Moon-Pluto. What distinguishes Saturn-BPM II experiences, as we have seen, is that journeyers identify solely with victims, whereas in Plutonic-BPM III experiences, they tend to identify, simultaneously, with both the victims and the perpetrating forces.

A blessedly positive experience related to Moon-Saturn is the *Hag* or *Crone* archetype, explored in this supervised and internalized LSD session undertaken with Saturn trine the subject's natal Moon:

> For a long period at the end, I was failing and losing again. Both sitters lay down next to me in a comforting way, like mom and dad. This nurture helped to heal more of my toxic-womb feelings. As I was failing and felt that I had blown the healing chances of an entire lifetime, I began to identify with the archetype of the Old Crone. Rather than her harmful energies being liberated out of my psyche and returning back into the transpersonal, I perceived that they would now stay stuck inside me and carried through into my next life. The material attachments she represented were now depicted by her/my fingernails, which began to extend across time into my next incarnation. I identified with a bitter old woman, sitting alone in an apartment and waiting for death, feeling malice toward all living things, especially children and cats.

Later in the evening, I felt the Crone emerging inside me again. Her finger-nails began to grow and grow unstoppably, and I just let it happen. They soon reached into every part of the cosmos, touching and connecting with all things. The boundaries between the physical world and the surrounding Divine suddenly opened, and everything was lightened and freed. I felt at that moment—about thirteen or fourteen hours into the session—a fundamental shift occurring, from being locked into my own boundaries to being radically connected now with the entire universe. It was a dramatically positive shift in a day of incredible surprises. I appreciated so deeply the care of my sitters and friends. It was the best post-session period I have ever experienced, and the feelings of universal connection continued in a diminished form from that point onward in my life.

A strange and oddly ironic sequence that can occur under Moon-Saturn alignments is an identification with the loneliness of the cosmic creative principle itself, accompanied by passing feelings of embarrass-ment or disappointment that: *"This is all there is?. . ."* But these deflating moments quickly resolve into a feeling of gratefulness that we—the divine and humanity—have each other. Journeyers then look forward to doing all the little daily things in their lives that they enjoy, such as eating, working, watching favorite shows, or being in nature because, in a very real way, every moment they experience is being enjoyed by two.

In the end, they realize that, while people in modern society often seem indifferent and uncaring toward each other, in times of emergency, such as the induced healing "emergency" of a supervised holotropic ses-sion, human beings are there for each other. The act of turning one's chronic, static symptoms back into a dynamic flow of experiences enables people to receive concentrated human support in a sustained and deliber-ate way.

Sometimes, during Moon-Saturn transits, journeyers may also feel that, although the physical setting of their sessions may not be overflowing with luxury and frills, it is adequate to allow them to have the experiences they need to have. The following holotropic session during a world transit of Moon trine Saturn conveys some of the maturing insights yielded from these archetypes:

I felt for a while that I was being abandoned by the female sitter. Even while I imagined that she was tired of me, another part of my mind maintained the possibility that I was just projecting and hooking in. Gradually I realized that it was I who needed a break, who was looking for a way out of continuing to face the material.

I began to understand that sitters—or anyone—can only make our experi-ence of the world so safe. At certain points in the inner journey, the death-rebirth process feels completely *unsafe*. I perceived that in all the pos-sible combinations of good and bad karma in a human lifetime, sitters as well as parents can be too protective, overprotective in a smothering way. I don't want my sitters to try and take away my suffering and humbling experiences, but rather to provide a safe and supportive neutral space in which I can suffer and learn for myself.

However self-reliant that journeyers might profess to be, Grof recommends that sitters and friends plan a "positive structured experience" at the end of the day centered around the participant. This tends to be especially important during Moon-Saturn transits, in order to compensate for the depressive and isolating character of these archetypes. In breathwork sessions, the optional group sharing at the end provides a positive bonding experience. After psychedelic sessions, a special dinner or rebirthday party of friends and family can have a gratefully received healing effect. However, the people supporting journeyers need to be sensitive to last-minute changes in his or her needs, such as wanting friends but not family to be in the room. These emotional qualifications can also change back fairly quickly.

Mercury-Saturn

Every man takes the limits of his own field of vision for the limits of the world.
Arthur Schopenhauer (Mercury conjunct Saturn 10°38') *Studies in Pessimism*, 1851

All is to be doubted.
René Descartes (Mercury trine Saturn, date only, calc. for noon: 2°19') *Discourse on Method*, 1637

I'm not denyin' the women are foolish: God Almighty made 'em to match the men.
George Eliot (Mercury square Saturn 7°35') *Adam Bede*, 1859

Mercury-Saturn Transits in Everyday Life

During transits of Mercury-Saturn, people's thought and communication often turn more toward practical concerns. Somewhat less idealistic, they feel drawn to what is useful and productive in the here-and-now world. The Saturn archetype focuses people's minds on specific concrete problems and tasks, making these good times for hard intellectual work and study. People's thinking tends to be more methodical, careful, and precise than usual and they may have a better eye for numbers and details. Saturn's minimalist character is also helpful for pruning or editing out unnecessary clutter in people's lives. Mercury acting on Saturn will enable them to step back and look objectively at serious issues and problems in their world, at what is not working and how to fix it.

On the shadow side, Saturn's constricting nature can give rise to more rigid or unimaginative modes of thought. Cautious conservatism can slide into repressive control, criticism, or nitpicking. Unable to see the big picture, people may also miss out on healing and liberating opportunities. Finally, a tendency toward pessimism, worry, or seeing the cup as half empty can indicate that their minds are being influenced by challenging perinatal or transpersonal themes.

Mercury-Saturn Transits in Deep Self-Exploration

The Mercury-Saturn field has a moderately strong effect in self-exploration. Although these archetypes may create a brief resistance to surrendering into holotropic states, they are not an important factor in choosing days for sessions. On the positive side, the rationality of mind associated with them can help people to step back and be more objective about their emotional material. These archetypes will also focus people's awareness on specific mental issues or problems that need to be addressed.

The *dynamic* Mercury-Saturn transits may also coincide with a more pessimistic outlook going into sessions. This is not usually a problem before breathwork workshops. However, as journeyers approach the more intense and demanding psychedelic experiences, they may, at times, have grim doubts or obsessions about the timing of the session, including the transits on that day. Their inner voice can have a grave warning quality. In general, concerns about the date and timing of sessions can usually be interpreted as the emergence of past traumatic events being projected onto the present situation. People often have very positive experiences despite strong doubts about the timing. In contrast, any outstanding trust issues with the sitters should be fully discussed and resolved before proceeding.

Once sessions are underway, journeyers with dynamic Saturn-to-Mercury transits may be more likely to project and imagine critical attitudes coming from their sitters, or interpret comments made by them in a negative way. They can perceive their sitters' words as negative and judging, or their explanations as inept and their voices as mumbling. Comments by the sitters, as always, should be kept to an absolute minimum. They need to exercise great care with every word, offering only short, positive, and supportive statements in response to the breather's own requests, such as: "You're doing great" "We're totally here for you" "We won't abandon you" and "You've got lots of time."

At the biographical layer of exploration, journeyers can work through memories of verbal abuse or criticism from their parents, reprimands for being slow or stupid, or of not being allowed to talk back. As this material surfaces, they may develop a desperate fear of making sound or of upsetting the people supporting them. They can also resolve issues around dogmatic religious or scholastic agendas that promoted obedience and memorization over personal unfolding, awakening of imagination, and creative initiative.

Perinatal Experiences

Tarnas observed that, as exploration reaches the perinatal realm of the psyche, the dynamic Saturn-Mercury transits will support the emergence of material from Grof's BPM II, although this is more likely when Saturn-Mercury is intensified by other Saturn transits. Reflecting the state of the fetus pressed inside the uterine walls—or in the birth canal during BPM III sequences—people can experience a radical contraction of their mental horizons, feelings of pessimism, and anguished self-doubt. These are understandable experiences of the suffering infant, unable to control or change the situation through any imaginable strategy of its own, a bad state that continues for what feels like an eternity. Time can have a grimly compressed quality. Tarnas notes that it is not uncommon to fall into a repetitive tape loop of negative thoughts, resembling a kind of circular mental hell. Journeyers may dwell on seemingly insurmountable problems, the attempted solutions of which only seem to escalate and compound the problems in their minds.

People influenced by BPM II can perceive the very act of thinking, let alone higher intellectual pursuits, as being absolutely pointless and futile. Penetrating beyond the opaque walls that separate human beings from any kind of higher meaning or truth might seem impossible or ludicrous. They have the glaring realization that when they get older, they may not even be able to remember their own names. During these experiences, sophisticated subjects may identify with artists who convey Mercury-Saturn themes in graphic ways, such as Francisco de Goya born with Sun-Mercury opposition Saturn, with his depictions of the mind tortured by demonic figures—for example, in his painting "Conjuration."

The following holotropic session undertaken with Saturn sextile natal Mercury, Mars opposition Mercury, and Saturn opposition Ascendant, illustrates some possible effects of Mercury-Saturn in the perinatal realm of exploration:

> For what felt like an eternity, I felt catastrophically vulnerable and unable to convey my deep and consuming fear that the sitters might abandon me—even though some emerging "bad" part of me felt that I deserved to be. Despite having headphones on with loud music, I believed that I could hear the sitters making negative comments such as *"Oh, God!"* and *"Oh, no!"* and sighing

impatiently. When I asked them about this later, they said they were in a relaxed and quiet place the entire time. I had been totally projecting.[5]

Full experience of this material releases it from the psyche, leading to a dramatic lifting of mental burdens, opening of horizons, and reconnection with the Universal Mind, states in which the operations of the human intellect and higher spirituality no longer seem to contradict each other.

Transpersonal Experiences

As exploration reaches the transpersonal realms, journeyers can identify with people who suffer from sensory impairments such as blindness, deafness, or inability to speak. They can also explore tendencies within the human psyche toward ignorance, blindness, and inertia in responding to its many pressing challenges.

At the highest levels, journeyers gain insight into the creation of what the Vedic philosophers refer to as *Maya*: the virtual reality or illusion of the material universe. They can explore the screenworks or boundaries that the Absolute Consciousness erects within itself to create the separate units of consciousness in the phenomenal realm. Ultimately, these cosmic screenworks translate into human experience as an exclusive identification with the material world and a deep reluctance to explore the psyche—as Alan Watts puts it: "the taboo against knowing who we are." People may also explore the convincing illusions of time and causality.

Venus-Saturn

Lots of people want to ride with you in the limo, but what you want is someone who will take the bus with you when the limo breaks down.
   Oprah Winfrey (Venus square Saturn 0°36′)

Loneliness and the feeling of being unwanted is the most terrible poverty.
   Mother Teresa (Venus square Saturn 2°21′; with Moon conjunct Saturn)
   "Saints Among Us"

'Tis better to have loved and lost
Than never to have loved at all.
   Alfred Lord Tennyson (Venus quincunx Saturn 0°11′) "In Memoriam" 1850

Venus-Saturn Transits in Everyday Life

Transits of Venus-Saturn combine the friendship, love, and enjoyment of the Venus archetype with the worldly responsibilities, practical concerns, and material boundaries of Saturn. Occurring every seven years, the dynamic Saturn-to-Venus transits can be cooling times in people's affections, as they ask serious questions about the long-term security and stability of their relationships. Those that are felt to be shallow, unstable, or to have run their course sometimes end under these influences— ongoing concerns that were tolerated before may now seem to be just too much. And in a more routine way, even the dynamic, short-term Venus-to-Saturn transits are not especially supportive for dealing with everyday relationship issues. It is often better to identify the problem and then wait until after the transit passes to try and resolve it.

At the same time, relationships that are deemed to be sound will undergo a firming and solidifying process, as people deepen their commitments to each other. Under Venus-Saturn they come to appreciate the Saturnian virtues of loyalty and steadfastness. Valuing quality over quantity, they hold dear the dependable and mature side of their partners, more attracted to a steady and reliable supply of affection—"stirring the oatmeal" love—than random bursts of excitement or variety. These are also good times for focused creative projects. The Venus-Saturn complex is especially conducive for work in hard materials such as wood, metal or stone, for utilitarian art, or for the business side of the arts.

If people already have issues around emotional deprivation, Venus-Saturn transits might increase their feelings of loneliness or unlovability. Acute suffering around these issues, however, can evoke a serious determination to work on the underlying issues. At times taking the opposite response, people's feelings of unworthiness may lead them to hide behind veils of prestige or vanity.

Venus-Saturn Transits in Deep Self-Exploration

Venus-Saturn transits correspond to moderately strong, more sobering influences in holotropic exploration. On the positive side, they help to foster clear professional boundaries and a sense of responsibility in everyone involved in the healing experience. The flowing transits, especially, work to stabilize the quality of contact between journeyers and sitters, creating an anchor around which people can face their emotional pain without concerns that the rejecting pattern will be repeated in the present situation.

Experiences occurring during the *dynamic* transits may also have a somewhat more challenging side. They do not pose a problem for breathwork workshops or for regular psychedelic sessions planned in a series. However, these are not the ideal influences for a first session with clients who have serious trust issues, although with caring sitters people can still have good results. The dynamic transits are also not supportive for individuals who are romantically involved to sit for each other, as ongoing emotional dynamics between them might affect their ability to fully surrender, or to objectively support the other's process.

This is especially true in psychedelic sessions. This concern would apply to dynamic Venus-to-Saturn or Saturn-to-Venus transits in either person's chart, or in the sky by world transit—as well as to many other Saturn, Pluto, and Mars transits. It is better for a person's spouse or partner to come in at the *end* of a session to help with the integration phase. As always, trust issues should be talked about beforehand and sitters need to ensure that they do not harbor any outstanding expectations of the client. The matter of fair compensation or trade for the service of sitting should also be addressed ahead of time. Two or more spiritual friends sitting for each other at regular intervals will enjoy a very solid and dependable depth of support in the long run.

In terms of content, journeyers with Venus-Saturn transits can explore issues around loneliness, selfishness, or materialism. They realize that, in order to heal their relationship problems, they have to be willing to face any selfish or grasping feelings they may harbor, but without acting them out any further in the social world. People often trace some of the roots of their relationship problems to painful experiences in childhood, as in this holotropic session conducted with Venus square the subject's natal Saturn:

> I felt warm, loving feelings for my dad while I worked through memories of needing attention from him, in the atmosphere of severe sibling rivalry and pressure that dominated my childhood. These warm feelings then shifted into the Oedipal problem and the ways I got emotionally massacred in the struggle for affection from my mom. With unrelenting competition from my charismatic and extroverted father on one side and lovable star brother on the other, it was almost impossible for me to get the attention I needed. I was grateful for the steady presence of my sitters in creating the space within which I could face these issues.

The most important cause of people's loneliness is not having a loving relationship in their present lives. The challenge then is to heal the wounds that prevent them from having a partner. Some of these problems are of the *omission* type—in which people did not get their needs for nurture met in infancy, and are thus unable to emotionally bond with others in the present. These issues can also create a feeling that their beauty and sexuality are their only appealing features and that they are not loved as a whole person. These problems can be resolved by regressing to the earlier point of need, in holotropic states, and then receiving the warm contact they missed as infants.

Venus-Saturn memories of the *commission* type that journeyers can resolve include episodes of sexual abuse, parental judgments on their sexuality, or the painful ending of relationships. Journeyers can also work through issues around beauty and ugliness, the problem of unwanted attractions, or the relationship between love and hate.

Perinatal Experiences

As self-exploration reaches the perinatal tier, the painful and judging forces in the psyche are revealed to be, on a deeper level, rooted in the contracting uterine walls during labor—expelling the fetus from its oceanic, paradisean state and out into the world of separate existence and mortality. People can have overwhelming feelings of emotional and romantic failure as this process completes itself. Perinatal sequences often include deep fears around losing one's beauty and lovability during the process of aging. The following excerpt is from a holotropic session conducted with Venus square natal Saturn:

> I identified with women tragically obsessed by the demands of the beauty culture—on a deeper level, driven by attempts to repress and stay on top of their threatening perinatal emotions and fear of death. In the next sequence, I was a female sturgeon in a Russian caviar plant being squeezed for her eggs—the feminine enslaved and milked for all she was worth.

These painful human fears and vanities gradually resolve as people let go of their attachment to personal beauty and embrace, instead, a generous and harmonious relationship with other people and all of life. The lower Aphrodite's glorification of attractiveness gives way to the higher Aphrodite's celebration of the beautiful and harmonious cosmos.

Transpersonal Experiences

As inner work continues in the transpersonal realms, journeyers explore themes of a similar kind but from the point of view of various collective, karmic, ancestral, and mythological protagonists. They may confront scenes around patriarchal cultures' judgments of sex, and on women's sexuality, in particular. They can explore the unique mixtures of beauty and pain-inflicting boundaries contained in aspects of nature such as a rose and its thorns. They can also see mythological or fairy tale images of various ugly creatures, fairies, or spirits.

Other archetypal experiences include the absence of the Beloved, the loyalty of Odysseus' Penelope, or the Hag-Crone. Journeyers may also encounter the rivalry between mythological brothers such as Abel and Cain or Osiris and Set. The following supervised and internalized psilocybin mushroom session was undertaken with Saturn square natal Venus:

> I had a vivid perception of being back in ancient Egypt where I did something wicked that has followed me ever since. This uncanny experience then deepened into a mythological scene: I am Seth, the Evil Brother who killed his good brother Osiris. In a strange interdimensional way, I perceived this mythological sequence as a source of deep, chronic problems in my current life.

After this blessed session, I noticed a distinct healing and releasing of karma in my relationships with my brothers and with males in general.

Allowing painful emotions to surface has an opening effect on people's hearts, reminding them that warm relationships and friendships are essential for a happy life. As this releasing unfolds, especially in psychedelic sessions, they will be extremely vulnerable to any sense of coolness or rejection coming from the people around them. To ensure that sitters' tiredness or hunger does not interfere with the flow of support, it is preferable that at least one backup sitter comes in to relieve the primary sitters when the dynamic phase of the session is nearing completion. A positive, structured experience planned in advance, such as a special birthday dinner will ensure that journeyers have an opportunity for warm social contact without the burden of having to make decisions or be responsible for other people's feelings.

Mars-Saturn

I have nothing to offer but blood, toil, tears, and sweat.
    Winston Churchill (Mars trine Saturn 7°57') First statement as British Prime Minister to the House of Commons, May 1940.

A small daily task, if it be really daily, will beat the labors of a spasmodic Hercules.
    Anthony Trollope (Mars conjunct Saturn, date only, calc. for noon: 5°31')
    An Autobiography, 1883

If you hate a person, you hate something in him that is part of yourself. What isn't part of ourselves doesn't disturb us.
    Hermann Hesse (Mars conjunct Saturn 8°36') *Demian,* 1919

Mars-Saturn Transits in Everyday Life

During Mars-Saturn transits, the impulses toward action, assertion, and aggression of the Mars archetype are confronted by the worldly priorities, boundaries, and consequences of Saturn. On the positive side, Saturn can focus people's output into useful, constructive channels. They are able to buckle down and put their noses to the grindstone, applying themselves with steady, unremitting discipline toward accomplishing the most arduous and demanding tasks. The Saturn principle helps to regulate the flow of energy in people's psyches so they can access a steady supply over a long period.

The *dynamic* transits are not the most helpful influences for initiating new projects, however, especially those that may need bursts of energy and enthusiasm, but all Mars-Saturn transits can be very supportive for finishing and completing tasks. They are also conducive for work in wood, metal or stone such as sawing, cutting, breaking, grinding or hammering. As always, though, if people are angry, it is important to be careful around machinery and sharp tools. Individuals may also have a tendency to wrench their muscles and joints.

The challenging side of the Mars-Saturn field emerges when Saturn's tendencies toward discipline are perceived as frustrating or defeating. Bosses, authority figures, or spouses may seem to be unduly demanding or punishing, or individuals themselves may project these attitudes. Work can feel like a harsh rat-race or grind. Subject to ongoing boundary collisions, some people may also feel a kind of cold smouldering anger or bitterness. However, these are not good times to lash out at others, as confrontations can take a decidedly nasty and acrimonious tone. It is usually better to step back, forbear and endure frustrating situations for a while, and then seek a solution or compromise later on.

During these episodes, however, it can be helpful to find a soundproof space to process some of the feelings of anger or hate that the Mars-Saturn complex can bring up. The quickest way to resolve these emotions is to actively feel both the aggressive force of Mars and the limiting focus of Saturn—mobilizing and holding both energies in a kind of sustained "dynamic tension." A good exercise is to press one's palms together while feeling Mars' centrifugal power and Saturn's constricting pressure at the same time. Allow the feelings to focus into a point in front of oneself, while actively pushing the pointed energy out of one's system through deliberate exhales. Coughing, growling, or shaking fists can also help to consume and release the energy. When these conditions of forbearance and effective processing are met, Mars influencing Saturn can help people to actively confront their deepest fears and resistances.

In general, the dynamic Mars-Saturn transits can also have a deflating or constricting effect on sexual energies. Finally, these are not the most supportive times to make romantic overtures toward someone new, as he or she is more likely to feel irritated or threatened.

Mars-Saturn Transits in Deep Self-Exploration

The archetypal field associated with Mars-Saturn alignments can help journeyers to stay focused on their emotional process and keep facing whatever comes up. The trines and, to a lesser extent the sextiles, represent moderately strong and positive influences for deep work. They mobilize tremendous tenacity and staying power, ensuring that people will stay committed until the end of the day and their material is completed.

The *dynamic* transits are important influences that also confer great resolve and steadfastness. They can help people to work through very difficult and trying emotional material. However, because of Saturn's tendency to constrict Mars' dynamic and expressive energies, these are not the ideal influences for a first psychedelic session, although, they will not pose a problem for experienced sitters. Mars-Saturn transits are also not an issue for sessions that are part of a pre-planned series of sessions, though their unique character will certainly register.

It is with individuals ingesting psychedelics in a casual or recreational way that heavy Mars-to-Saturn or Saturn-to-Mars transits can sometimes present some challenges. These archetypes can impart a distinctly harsh and punishing flavor to people's emerging process. Primal energies do not flow out automatically in a smooth and unimpeded way, but seem to need to encounter some kind of dynamic resistance in order to be released. For this to be a healing process, however, the resisting force ultimately needs to come from within the participant's own psyche, or be perceived as cooperating with it. Stressed-out young people in social settings may project and feel that these archetypal resistances and boundary pressures are coming from the external environment and, occasionally, push back. Finally, dynamic Mars-Saturn alignments—in either person's chart or by world transit—are not conducive for romantic partners planning to sit for each other. The experience of "boundaries with teeth" associated with this complex can be extremely unpleasant and could lead, in certain situations, to a highly damaging feedback loop of reinforcing, negative responses.

The basic character of the Mars-Saturn field is of focused passion or aggression (Mars) in an enclosed space (Saturn). On occasion, journeyers may find the perfect intersection of these energies by holding pillows over their faces and yelling, though the use of pillows should be suggested by the participant rather than the sitters. They can also release tension by actively pressing their palms together, squeezing a towel, making fists, growling, or coughing.

In terms of content, journeyers may face and release feelings of bitterness or hate leftover from interpersonal conflicts in their lives. They may also work through the damaging effects of rape, abuse, or other violence subjected upon them. Finally, people can encounter leftover traces from serious injuries, illnesses, or operations. The following memory of a tonsillectomy from a supervised and internalized LSD session was conducted with Mars trine Saturn in the sky:

> About six hours into the session, without warning, I was reliving my tonsillectomy as a child. As plain as if it was happening right then, I could feel an intrusive sharp object reaching down into my throat and cutting. I began to gag and cough intensely. So harsh and disruptive, I could feel that this surgery, deep in my throat, has probably been a source of disharmony in my communications all my life.

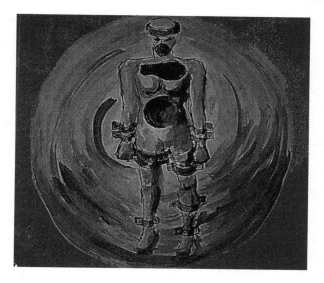

Figure 12. "Hyperventilation Armor" Mojca Studen (Mars square natal Saturn, and Saturn square natal Mars). This Holotropic Breathwork session of a Slovenian participant illustrates one of the major Mars-Saturn themes of machinelike tension and constriction. After surrendering to this pressure, the armor and darkness began to melt away and she felt newly liberated, with a sense of pleasant physical freedom and movement in her body.

On one level, an activated Mars-Saturn can indicate a Saturnian reluctance to face the more intense Mars energies. People may have conflicts about letting go and revealing their aggressive feelings. They can also display alternations between their aggressive and controlling impulses. As the process deepens, the ambivalent back-and-forth conflict between these archetypes is recognized as being inherent in the material itself.

Perinatal Experiences

As exploration reaches the perinatal region, the dynamic tensions between Mars and Saturn are revealed to be, on a deeper level, based on the rage and struggle to survive of the fetus compressed within the narrow birth canal. Grof found that feelings of claustrophobia, anxiety and aggression are understandable reactions of any organism exposed to life-threatening suffocation and excruciating pain such as those involved in delivery. If journeyers' emotional material is dominated by *Saturn and BPM II*, they will tend to relate exclusively with victims, identifying with human beings or other life forms who have had their assertive drives and boundaries ruthlessly assaulted or punctured by external forces.

When *Pluto and BPM III* dominate, the Mars-Saturn field will help to focus people's attention on specific difficult energy blocks in the death-rebirth process in order to release them. It is helpful to remember that feelings of frustration and of being stuck are intrinsic to this archetypal complex. There is a tendency for individuals to try to control and override the energies, for example, by sitting up and hitting pillows or by yelling in a forced way—which then results in a hoarse voice and sore throat afterward. People may also try to avoid their perinatal emotions by seeking to move somewhere else with "more space." They need, as much as possible, to simply lie back, breathe, and surrender to the emerging feelings and sensations as they unpack themselves from their unconscious. Lying down is the most effective position for working through any emotion.

Introjected pressures from the birth canal provide much of the energy behind judging, punishing, and self-limiting attitudes in later life. Freud called this part of the psyche the *superego*. In order to consume these punishing inner structures, people must be willing to feel both the aggressive fury of the infant and the constricting force of the birth canal, as the psyche presents them in alternation or simultaneously. They can also discharge the punishing and judging energies inside them by imagining a medium-sized ball in front of their abdomens, and then jamming their hands down and onto it from both sides, over and over, while exhaling in short aggressive bursts. This approximates the force of the mother's contracting body around the fetus' head during birth.

The following is from a holotropic session conducted with Saturn conjunct natal Mars:

> The morning of the session, the words "He will hurt you" played over and over through my mind. I was paralyzed with fear as I projected these apparent warnings onto fears about my male sitter. When the words deepened into, "He will kill you!" I was finally able to interpret them as originating from a surfacing archetypal complex of the *Punishing Father/Constricting Birth Canal*. Throughout the session, whenever I imagined that the male sitter might be mad at me, I focused in and became the compressing forces myself, mobilizing and aiming them at my own being, resulting in enormous releases of tension. Of course, my sitter was completely supportive through this process, and I was able to heal some very deep parental and perinatal wounds.

As this material floods out of the psyche in high-dose psychedelic sessions, journeyers can at the outset feel excruciating fears of what they might do, if they really let go of control. This seems to be a kind of barrier or prelude to the emergence of the deeper BPM III material. As aggressive energies break through, they can then see grotesque underworld images such as weird angry fetuses marching in Nazi jackboots, that clearly reveal the source of their feelings to be in the perinatal layer of the psyche. By letting the energies explode out of their systems, journeyers can greatly diminish and then virtually eliminate the effects of anger and aggression in their everyday lives.

BPM III *sadomasochistic material* that emerges during Mars-Saturn transits can also include especially harsh or vicious mixtures of sex and aggression, the acted-out corollaries of which can be seen in the headlines of any major newspaper. As we have seen, the combination of sex and aggression is based on the suffocation and sexual arousal of the fetus during labor. Additionally, some babies are born with the umbilical cord wrapped around their necks or squeezed against the mother's pelvic bone.

Grof found that one of the reasons that rape is so damaging is that the victim suffers not only from the event itself, but that it opens a pathway for the reservoir of perinatal emotions to reach present awareness. He discovered that, in order to fully heal from the effects of sexual violence, his patients had to work through not only these traumatic events but their unresolved perinatal material as well.

Transpersonal Experiences

As exploration continues in the transpersonal strata, sequences of animal consciousness tend to center around cold-blooded or armored predators such as sharks or crocodiles. Typical scenes include predators ripping out the throats of their prey, as in this holotropic session conducted with Mars trine Saturn in the sky:

> In another scene, I was a big cat on some primal savannah grassland, ripping out the throat of an antelope-like creature, as archetypal blood gushed out all over. This seemed somehow related to the unusual enjoyment I felt eating dinner the next day.

Journeyers may also identify with various birds of prey such as eagles, hawks or owls, focusing on the sharp definition of their beaks and talons.

They can identify with the murderous cruelty of dictators espousing their cold philosophies of blood and steel, or explore the consciousness of the element iron and its role in human history, as in this session during a world transit of Mars sextile Saturn:

> I felt the wounding effect of all the needles that have ever been poked into me in my life, as well as the collective pain of humanity, especially children,

during the stage of technological development when needles are routinely used in medicine and dentistry. At the same time, I identified with all the people who have ever been killed or wounded by chopping swords and other iron weapons. I felt that when a species reaches the Iron Age stage of development, the death and suffering from these hard weapons and from steel needles indicate a new kind of wake-up call, an alerting shock to the collective psyche that the need for mass awakening is urgent and close at hand.

Individuals in holotropic states can also identify with the consciousness of barbed wire, wrought iron, or the medieval Iron Maiden. Related figures include the blacksmith Hephaestus, the Vicious Spoiler, or the vengeful furies. Some people may also reflect on modern fantasy characters such as the Klingons or Cardassians from the *Star Trek* series or the orcs and dwarves from *The Lord of the Rings*.

Focused bodywork is often needed at the end of Mars-Saturn sessions. The sitter applies steady pressure to an identified spot while the breather tenses up against the resistance, while making any sounds or movements that want to emerge. Expert sitters may also, in the final stages of a session, suggest dynamic-tension exercises such as pressing down on the journeyer's palms while he or she presses upward, to mobilize and release leftover tension. During this process, sitters need to exercise special care in not crossing boundaries or pushing too hard. They also need to be sensitive to changes in the breather's needs, such as alternately wanting and then not wanting bodywork, and not force anything—as people with Mars-Saturn transits will be more susceptible to external pressure of any kind. Finally, it is always recommended to have an ample supply of pillows around breathers, to protect them from accidentally hitting or kicking the floors and walls during cathartic bursts.

Jupiter-Saturn

A mature person is one who does not think only in absolutes, who is able to be objective even when deeply stirred emotionally, who has learned that there is both good and bad in all people and in all things, and who walks humbly and deals charitably with the circumstances of life, knowing that in this world no one is all-knowing and therefore all of us need both love and charity.
Eleanor Roosevelt (Jupiter sextile Saturn 4°40') *It Seems to Me*, 1954

Character cannot be developed in ease and quiet. Only through experience of trial and suffering can the soul be strengthened, vision cleared, ambition inspired, and success achieved.
Helen Keller (Jupiter conjunct Saturn 10°32'; with SA=JU/NE)
Helen Keller's Journal, 1938

Jupiter-Saturn Transits in Everyday Life

Jupiter-Saturn transits are the least glamorous of Jupiter influences, but one of the most beneficial. Aligning at regular intervals in everyone's lives, they seem to occur at times when people need some kind of rebalancing reality check or reminder of their human limitations, bringing them down to earth. The Saturn archetype acting on Jupiter helps to deflate Jupiter's ongoing tendencies toward excess and inflation. Feelings of shortage or deficiency in various areas of life make these appropriate times to edit and prune out what is unnecessary and focus on essential priorities, on quality over quantity.

At the same time, Jupiter helps people to see the positive side of Saturn's boundaries, limitations, and challenges. They discover what Tarnas describes as a "sober, mature" appreciation for the various obstacles and adversities in their lives as builders of character, reminding them of their mortality and keeping them on track. With a clearer perception of what really brings them satisfaction, individuals can let go of unrealistic, grandiose fantasies and focus on what is actually happening and what is truly possible. They gain a new respect for integrity, the ring of truth, and solid rewards earned honestly over time.

Jupiter-Saturn Transits in Deep Self-Exploration

The flowing transits of Jupiter-Saturn represent mild but positive influences in deep inner work. They support proper planning and preparation, thus helping to ensure that logistical details before and after sessions work out smoothly. The dynamic alignments, although usually contributing some Saturnian themes, are not considered a problem either for a first session or for sessions that are scheduled in a series.

However, it is important that people plan ahead and have enough of everything essential for a smooth event, especially, adequate time and support, in order to compensate for the feelings of scarcity and shortage that can sometimes arise during any Saturn transit. In psychedelic sessions, according to Grof, there should ideally be expert sitters on duty for at least the beginning and middle phases of the day—about four-five hours for psilocybin mushroom sessions, and six to seven hours for LSD sessions.[6] Additionally, journeyers should make arrangements with their partners, spiritual friends, or trusted family members to come in and relieve the primary sitters at that point for the rest of the evening. Equally important is to have a soundproof space with no one coming or going who is not directly supporting the participant.

Even when resources are scarce, however, some highly motivated individuals may feel tempted to go ahead with inner journeys without having the ideal amount of time or support they might need. Everyone seems to need to learn these things for him or herself, but experience suggests that it is better when people set things up carefully ahead of time. It can be very painful when a person's only sitter, contracted for a set number of hours, gets up and leaves when that time is over and the vulnerable person finds that he or she still needs human contact. If possible, journeyers should try to have relief support planned in advance.

At the *biographical* layer of exploration, subjects can remember episodes of constriction or cutbacks in their lives, periods when the universe seemed to be reining in their excesses. They can also work through conflicts about expanding or putting themselves out into the world.

Perinatal Experiences

Tarnas realized that as self-exploration reaches the perinatal layer, the Jupiter-Saturn field can activate feelings of being stuck or held back, failure, loss, or compression of space—all characteristic of Grof's Basic Perinatal Matrix II. Sequences of being ruthlessly exposed by a supreme deity in scenes of Judgment press on individuals the fact that we cannot ultimately escape responsibility for our actions in any way.

During these humbling episodes, people realize that much of the worldly bluster and egotism of human beings is just a wishful compensation against the unconscious memory of birth and fear of death. The following holotropic session with Jupiter square natal Saturn illustrates this kind of grandiose compensation against primal fear:

> I could feel my jaws helplessly pressed together in the birth canal, while at the same time, seeing images of a ruthless and paranoid South American dictator. He/I was sitting on a smoky restaurant veranda projecting largeness and strength, but in this moment I knew that his real, deeper feelings were just the opposite.

Similar to Saturn-Uranus in some ways, journeyers with Jupiter-Saturn transits may also feel alternating urges to expand and contract, as a part of their being struggles to grow and break free (Jupiter) while another part seems to hold them back (Saturn). Sometimes they can feel that their inner beings are being worked on to explode open, but that they will never be able to let go and let it happen. If breathers ask for support in these moments, sitters can remind them simply to stay with whatever is happening, without trying to change the experience. The alternating feelings of expansion and contraction are then revealed to be the introjected pressures of the birth canal itself, alternating with the fetus' desperate urge to escape from it and reach birth. Allowing these two forces to play themselves out automatically resolves the pressure.

Transpersonal Experiences

In the transpersonal realms of discovery, journeyers continue to explore the interplay of various opposites and polarities in the universe such as growth and compression, success and failure, or good and evil. They can experience the effects of many kinds of deflating and rebalancing processes in human life, increasing their ability to trust exactly where the universe takes them and when. The resolution of opposites may also be depicted in mythological or fairy tale sequences such as Goldilocks finding the porridge that is just right, or an appreciation of the Greek and Chinese ideals of the Golden Mean: "nothing to excess."

Journeyers also continue to explore the theme of cosmic justice. They may encounter various gods and goddesses of justice, or givers of law, such as the Babylonian Tiamat, the Egyptian Maat, the Indian Vishnu, the Greek Themis, or the Arabian Allah. People also develop a profound respect for the Saturnian processes of maturation, delay, and karmic rewards over time. The following holotropic experience of an artist was undertaken with Jupiter conjunct Saturn in the sky:

> I flashed on my creative projects and was grateful for the many times that the universe has stopped or slowed me down. In this state, I perceived that the worst kind of karma in human life is when the universe gives us an opportunity to move in directions that would ultimately be harmful to ourself or others. A more fortunate type of karma is where the universe won't let us get away with damaging or inflating kinds of success in the world before we have been emotionally healed.

Journeyers come to realize that all delays and obstacles to human awakening are ultimately put there by the Universal Mind itself, in just the right mixtures to keep things interesting. As one veteran connoisseur explorer put it: "Nobody gives away a good plot."

*   *   *

Transits of Pluto

The overlap of content in these sections becomes especially apparent in the sections on Pluto. I have tried to strike a balance between not repeating material unnecessarily and making each description comprehensive in itself, so that journeyers can access all the support and information they might need before approaching sessions during any given transit. The most helpful use of this book, rather than reading it sequentially from beginning to end, would be for readers to look at those chapters that apply to their own current transits.

Sun-Pluto

[Every ideology can be seen as] the personal confession of its author. . . . Psychology shall be recognized again as the queen of the sciences, for whose service and preparation the other sciences exist. For psychology is now again the path to the fundamental problems.
    Friedrich Nietzsche (Sun opposition Pluto 0°50′)
    Beyond Good and Evil, 1886

There is strong shadow where there is much light.
    Johann von Goethe (Sun square Pluto 6°0′) *Gotz von Berlichingen*, 1773

Sun-Pluto Transits in Everyday Life

Sun-Pluto transits represent six-to-ten-day periods (Sun to natal Pluto) or three-to five-year epochs (Pluto to natal Sun) when the solar side of people's psyches—their sense of basic selfhood and autonomy, light, warmth, and goodness—may be challenged to face and integrate various Plutonic energies and themes in the universe, including those around power, shadow, death, sex, aggression, rebirth, and renewal.

At best, people will directly face these deeper human issues without getting carried away or acting them out in the social world. They may feel strongly compelled to make improvements in themselves or in the world around them. Whatever external projects they become involved in, it is essential that they also take some time to look at the subterranean forces in their psyches. Joseph Campbell refers to this act of descent into the psychological underworld, facing the repressed contents, and then returning to contribute something positive to society as the *hero's journey*, a quest that is essential for both men and women.[7] Without ongoing introspection, the obsessive energies associated with Pluto may have a damaging effect on people's relationships and career efforts.

Forces within the inner life may seem to conspire with external events to bring up buried feelings with great pressure until they are consciously faced. The precipitating events might include feelings of breakdown, power struggles, or heavy emotional encounters. Unilaterally withdrawing from these situations and finding cathartic outlets is always helpful. Individuals may also experience an activation of their *kundalini*, primal energies that rise up their spines, opening the energy centers or *chakras*.

At the same time, Pluto compels people's natural impulses toward personal autonomy, vitality and self-expression, associated with the Sun, into full manifestation. These can be periods of profound creativity, sense of capability, and coming into one's own. However, it is important that individuals do not become ruthless or domineering, or they may end up sabotaging themselves and undoing their creative efforts and projects with just as much force as they initiated them.

The *flowing* transits also offer sustained avenues for rebuilding or remaking situations, creative work, and self-exploration. Although people may still have some obsessive tendencies, the overall feeling tends to be one of renewal, regeneration, and empowerment. By getting the primal energies flowing again, all Pluto trines, and to a lesser extent sextiles, are helpful for emotional and physical healing after periods of crisis.

Sun-Pluto Transits in Deep Self-Exploration

The Sun-Pluto field is highly supportive for holotropic exploration. As we saw, these fiery archetypes help people go deeply into the inner terrains of the psyche where great healing potentials await. At the *biographical* layer of exploration, Sun-Pluto can bring up issues around willpower and domination, authentic self-expression, and integrity. If role models in the person's early life abused power or acted out their own emotions in a ruthless way, these memories may surface for conscious processing. Journeyers may also work through traces left over from episodes of intense struggle, violence, or life-threatening illnesses such as diphtheria or whooping cough.

Perinatal Experiences

As exploration reaches the perinatal domain, Tarnas observed that the Sun-Pluto field will help to bring up material from Grof's Basic Perinatal Matrix III, a cluster of experiences centered around the dynamic stage of labor. At this point, the cervix is now dilated and the fetus is slowly forced down the birth canal by powerful uterine contractions.

Journeyers experience waves of aggressive feelings in the context of a determined *titanic fight*. Grof found that aggression is an understandable reaction of any organism exposed to prolonged mechanical pressures, physical pain, and suffocation such as those involved in delivery. The infant's body and psyche also introject the powerful driving forces of the uterine contractions themselves. In holotropic sessions during any Pluto transit, people may experience frantic motor phenomena, complex twisting

Figure 13. Ayahuasca session of a female subject. "To live, you must die." (Pluto conjunct natal Sun, Sun opposition natal Pluto, and Uranus conjunct natal Moon). "It had to do with the terror and anguish of the unknown I was going through in my life. A white horse with the 'parca' (*Death* figure) came up and said the words: 'To live, you must die.' I couldn't decide what to do but finally got up behind Death. We galloped towards a furnace so hot it was white. And there, my flesh melted away until I was only bones and then these were burned too. Death and the horse disappeared, and I arrived at a calm and fresh oceanic place where, mysteriously, I came back together with a reborn sense of myself."

movements, twitches and tremors, hypersalivation, and profuse sweating as these energies are released from the system. This catharsis is profoundly healing and should be encouraged for as long as necessary until people reach a calm and resolved state. The transpersonal side of the experience can include images of active attacks in wars or revolutions, mythological battle scenes, erupting volcanoes, or violent storms.

The *sadomasochistic* themes that emerge under Pluto transits are also related to suffocation. During each uterine contraction, the blood flowing through the umbilical cord is cut or interrupted and this is experienced as choking, which, as we have seen, creates a strange form of obsessive, Dionysian arousal. Grof's discovery that our first sexual experience occurs in the context of the physical pain, activation of aggression, and vital threat of birth provides a logical explanation for the often observed, negative relationship between sex and aggression in human society.[8]

The *scatological* sequences of BPM III reflect the fetus' encounter with blood, mucus, fetal liquid, and sometimes feces and urine in the final stages of delivery. However, these sequences go far beyond what it could have actually experienced. Journeyers may see piles of rotting corpses, feel that they are wallowing in pools of excrement, or swimming through all the septic lines on the planet. These are often accompanied by intense nausea and projectile vomiting. *Demonic* experiences involve a serious examination of the problems of duality and shadow in the universe, the relationship between good and evil, and confrontation with demonic archetypes. Facing this uncanny material consumes its effects in people's everyday lives.

In *pyrocathartic* sequences, journeyers pass through states of purifying fire. They may see images of vast conflagrations, bursting rockets, or fire in a more symbolic form and sense that it has a deeply purifying effect. The following holotropic session, undertaken with Pluto trine natal Sun, illustrates sadomasochistic and demonic elements which resolved into purifying fire:

> I entered into a dark, S&M underworld where a multitude of naked figures were engaged in every imaginable kind of sexual practice. Yet rather than finding it disturbing, as I might have in my normal state of mind, I felt a weirdly positive overtone from this scene. I had the sense that in this archetypal place, all the energies and structures within my psyche could now be blended together and transcended in divine peace. I saw the boundaries of my ego slowly burning from the outside in, consumed and purified toward the spiritual center. As this was happening, I saw images of peacock feathers and felt brotherly feelings for all humanity.
>
> In the days afterward I noticed a deep sense that two halves of my psyche were now re-knitted back together in wholeness. Some part of my ego has, for my entire life, been fearfully repressing this underworld experience.

Transpersonal Experiences

People may also explore wide-ranging themes in the historical and archetypal unconscious, around issues of power, domination, aggression, purging, renewal, and regeneration. Sessions during all Pluto transits can center around the transformation of forms in the universe, the effects of perinatal energies in human history, or encounters with the negative side of the cosmic creative principle or *Cosmic Shadow*. Journeyers explore the relationship between the archetypal principles of light and shadow, spirit and nature, or Apollo and Dionysus and a transcendence of these polarities in openings to divine consciousness. They may also experience deities symbolizing cosmic renewing and transformative power such as Shiva or Kali.

Moon-Pluto

The place of magic transformation and rebirth, together with the underworld and its inhabitants, are presided over by the Mother. On the negative side, the Mother archetype may connote anything secret, hidden, dark; the abyss, the world of the dead, anything that devours, seduces and poisons, that is terrifying and inescapable like fate.
C. G. Jung (Moon conjunct Pluto 8°03') *The Archetypes and the Collective Unconscious*, 1981

Everyone is a moon, and has a dark side which he never shows to anybody.
Mark Twain (Moon conjunct Pluto 2°40')
"Following the Equator" 1897

Only that which is deeply felt changes us.
Marilyn Ferguson (Moon semisextile Pluto 0°27')
The Aquarian Conspiracy, 1980

Moon-Pluto Transits in Everyday Life

During these intense alignments, people often have a greater exposure to Pluto's regenerating themes. The process can begin with inner or outer events which seem to alter or threaten people's feelings of nurture, connection, or rootedness. Although there are similarities between Pluto-Moon and other Pluto transits, the influence of the Moon archetype is to channel many of Pluto's archetypal energies through the lunar areas of life, including the body, the emotions, the home, family, and community. Very often, people do not feel exclusively victimized by these forces, but feel actively part of them—persuaded by their own emotional behavior that more self-discovery and self-knowledge are needed.

People with the *dynamic* transits, especially, will be prone to much deeper layers of emotion, as Plutonic elements in the psyche attempt to push buried feelings up into awareness. Even minor stimuli can set off intense reactions which then implode or explode toxically into the world around them. These scenes may revolve around jealousy, passive aggression, power struggles or, at their most difficult, feelings of biological crisis—whether or not there is a real problem. Purging encounters with the shadow side of human nature involving dark and heavy energies, feelings of obsessive struggle, or breakdown are then followed by powerful surges of renewal, regeneration, and transformation. These episodes are not always easy at the time, but in retrospect, as people feel the healing and opening which follow from them, they recognize that the transforming experiences are being driven by their own inner wisdom, in the service of a far-reaching evolutionary process.

The archetypal field associated with Moon-Pluto transits is thus one of the most conducive for deep emotional-release work and people experiencing them, or subject to them through a family member, should make every effort to seek out avenues for holotropic work. Even if the offensive emotions seem to be emerging through the behavior of others, the most helpful response for people is to withdraw their aggressive feelings from the social sphere and do some of their own processing. Attempts to repress or redirect Pluto's energies will be, in the long run, less than successful. The inner volcano simply needs to let off pressure at times, and this is one of those times. The Moon archetype brings elements of profound nurture and kindness to this releasing cycle, and people may appear who can offer help during these periods.

The *flowing* transits provide similar avenues for emotional exploration. They can also assist people with efforts to upgrade or regenerate conditions around their homes. All Moon-Pluto transits support healing or consciousness-raising groups in the home space.

Moon-Pluto Transits in Deep Self-Exploration

At the biographical layer of exploration, journeyers may work through memories around aggression in the family, situations in which they were either the perpetrator, the victim, or both. *COEX systems* involving feelings of jealousy, humiliation, or domination may also surface for processing. People who in childhood experienced the flow of nurture in a controlling or manipulative way can heal these issues as they take in the emotional support of their sitters. They may also deal with relationship problems from their present lives, recognizing that only by feeling the emotions on all sides of these issues can they fully resolve them. Finally, journeyers can work through leftover traces from serious accidents, illnesses, or operations.

The safe setting in holotropic work turns the challenge of the ego completely around. Instead of needing to repress and endure the forces of the unconscious—which commandeers vast amounts of energy and leaves people chronically tired and worn out—journeyers can let go and allow their emotional contents to fully emerge and express themselves, freeing them from their systems. As always, sitters should be comfortable with the entire range of material that can arise in these states, allowing it to surface without judgment. Negative reactions to someone's process should be seen as an invitation for more of one's own inner work.

The best results in internalized sessions, according to Grof, occur with supervision from a male-female team or *dyad*. If journeyers begin to project onto one sitter, the other remains as a safe emotional anchor. Although it is not recommended for people in romantic relationships to sit for each other, if attempted, they should have, at the very least, a second, emotionally neutral sitter present.

The following is from an internalized LSD session of a young male student with Pluto square natal Moon, whose only sitter was his girlfriend:

> For a long time, I alternated between deep human sorrow and ecstatic religious feelings. I laughed and cried, over and over, in sequences of euphoric release. After a while, the outpourings began to sour and darken, as I felt a kind of desperate, toxic jealousy growing inside me. I asked my girlfriend if she loved me. She kept saying that she did, but in my altered state I was unpersuaded. Though she tried, she was unable to convince me that she loved me.
>
> In retrospect, I realize that my feelings of insecurity were emerging from a pool in my psyche and could not have been resolved by anything my girlfriend might have said or done. Eventually I sat up and removed my eyeshades and headphones, as the session basically derailed. Fortunately by the end of the evening my emotions smoothed out, but I vowed never to have a romantic partner sit for me in a session again.

Perinatal Experiences

Although helpful for facing any part of the transformative journey, Tarnas found that Moon-Pluto transits have a special resonance with Grof's BPM III, based on the dynamic stage of labor. At this point, the cervix is open and the long propulsion down the birth canal begins. As we have seen, for the fetus, the life-threatening event of labor arouses an enormous aggressive response, and when people face this material it is accompanied by a sense of *titanic fight*. They may emotionally identify with both the victims and the perpetrators in these scenes, with both sides experienced as being parts within themselves. They may also feel torn between their desperate needs for nurturing support, and agonizing concerns that they may hurt the sitters somehow. This mixture of aggressive danger and vulnerability indicates that BPM III material is about to break through. As well as explosive discharges of aggression, people can experience pressures and pain in various parts of their bodies, profuse sweating, muscular tremors, and complex twisting movements that closely resemble delivery.

Another theme that emerges is the *sadomasochistic*. This complex amalgam of sexual arousal, suffering, and aggression is also related to suffocation and pain in labor. *Scatological experiences* are based on the fetus' confrontation with biological materials and are often accompanied by nausea and projectile vomiting. A number of Grof's patients with severe menstrual symptoms experienced a dramatic and permanent relief from these problems as they worked through their leftover perinatal material.[9]

Demonic sequences are possible during any Pluto transit. As journeyers move toward greater spiritual wholeness, they begin to identify less with the boundaries of their ego and more with the entire field of cosmic consciousness. They realize that our true identity is ultimately every part of the cosmic field, including the negative, shadow elements within it. As demonic archetypes begin to surface, people may fixate on unbearable expectations of being abandoned, while at the same time feel that they somehow deserve it.

In one of its most uncanny forms, journeyers pass through the experiential prototype of what was acted out at certain points in history as the Witches' Sabbath or Walpurgis Night. These widespread rituals were an externalized expression of many of the standard BPM III themes, including an atmosphere of darkness and foreboding, inverted spirituality, sexual arousal, excitement, and encounter with biological materials. When allowed to unfold internally, the demonic elements automatically resolve and disappear as divine consciousness in the form of Jesus, Mary, God, Buddha, Shiva, Allah, Parvati, or other cultural forms breaks through and cleanses away the dark energies.

The following holotropic session undertaken with Pluto sextile natal Moon illustrates several aspects of demonic experiences:

> The usual bad emotions I feel about myself began to intensify and then shift to a completely different kind of feeling. It was as if something that was always inside of me was now coming forward, revealing itself, and taking over control. I felt a sense of unstoppable malevolent intentions expand past my boundaries and overlap with the awareness of my sitters. I imagined that *It* /I was in control and manipulating the sitters psychically, so that they wouldn't abandon me.
>
> This uncanny experience then passed to more familiar territory and by the end of the evening I felt peaceful and relaxed. I checked with my sitters later, and they said they hadn't noticed anything particularly difficult or threatening during the experience.

The final theme of an activated Pluto is *pyrocatharsis*. Here feelings of corruption and impurity are consumed by passing through states of purifying fire.

In all these sequences, detailed obstetric elements tend to be overlaid with collective, karmic, and mythological themes that share with delivery the same characteristics of death and rebirth. Thus perinatal scenes can open out into images of animals slaughtering their prey, active attacks in wars and revolutions, or the death and rebirth of various deities. Journeyers may identify with every fetus who has ever been born, or with their delivering mother, or all mothers. The following is from an internalized LSD session of a male subject with Pluto sextile natal Moon:

> I saw an image of all these zipped-shut wounds in my body and psyche finally opening, as the emotions inside them spilled out into the unconditional presence of the people supporting me. After the birth, my mom and I had to bite down on so much unprocessed pain, just to get on with the demands of modern living.
>
> I felt how her desperate emotional needs around the delivery were not met by the impersonal treatment of the hospital staff—I identified profoundly with her suffering. Neither of us had anything like enough time to process what we had just been through.

As people complete this material, a doorway permanently opens in their psyches to experiences of the entire cosmic field.

Transpersonal Experiences

In the transpersonal realms, people explore destructive, transformative, and evolutionary themes and processes in the universe at large. *Racial and collective memories* include the resolution of chronic problems and conflicts in human history, or the long-term power of maternal bloodlines. Participants can experience scenes around the onset of patriarchy in the Middle East, or long sequences from the slave trade in which they identify with a number of protagonists over many centuries. They can perceive that working through these traumas from events in our shared history may be a necessary component in bridging the world's pressing ethnic and racial divisions. Sequences of *animal consciousness* tend to center around nocturnal creatures such as owls, cats, foxes, wolves, coyotes, or bats.

Journeyers may also encounter the figure of the Earth Mother or her destructive form, the Terrible Mother. They explore every facet of the triple goddess who symbolizes the archetypal Feminine's rule over biological life, from youth to maturity to old age. This goddess, often referred to as the *Creator-Preserver-Destroyer* or *Virgin-Mother-Crone*, can take many cultural forms, including Parvati-Durga-Uma, Hebe-Hera-Hecate, the Three Fates, or the Norns. The same tripartite figure may also appear in its masculine personas such as Brahma-Vishnu-Shiva. Finally, journeyers can face mythic monsters such as the Furies, the Gorgons, or the Sphinx.

In the final hours of sessions, journeyers may alternate between needing to process residual bursts of material and receiving nurturing support from their sitters, friends, and family.

Figure 14. Holotropic Breathwork experience. "The Cauldron of Transformation" John Ablett (Pluto conjunct natal Moon, and Pluto square natal Pluto). Time stands still in a moment between life and death. Three crones—a Wise Woman, a Witch, and Kali—stir a cauldron of transformation.

Mercury-Pluto

Miss Bart had the gift of following an undercurrent of thought while she appeared to be sailing on the surface of conversation.
   Edith Wharton (Mercury square Pluto 4°35′)
   The House of Mirth, 1905

A fanatic is one who can't change his mind and won't change the subject.
   Winston Churchill (Mercury opposition Pluto 3°50′)

Mercury-Pluto Transits in Everyday Life

At these times, the driving emotional forces associated with Pluto have a tendency to obsess and compel people's thought processes and communication. The atmosphere in their minds may become more intense and pressured as they think about serious problems and their potential deep solutions. These are supportive transits for sustained mental work, penetrating research, or troubleshooting. Individuals can keep their minds engaged on one course of thought, following it all the way through to resolution;

they will also have heightened instincts to look below the surface of events to their underlying causes and motivations.

Tarnas calls this the "archetypal detective" alignment and people sometimes develop an interest in detective novels or themes. They may also discover a capacity to write and speak more effectively. At the same time, with their attention turned more toward the Plutonic underworlds—in both their psychological and societal forms—they may become interested in depth psychology, psychopathology, or criminology.

The shadow side of the Mercury-Pluto field emerges when driving energies pressing upward from within warp the balance and serenity of people's mental state. They may become fixated on one train of thought. They might also be tempted to engage in intellectual power struggles, devastating criticism, or the moral and psychological analysis of others. Even when these perceptions are accurate, it is generally more helpful to turn the penetrating insight associated with Mercury-Pluto on oneself and one's own deeper motivations. During each Pluto cycle, there is always another layer to uncover.

Mercury-Pluto Transits in Deep Self-Exploration

These transits are fairly powerful and very supportive in holotropic states, though they become more potent when they are part of a larger field of transits. With people's minds naturally tuned toward the shadow side of their psyches, Mercury-Pluto will help them to zero in and face their deeper material. These archetypes also support full catharsis of the emerging emotions. If journeyers have issues from their past around verbal or intellectual suppression, these transits will help them to explode through the old barriers and conditioning.

At times, people undergoing sessions may have an ongoing need to speak and share with their sitters. Unless they are directly asking for reassurance, not all of these comments will need a response. As long as journeyers stay lying down with their eyeshades and headphones on, sitters can just sit back and trust the deepening process. At the *biographical* layer of exploration, people may remember episodes of verbal abuse or the dangerous questioning of various assumptions and taboos. The following is from a holotropic session with Mercury conjunct the subject's natal Pluto:

> Memories of my father returned and his strong desire that I just forget the past. He desperately wanted me to forget and stop probing.

Perinatal Experiences

As exploration reaches the perinatal tier, people have the sense of entering a more dark and ominous landscape. This region of the psyche may announce itself with grotesque imagery such as angry fetuses dressed in Nazi uniform or other demonic motifs. The Vedic tradition in India refers to the five-thousand images that pass through the baby's mind during labor. Though it may not be possible to verify with certainty what the baby experiences, I believe that Grof's research work has essentially documented the full range of these perinatal themes.

Journeyers pass through a succession of inner states which contain both standardized features—the core elements of the BPMs—as well as variations and inflections based on their obstetric and biographical history, their astrological transits, and other factors. People have compared this clearing process to watching, one by one, a finite series of DVDs. The difference between holotropic states and watching a movie, of course, is that holotropic states are multidimensional and affect every perceptual channel with incredible power and intensity. They are the ultimate *Reality TV.*

The effect of the Mercury-Pluto field is to arouse an obsessive death-rebirth struggle involving people's thought and perception. The source of these struggles is revealed to be the infant's head pressed forcefully down the birth canal and struggling to escape, while its awareness is barraged with an onslaught of extreme thoughts, images, emotions, and sensations. Subject to these pressures, people become willing to face whatever is emerging inside them.

The mouth may become a channel for nasty, profane, or inhuman sounds as they blurt out repeated ribald obscenities, complex ironies, or dire warnings. These experiences release enormous amounts of negative energy and have a purging and cleansing effect on awareness, leading to higher levels of balance, serenity, and perspective in everyday life. Journeyers see that their minds resemble something like a receiver or channel of cosmic input, and not an organ that can ultimately choose its own reality. Our egos cannot control the contents of the unconscious.

The following is from a holotropic session undertaken with Mercury sextile Pluto, and Pluto square Mars:

> Finally releasing tension from my poor scrunched-up face, next I passed through some choking and breakthrough coughing which felt surprisingly good. I'm just not afraid of it anymore. As the process exploded my puritanical religious and then feminist training, I was saying, "c*nt, c*nt, c*nt," over and over. I realized that my entire perspective on the vagina and sex in general was based on the life-threatening pressures of delivery.

Transpersonal Experiences

As exploration proceeds, people explore various effects of communication and intelligence through human history. The following session of a former member of a fundamentalist church—undertaken during a world transit of Jupiter-Pluto square natal Mercury—illustrates both perinatal and collective elements:

> I went through a long sequence of hypersalivation accompanied by a feeling that karma in the collective psyche was lifting, not only for me but for the entire fundamentalist community. The hypersalivation and sounds I was making were expelling the source of verbal hype and intensity that the leaders of many fundamentalist sects pass off as righteous sermonizing.
>
> Now appearing so immature and wishful, their routine "frothing at the mouth" was revealed to be only the reflex salivation and mental obsessions of a fetus under duress in the birth canal.

Journeyers also face themes around the loaded questions of the Sphinx, the dangerous questioning of Oedipus, or the wishful schemes of the evil-magician archetype. Finally, they can discover a deeply penetrating insight, allowing them to see the world as flows of energy and consciousness.

Venus-Pluto

Love opens the doors into everything, as far as I can see, including and perhaps most of all, the door into one's own secret, and often terrible and frightening, real self.
  May Sarton (Venus sextile Pluto 1°19′)
  Mrs. Stevens Hears the Mermaids Singing, 1965

'Fair and foul are near of kin,
And fair needs foul,' I cried....
But Love has pitched his mansion in
The place of excrement
For nothing can be sole or whole
That has not been rent.
  William Butler Yeats (Venus conjunct Pluto 0°16′)
  "Crazy Jane Talks with the Bishop"

Venus-Pluto Transits in Everyday Life

These fascinating transits combine the yearning for love, beauty, and pleasure associated with Venus, with the shadowy depths, underworld intensity, and healing empowerment of Pluto. The Pluto archetype intensifies people's intimate lives, enabling them to feel their emotions more passionately and bringing up into awareness any unfaced material that prevents them from enjoying deeper levels of bonding and connection.

The Venus archetype acting on Pluto brings elements of divine grace and kindness to this renewing process. Ideally, people embrace the healing power of love, supporting the transformational efforts of their friends and family. Venus-Pluto can have a profoundly regenerating effect on relationships, helping people to see love and sex as sacred healing and bonding opportunities. Challenging emotions will always come up, but as long as people are willing to stay with the emotions and keep feeling them, they are inevitably consumed. These transits also support deep and passionate forms of creativity.

When people do not have outlets for their darker feelings and aim them at each other instead, the *dynamic* Venus-Pluto transits can have a toxic and spoiling effect on their relationships. Passive forms of aggression are possible as Venus' gentle, yin nature, driven by unhealed trauma and jealousy, turns to grasping and manipulating behavior. People may feel mixtures of attraction and repulsion for the same person. Any tendencies they may have toward sadomasochistic emotions could surface at this time. People may also experience themes of death and rebirth through their friendships.

And finally, with the Venus and Pluto archetypes compelling each others' sexual natures, people sometimes encounter romantic obsessions, on either the pursuing or the receiving side. Even if the offending force is coming from the outer world, it will still be helpful for people to face the driving Plutonic material in their own psyches.

Venus-Pluto Transits in Deep Self-Exploration

Venus-Pluto transits correspond to moderately powerful, highly desirable influences in holotropic states. The yielding grace of the Venus archetype helps people to accept and even enjoy the darker emotions emerging from their unconscious, while Pluto clears out any leftover wounds and blocked energies that prevent a deeper experience of divine love.

In the early stage of exploration, journeyers can face issues around jealousy, betrayal, offended vanity, or problems related to attraction. They may also recall feelings of deep passion, healing love, or powerfully beautiful nature or music. As the process deepens, the Venus-Pluto field will help them to face acceptingly the content at every point in the perinatal journey. However, it seems to have a special resonance with the sadomasochistic aspects of BPM III.

Perinatal Experiences

As we have seen, the fact that our first sexual experience occurs during the prolonged suffering, activation of aggression and fear, and encounter with biological materials during labor provides an understandable basis for many types of sexual variations and dysfunctions. Grof observed that if these emotions are then reinforced by sexual traumas in the lifetime, the individual has to deal with not only the effect of those traumas but also the reservoir of perinatal energies in their psyches. Rape and abuse create pathways for perinatal themes to reach present-day awareness. Full experience of the BPM III material and connection with positive transpersonal states clears the emotional channels so that people can again enjoy love and sexuality without the heavy influence of perinatal themes.

At the outset of discovery, journeyers may pass through scenes depicting sex as the root of all evil, sometimes personified as archetypal temptresses. They gain insight into the deep terror of female empowerment at the heart of patriarchal cultures—seen to be ultimately rooted in a fear of the delivering birth canal and accompanying fear of death. They may also face the archetype of the *Death Marriage*, in scenes that embody strange mixtures of sex and death. These are based on the shattering encounter with dying along with sexual arousal that occurs in labor. All thoughts of male superiority are permanently exploded and revealed to be desperate wishful thinking, as journeyers work through these complex feelings and experience reunion with the divine Feminine.

We can see early BPM III themes in the following psilocybin-mushroom session undertaken with Venus trine the subject's natal Pluto, and a world transit of Venus conjunct Pluto:

As the process moved into the sadomasochistic realm, I began to see images of nonconsensual cunnilingus. I realized that these unsavoury scenes depict the actions of people unconsciously driven by the memory of delivery, specifically, of coming in contact with the maternal vagina at the moment of crowning.

In the next tableau, I was in ancient Egypt, a female member of the royal family about to be made love to by her brother. I recalled that the royalty of some cultures married and practiced incest with each other for millennia as an established and even glorified tradition. I felt certain that the motive was to keep power in the family, and the overall feeling was not pleasant. Through these experiences, I felt the divine trying to show me that the agony and failure of the sadomasochistic sequences are actually safe, something which I can now fully surrender to and trust.

Finally I had images of gorgeous ornate temples in central India—some of the few which the Mogul invaders did not destroy—that depict scenes of orgiastic sexual liberation and fulfillment. I felt that this pre-invasion culture of India must have been, in some ways and for some, a paradise on earth. In harsh contrast, the arrival of the conquering patriarchs from the north with their intensely monistic religion was experienced as a spiritual, emotional, and aesthetic catastrophe. I had to somehow reconcile these two extremes of human experience within my being. Through this entire process, I could feel the gluteus muscles of my buttocks gripped in a long releasing spasm.

As the threatening leftover emotions are consumed, the sexual allure that patriarchal cultures view as the temptations of the Feminine are then seen in a new light, as the draw toward a fuller existence—the mother's contracting body pressing the infant down and out, through the orgasm of birth, into the joy of a new life. The patriarchal stage of history is then itself recognized, as Tarnas suggests, as a kind of titanic birth labor in human consciousness—"the five-thousand-year birth canal of the Great Mother Goddess."[10]

Transpersonal Experiences

Journeyers in sessions may explore the interplay of love and hate through human history. They may also perceive sexuality as a cosmic force of immense magnitude and scope. Feeling the primal drive to unite, they access a universal love which transcends all darkness and divisions, a powerful healing wave opening new channels for connections with humanity. The following is from a session with Pluto trine natal Venus:

I felt loving connections with my sitters and with everyone in my life. I had the sense of a higher, cosmic love healing and regenerating me. It's working! The healing is working!

The archetypal field associated with these transits can enhance unusually deep bonding with friends and family in the later phases of the day. Long walks in nature will also have a profoundly integrating effect. If journeyers have concerns about emotional or sexual boundaries with anyone who will be in the session space afterward, for example a new or former partner, it is best to resolve these issues beforehand.

Mars-Pluto

We cannot cure the evils of politics with politics. . . . Fifty years ago if we had gone the way of Freud (to study and tackle hostility within ourselves) instead of Marx, we might be closer to peace than we are.
Anaïs Nin (Mars trine Pluto 1°29′) Letter, 1974

To reach the port of heaven, we must sail sometimes with the wind and sometimes against it—but we must sail, and not drift, nor lie at anchor.
Oliver Wendell Holmes (Mars trine Pluto 5°13′)
The Autocrat of the Breakfast Table, 1858

Mars-Pluto Transits in Everyday Life

During these transits, Pluto compels the Mars archetypal principle into being with great intensity, and people often feel powerful surges of martial energy and drive. These can be supportive times to adopt new yoga or fitness regimens, discard bad habits, and get one's primal vitality flowing again. The trines and to a lesser extent, the sextiles, have a special renewing effect on the body after periods of crisis or illness. The effect of Mars on Pluto is to help people actively pursue goals with an aim of regeneration or transformation, from renovating in the home or cleaning up old messes and problems, to self-exploration and psychotherapy. These archetypes also give them the courage to face difficult and demanding situations. At times, these transits can begin with a breakdown of people's basic sense of energy and vitality, and then after a period of struggle, feelings of rebirth.

The shadow side of the Mars-Pluto field can be intense and destructive when acted out. Some people may seriously overexert and strain themselves. Issues around willpower, brute strength, and emotional domination may also arise—as usual, any impulse toward forcing things should be seriously questioned and probably resisted. Sometimes other people or situations seem to embody the aggressive energy. Whatever its apparent source, a dependably helpful response is to find a soundproof room and give the energies full expression, becoming all the parts in turn. Sexual experiences may also be tainted with perinatal themes, until the underlying material is confronted and worked through.

Mars-Pluto Transits in Deep Self-Exploration

Mars-Pluto transits correspond to powerful and desirable influences in self-exploration and experienced sitters will greatly value their effects. As always, it is essential to have an adequate ratio of sitters to participants so that the cathartic potential of these archetypes can be channelled in the safest possible way. In the internalized approach that Grof describes, there is only one participant at a time supported by two experienced sitters.

Mars heightens the releasing effects associated with Pluto, giving sessions more dynamic power, expressiveness, and straight-ahead momentum. Journeyers find the focus and resolve to aim one-hundred percent of their energies at transcendence, like a missile going back to the gods that sent it. These archetypes push consciousness down through the emotional underworld and out into explosive rebirth.

At times, people may struggle between their biological instincts toward self-preservation and their spiritual impulses to surrender, trust the process, and let go. But sooner or later, the ego's well-worn urges to control things are overwhelmed by Pluto's healing pressure. In holotropic states, the sitters take a passive support role, trusting the participant's own inner healer to do the work and choose the relevant material for that session. The exceptions to this are: first, if a person develops trouble breathing, in which case active bodywork becomes necessary to release tensions around the throat; and, second, if he or she gets up and tries to leave the session room. In that case, sitters need to actively intervene and interpret the source of the person's fear. For example, it can be helpful to offer comments such as: "You're reliving traumatic memories" "The quickest way through this is to surrender to its most difficult parts" or "You're in a healing session and these feelings will pass."

Perinatal Experiences

Tarnas found that these archetypes have a special resonance with the aggressive facets of BPM III. As we have seen, alarming compression and life-threatening suffocation arouse a determined aggressive response in the fetus. At the same time, its body introjects the driving and contracting forces of the uterine walls themselves. People facing this material display frantic motor phenomena, projectile vomiting, and powerful aggressive discharges.

Figure 15. Holotropic Breathwork session. "I am a POWER ENGINE" Heike Daniel (Mars trine natal Pluto, Neptune trine Venus, and Venus square Mars). "There were waves of wild and fierce feelings and still—in the middle of all that— I felt the power of love, which dwells in the heart." In this image, we can see the aggressive martial energies associated with her Mars-Pluto transit, as well as the transcendent love of the Venus-Neptune.

As these stored energies release from their psyches, obstetric elements are also overlaid with themes from the natural world, from history, and from mythological realms which embody the same qualities of raging aggression, destruction, and transformation. Themes from nature include ferocious polar bears battling Inuit hunters, predators slaughtering their prey, or volcanic eruptions. Historical episodes center around active attacks in the wars of all ages such as out-of-control Nordic invaders dying with their swords in their hands, dive-bombing kamikazes, or onslaughts of "Stalin's Organ" rockets. Mythological themes include the calamitous raging of thundergods such as Thor or Zeus, the wrath of Achilles, or the Clash of the Titans.

The following supervised ibogaine session of a sixty-four-year-old physician—illustrating classic BPM III elements overlaid with collective themes—was undertaken with Mars conjunct natal Pluto, and Pluto square natal Jupiter.

The session was probably the most dramatic of my life. The first part was a typical sort of holotropic session in terms of sensory and visual material. We were in a rural location and there were some deer walking around outside, and deer in the native tradition are the bringers of visions. So that put me into a connection with the film, *The Deerhunter*. In *The Deerhunter,* there's a scene where some American soldiers have been captured by the Viet Cong and are kept in a cage, submerged up to their necks in water, and they're taken out and made to play Russian roulette.

I suddenly found myself in the session sitting with a pistol at my temple, mimicking that scene. And then ***bang!*** I was just catapulted into, I would say, a good four hours of killing, just killing. It was close-range killing with handguns and machine guns. There were drug deals gone wrong, there were lover's quarrels, random violence on the street, wrong place at the wrong time. But the vast majority of it was military killing. Assaults, going over the top, shooting up people, bursting into rooms, killing Germans, Germans killing me . . . Japanese. . . . But I wound up and kept going back into a particular battle that took place on Omaha Beach during D-Day. It was the scene portrayed in the opening part of the movie *Saving Private Ryan.*

In one subset of that battle, the U.S. Rangers had to scale a cliff using ropes and pinions, and the German soldiers were dropping grenades down on them and blowing them off the ropes and more of them were running up. And that's the battle that I kept coming back to. I wound up in the personality, sharing the personality, and watching the personality of a United States officer, probably of Brigadier rank, just ruddy, red-faced, bucolic, full of rage, and urging his men on to the guns and killing, killing, blood, blood, blood, blood, blood! It was just unbelievable! I've never experienced anything like it. I opened my eyes and the killing was going on. I closed my eyes and the killing was going on. Just killing, killing, killing, killing, that's all it was. There was no fear, zero fear. There was just the tension of being in the battle, kill or be killed. Instant responses.

What the Bwiti teacher said is that the medicine was just emptying that stuff out of me. It made absolute experiential sense because I didn't have any revulsion at the killing, nothing but the urge to survive, and to kill or be killed. It was way beyond any moral or ethical interpretation of the situation I was in. That had all been done in the landing craft coming up to the beach. Now you were in the battle, which is a metaphor also often used by the Santo Daime: "Being in the battle."[11]

Manifestations of the *sadomasochistic* aspects of BPM III are often intense under Mars-Pluto transits. This material can be safely released in holotropic states, whereas the same energies acted out in the social world would have very damaging consequences. Sexual feelings can reach orgiastic levels of arousal as journeyers pass through inner states depicting every act in human sexual behavior, from every position and point of view. The sadomasochistic side of BPM III eventually culminates in a type of driving ecstasy which transcends pain and pleasure, followed by permanent breakthroughs as people relive the moment of crowning and connect with positive transpersonal states.

Grof's research determined that problems of impotence and frigidity, for example, are not caused by a *lack* of sexual energy, but by individuals containing too much of the threatening perinatal energies in their psyches, especially fear and aggression. Whenever they become sexually aroused, their inner repositories of fear and aggression—which were part of their first sexual experience during birth—emerge along with the sexual feelings. Because these emotions are inappropriate in a romantic context, people repress them, which then represses their sexual feelings as well. Grof found that, in order to resolve these problems, individuals need to work through enough of their perinatal material so that they can again feel comfortable with their sexual energies. The exception, of course, would be the less-common situations that have a physiological component such as vascular disease or nerve damage.[12]

The following internalized LSD session of a male graduate student occurred with transiting Pluto square natal Mars:

I saw that my entire sexual life was colored by experiences during labor. Complex homosexual feelings began to surface, which I saw later to be understandable emotions of a vulnerable fetus, desperate for protection against the delivering birth canal and accompanying Terrible Mother archetype—people influenced by this memory in everyday life are basically unable to see the vagina as a source of pleasure. Then I began to project predatory sexual energies onto one of my sitters, praying that he didn't cross the boundary while I let my emotions play themselves out. I was deeply relieved that he was just my sitter.

I felt the impossibility of trying to have a romantic relationship, given all these unfinished emotions, and that I need supportive, detached sitters so much more now than intimate relationships. Through the wounded perspective of the perinatal matrices, sex is just one loser on death row doing it with another mortal loser—death f*cking death. What's the fun of that? . . . Then I was looking at the male genitals through the same wounded perinatal stencil, this time from a female point of view. From this traumatized perspective, the penis is the big problem—the vicious and insensitive penetrator. I could see how male energy in the universe shakes things up and keeps emotional processes activated, but just how threatening and destroying it can be at times.

Next I was facing issues from the phallic stage of development: I was a toddler getting used to having a penis. Though I generally feel comfortable in my masculine vitality, I saw how ludicrous it was to perceive any kind of ultimate strength or power coming from the male sex organs. I felt the pathetic weakness of the infant in the face of the delivering feminine and the wishful thinking of all forms of male machismo and dominance. Males' bigger physical size may be nature's necessary compensation for the stronger emotional power of females. The process then began to move toward a strange mixture of pain and pleasure. After some reluctance, I realized that, with the pleasure element, I could now find a way to enjoy any amount of suffering, even dying.

At another point, I was back in the birth canal and surrendering any thoughts of male superiority. I was conceding the battle of the sexes, and just wondered in endearing acknowledgment: "How does She do it, always come out on top?" I saw no need to change the situation. Gradually, as the feeling of spiritual surrender progressed, I felt the masculine to be an equal partner of the feminine.

Scatological experiences are based on the infant's confrontation with biological materials during labor. However they have an intensity that far surpasses the physical realm. Journeyers may also gain insight into many people's antagonistic relationship with the natural world—seen ultimately as a need to suppress and pave over their fear of the Feminine and "Mother" Nature, left over from the birth process.

Demonic experiences may include feelings of sinking moral failure, malignant evil, and confrontation with demonic archetypes. These then transform into sequences of triumphant release, as Dionysus, Christ, or Persephone liberate the suffering souls from the underworld. Its final resolution appears in dramatic scenes of the principle of good in the universe overcoming and transmuting that of evil.

Finally, elements of *pyrocatharsis* have a magical sense of purifying the outmoded and corrupt elements in the psyche. Just as fire in the physical realm turns matter into energy, fire in its symbolic form liberates traumatized inner structures back into free-flowing spiritual energy. As this Plutonic material reaches culmination, people can feel cosmic energies flowing through their bodies from all directions, breaking up old patterns of control and widening the pathway for Uranus' rebirth matrix to fully manifest.

Transpersonal Experiences

In transpersonal experiences, journeyers continue to explore the effects of sexual, aggressive, and destructive impulses in different periods of history and through various layers of the universe. These scenes are then followed by those of profound creation, rebirth, renewal, and regeneration. Grof found that although the bulk of the unnecessary or *malignant* type of aggression in the psyche is rooted in the perinatal layer, additional sources emerge from various transpersonal sources. These include embryonic crises; traumatic ancestral, racial, collective, and past life memories; identification with various fighting or hunting animal species; violent mythological sequences; and identification with inorganic processes such as volcanic eruptions, earthquakes, ocean storms, the destruction of celestial bodies, and the consciousness of black holes.[13]

Bodywork maneuvers during Mars-Pluto transits tend to be highly effective. Breathers may also process any leftover material the following day by taking a few deep breaths and allowing the material to express itself through their voices and hands.

Jupiter-Pluto

The twentieth century's massive and radical breakdown of so many structures—cultural, philosophical, scientific, religious, moral, artistic, social, economic, political, atomic, ecological—all this suggests the necessary deconstruction prior to a new birth.
   Richard Tarnas (Jupiter opposition Pluto 1°59′)
   The Passion of the Western Mind, 1991

Life, forever, dying to be born afresh, forever young and eager, will presently stand upon this earth as upon a footstool, and stretch out its realm amidst the stars.
   H. G. Wells (Jupiter trine Pluto 7°31′) *The Outline of History,* 1920

Jupiter-Pluto Transits in Everyday Life

During these intensely renewing transits, Jupiter has the potential to broaden and expand all the beneficial qualities associated with Pluto. These are times when people often feel empowered to make positive changes and improvements in their lives. They can let go of old emotional baggage, unhealthy relationship patterns, and dissatisfying career choices. Carried along by a primal healing wave, they may also breathe deeper, adopt new physical regimens, and eliminate negative habits. These transits support all projects with an aim of "cleaning up or clearing out" old situations, bodily regeneration, and spiritual renewal.

At the same time, the Pluto archetype works to transform people's sense of what actually constitutes success in human life, by direct healing of the emotional issues underlying their feelings of insecurity and dissatisfaction. These are good times to actualize realistic and attainable life goals. However, as Hand notes, for these aims to have lasting results, they need to benefit everyone and not just oneself. If people's ideals of success are selfishly motivated or extreme, and they insist on going in directions that might be harmful to themselves or others, these transits may give them the opportunity to go off course for a while and experience the results of those actions. This often then leads to a new sense of personal responsibility and awareness of others' needs.

The shadow side of the Jupiter-Pluto field includes feelings that the old and weak must die so the new and strong can survive, postures of superiority, and various forms of power abuse. Cycles of ruthless acting out in the world followed by the inevitable consequences and a renewed commitment to self-work can have positive effects in the long run. People eventually see that the urge for growth and improvement of this obsessive combination can only be realized when they include, in their life strategy, facing and owning the shadow material in the unconscious.

Jupiter-Pluto Transits in Deep Self-Exploration

Personal and world transits of Jupiter-Pluto are very powerful and desirable markers for self-exploration, and journeyers, sitters, and therapists conducting sessions will greatly look forward to them. They often coincide with a whole new wave of deep releasing in people's psyches as the regenerating process goes into overdrive.

The Jupiter-Pluto field can usher in profound experiences of death and rebirth, far-reaching renewal, and the successful completion of entire cycles of healing. It represents the threshold moment in Pluto's transformational process when decay turns into fertilizer, death to new life. Tarnas found that people undergoing sessions at these times have a feeling of being pulled upward by a higher evolutionary force—as if bound to a "divinely guided missile."[14]

These archetypes can push up and make available for processing even the most fundamental lifetime traumas. The following holotropic session, undertaken with Pluto conjunct natal Jupiter, illustrates the healing of severe emotional and physical abuse during infancy, which then deepened into perinatal elements:

> At critical points, I let the father energy come in much closer than usual, as my male sitter did bodywork on my solar plexus and chest. I remember saying, "And this is the point where dad puts his hands around my throat." I felt unspeakably grateful that my sitters didn't hurt me the way my father did in those terrible karmic moments as an infant, when he would go to any length to make me stop crying in the night. I was finally able to release this deep karma that has crippled my life.
>
> As the process moved into the perinatal layer, I could feel a higher presence permeated through my windpipe and lungs, and surrendered to the Divine Mother in her oxygen-providing and depriving capacity. I recognized that a vastly more powerful force was, ultimately, in charge of my oxygen supply and could suffocate me at will.

Journeyers confront issues around insatiable greed, overweening ambition, and abuse of power, and the end of any delusions they may harbor about gender or racial superiority. They also recognize that, under certain conditions, all humans have the potential to make mistakes and commit harmful actions. Rather than being a steady, incremental ascent toward the light, spiritual awakening often includes experiences of breakdown and failure during the early phases of each cycle.

Perinatal Experiences

As exploration reaches the perinatal region of the psyche, Jupiter-Pluto transits are a tremendous asset for facing every stage in the process. If people are working through Saturn's "no exit" material, these archetypes create a feeling of divine empowerment that can force them into full experience and resolution of that stage. If their inner journeys are dominated by Pluto's death-rebirth struggle, Jupiter adds an overdrive quality to Pluto's releasing cycle, a vast cosmic force unlocking and pressing out their buried material.

The initial character of perinatal sessions during any Pluto transit can feel for periods of time like an unfolding catastrophe. The Jupiter complex adds an epic character to people's experiences: a sense of runaway power trips and greed, irreversible moral disaster, and "absolute damnation of transcendental proportions." These scenes are accompanied by surges of aggression, nausea and projectile vomiting, feelings of suffocation, and breakthrough coughing. Jupiter-Pluto sessions can include any of the classic BPM III themes—demonic, sadomasochistic, scatological, and pyrocathartic—but with a special resonance with that of *titanic struggle*, the

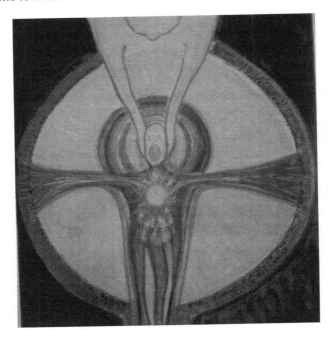

Figure 16. Holotropic Breathwork session. "Surrender" Anne Høivik (Pluto square natal Jupiter-Mars, Jupiter trine Pluto, and Uranus-Neptune opposition Sun). An image of crucifixion and explosive transcendence of boundaries in a perinatal session of a Norwegian participant.

sense of being engaged in a massive transformational process of cosmic dimensions.

In *demonic* scenes, people perceive the tendency in stressful events for the Plutonic unconscious to overwhelm Jupiter's higher idealism. This shattering insight eventually deepens into full confrontation with demonic archetypes, which releases the negative cosmic energies from people's psyches. In *sadomasochistic* experiences, journeyers experience sexual arousal mixed with suffering, fear, and aggression, reaching orgiastic levels of intensity. Full surrender to this material leads to a clearing of the sexual channels and profound healing of relationship issues.

Scatological themes have a similar epic quality, as well as the potential for a permanent resolution of the material. The following is from a supervised and internalized LSD session with Jupiter conjunct the subject's natal Pluto:

> Out of the blue, I perceived that I stank . . . really bad! So vivid and overwhelming. . . . I mentioned it to my sitters and one of them said acceptingly,

"That's a part of the process." Next I was sure I could smell what seemed like fluids from a vagina all around me, and then something more serious and unmistakable: SHIT!! Somehow I could taste it, as plainly as day.

This then shifted to a highly vigorous and accelerated, swarming type of consciousness which I realized was the consciousness of germs. *"We mean business!"* I perceived that germs break down what is old and outworn in the cyclical processes of nature. I could also see that man-made chemicals often disrupt this cycle of organic purification. My feelings about the excrement that seemed to be all around me suddenly changed into something completely different. For bacteria, our waste products are a perfect and desirable milieu.

Broadened by the Jupiter archetype, Pluto's *pyrocathartic* elements may also have a grandly mythic character, as embodied in this internalized marijuana session with Mars-Jupiter conjunct the subject's natal Pluto:

Some part of my consciousness was now represented by the ring from J. R. R. Tolkien's *The Lord of the Rings*. The ring depicted my greed and attachments in the world as well as the archetypal divine fire burning away those attachments. It was in front of me, made partly of shining gold and partly of fire, which seemed to represent the interface between fixed Saturnian reality and Pluto's transpersonal liberation.

I was travelling head-first, relentlessly forward, led by and pursuing the ring as it sliced a tube through space—like some kind of cosmic birth canal that I was falling through. I could see that in order to consume my ego's attachments, I would have to pursue this transforming process all the way to the archetypal fires of Mt. Doom—and that the perinatal-shadow side of my psyche, symbolized by Gollum, would be an ever-present threat until the end.

During the resolution phase of all sessions, journeyers may project positive feelings onto their sitters, perceiving them in a magical way as the delivering birth canal, the forces of good in the universe, or the archetype of the Great Mother. At the blessed moment of crowning, they may also identify with kingship or regicide. After the long death-rebirth struggle, neophytes emerge from the birth canal with what Tarnas calls "titanic orgiastic force."[15]

The following session containing themes from the biographical, perinatal, and transpersonal layers of the psyche was undertaken with Pluto conjunct natal Jupiter:

As the session climaxed in the third hour, I had a few unbearable moments that the male sitter—"dad"—might be abandoning me and then, as this terror resolved, I went through a powerful sequence of *"God Hates Me!!"* I felt enormous negative forces aimed at my ego, that I have understandably repressed all my life—just as any young person would because they are so unimaginably threatening. The pressure that was so constant from my dad was finally forcing its way through my entire being from top to bottom. How can an infant accept this kind of threat coming from its father? It was just too close to home at the time.

Yet incredibly I now recognized that my dad's rage and domination, as well as the oppressing forces of the birth canal, were actually manifestations, on a deeper level, of liberating pressure of the Hindu god Shiva aimed at the false structures of my ego. I was surrendering to the negating force and it was decidedly winning. All the energies of my being were vibrating out sideways beyond the boundaries of my psyche, as the divine completely took over my awareness. The message came clearly: "You think transformation is a gentle process? At times—it is brutal!"

As I heard this voice, I felt a profound sense of accomplishment as if something that had been trying to happen all my life was now coming to pass. My ego structures were being ecstatically ripped open. The sideways energy loops suddenly arranged themselves into a giant Zeus-like motif, carrying the feeling of a higher, integrated Jupiter energy. This archetypal pattern extended from the conscious space above my head to the space below my feet. All the energies and atoms of my body were now included in this archetype of wholeness and transcendence that was restructuring my entire being. I saw that this benevolent, Platonic Form had been drawing my entire life toward itself for years and had finally succeeded. The feeling of impressed amazement at what the divine can accomplish has continued since this session. I still marvel at the positive forces operating behind the scenes in human life.

Transpersonal Experiences

As explorations continue, people may face deities from the collective unconscious who personify the supreme power in the universe such as Kali, Inanna, Zeus, Shiva, Yahweh, Woden, or Shangdi. They may also encounter kings and queens of the underworld in the form of Yama, Hades, Satan, Nepthys, Persephone, or Hecate, or gods and goddesses symbolizing sexual potency such as Dionysus, Shiva, or Shakti.

The following is from a ceremonial ayahuasca session of a female writer with Pluto trine her natal Jupiter:

> In the end, after all the healing and releasing was done, my twin flame was transformed into a king, and he was presented with a very special crown and outfitted in robes of white and gold. He raised me up as his queen, and we were swept up into the most exquisite *hieros gamos* ceremony—with many great beings of light heralding, praising, blessing and enfolding us in their light and love. The whole process was truly alchemical. We were cooked,

transmuted and ultimately reunited as Rex and Regina, sun and moon, gold and silver, fire and water.

The guiding direction of the Jupiter-Pluto field is toward an integration of the lower Plutonic and higher Jupiterian impulses in the psyche. With Jupiter glorifying and celebrating the primal energies associated with Pluto, people often feel drawn to embrace the more grounded, earthy, and feminine aspects of their spirituality. The following is from a ceremonial ayahuasca session with Pluto trine the subject's natal Jupiter, and Neptune conjunct her natal Moon:

> I felt the most sublime and devoted love for the overwhelmingly powerful spiritual force that inhabits this planet—which was, without a doubt, a Supreme Mother power. I felt so enormously minute in the face of this awesome presence; I was utterly humbled. I bowed down before Her and begged Her to teach me Her ways.
>
> But I recognized that in service of such a pledge, I need to bring forth the energies of the Tantric Deva, the Mediterranean Fertility Goddess, and the High Priestess—those who do not sit on the stone cold floor and pray to a sky god (as I saw myself doing a few times) but who dance the energies of the Christ consciousness onto the Earth plane, and who use the vital forces of the root, of the Earth, and of nature to do so! I think that the Nun has served her purpose on my path . . .

People may also explore evolutionary themes and meta-trajectories in the larger universe, seen to be, ultimately, in the service of an infinitely entertaining cosmic game. They may directly encounter the forces of teleology: of human history as being led or drawn toward a more evolved and integrated state of being. And, finally, during any Pluto transit, people can experience kundalini energy flowing up their energy centers and putting the healing process into overdrive.

The Jupiter-Pluto field engages a titanic struggle for renewal and purification through profound journeys down and through the underworld of the psyche. The observed benefits of these experiences are in Grof's words "undreamed of" in traditional psychotherapy and psychiatry.[16] And referring to Ebertin's handbook *The Combination of Stellar Influences*, Tarnas describes the influence of Jupiter-Pluto as: *restitutio ad integrum*—resembling a "spiritual blood transfusion."[17] Completion of this regenerating process has far-reaching healing potential, not only in individuals' lives but for the world around them.

The following is from a session with Pluto conjunct the subject's natal Jupiter: "My goal is the collective goal—to open."

*   *   *

Transits of Uranus

Sun-Uranus

So happy just to be alive
Underneath this sky of blue
On this new morning with you.
    Bob Dylan (Sun conjunct Uranus 6°53′) "New Morning"

Life is either a daring adventure or nothing. To keep our faces toward change
and behave like free spirits in the presence of fate is strength undefeatable.
    Helen Keller (Sun sextile Uranus 1°43′) *Let Us Have Faith*, 1940

Two roads diverged in a wood, and I,
I took the one less traveled by,
And that has made all the difference.
    Robert Frost (Sun trine Uranus, date only, calc. for noon: 6°34′)
"The Road Not Taken" 1916

Sun-Uranus Transits in Everyday Life

Sun-Uranus transits combine the bright selfhood, autonomy, and vitality of the Sun archetype with the emancipation, rebirth, and breakthroughs related to Uranus. These transits often seem to occur as people are feeling a sudden resolution of problems in their lives, new inspiration, and creative enthusiasm. The Uranus archetype liberates their natural autonomy and self-expression, helping them to reconnect with a sense of confidence, transcend old limiting patterns, and find new talents. The Sun seems to shine a little more brightly.

The effect of the solar archetype on Uranus is to heighten people's innate, Promethean yearnings for freedom, innovation, and progress. They may feel strong urges to follow new directions, take untried risks, or change vocations—to discover the path less trodden. No longer content with the status quo, they are drawn to what inspires and excites them.

If people adopt a too one-sided or extreme identification with Uranus' eccentric energies, however, they may display the shadow side of this complex. The Sun's egocentrism combined with Uranus' individualism may make it difficult for them to cooperate or compromise. They may rebel simply for the sake of rebelling, whether there are any real or serious issues at stake. An aversion to any kind of structure or routine can also make life in the real world difficult. Manic hyperactivity or nervous tensions are possible, reflecting the influence of perinatal material pressing upward from within.

Sun-Uranus Transits in Deep Self-Exploration

Transits of Sun-Uranus correspond to powerful archetypal forces in self-exploration. They add a warm, exciting, and inspiring quality to sessions, greatly increasing the potential for dynamic breakthroughs. In general, people with these transits will be more open to having new experiences and to exerting the effort necessary to break out of chronic holding patterns rooted in their past. People often reach entirely new levels of experience, such as their first perinatal session, their first identification with animal or plant consciousness, or first encounter with an archetype or mythological sequence. Regardless of the depth or intensity of the emerging process, the activated Uranus principle is an indicator of sudden, dramatic resolution of the material, drawing consciousness out the other side in transcendent release.

In the *biographical* realm of exploration, journeyers may remember positive experiences around their fathers, personal breakthroughs, and other successes in their lives. These transits are helpful for healing father issues or problems with men in general. Attuned to the encouraging qualities of the divine masculine principle, people will be more open to receiving emotional support from their male sitters and to appreciating the solar qualities in their female sitters.

Perinatal Experiences

While helpful for facing any part of the transformative journey, Tarnas found that these archetypes enhance special access to the states of rebirth which Grof terms the Basic Perinatal Matrix IV. BPM IV centers around the sudden intensification of pressure in the birth canal, the moment of crowning, and completed delivery, as the infant leaves the mother's body and begins life as a separate organism. These sequences include clear obstetric features which experienced sitters can support.

When a breather reliving birth begins to arch and flex the head backward, this is an indication that the process is reaching its final stage; it reflects the situation when the base of the fetus' skull is leaning against the mother's pubic bone and the perineum is being pulled over its face. Since this typically means encountering various forms of biological material, we can often see the breather grimacing, spitting, and attempting to wipe some imaginary material from his or her face. Here it might be very helpful to slide the palm of one's hand slowly over the breather's face from the forehead to the chin and with the other hand apply pressure at the base of the breather's skull. This can greatly facilitate the completion of the birth process.[18]

Subjects undergoing rebirth experiences see the inside of great halls and cathedrals, blinding white or golden light, and peacock spectra patterns. They may encounter scenes around the end of wars or revolutions, the calm after raging storms, or the discovery of a medicine that will help both sides in a conflict. Accompanying archetypal themes include heroes slaying the dragon, the ascension of deities, or reborn souls drinking ambrosia with the gods on Mount Olympus.

In a blessed atmosphere of redemption, salvation, and forgiveness, people experience brotherly and sisterly feelings for all humanity. Their basic priorities in life undergo a fundamental shift, with a new value placed on warm human relationships, meaningful work, and sensitivity to ecological concerns. With renewed feelings of autonomy and enthusiasm, their own unique talents and character also shine through more fully. At the same time, they have critical attitudes toward the abuse of power.

Any engagement of the Sun-Uranus field will be an asset for journeyers in reaching a more integrated state of rebirth. The following is from a guided ayahuasca session of a female artist with Uranus conjunct her natal Sun:

> As this primal purge/cosmic cleanse was happening, I was simultaneously being deluged with LIGHT, LIGHT and more LIGHT. It was as though the floodgates of heaven opened up and inundated me with cosmic life force. And the more compacted debris I released, the more I was besieged and overwhelmed with light. I could feel it going through me and seeding its way through my very cells and DNA—to the point where I was literally vibrating! . . . I felt as though a sacred mystery was being performed through my body, and I had a sense of what it means to be resurrected.

Transpersonal Experiences

Sessions also tend to have an exciting, awakening, and liberating character in the transpersonal realms. The awakened solar principle helps journeyers to tap directly into the life experience of their fathers or other male ancestors. The following is from a holotropic session undertaken with Uranus trine natal Sun:

> I saw images of my father and the message came clearly: "no blame, no blame." Then I was my dad at six weeks old, coughing violently with whooping cough and feeling that no one could or would help him. I could feel deeply the heartache of his parents during this terrifying ordeal. He almost died then, and I saw how it shaped his personality in some difficult ways that now made perfect sense. I also felt sorry for the suffering of my grandfather as a boy. Then I experienced, through my back and chest, the sorrow of our

entire ancestral lineage. There were images of father-son, father-son problems going back many generations to some royalty figure tormenting his son.

Other themes include the liberating side of Promethean, Western society, or racial and collective memories of good fathering from around the world. These archetypes can also help people to resolve *karmic memories* as they feel the emotions on both sides of bitter conflicts from what are perceived as other lifetimes and reach states of forgiveness and willingness to be forgiven. The following is from a ceremonial ayahuasca session of a female writer with Uranus conjunct her natal Sun:

> One of my intentions for this journey was to forgive all those, past, present and future, who have ever caused me grief or pain, in this life or any other. There is one past life that has been haunting me throughout all of these sessions and I have often found myself begging for forgiveness for the wrong that I committed in that life. But I finally recognized that it was myself that I had to forgive. And when I truly did this, I was finally able to release it. After this I lined up all of those who had ever hurt me . . . stretching back through eons and eons of time. I lined them up and forgave them all. I also saw myself peeling off layers and layers of my skin—peeling off the outworn mantle of myself—and hurling it down the cosmic abyss.

Figure 17. Holotropic Breathwork session of an English participant. "Spirit of the Forest" John Ablett (Uranus square natal Sun, a world transit of Sun square Uranus, and Mars conjunct natal Neptune). "A shamanic male figure, part human, part animal, invites me to engage in a test of strength, forehead to forehead. The energy of male aggression then transforms into a more spiritually balanced and positive form."

Sessions in the *archetypal* realm of exploration center around the masculine personas of divine consciousness. Journeyers may encounter the Sun Hero, the Cosmic Sun, the Divine Child, Apollo, Christ, or God. Experiences of the divine as radiant light or a warm, loving presence are also common. A psychological condition that seems to be related to Uranus transits, in general, is the *Christ complex*. People may have feelings of spiritual self-importance until they face and complete the remaining death-rebirth material.

The following is from a supervised and internalized LSD session with Uranus trine the subject's natal Sun:

> After this long and trying day with many challenges, I gathered with my friends and enjoyed some bonding time around the fireplace. Later in bed, I saw a flow of unsettling scenes accompanied with more anxiety. In one, I was flame-throwing an Asian village.
>
> Finally, I had an image of Christ struggling to reach his way to heaven. I saw a male figure of divinity cradling the wretched figure of Death, his beloved child. Then I perceived God the Father, bearded and integrated, with arms outstretched in peace, completeness, and mercy and passed into a relieved sleep.

In what are experienced as the ultimate layers of exploration, the Uranus archetype corresponds to that moment in the incarnational cycle when the separate units of awareness in the material world begin to transcend their outmoded boundaries and reawaken to their identity as Absolute Consciousness.

The final stage of sessions is more likely to have the character of ecstatic reentry, as journeyers celebrate in feelings of electrifying freedom and rebirth. Manic emotions may also persist in some form until the driving Plutonic energies underlying them have been worked through and digested. Long walks in nature will help to smooth out any residual material and integrate the experience. Sunlight in particular may be perceived as having special magical and uplifting qualities.

The following is from a supervised and internalized psilocybin-mushroom session during a world transit of Sun trine Uranus:

> Around the three-hour point, I found myself suddenly in the terrifying, archetypal *Dying Place* with urgent feelings of danger and threat. It's too late in the session for ego death! The timing is wrong and way off! **Danger! Danger!!** . . .
>
> The feelings then immediately passed and I saw an image of Hindu lattice-work, comprised of plant, animal, human, and divine elements all in light, resolving up to a central source of Higher Light that contains all things. Sweet blessed relief.

Moon-Uranus

True emancipation begins neither at the polls nor in courts. It begins in woman's soul.

Emma Goldman (Moon conjunct Uranus, date only, calc. for noon: 2°13′) *Anarchism and Other Essays*, 1911

Emotion is the chief source of all becoming-conscious. There can be no transforming of darkness into light and of apathy into movement without emotion.

C. G. Jung (Moon square Uranus 0°39′) *Psychological Aspects of the Modern Archetype*, 1938

Moon-Uranus Transits in Everyday Life

During these transits, people's inner emotional worlds and abilities to take care of themselves are awakened in new ways by powerful impulses toward freedom, independence, change, and excitement. The electrified feminine principle helps them to appreciate the flow of their emotions as healing and liberating. They may have heightened emotional responses to everyday events. They may also discover long-forgotten or entirely new kinds of feelings within themselves such as exhilaration, aliveness, and spontaneity.

People's home lives and relationships also tend to be more interesting and stimulating. These are generally good times for cherishing fun activities in the family, pursuing hobbies, or enjoying meals together, provided that everyone's unique self-expression and needs are respected. Moon-Uranus transits also support awareness-raising groups in the home space.

The Moon principle acting on Uranus will help people to apply themselves with kindness and passion to various progressive causes or the work of spiritual awakening. They may also feel nourished by the inspiring and uplifting qualities of motherhood and sisterhood. Finally, they can feel a renewed trust in the liberating guidance of their own "inner healer," surrendering to it more deeply.[19]

The shadow qualities of the Moon-Uranus field include feelings of manic restlessness, wired agitation, and nervous tension. People may have trouble sitting still and relaxing, often caused by perinatal energies bursting through their psyches. They might feel conflicts between their needs for intimacy and connection, and those of freedom and variety. At times, Uranus' impulse toward awakening change and shakeup can also appear in chaotic or disruptive ways until the emotional energies underlying these events are made conscious.

Moon-Uranus Transits in Deep Self-Exploration

Moon-Uranus transits are highly desirable in holotropic states, representing periods when people's psyches are essentially splitting open, allowing buried trauma to surface and release itself. In their book *Holotropic Breathwork*, the Grofs discuss the issue of why facing painful memories is so healing:

Frequently asked questions about reliving of childhood traumas are: What makes this process therapeutic? Why does it not represent retraumatization rather than being conducive to healing? The unique nature of the holotropic state allows the breather to simultaneously play two very different roles. A person who is experiencing full age regression to the period of childhood when the traumatic event took place, identifies in a very authentic and convincing way with the child or the infant involved. At the same time, he or she retains the stamina and reasoning capacity of a mature adult. This situation makes it possible to fully experience the original event with the primitive emotions and sensations of the small child and, at the same time, process and evaluate it from the position of an adult. It is obvious that an adult is capable of coping with many experiences that during childhood were incomprehensible, confusing, and intolerable. In addition, the therapeutic context and support from people whom the breather trusts makes this situation vastly different from the circumstances under which the original trauma occurred.

This might be an adequate explanation for the healing . . . [effect that] conscious reliving has on some less extreme traumas. However, the healing of major traumas—particularly those that threatened survival and body integrity of the individual—seems to involve yet another therapeutic mechanism. It is likely that in situations of this kind, the original traumatic event was recorded in the organism, but its impact was not fully experienced at the time when it happened. On occasion, massive psychological shock can lead to blacking out and fainting.

It is conceivable that the experience can also be shut off partially, rather than completely; the individual then does not lose consciousness, yet does not . . . [register] the full impact of the trauma. As a result, the traumatic event cannot be fully psychologically "digested" and integrated; it is dissociated and remains in the unconscious as a foreign element. This does not prevent it from having a disturbing influence on the person's emotional and psychosomatic condition and behavior.[20]

Perinatal Experiences

As we have seen, the Uranus principle acts as a kind of cosmic midwife, helping people to face the emotional material engaged by their challenging Saturn and Pluto transits, and pull consciousness out the other side into states of rebirth. Rebirth experiences often include clear obstetric elements. People may relive factors such as the type of anaesthesia used, forceps delivery, or breech birth. They may also identify specific conditions in the delivery room, details which can sometimes be verified later. Finally, it is possible to remember moments of sweet bonding and breastfeeding with the mother, experiences which often have deeply mystical overtones.

The following is from a holotropic session of a male subject with Uranus conjunct natal Moon, and Pluto square natal Uranus:

> Passing through a dark place of fear and aggression, I suddenly identified with the goddess Persephone being carried out of the underworld and into the light of day by her grateful father. She//I was limp and groggy as I also identified with my own delivery as a newborn, still drugged by my mother's anaesthetic. The visual field suddenly brightened, as all around was the lush green of springtime in a deep mountain valley. My father rejoiced exultantly as he cried out to a multitude of figures lining the top of the valley: *"I've brought her home! I've brought her home!"* It was the cherished rebirth of the divine Feminine out of the perinatal underworld.
>
> Recalling this decades later, I still feel tears of joy. As an intellectual male raised in a masculine and materialistic culture to be able to participate in the rebirth of Persephone was a profound act of grace. It was one of the highlights of my entire life and I still feel deeply privileged and grateful.

Grof found that as people decrease the repository of pain in their psyches, they gain access to much wider channels for positive feelings. They also tap into basic human values, including altruistic and humanitarian impulses and a desire to live in a more close and satisfying way with nature. They recognize that there can be no higher societal priorities than having clean air, clean water, and clean soil. The following is from a holotropic session undertaken with Uranus sextile natal Moon, and Pluto conjunct natal Jupiter:

> Struggling with a feeling of abysmal failure centered around pressures in my mouth, I had a sense of losing my teeth and existing in that part of life when the teeth are often gone: old age. I was grappling with the question of what ultimately gives meaning to human life.
>
> The obsessive pursuit of power, wealth and fame, enacted by so many in our society, from this perspective, now seemed incredibly shortsighted and futile. I could see that acts of giving and caring, rather than being a subset of the main pursuits of life, are the only worthwhile strategy, the real purpose of life. I also vowed not to focus on others' shortcomings, but to see the spiritual wholeness in every person.

Transpersonal Experiences

As exploration deepens, people have the sense of accessing experiences normally considered beyond the range of human perception. In sequences that transcend *spatial* boundaries, they can identify with other people or groups of people, and perceive that their experiences are helping to liberate those individuals. Journeyers may also identify with the maternal instincts in all of nature or in specific animals, such as the overwhelming drive of mice to care for their young, fretting with thoughts of *"**Babies!** . . . **babies!** . . . **babies!**"* In scenes that transcend *temporal* boundaries, they may participate in the resolution of various racial, collective, or karmic memories and problems. People of both genders can feel the uniting bonds of maternal bloodlines through human history or identify with the spiritual awakening of women in our time.

Archetypal experiences include the death and rebirth of deities, the humanitarian aspects of Prometheus, or the plenitude of the inner Holy Grail. Encounters with the Great Mother Goddess personified as Isis, Demeter, Parvati, Lakshmi, or Mary are also relatively common. The following is from a psilocybin mushroom session undertaken with Moon trine Uranus, and Neptune opposition Uranus:

> After the long period of suffering, an archetypal Sister leads me by the hand, away from the problems of my biography and up into the divine realm. There is no separation between us. Her boundaries are made of fire, then mine also, as we merge into the blessed numinous realms together.
>
> I see a cosmic vagina made of peacock-spectra patterns and recognize it as the *Virgin* archetype, the eternal and pristine Feminine, unsullied by the biological mess of delivery.

In the later phase of the day, Moon-Uranus transits support ecstatic reentry and bonding experiences with friends and family. Journeyers may perceive moonlight, moonbeams, and the starry night sky as having especially magical and soothing properties. Long walks in nature or lying out under the stars can also have a profoundly integrating effect.

Mercury-Uranus

Loyalty to petrified opinion never yet broke a chain or freed a human soul.
    Mark Twain (Mercury square Uranus 8°06′)
    Inscription beneath his bust in the Hall of Fame.

I tore myself away from the safe comfort of certainties through my love for truth; and truth rewarded me.
    Simone de Beauvoir (Mercury conjunct Uranus 1°09′)
    All Said and Done, 1974

The mind is not sex-typed.
    Margaret Mead (Mercury conjunct Uranus 2°50′) *Blackberry Winter*, 1972

Mercury-Uranus Transits in Everyday Life

At these times, the Uranus archetype awakens the perceptual, cognitive, and intuitive elements of people's minds, while Mercury provides a mental channel for Uranus' liberating forces to manifest. People often feel a quickening of their thought processes, accompanied by mental breakthroughs, new perspectives, and inspired ideas. They may crave higher levels of stimulation, drawing them to the internet, games, and channel surfing— novelties where their curious minds can engage in multiple inputs. Their enjoyment of humor and wordplay may also be enhanced.

These transits are good times to study new subjects, with individuals showing a special aptitude for mathematics, electronics, languages, or programming. Drawn to progressive new ideas, they may also seek to break out of limiting patterns of thought, and ways of seeing the world, left over from their childhoods, education, or religious traditions and discover for themselves the liberating power of direct inquiry. Freedom of thought, excitement in learning, and celebration of the mind become their mantra.

The challenging side of these archetypes includes racing thoughts, manic restlessness, and nervous tension. People may have trouble turning off their minds and relaxing. To reduce these tensions, it can be helpful for them to move their wrists and fingers around, while making any sounds that want to emerge. Some people may also come up with a series of impractical, eccentric plans with little chance of realization, exasperating their friends. Sometimes they are attracted to every passing gimmick or novelty, regardless of its merit.

Mercury-Uranus Transits in Deep Self-Exploration

Mercury-Uranus transits are moderately strong markers for self-exploration, adding interesting narratives and unexpected plot turns as the healing journey unfolds. Freeing people's awareness through astonishing synchronicities and playful surprises, they see that they never know for sure what is going to happen next in life, but that some kind of Higher Intelligence seems to be orchestrating events in a deeply meaningful way. Enjoying "sudden flashes of insight" and inspiration, they may see their minds not as an impediment to spirituality, but as a lightning rod or vessel of the universe's own adventure of self-discovery. The human brain can be experienced as a direct doorway to cosmic consciousness.

Under any astrological transit, unexpected material may emerge in sessions, which is why it is always recommended to have trustworthy sitters. Reliable conditions in the session room will allow the inner electric play to unfold without reservation. The dynamic Mercury-Uranus transits also seem to coincide, on occasion, with electronic glitches such as trouble with the sound system. As always, it is advisable to have a backup music source. However, if necessary, a steady drumbeat on any hollow object will help to carry people through their experiences.

Perinatal Experiences

These archetypes inspire people with the basic faith and optimism that breakthroughs are possible, a mind that won't settle for the status quo but keeps looking and questing until the liberating higher truth is revealed. Journeyers can perceive words or phrases thunderbolting into their awareness, or temporary loss of reference as their rational minds let go. In a deeply regressed state, they may utter bursts of childlike vocalizing or gibberish. They can also release nervous tension in complex twisting movements or shaking of their bodies, wrists, and fingers.

It is important to allow these wired, chaotic energies to emerge from the system in whatever form they want to be expressed. The Greeks knew from experience that without the emotional outlets of their honored mystery religions—most famously, the Eleusinian, Orphic, and Dionysian sites—people were more likely to fall sway to dangerous collective hysterias. They saw that the *lesser insanity* of these well-established healing ceremonies was necessary to prevent the *greater insanity* of societal madness.[21]

As people reach the rebirth states of BPM IV and the confining pressures of the birth canal suddenly lift out into infinity, they undergo a dramatic cleansing of their mental and sensory channels. They may see images of medical and scientific breakthroughs that benefit all humanity, or experience what Grof and Tarnas term the *Promethean* form of ecstasy, as their crown chakras open and they receive direct insights into the cosmic nature of reality.

The following is from an internalized psilocybin mushroom session with Mercury square the subject's natal Uranus, and Mercury trine Uranus in the sky:

> I saw an image of windshield wipers removing thick mud from a car window, which seemed to represent a clearing of inner vision. I could feel my sixth chakra opening, the center of higher insight, and perceived that while the perinatal unfolding centers around the opening of the heart chakra, the other chakras also open during this process.
>
> Later, my entire being became a flow of moving fractal patterns, with the points of the energy designs flowing out through my fingers. I could see that, in these states, simply facing the material that the psyche presents leads automatically to resolution. Just as the Buddha-like figures perpetually reappear in fractal patterns, all inner experiences lead inexorably to Absolute Consciousness.

Transpersonal Experiences

Journeyers can have a sense of participating in the ongoing intellectual liberation of humanity. They may comprehend the scientific and philosophical progress of *Homo sapiens* as a kind of collective birth labor, with incremental leaps in knowledge and awareness leading toward some future omega point of species awakening. They may also encounter the archetype of the trickster in the form of Loki, Monkey, or Coyote.

People may enter states where the highest motive of Absolute Consciousness in creating the material universe seems to be something like cosmic boredom and a craving for adventure and play. The divine may also be seen to embody the unquenchable curiosity of a scientist—savoring its own self-discoveries, variations, anomalies, and experiments. Finally, they may enjoy celebrations of cosmic humor and perceive the Universal Mind as having a wide-ranging and well-developed sense of irony and comedy.

The Mercury-Uranus field will help sessions to end on a positive note. Euphoric journeyers may laugh in abject amazement at the trials of the day, and the way their minds were so utterly convinced by the emerging material. They discover a wide-eyed regard for the psyche's pattern of all-encompassing pressure followed by surprising release. They may also display some manic tendencies, talking fast and sharing enthusiastically until the material smooths itself out and they reach a calm and relaxed state. If tensions persist, it can be helpful to lie down and do some wrist- and finger-twisting movements along with verbal expression.

Venus-Uranus

Each friend represents a world in us, a world possibly not born until they arrive, and it is only by this meeting that a new world is born.
Anaïs Nin (Venus square Uranus 2°49′)
The Diary of Anaïs Nin, vol. 2, 1939–1949

A good marriage is one which allows for change and growth in the way they express their love.
Pearl Buck (Venus square Uranus 7°10′)
To My Daughters, With Love, 1967

Venus-Uranus Transits in Everyday Life

These entertaining transits combine Venus' yearnings for love, beauty, and fun with Uranus' needs for freedom, variety, and excitement. The Venus-Uranus field awakens people's social and romantic lives, giving love, sex, and friendship the quality of irrepressible, liberating forces. Relationships can undergo periods of magical rebirth as people experience each other in new ways or break out of old emotional patterns together. The dynamic transits in particular may also correspond to romantic-triangle situations, as someone in the couple becomes attracted to a third person who seems to offer the novelty or inspiration that he or she is looking for.

For single people, Venus-Uranus transits may represent new relationships or a series of stirring encounters. They can feel sudden attractions, often to those who are very different from their usual pattern, such as from a different ethnic background, social situation, age, or gender. It is almost impossible to know, however, whether infatuations begun during the dynamic Uranus-to-Venus alignments will settle into a stable routine until after the transit passes. Sometimes they end just as suddenly as they begin.

These transits also support interesting and liberating friendships. Individuals may enjoy new kinds of social situations and connecting with different types of people. Artistic creativity and appreciation of beauty are also awakened, especially those employing electronic or other innovative media and bright or striking color. Some individuals may feel rapture in the presence of gorgeous music, art, or nature.

The challenging side of the Venus-Uranus field emerges when people's needs for social and emotional novelty manifest in selfish or disharmonious ways. Their yearning for excitement may have a disruptive effect on their relationships. Holding freedom above intimacy, they may glide from one social contact to another, staying always on the emotional surface.

Venus-Uranus Transits in Deep Self-Exploration

In self-exploration, the Uranus archetype awakens feelings of love, kindness, and harmony, while Venus offers a loving channel for Uranian emotional breakthroughs to surface. People can heal problems around bonding and nurture. They can also have strikingly positive reactions to evocative music. At the biographical layer of exploration, they may remember impulsive attractions or romantic-triangle situations in their lives.

Perinatal Experiences

As journeyers reach transcendence, they experience the electrifying victory of love over the depression, aggression, scatology, and demonic energies of the previous stages of birth (BPM II and III). The eternal Feminine rises majestically over the dying elements of the outmoded ego, untarnished by illusions of imperfection, decay, or death.

Explorers may see brightly colored rebirth motifs, glowing radiant mandalas, and beautiful peacock-spectra patterns depicting free cosmic energy reorganizing back into its divine source. These brilliant visions are one of the most recognizable features of any archetypal influence. The following is from a guided ayahuasca session undertaken with Venus square the subject's natal Uranus:

> I experienced my whole body as a diamond-fire, crystalline web of rainbow light. Undulating streams of light vibrated and pulsated around me and I could feel how this web of energy was not only expressive of a personal energetic imprint that was unique to me, but was also interwoven through and interlinked with the greater electromagnetic tapestry of the cosmos.

Figure 18. "Peacock Great Mother Goddess" Stanislav Grof (Uranus-Pluto square natal Venus, and Neptune trine natal Jupiter). A psychedelic session that embodied "an entire range of expressions of the Feminine and my relation to them: devouring Feminine, Amazonian Feminine, Feminine as lover, as mother, and the culmination was connection with the Peacock Great Mother Goddess and a sense of being nourished by her milk—an archetypal version of milk or Ambrosia—not through her breast, but somehow imbibing it through my entire body or being."

The manic side of the Venus-Uranus field emerges when individuals desire and may be partly in touch with transcendence, but have not yet worked through the powerful, driving energies from the preceding stage of delivery (BPM III). They may feel constantly restless in love, addicted to the excitement of new adventures but unwilling to accept any challenge that reminds them of the life-threatening confinement of the birth canal.

As journeyers face these emotions and reach states of loving reunion with the divine, they reduce the manic pressure in their psyches, enabling them to accept the inevitable ups and downs of real human relationships. They will enjoy an enhanced sense of both love and freedom, with access to rich varieties of emotional experience even with the same partner. For many on a spiritual path, the most interesting and satisfying part of sex is the feeling of making love with the divine principle itself, personified as various gods or goddesses of the collective pantheon. The partner can be experienced as a doorway to or embodiment of the sacred realm.

People also gain insight into the psychology of exhibitionism and its relationship with the consciousness of the naked newborn, freed from the confining pressures of delivery.

Transpersonal Experiences

Journeyers in sessions may also identify with the universal emancipation of women. Breakthrough experiences can at times include both a liberation of sexual energies, and a liberation from sexual energies. The following holotropic session of a male graduate student occurred with Venus trine natal Uranus, and Venus sextile Uranus in the sky:

> I identified with a specific, unknown woman and from her point of view what felt like the negative side of her/my hormones and monthly cycles. In this negative, perinatal-influenced state, it felt like a karma to have to go through the child-bearing years. Finally menopause came and I felt deeply relieved, unlike what our male- and youth-dominated culture might suppose. My spirit was free from the shackles of all those biological imperatives and unwanted, hormone-driven attractions.

Journeyers may also experientially identify with the mating behavior of various animal or plant species. They can explore love and sex as universal forces of immense range and scope, or the effects of divine grace in human history. They may see ravishing goddesses embodying sexual allure and maternal compassion, hear angelic music in heavenly choirs, or behold breathtaking displays of cosmic beauty. Other mythological and fairytale sequences include the redemption of Cinderella and the birth of Venus.

The following internalized LSD session was undertaken with Uranus square natal Venus, and Neptune conjunct natal Moon:

My feelings gradually smoothed out and became more serene. I saw a loving, ancient desert goddess reclining on her side above a timeless Middle-Eastern city. She appeared in the costume of classic Arabian belly-dancers, emanating divine sexual warmth, comfort, and nurture. Months later I recognized her as the goddess Ishtar—who was with her cognates Inanna and Astarte adored as the queen of heaven for thousands of years in the Sumerian, Babylonian, Assyrian, and Semitic cultures. It seems incredible that a face of the divine this beautiful could ever be forgotten! It was one of the most sublime revelations of my entire life.

Then for several hours I saw brilliant Eastern motifs and mandalas in vibrant color, which seemed to represent cosmic energies returning ecstatically to their divine source. I felt surrounded by love and beauty for the rest of the evening. The whole day was a healing miracle.

In the integration phase, journeyers may respond with unusual appreciation to a loving gathering of friends and family, such as a special psychedelic feast, rebirthday party, or dancing. With their sensory channels cleansed and awakened, they will savor sparkling natural scenes, inspiring music, and warm human contact. They will also be open to appreciating art objects and pictures of a high aesthetic value.

Rebirth experiences correspond to an opening of the heart chakra and people may experience warm rushes of energy and positive affect that continue into the next day and in some form indefinitely.

Mars-Uranus

The only people for me are the mad ones, the ones who are mad to live, mad to talk, mad to be saved, desirous of everything at the same time, the ones who never yawn or say a commonplace thing, but burn, burn, burn, like fabulous yellow roman candles exploding like spiders across the stars and in the middle you see the blue centerlight pop and everybody goes "Awww!"
Jack Kerouac (Mars square Uranus 0°18′) *On the Road,* 1957

The only thing I regret about my past is the length of it. If I had to live my life over again I'd make all the same mistakes—only sooner.
Tallulah Bankhead (Mars sextile Uranus, date only, calc. for noon: 3°27′)

Mars-Uranus Transits in Everyday Life

During these engaging transits, the archetypal field related to Mars catalyzes people's yearnings for freedom and excitement, while Uranus liberates their martial energy and courage. The meeting of these fiery archetypes can have dramatic effects. It often occurs as pressures have been building in some area of people's lives, providing the sudden eruptive force to release the tension. Mars-Uranus can help individuals to get in touch with their anger. As always, it is best to find effective outlets for these energies rather than aiming them at others.

Some people may also find themselves drawn to thrilling adventures, daring risks, or high speed. A craving for martial excitement make these generally rewarding times for physical activity and sports as long as people show reasonable caution, especially around machinery. Mars-Uranus provides the dynamic spark to break out of oppressive or confining states. An important source of many people's limitations is on the inside, in the form of unresolved fear and conflicts in their psyches—these archetypes can help them to face this baggage and clear it out.

The shadow side of the Mars-Uranus field emerges when its volatile impulses are acted out in the social world. Flashes of anger can lead to upsetting scenes and confrontations. Wantonly playing out the macho-rebel side of these archetypes, some people may also take undue physical risks. And finally, a misplaced sense of fighting spirit can result in an angry defiance of all good sense. Even activists and environmentalists working for good causes may find that they can be more calm, persuasive, and effective in the long run when they clear out their own repository of unconscious aggression.

Mars-Uranus Transits in Deep Self-Exploration

All Mars-Uranus transits are powerful and exciting indicators in holotropic exploration, giving sessions an intense breakout quality. They are certainly one of the factors an experienced sitting team would seek out in planning dates. These archetypes forcibly catalyze each other, heightening feelings of courage, energy, and explosive liberation. Sessions tend to move quickly, with fast encounters and sudden, decisive release from the material, what Tarnas calls "transcendent breakthrough speed." Participants' inner healer zeros in on its target, taking them through the experience and reaching the other side before their minds even know what has happened.

During the *dynamic* transits of Mars-Uranus, it is recommended that journeyers and sitters adhere to the strict protocols of internalized sessions. This is especially important for those with a history of aggressive acting out. For their own and others' safety, journeyers commit to staying in the reclining position with eyeshades and headphones on, and not, for example, running through the woods acting out a Viking racial memory, proclaiming world peace in traffic, or attempting to defy the laws of physics. These energies can be rash and dangerous when acted out in the wrong setting. Many of the deepest inner experiences simply cannot be faced if people are standing up or interacting with the outer world.

This is not just a question of their minds being distracted by the environment. Some of the accidents and suicides of the 1960s that brought on the drug hysteria and backlash were based on a serious confusion by users of psychedelics between inner and outer realities. People facing the life-threatening pressure of the birth canal might, for example, project and see an open window as a way out of their confinement, leading to tragic consequences. Lying down and facing the emerging memory, on the other hand, consumes it from the system and leads to states of rebirth and transcendence.

Perinatal Experiences

The direction of the Mars-Uranus field is toward a powerful eruption of repressed energies, like a volcano blowing its top as the emotional lava finally breaks through. These archetypes support fast resolutions of material at every stage of exploration. They engage at decisive moments, giving people dynamic, positive boosts of energy and courage. The following is from a session with Uranus conjunct natal Mars:

> Thrashing around with high energy, I experienced wave after wave of aggressive release, with many crescendos of shuddering, coughing, and heaving on an empty stomach, and my legs shaking continuously for over eight hours.

When combined with other Uranus or Pluto transits, Tarnas found that Mars-Uranus can help mediate access to states of rebirth and transcendence, what Grof calls the fourth perinatal matrix (BPM IV).

During this cathartic process, journeyers may identify with rebels or freedom fighters from various eras in history. Themes of aggressive liberation are also common, in scenes of swordplay and evisceration, escaping from prison, bloody revolution, or killing the tyrant. They may see images of ripping, tearing, or cutting their way to freedom. Mythological themes include the feats of legendary heroes slaying the dragon, capturing the Golden Fleece, or defying false suitors. Journeyers may also encounter fiercely independent figures such as Artemis or Atalanta. As the martial energies begin to resolve, they exult in a growing freedom, often accompanied by scenes of Olympic champions winning races, rockets accelerating past the speed of light, or a euphoric transcendence of conflict.

Finally, these archetypes facilitate ecstatic rushes of energy and in perinatal sessions can liberate sexual material. People feel currents of

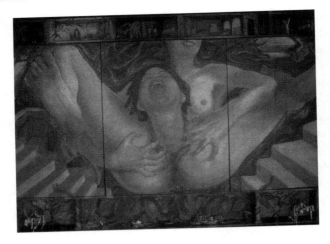

Figure 19. "Out of the Darkness" Amina Re (Uranus conjunct natal Mars, and Pluto conjunct natal Moon). A powerful experience of being born and giving birth to a new self in a Holotropic Breathwork session of an American participant.

cosmic energy surging through their bodies, breaking through old repressions and inertias.

Transpersonal Experiences

Journeyers can help, in a synchronistic way, to release further pressure from the collective psyche through various ancestral, collective, or karmic experiences. They may also explore the consciousness of birds of prey or other swift predators which are untouchable by other animals. The following is from a holotropic session with Uranus conjunct the subject's natal Mars:

> I saw the consciousness of eagles as being highly transcended. Their awareness has not evolved upward out of the physical realm in the simple way that Darwinian biology proposes. Rather I experienced it, also, as the boundaries of definition where divine consciousness dips down fully into the physical realm. The consciousness of eagles is clearly and self-awarely Absolute Consciousness defined into a material shape.[22]

The consciousness of eagles or hawks can also appear at the beginning and end of sessions as a kind of master of ceremonies of the entire day. Finally, journeyers may identify with inanimate objects, including those made by human beings, or with natural processes such as lightning.

Focused bodywork can be highly effective in releasing any remaining tension. Sometimes these final energies can be depicted as sharks gliding menacingly in otherwise serene water, and then following the release, the water is experienced as clear again. After well-integrated sessions, people will feel vibrantly free and alive.

Jupiter-Uranus

Oh, the glory of growth, silent, mighty, persistent, inevitable! To awaken, to open up like a flower to the light of a fuller consciousness!
　　Emily Carr (Jupiter conjunct Uranus 1°53'; both in square with Venus)
　　Hundreds and Thousands, 1966

Let the winds of change blow through my life, bringing the most radically enlivening thing that could possibly happen. I am hoisting my sails.
　　Caroline W. Casey (Jupiter sextile Uranus 0°32')
　　Making the Gods Work for You, 1998

Jupiter-Uranus Transits in Everyday Life

In these liberating alignments, Uranus brings a sense of unexpected new freedoms, dramatic awakening, and resolution of problems, while Jupiter one of divine benevolence, expansion, and success. The Jupiter archetype heightens people's natural impulses toward innovation, experimentation, and change. They may be graced with exciting new opportunities, releases of pressure, or various kinds of peak experiences. Dissatisfied with the stagnant routines and compromises of the past, their yearning for broadened adventures make these generally good times to travel, take courses, or engage in inspiring self-exploration. Jupiter-Uranus transits seem to occur just as people have done their work and paid their dues, and the universe suddenly opens doors to new levels of experience.

　　The Uranus archetype acting on Jupiter helps to awaken a sense of beneficial effects and positive outcomes. Jupiter-Uranus represents the lightning strikes of divine grace that turn things around and offers to humanity second chances. Moments of "Eureka!" and "Aha!" are possible, although these rarely take the financial forms that people are expecting. Some astrologers refer to Jupiter-Uranus as the "Thank the Lord" alignment, because so many people exclaim those words at these times. In *Cosmos and Psyche*, Tarnas also documents the remarkable correlations, spanning centuries, between Jupiter-Uranus *world transits* and periods of social and political rebellions and awakenings, scientific quantum leaps, artistic breakthroughs, and opening of horizons across the entire world culture.[23]

　　Given the restless nature of these archetypes, it is understandable that they have significant shadow qualities. People may have strong urges to throw aside various routines and structures in their lives, including those they might still need for security. They may also have a tendency to glorify anything that seems novel or flashy. Of special appeal are new-age gadgets, technologies, and philosophies that offer quick and easy enlightenment without the slightest degree of pain or effort. Uranus lighting up Jupiter can also lead to various kinds of immoderation and "impulsive excess."[24] People may get carried away by a kind of golden-rebirth, breakthrough feeling. Episodes of unbound "Midas touch" inflation are possible, until Saturn again bursts the bubble and brings them down to earth.

Jupiter-Uranus Transits in Deep Self-Exploration

Transits of Jupiter-Uranus are some of the most desirable markers for self-exploration. They correspond to fantastic, almost miraculous influences for a first breathwork session or a first internalized psychedelic session. And as noted, the years when these planets align by world transit signify an increased spirit of adventure and breakthrough potential across the entire world psyche.

Jupiter-Uranus transits frequently correlate with major turning points, quantum leaps, and awakenings to new layers of experience in people's inner lives. These openings might include their first perinatal sequence, their first contact with animal or plant consciousness, or their first confrontation with an archetype or past-life memory. Jupiter-Uranus represents the *deus ex machina*, the sudden intercession of divine grace leading to a complete and unexpected resolution of the emerging material. Of course, the deepest breakthroughs occur along with powerful Pluto transits and an ongoing, systematic approach.

People may see a series of vignettes celebrating successes in their lives. On the challenging side, they can also face memories in which their parents built up their expectations to achieve great things in the world, a contributing factor in the onset of manic depression. Grof's research found that another clear etiological root of manic depression is the practice of swaddling infants.[25] People may also confront in themselves feelings of grandiose inflation or *hubris*, a state of overweening pride that results from living too far from conscious dependence on the divine—one justifiably feared by the ancient Greeks.

Perinatal Experiences

These transits also correspond to important incremental breakthroughs in the perinatal unfolding itself, such as the completion of the no-exit stage, the first demonic or sadomasochistic experience, or the first willingness to allow oneself to throw up or lose control. For people who have already encountered some of the biological and emotional aspects of the perinatal realm, these archetypes may grant access to its rich archetypal facets.

Conversely, those who have experienced the death-rebirth material primarily in a Jungian way, as a flow of symbolic images, can undergo openings into the more primal, biological, and obstetric elements of birth and death. Tarnas found that Jupiter-Uranus alignments have a special resonance with the states of overall transcendence which Grof terms BPM IV. They represent the rebirth matrix in its most expanded and celebrated form: the successful delivery and spiritual deliverance from the nightmare of a fear-based mode of being.

As these breakthroughs unfold, people may also have feelings of inflated self-importance, exaggerated freedom, or special privilege, even identifying personally with figures such as Midas, Icarus, Christ, or God. While in everyday life, these emotions might be responded to with censure, in holotropic sessions, sitters just allow the inflationary pockets to emerge and dissipate themselves. Arrogant or exclusionary feelings are soon replaced by those of win-win, shared breakthrough. Ideally, sitters also let journeyers laugh for as long as they need to. Feelings of triumph are natural emotions for a newborn, and it is okay to feel and express them.

The following internalized session of a male subject with Jupiter trine natal Uranus, and Pluto square natal Pluto, illustrates BPM III elements resolving into BPM IV:

After the nightmarish sequence in which the energies inside me were destroying the whole world and then the entire universe, I suddenly realized that the nightmare was over . . . Unbelievable relief! . . . I saw that it had all been just a projection of my birth struggle inside the mother, as the old universe of the womb was forever destroyed.

The process then cycled back into a distinctly sadomasochistic facet of delivery. I identified with a specific, unknown young woman somewhere in Holland not wanting to give birth and resisting the process. I could feel a head stuck in my vagina and sharp tensions along the inside of my thighs. Finally, all I could think of was to push! *Push!* The process then shifted to more pleasurable territory. I was a woman urgently craving pressure in my vagina. This perinatal-based experience certainly demystified certain aspects of female sexuality for me.

The feelings of relief and liberation continued through the evening. What I thought earlier was the desperate alarm of all humanity now changed to a sense of shared credit and celebration for my successful delivery. I felt a redemption for all the friends who have supported me over the years. The world appeared fresh and pristine and the sounds of the owls, frogs, and coyotes outside the cabin that night—sweet life!—were exquisitely reassuring.

Individuals who reach the rebirth states of BPM IV feel a sense of universal redemption, salvation, forgiveness, and atonement. Reflecting the decompression of space at the moment of birth, they may see images of the inside of great halls and cathedrals. The world around them suddenly seems to come alive, permeated with sparkling flows of divine energy. Euphoric explorers may also identify with star mountain climbers attaining the highest peaks, scientists making discoveries that will benefit all humanity, or the end of wars, revolutions, or deadly storms.

The archetypal side of rebirth experiences includes stealing fire from the gods to give to humanity, alchemists turning lead into gold, or gods and goddesses such as Persephone, Dionysus, or Christ rising triumphantly from the underworld. Journeyers may feel an electrifying inspiration as their higher chakras open, in what Grof and Tarnas refer to as the *Promethean* or *illuminative* type of ecstasy. Related transpersonal themes include reaching the light at the end of the tunnel, the Ascension, enlightenment, or satori. With brotherly and sisterly feelings for all humanity, people's spiritual feelings tend to have a universal, all-encompassing and inclusive, rather than a denominational or sectarian character.

While savoring the incomparably more peaceful atmosphere of BPM IV and conditions in the delivery room, journeyers may still work through some minor challenges to their newborn spiritual awareness. However, these feel easily overcome by quicker and superior insight. The heroic feelings in rebirth experiences are based in the realization that the eternal Absolute Consciousness has overcome the limiting boundaries of the separate ego and fear of death. Sequences of rebirth and connection with positive transpersonal elements lead to a state of what Grof calls "higher sanity," a more connected and selfless way of functioning in the world.[26]

Transpersonal Experiences

Transpersonal experiences during these transits also tend to have an exciting and emancipatory quality. People can participate in the resolution of family problems and dynamics going back many generations. They can reach states of forgiveness and release of karmic burdens in traumatic racial or collective memories. The ability to identify with the emotional experience of other people, groups of people, and other life forms also provides new information for solving shared social and ecological problems.

Accessing further back in time, journeyers may experience the redemption of arduous passages in phylogenetic evolution, such as the first living cells, the first animals, the development of vertebrae, or primates leaving the safety of the trees. They may also celebrate quantum leaps in human history, such as the harnessing of fire, the beginning of agriculture, the adoption of the wheel, or the development of writing, electricity, and the internet. They can glimpse early resolutions in the great meta-trajectory of human ego consciousness—as the nightmarish, high-pressure era of postmodernism (c. 1900–) gives way, slowly and painfully, to the birth of a genuine, caring planetary consciousness.[27]

The integration phase of Jupiter-Uranus sessions is more likely to have the character of high liberation and ecstatic reentry. People feel incredulous amazement about the experience they have just been through, as well as some possible manic tendencies until any remaining material has been processed and digested. Enthusiastic journeyers may proclaim not only their own freedom, but insist that everyone in the world should have the same experience as soon as possible. They can feel a great need to call the President, the Pope, or other world leaders to share their incredible new discovery that will benefit all humanity. Needless to say, cell phones should be stowed safely away until people reach a more integrated state of rebirth.

These archetypes support the reawakening to divine consciousness, the *felix culpa* or blessed reward for enduring the loss of the womb paradise. They symbolize the "sacred Yes," the eternal natural exuberance that affirms life and electrifies it with higher meaning and possibilities. Under Jupiter-Uranus, the world is made new.

*   *   *

The Fundamental Alignments

The following section explores the archetypal fields represented by the powerful pair alignments of the outer planets: those of Saturn-Neptune, Saturn-Pluto, Saturn-Uranus, Uranus-Pluto, Neptune-Pluto, and Uranus-Neptune. These alignments, especially when they occur by conjunction, opposition or square, symbolize profound patterns of consciousness that will tend to dominate people's experiential fields when they are activated. And similarly, when they combine by *world transit*, they represent long-term evolutionary processes that affect the entire collective psyche.

In *Cosmos and Psyche*, Tarnas documents the broad range of cultural, political, and psychological manifestations associated with the following transit combinations. By integrating a wider orb on world transits, he demonstrates that humanity is always under the influence of at least one of these primary patterns of experience. Explorers of the psyche will come to honor these fundamental landscapes of consciousness, knowing them directly from the inside.

Saturn-Neptune

[Our] prenatal and perinatal history . . . has important implications for our spiritual life. As we have seen earlier, incarnation and birth represent separation and alienation from our true nature, which is Absolute Consciousness. Positive experiences in the womb and after birth are the closest contacts with the Divine that we can experience during our embryonal life or in infancy. The "good womb" and "good breast" thus represent experiential bridges to the transcendental level. Conversely, negative and painful experiences that we encounter in the intrauterine period, during birth, and in the early postnatal period send us deeper into the state of alienation from the divine source.
    Stanislav Grof (Saturn sesquiquadrate Neptune 2°13′)
    The Cosmic Game, 1998

Where there is sorrow there is holy ground.
    Oscar Wilde (Saturn square Neptune 2°0′) *"De Profundis"* 1905

Saturn-Neptune Transits in Everyday Life

Saturn-Neptune transits combine, in various ways, the yearning for higher meaning, unity, and connection associated with Neptune, with the forces of separation, boundaries, and concrete reality related to Saturn. Neptune represents an important part of the *holotropic* or "moving toward wholeness" principle in the universe, while Saturn is tied to the *hylotropic* or "moving toward matter" impulse.

The *flowing transits* provide opportunities to merge and balance these exceptionally different archetypal principles in people's life experience. They can be good times to bring imagination into form, show more compassion at work, or adopt a daily meditation practice. People may also make Saturnian edits to Neptunian areas of their lives, such as discarding a shallow esoteric routine, letting go of unrealistic fantasies, or weaning themselves from recreational drug use. As always, we can see the complex, multileveled, and multivalent ways in which the archetypes might manifest at any given time.

Along with these positive effects, the *dynamic transits* also represent periods when people may feel a disparity between their higher ideals and actual reality, or their needs for integrity versus those of security. The issue of selling out can arise. Sometimes they have a sinking feeling they have lost something precious or irreplaceable. At other times, they might feel drawn to leave a perfectly sound situation to follow a womb-like dream. As if floating in a misty haze, individuals can feel disoriented and confused, and it may be harder to make clear decisions. These archetypes often have a poignant, anguished quality. People may feel deeply vulnerable as Neptune dissolves away Saturn's old boundaries and attachments.

The archetypal field associated with these transits also has a helpful deflating effect on any tendencies people may harbor toward "spiritual materialism." Through disappointments in the world they discover a profound yearning to cut through these pretensions and connect more authentically with the cosmic source. Saturn-Neptune alignments support a humble, grounded, one-day-at-a-time approach to life, encouraging people to make an honest and sober appraisal of their relationship with the inner divine. In transpersonal psychology, as we have seen, drug and alcohol abuse are seen as attempts to fill a spiritual void and regain wholeness. Individuals with these problems will often benefit from 12-Step or other programs that encourage them to rediscover a relationship with Higher Power, as they see it. Even non-addicts may find value in attending a 12-Step meeting at least once in their lives.

Saturn-Neptune Transits in Deep Self-Exploration

The flowing Saturn-Neptune transits are mildly supportive for holotropic states. They help people to appreciate the strict protocols around internalized sessions that will enable them to let go and allow their emotions to safely unfold. They also help journeyers to maintain a distinction between their inner material and the outer reality of the session room.

The *dynamic* transits have a similar effect, in bringing attention to protocol issues beforehand. Once underway, it is normal in psychedelic sessions during any transit for people to temporarily project their emerging material onto the sitters, at certain points. This is not a problem as long as they stay lying down with their eyeshades on. However, as always, sitters need to stay clear and up to date with their own inner process, so they do not hook into journeyers' projections and begin projecting back themselves. In psychotherapy, this kind of negative feedback loop is referred to as the *circulus diaboli* or "diabolic circle" and needs to be prevented.

In general, the dynamic Saturn-Neptune alignments can be a somewhat more deflating influence in holotropic work. Unless very supportive other transits are also in effect, these are not the best times for a first psychedelic session with clients prone to chronic depression, as they might become unduly discouraged by their initial experience. This would apply especially to dynamic Saturn-Neptune transits that also involve *Mars*. It might also be preferable not to schedule group medicine-work or breathwork sessions under dynamic *Saturn-Neptune-Mars* world transits. Although these archetypes are not considered especially dangerous, they can be confusing and demoralizing to people, undermining their basic feelings of confidence in the process.

As with all Saturn transits, people can have helpful sessions if they are willing to temporarily face discouraging or humbling states of consciousness. The type of suffering associated with Saturn-Neptune does not, by itself, usually have a breakthrough cathartic quality, but rather a sense of slow and anguished dissolving of the old ego—the washing away of outmoded inner patterns in preparation for Neptune's melted ecstasy. The Neptune archetype grants divine compassion to this softening process. People can sink trustingly into their pain, feel, and melt through it—these transits are unusually conducive for deep crying.

Biographical memories that surface include the interruption of nourishing and comforting situations, or the loss of something precious such as the end of a relationship, the breakup of a family, or the departure of a beloved parent.

Perinatal Experiences

Tarnas found that when exploration reaches the perinatal tier of the psyche, an engaged Saturn-Neptune field will enhance the emergence of both Neptune's BPM I (*the Amniotic Universe*) and Saturn's BPM II (*No Exit*). Sometimes, combinations of BPM I and II can manifest as Oedipus- or Electra-type projections on the sitters, with one appearing to embody the nurturing good-womb energy and the other, the hellish uterine contractions.

When journeyers' process is dominated by *Neptune and BPM I*, their womb experiences may include elements of Saturnian intrusion, disruption, or complication, as they resolve memories around maternal stress or illness, chemical toxicity, or feelings of being unwanted. Grof found that these are often accompanied by experiences of polluted streams and underwater dangers, negative astral influences, or perceptions of "bad karma." Full surrender to this material leads to a sense of having consumed the negative karma. Toxic-womb sequences during any transit can include authentic biological elements, as well as emotions ranging from anguish and distress to, in the case of attempted abortions that were unsuccessful, apocalyptic terror.

Tarnas found that strong Saturn transits, in general—as well as those of Neptune-Pluto—can also engage memories around the transition from BPM I to the alarming onset of labor of *BPM II*. The fetus' amniotic heaven is interrupted by first noxious chemicals and then powerful uterine contractions. As these memories surface, people can feel an overwhelming sense of fear, danger and threat, experiences which are an important source of paranoia in later life.[28] The onset of labor may also take the form of being devoured by a giant spider, whale or octopus, descent into a menacing whirlpool or maelstrom, or cosmic engulfment. Many journeyers facing this material have independently referred to the biblical story of the fall from paradise and God's curse on Adam and Eve that "in pain and sorrow thou shalt bring forth children."

Saturn-Neptune symbolizes that stage in the perinatal journey where the Fall has happened, but the individual is still close enough to paradise to feel its loss most acutely. The potential for blissful security is still in the picture but the individual is unable to regain it, like seeing heaven but knowing one cannot be there. The state of separation is that much harder to bear because its remedy still looms in the background. Journeyers may feel an unbridgeable gulf between suffering humanity and unreachable divinity, or utter despair in a meaningless cardboard world.

Saturn's BPM II experiences may also include elements of Neptunian uncertainty, disorientation, or confusion. As these sequences slowly dissolve the archetype of hell from the psyche, people discover in themselves a mature acceptance of the entire trajectory of human life, from womb to tomb. They gradually let go and relax into their place in the fabric of the universe. The following is from a session undertaken with Neptune conjunct natal Saturn:

> I am interwoven on the tapestry of life. There is no need to worry anymore about my part in this tapestry and how or when I will be extinguished. I was created exactly here for a reason. Relaxing . . .

Direct emotional merging with the numinous, however, can feel somewhat leaner and more precious under these influences. The feeling tends to be that of the divine's mercy for his or her unworthy sinner rather than seamless mystical union. Even a modest contact with the gods and goddesses who embody divine compassion, such as Mary, Parvati, Demeter, Kwan Yin, Buddha, or Christ can be deeply nourishing in these moments.

Transpersonal Experiences

As exploration deepens in the transpersonal realms, subjects can identify with salt-of-the-earth humanity or with life forms that play a humble yet fundamental role in the great food chains of life, such as plankton or earthworms. They may also experience the awareness of animals who embody strange or unusual mixtures of self- and selfless consciousness.

At the archetypal level, journeyers may encounter mythological figures such as Tantalos who was condemned to eternal thirst. They can also experience Cronos being urged on by his mother Earth to castrate his father Ouranos, representing the lost majesty and potency of the heavenly realm that human beings must endure to enter earthly incarnation. The separation between earth and heaven, or time and eternity, can also be portrayed as the relationship between Tezcatlipoca and Quetzalcoatl, the Aztec deities representing matter and spirit. People explore the interplay between these fundamental vectors in the universe—the hylotropic and holotropic or material and spiritual—and recognize that, ultimately, humanity and the divine need each other to be fulfilled.

Journeyers also explore the effects of *Maya*, the illusory screenworks in the material world that keep Absolute Consciousness hidden from our everyday minds. They discover the means for a deeply committed yet detached approach to life, described in Buddhism as: "being in the world but not of it, like a lotus leaf floating in a pond of muddy water." The lotus is cherished in Eastern philosophy because its roots reach deeply into the muddy bottom while its leaves float pristinely above the surface of the water.

During the more severe Saturn-Neptune transits, minor complications or projections may persist into the later stages of the day. The following holotropic session undergone with Neptune conjunct natal Saturn, illustrates the effect of residual perinatal elements:

> The session first broke into rebirth around the third hour, although waves of threatening material continued to surface through the day. I was a newborn, needing a lot of quiet time with mom and dad. My sitters were totally there for me and I felt loved and nourished.
>
> At the same time, I was projecting negative energy on my friend next door in the kitchen, feeling that she was trying to spoil these special moments by insisting that it was now time for dinner. Gradually I realized that the sitters were embodying the memory of the Nourishing Mother and womb, while my friend was carrying the projection of the Spoiler or Terrible Mother—at root, my fear that the hellish uterine contractions would return.

Saturn-Pluto

Saturn is seen as being an instrument in the service of the all-powerful Plutonic Deity, Shiva, the Great Destroyer and Creator. . . . In Shiva's feminine form, Pluto is Shakti, the Supreme Goddess, Mother Nature, the power and energy of the Universe, Kundalini; while Her destructive aspect is black Kali, the fierce devouring Mother. Thus the Plutonic process of death and rebirth can be understood as an expression of Shiva's feminine aspect—the Divine Mother's birth process, the positive erotic Kundalini arousal, the destructive birth canal's contractions, Mother Nature's eternal regenerative power which

bestows rebirth. Manifestations of Saturn-Pluto are her labor contractions, Jupiter-Pluto her birth orgasm.
  Richard Tarnas (SU=SA/PL 0°23') *Prometheus the Awakener,*
  original unpublished version, 1980

Long is the way
And hard, that out of hell leads up to light. John Milton
  (Saturn square Pluto 1°32') *Paradise Lost,* 1667

I am become death, the destroyer of worlds.
  Robert Oppenheimer (Saturn trine Pluto 0°39') Quoting Vishnu
  from the *Bhagavad Gita* at the exploding of the first
  atomic bomb, July 1945, at Alamogordo, New Mexico.

Saturn-Pluto Transits in Everyday Life

The *dynamic* Saturn-Pluto transits represent some of the most serious and intense archetypal energies that human beings can experience. Pluto acting on the Saturn principle can heighten feelings of compression, constriction and challenge, as well as marshal deep reserves of endurance to survive and outlast demanding conditions. The empowered Saturn also enables people to exert enormous levels of discipline toward accomplishing the most strenuous goals and tasks. The strict, Saturnian side of human nature may also get carried away on occasion, manifesting as ruthless levels of self-control or the impulse to control and punish others.

At the same time, the archetypal Saturn acting on Pluto (Saturn→Pluto) can bring sustained attention to the shadow side of the psyche associated with Pluto, forcing people to let go and face their emotional pain. The focused Pluto archetype may also help them to work long and hard on projects with an aim of regeneration or renewal. At best, they will take responsibility for any impulses they may feel toward power and domination over others, and make a long-term effort to face the psychological forces underlying them.

Saturn-Pluto transits sometimes have two stages. In the first stage, people feel a strong urge to monitor their negative qualities, especially not to abuse power or backslide into overbearing behavior (i.e., Saturn controlling Pluto). In the second phase, they begin to feel that their own rigid self-control is an even bigger problem. They often then forge a commitment to let go and allow Pluto's primal energies to break through in safe ways (i.e., Pluto integrating Saturn).

The trine and sextile transits tend to be less severe and obsessive, while providing similar opportunities for sustained, incremental transformation and hard work. They represent times when people can be successful at structuring their worlds, in both constructive and ultimately self-repressive ways.

In *Cosmos and Psyche*, Tarnas documents the relationship between Saturn-Pluto *world transits* and important events in world history and culture. The themes he describes as routinely corresponding to these alignments include an intensification of the forces of war and terrorism— recent examples of which include the Saturn-Pluto conjunction of 1914 at the beginning of World War I, the Saturn-Pluto square in 1939 at the start of World War II, the series of Mideast wars which coincided with sequential Saturn-Pluto alignments of 1948 (the conjunction), 1956 (the square), 1967 (the opposition), 1973 (the square)—and the Saturn opposition Pluto in the early 2000s during the attack on the World Trade Center, in 2001.

Saturn-Pluto alignments also regularly occur during times of severe cultural tension and splitting, such as the conjunction of 1947–1948 at the onset of the Cold War when the U.S. and U.S.S.R., former allies against the Nazis, began the long faceoff of the Cold War—or the opposition of the mid-1960s which saw the assassination of President Kennedy, the deep dividing of American society over the issue of the Vietnam War, and the start of what became known as the "culture wars."

These transits also correspond to periods of conservative empowerment and Realpolitik, such as the Saturn conjunct Pluto of the early 1980s during the onset of the Reagan era, or the Saturn opposition Pluto of the early 2000s which saw the intense political aftermath and responses to 9–11, including the invasion of Iraq. Tarnas illustrates how Saturn-Pluto transits also manifest in a profound commitment to moral courage and facing the shadow, the creation of paradigmatic works of art, and the forging of deep cultural and artistic structures.[29]

Saturn-Pluto Transits in Deep Self-Exploration

Saturn-Pluto transits represent extremely powerful forces in holotropic work which cut through the surface layer of the psyche and take journeyers into their deepest emotional material. These archetypes invoke both the need and the capacity for sustained inner exploration, offering avenues to work through some of the most rigid and self-punishing structures in the psyche. They can help people to access enormous reserves of staying power and determination.

At the *biographical* layer of exploration, journeyers may work through leftover traces from events in their lifetimes around sustained aggression, abuse, or domination. These might include memories in which they were either the victim (archetypally related to Saturn) or the perpetrator (associated with Pluto). Grof suggests that breathers with heavy Saturn-Pluto transits could be held and comforted by female facilitators with a loving earth-mother, Venus-of-Willendorf type of physique. This kind of soft cradling in an ample, grounded body would help to compensate for the punishing side of these archetypes and create a supportive medium in which the Saturn-Pluto, hard-labor nightmare could be faced internally. The following is from a supervised and internalized session with Saturn square Pluto in the sky:

> I passed through places of feeling utterly hated, despised, and undeserving of help. I imagined that the sitters were disgusted by me and on the verge of withdrawing their support and leaving. In this state of desperate vulnerability, I prayed that they wouldn't abandon me. As the underlying material finally broke through and released, I was very grateful for their professionalism and human compassion, because I don't think I could have recovered from being rejected in that moment.

Perinatal Experiences

As exploration deepens, Tarnas found that these archetypes can manifest as either a Plutonic intensifying of Saturn's no-exit state (BPM II), or a Saturnian focusing of Pluto's death-rebirth struggle (BPM III), or both. In either case, the second archetype acts as a powerful adjective on the other, evoking highly concentrated forms of that matrix.

When sessions are dominated by *Saturn and BPM II*, the Pluto archetype will help to compel Saturn's no-exit ordeal to its most unbearable extremes, thus consuming it from the psyche. Journeyers pass through states of inhuman suffering and hellish torture, what Tarnas calls the "concentration camp archetype." Life is seen as being utterly pointless and futile, with misery, pain, and death all that really exist in the universe. Full surrender to these states liberates them from people's consciousness.

Saturn-Pluto subsumes the most difficult phases of the birth process. The womb has been irretrievably lost and turned into a torture chamber, and yet the light at the end of the tunnel still seems so far away. Facing this "no man's land" of the soul, however, is where a new spirituality takes deep and lasting root. The full sense of being stuck—at the mercy of higher archetypal forces—opens the door to a profound releasing process. As Tarnas describes:

> All the powerful biological energies of self-preservation, aggression, vital anxiety, and orgasmic libido are aroused to the full in the infant by the birth process, and yet are unable to be discharged because of the totally constricting birth canal. In subsequent biographical existence, these energies seek discharge by recreating similar existential feelings of intolerable constriction,

strangulation, explosive frustration, biological danger and violence. But only by reliving this primal event at the archetypal level at which it was first experienced can the energies be released. One is "born again" only by surrendering to the original event's reality in the unconscious, only by, quite literally and in every detail, being born again.[30]

When people's sessions are dominated by *Pluto and BPM III*, the Saturn principle will help to engage the most severe features of the death-rebirth cycle, so the transformational process can finally get emotional traction and begin to complete itself. Journeyers encounter themes of *titanic aggression and struggle* in inner scenes of exploitation, revenge, torture, murder, and dismemberment. As in all BPM III material, they can experientially identify with both the victims and the perpetrators in these sequences, with a focus on the relationship between them. People also face the psychological roots behind many predatory and selfish ideologies in human society. Nature can appear in its most brutal and unforgiving form through the lens of something like a *Hobbesian-Spencerian* archetype—life in the state of nature as "nasty, brutish, and short." The law of the jungle and survival of the fittest can, from this perspective, seem to be the dominant imperatives in human culture.[31]

Archetypal themes that emerge include the hard labors of Sisyphus, Hercules or Samson, implacable judgment, or crucifixion. In its most extreme form, and particularly when Saturn-Pluto transits are combined with Mars, journeyers may experience God or the divine principle as a callous butcher and the world as a slaughterhouse. In retrospect, these experiences are perceived as being cathartic, of getting rid of energies that are already inside people and causing problems in their lives. Journeyers gain repeated insights that it is better to face the material internally than to act it out, or to wait for it to manifest in the outer world. The following holotropic session during a world transit of Saturn opposition Pluto illustrates aggressive elements of BPM III combined with transpersonal themes:

> I saw Hitler and the Nazis as approaching the ultimate personification and embodiment the negative BPM III themes: ruthless aggression, sadistic cruelty, demonic evil, an obsession with purification, and entrancement by fire. In one sequence, I was involved in the bombing of Dresden, from both sides. Then, I became all the bombing victims of the war. There were loud sirens, half-a-second of startled panic, more surprise than anything, then death. At the end of the war, I saw scenes of rape and evisceration.

Sadomasochistic elements during these transits tend to center around themes of sexual violence. People encounter the feelings of both masochists and sadists and see how these compulsions have deep roots in the birth process. Masochists relate primarily to the suffering fetus and equate suffering with the liberation of birth. In contrast, sadists also identify with the oppressing force of the uterine walls, and have a strong desire to turn things around, confine, and humiliate others. The following holotropic session of a male subject was undertaken with Saturn square natal Pluto:

> I identified with a virgin being penetrated for the first time, then someone being raped. It was like having a "psychotic bomb" exploding deep inside me. How could I ever recover from it? . . .
>
> The material then slowly moved toward a sadomasochistic mixture as I wondered: "*God, what fresh hell is this?!* . . ." Later, as the session began to resolve, I was dying and even that felt strangely good.

Demonic or *underworld* themes include the effects of attachment and lack of forgiveness, the dark side of ambition, and feelings of evil control. Journeyers can explore the archetypal heart of darkness, seeing humanity as something like "a teeming horde of infamies."[32] Facing this material makes it possible to change deep patterns of harmful behavior from the past. People feel the benefits of applying steady pressure on a karmic problem for a long period of time.

Scatological sequences center around the inability of law or structure to prevent the natural, cyclical processes of decay and breakdown. Journeyers also face scenes of ecological catastrophe, as in this session undergone with Pluto sextile natal Saturn:

> I explored the emotionality driving human and societal forces that are destroying the earth's environment. Some people spend their entire precious lifespans striving to convert nature's beauty and wholeness into landscapes of waste and degradation. I perceived that this may be because scenes of pollution match the unhealed perinatal material in their psyches. Driven by emotional motivations that go far beyond any economic rationale, ruthless industrialists, on an unconscious level, equate ugliness and despoilment with the memory of delivery which they are trying to complete.

As these sequences emerge and resolve themselves, journeyers begin to see that the severe contractions of labor that force the infant's head through what feels like the worst place in the universe become the very forces that propel it toward one of the greatest experiences in the universe, the ecstasy of rebirth.

Transpersonal Experiences

The nature of sessions in the transpersonal layers during Saturn-Pluto alignments is similar to those in the perinatal realm, but with wider and more encompassing protagonists. The overall feeling tends to be one of intensely compressed or powerfully unleashed cosmic energies. *Collective experiences* center around the unimaginable suffering of human groups through history, such as women burned at the stake during the Inquisition, Jews murdered in the concentration camps, or Africans brutalized in the slave trade. The following holotropic session with Saturn square Pluto, and a Uranus-conjunct-Neptune world transit, illustrates the deeply suffering character of these archetypes:

> During the period of trust crisis with the female sitter, she wisely put on music with a female First Nations singer. The singer's voice was full of suffering and strength, accusing me and all Europeans and demanding that I listen. I didn't want to at first, but as the process deepened I began to identify with countless First Nations mothers, unable to protect their children dying horrible deaths from smallpox. I relived the apocalyptic suffering of entire tribes in seventeenth-century Canada, especially focusing on the Hurons in what is now Quebec.
>
> I was grateful for the opportunity to help heal this buried trauma. Why does the divine perpetrate these kinds of catastrophes? What purpose could it possibly serve? After a long time, I felt that it could be for only one possibility—a sweeter rebirth later. Filled with justified elation and pride, I was participating in the rebirth of First Nations spirituality in our time.

Journeyers can experience collective memories that involve armoring responses to traumatic episodes in human life or karmic burdening over long periods. They may also face sequences that embody the Saturn-Pluto capacity to endure and survive even the most extreme ordeals.

The *consciousness of animals* experienced under Saturn-Pluto transits includes the suffering of deeply sentient beings such as elephants, as in this holotropic session with Saturn square Pluto in the sky:

> I identified with an elephant who was mortally wounded and had just watched his child killed by hunters, in an act of wanton greed and cruelty. His pain was unbearable and unjustified. Feeling his deep sorrow, I cried and cried, opening the grief pathways in my face and heart. I perceived elephants to be sensitive, profound beings who register heavily these tragedies inflicted on them. I also saw that the period in history when *Homo sapiens* has firearms has consciously heralded in for the elephants a terrible transition time when they suffer most deeply, but also the possibility that humans might evolve beyond that cruelty to become a compassionate race who can live in harmony with them.

Journeyers may also encounter the awareness of heavily armored, terminator-type predators such as sharks or crocodiles, as in this holotropic session with Saturn square natal Pluto:

> I was a shark, the clean-up archetype in the universe, and I could see that death is ultimately a release. These predators in nature are actually freeing divine consciousness to realize itself again.

Experiences of inorganic materials or processes can include an identification with heavy metals, barbed wire, or the undying, demonic consciousness of petroleum. The following session undertaken with Saturn square Pluto in the sky spans elements of animal consciousness, a species of octopus—and an inorganic material, the chemical dioxin:

> I experienced the uncanny intelligence and good-natured pride of the octopus in various ways, both through a direct identification with him and in what felt like a species-to-species communion. In one sequence I was inside a great seventeenth-century European hall, possibly in Holland, where octopus was being served and I could feel the pride of the species that they were considered a delicacy of the time.
>
> Then the scene shifted back to the present and I became the consciousness of what I recognized was the chemical dioxin, used to whiten paper for consumers. This was accompanied by emotions of terrible escalating danger. I felt the consciousness of dioxin to be molecularly unstable, which translates into a driving sense of: *Taking! Taking! Taking!!* I could feel the direct threat to the octopus from a multitude of chemicals and its fear for the entire ocean. The sense of fear and threat was terrible, so terrible. . . . I felt torn between facing this planetary horror and trying to have some other kind of experience, but I couldn't bargain or wish away the danger in any way. Having a heart means feeling everything the universe needs us to feel. The oceans are pleading for our help.

During any transit, people may find themselves participating in ingenious science-fiction or alternate-reality narratives resembling the best plots from *Star Trek*. Under Saturn-Pluto transits, these can include encounters with inhuman, machine-like terminator beings whose guiding motivation is to enslave others.

Archetypal and mythological sequences may involve confrontations with the destructive principle in the universe, what Grof refers to as the *Cosmic Shadow*. This can take various cultural forms including the archetypes Ahriman, Hades, Lilith, Moloch, Kali, Satan, Lucifer, Coatlicue, or Loki. Related experiences include doomsday, the Apocalypse, or fate, as in this holotropic session during a world transit of Saturn square Pluto:

> The perinatal elements suddenly took the form of a leering serpent's head. I fell into its mouth and then down, down, down for a surprisingly long way—through the tunnel into the serpent's belly. Inside, there were three demons, working out the negative fates and disasters of all people.

The archetype of the Apocalypse seems to have a special thematic correlation with Saturn-Pluto world transits. People accessing this material perceive that in order to prevent the Apocalypse from actually manifesting in human history, a sufficient number of people may have to experience it internally. Humanity encounters some degree of the Apocalypse archetype

Figure 20. Holotropic Breathwork session of a Russian participant, during a world transit of Saturn square Pluto.

every time these planets are aligned, though in a very real way it has already arrived for so many animal and plant species in our time. Another resonant theme is that of a *Cosmic Blast Furnace*, a crucible capable of evoking and melting through even the darkest fears and most rigid boundaries in the collective psyche.

The somewhat grimmer atmosphere associated with Saturn-Pluto transits may continue in a lesser form in the integration phase. A positive structured experience which includes plenty of warm bonding with family and friends will help to counteract the repressive nature of these archetypes. Because Saturn can at times prolong sessions and delay the resolution of material, journeyers may need to lie down and do some final brief processing later in the evening. Focused bodywork will help to mobilize and discharge any leftover energies. If people stabilize in a difficult place, however, another session should be scheduled as soon as possible.

Anyone who surrenders to the structure-breaking power of these archetypes will come away deeply impressed. The following is from a holotropic session with Pluto sextile the subject's natal Saturn:

Near the end of this long day, I saw angry bones fighting, clacking and smashing against each other until they turned to dust. I could feel deep emotional structures in my psyche being ground up and dissolved. As I let go and surrendered, I experienced feelings of profound peace and sacredness that lasted for the rest of the night and beyond into the following days.

Saturn-Pluto represents the darkest phase of the death-rebirth struggle, the furthest point from ecstatic union with the divine source. It represents the inside of the whale, of the *vagina dentata* of physical incarnation. Yet to undergo these experiences is to become fully human. Although journeyers may sometimes feel a less obvious sense of redemption during Saturn-Pluto transits, in retrospect, they are the great evolutionary watersheds in a human lifetime. Saturn-Pluto is the cosmic terminator of outmoded structures, the necessary tough love of an ultimately playful divine consciousness that endlessly loses and then rediscovers itself through human suffering and rebirth.

Saturn-Uranus

The most radical revolutionary will become a conservative on the day after the revolution.
  Hannah Arendt (Saturn sextile Uranus 4°47')
  In *New Yorker*, 1970

The liberty of the individual must be thus far limited; he must not make himself a nuisance to other people.
  John Stuart Mill (Saturn conjunct Uranus, date only, calc. for noon: 0°30')
  On Liberty, 1859

How glorious it is—and how painful also—to be an exception.
  Alfred de Musset (Saturn semisextile Uranus 1°14'; with Jupiter opposition Uranus) *La Merle Blanc*, 1842

Saturn-Uranus Transits in Everyday Life

Transits of Saturn-Uranus represent the often tense, sometimes flowing interplay—in the psyche and the world—between Saturnian impulses toward structure, stability, and rigidity and Uranian forces impelling freedom, awakening, and change. The *dynamic* transits almost always reflect some degree of confrontation between these archetypal vectors in people's life experience. In the outer world, this may show up as the meeting of various conservative versus liberal, controlling versus rebelling, or preserving versus chaotic aspects of society. A classic manifestation of such polarities is the generation gap, in which older people can embody a Saturnian adherence to cautious, established values and the young, a Promethean attraction to bold experimentation and new freedoms.

The Saturn and Uranus principles each have their shadow side. For every defensive and controlling structure in the world there seems to be an equal amount of erratic or irresponsible acting out. Each extremist point of view reflects, or may even create, its opposite mirror image—which is why it is important for people to discover in their beings the positive side of both archetypes and find a moderate balance between them. When Saturn-Uranus is activated, individuals who tend to identify more with the Uranian side of the polarity may feel a need to prune or edit out certain eccentricities or blind spots in their behavior to grow up in new ways. Those holding more habitually to the Saturnian side of the gestalt may be forced to become more flexible, tolerant, and compassionate. The ongoing confrontations between the Saturnian and Uranian opposites in society put pressure on each of us to reform and move toward the balanced emotional center and a higher integration of both forces.

The meeting of the Saturn and Uranus principles can also manifest primarily in people's inner lives as a struggle between various options or choices, some of which are secure yet stifling, and others exciting but uncertain. People may feel a tension between two opposing parts of themselves, one fear-based and defensive, and the other freedom-seeking and adventurous. In psychological terms, this reflects an interplay between memory complexes rooted in past experiences of pain and loss, and those based on freedom and success. These various memory systems, which Grof calls *COEX systems*, can manifest either simultaneously or in alternation.

It is helpful for people to feel deeply the swings of emotion engaged by the Saturn-Uranus field, holding the tension within their beings until a healing resolution presents itself from within. After a finite amount of struggle these archetypes eventually integrate in the psyche, with Saturn and Uranus bringing out the best sides in each other. At that point, people will tend to embody qualities of careful experimentation, disciplined change, and responsible freedom.

Saturn-Uranus Transits in Deep Self-Exploration

The flowing Saturn-Uranus transits are moderately strong and supportive markers in holotropic states. They help people to see the importance in creating a safe external container within which the breakthrough process can unfold internally. Holotropic states present opportunities to work through trauma-based inner structures in a safe and supported setting—as Grof, born with Saturn square Uranus, writes: "turning the static symptom back into a dynamic flow of experiences."[33]

The *dynamic* transits, although challenging, represent powerful and overall liberating influences in deep work that tend to manifest in several key ways. They occasionally coincide with disruptions around logistics. At times, people may need to make last-minute alterations such as changing locations, readjusting sitters, or switching to a backup music source. These nerve-wracking changes often require a razor's edge of tense patience, but are then just as often followed by surprising resolutions—with things working out as unexpectedly as they earlier seemed to fall apart. Ideally, sitters provide as much external consistency as possible so that journeyers can let go and allow the chaotic Uranian energies to play themselves out on the inside.

At the outset, Saturn-Uranus represents an interplay between the forces of inertia and the forces of liberation in the psyche, a tension between the ego's fearful need to keep control and the soul's yearning for freedom and transcendence. In the end, it is deep suffering that draws many people to inner work, seeing that the consequences of their holding on are greater than their fear of letting go. Once exploration begins, there is another level where the tense polarity between limitation and liberation is recognized as being intrinsic to the material itself. In the biographical layer of the psyche, this can manifest as memories in which people's independent or eccentric impulses were opposed by parents, teachers, and other authority figures or by circumstances beyond their control.

Perinatal Experiences

As uncovering work reaches the perinatal realm, the polarized oppo-sites of Saturn-Uranus tend to surface in distinct ways at each point in the process. When sessions are dominated by the *no-exit material of BPM II,* Saturn's states of anguished oppression tend to be extreme, short, and released quite suddenly—people may alternate between feelings of hope-less suffering and unexpected transcendence, in a quickly changing dialec-tic. A typical pattern is to perceive agonizing problems in one's life or body, rooted on a structural level which seems absolutely unchangeable and unbearable. These problems are then suddenly transcended as people experience energy flows, inner connections, or higher perspectives that introduce a new problem-solving avenue.

Uranus is ultimately a more encompassing archetype. Its resolutions integrate and subsume the problems of Saturn, making breakthroughs inevitable as long as people are willing to keep facing their emerging pro-cess. Uranus awakens and intensifies Saturnian pain and then reveals it as just another archetype, divine *Tragedy*, which has no ultimate relationship with people's actual circumstances. In one of life's most welcome sur-prises, suffering that seems to be deeply personal is revealed to be transper-sonal, i.e., an archetype whose negative effects can be consumed by being faced on an emotional level. Repeated sequences of distress and release eventually convince people that Saturn's pain is just another experience—that, for consciousness, nothing bad is actually happening. They learn to open more fully to their emotions in order to release them.

When heavy Pluto transits are also in effect and sessions are dominated by *BPM III death-rebirth material*, the Saturn-Uranus field tends to manifest as sharply alternating sequences of the baby stuck in the birth canal, followed by its forward thrusts during each uterine contraction, and back again. The following session, undertaken with Saturn trine Uranus and a world transit of Saturn conjunct Uranus, illustrates the effect of these alternating forces in a BPM III session:

> I felt a strong demonic presence and had images of grotesque demons and Nazi-like figures, a violent Nordic-type energy that needs to be stopped somehow. For several hours I experienced an intense self-limiting hatred toward myself, alternating with a kind of driving ambitious energy to *get ahead*! During the constricting phase, I felt that the whole world could plainly see that I was a scheming bad person up to no good, and I felt a desperate need to let go of control and surrender. Then the other part of my psyche would take over—a kind of driving evolutionary force, and I became scared that I was going way too far. I felt powerless to stop either of these processes emerging in alternation.
>
> Suddenly the oscillating struggle within me shifted to biological birth. I had instant knowledge of the influence of higher universal forces on every aspect of my being, from the most inhibited qualities to the most inflated. What I had always thought was a necessary, counterbalancing struggle within me, between parts inside *me*, was revealed to be simply an alternation between introjected pressure from the birth canal, and the driving cosmic energies pushing the baby toward birth. My rational thought processes were, in every last nuance, just the interplay of higher transpersonal forces. I had been tricked into thinking I had an individual ego at all. It was an utter surprise and I felt deeply humbled. The message came, "Leave the details and outcomes up to the universe. Your only job is to consciously experience." I was thrashing around ecstatically with images of the end of a war and the discovery of a medicine that would help both sides in a conflict.

In BPM III sessions, the tensions associated with Saturn-Uranus transits can also manifest as conflicts around urinating, or, occasionally, defecating. These conflicts reflect the urethral and anal tensions during labor that are not resolved until the decompression of the completed birth. The following is from a holotropic session with Saturn trine natal Uranus:

> I had a recurrent fear of peeing, making a mess, and losing the support of my sitters. After a while I began to realize that conflicts around urination might be intrinsic to the birth experience itself, caused by the biological tensions during labor. It seemed possible that the conflicts would automatically resolve as I reached the rebirth state of BPM IV. At several points later on, I was

finally able to pee but a recurring message seemed to be that every minutia of release and satisfaction in human life is cosmically ordained, i.e., we cannot make it happen.

As well as occurring in alternation, the polarized tensions in Saturn-Uranus sessions can manifest simultaneously, in the form of the classic Oedipal or Electra complexes. Here journeyers relive their positive emotions for one parent, while feeling a rivalry with or fear of the other. As the emotions surface, they can project these polarities onto the sitters, feeling strongly bonded with one sitter and wanting no contact with the other. In high-dose psychedelic sessions, where projections often become intense, journeyers may pass through states of excruciating mistrust and even occasionally want one of the sitters to leave the room. As long as the participant remains in the reclining position with his or her eyeshades on, sitters should use their judgment and possibly stand just outside the door, and the crisis will soon pass. An equally strong craving for the same sitter to return, and profound gratitude that he or she did not leave often follows shortly thereafter.

Grof's research demonstrated that the Oedipal and Electra complexes have deep roots in the perinatal layer of the psyche: consisting of an emotional triangle between the infant, the oppressive birth canal, and the nourishing good womb or breast. While the basic formal patterning of these issues often seems to correspond to biographical events, the primary source of the emotions behind them is the life-and-death struggle in the birth canal, the sexual arousal during labor, and the promise of satisfaction at the end of the process.

Journeyers with Saturn-Uranus transits may also work through ambivalent mixtures of love and fear, or love and hate for the *same* parent, for the delivering mother, or for an archetypal complex. The following is from a holotropic session during a world transit of Saturn opposition Uranus:

A sense of the supportive Father was with me through the entire day, except during a brief sequence as I projected *Judging Angry Father* onto one male sitter and *Supportive Father* onto the other. I integrated the possibility, so hard to accept in my childhood, that my dad could have both loved me and been angry with me at the same time. As this was happening, I began to see it as a kind of Good Feelings/Bad Feelings archetypal triangle and surrendered to it all the way.

When sessions include the *rebirth states* of *BPM IV*, the Saturn-Uranus field may take the form of delayed resolutions or mitigating factors around the birth. The range of conditions for the newborn, although incomparably less challenging than the preceding stage of labor, can include painful Saturnian elements such as harsh medical treatment, isolation from the mother, or illness. The following is from a supervised and internalized

LSD session with Uranus conjunct the subject's natal Moon-Saturn conjunction:

> Suddenly the relieved atmosphere of birth was interrupted and I felt intensely vulnerable. I am reborn as one individual, but the larger world is on the verge of destruction. *Danger! Danger!* Saturn's sense of responsibility was imposing itself prematurely on my tender lunar matrix. I realized that I didn't have anything like enough loving care or time to recover from my birth. I felt my desperation at my mother not being there, with each separation a reminder of the perinatal horror.
>
> Then without warning I saw hypodermic needles around me and reacted with instinctive fear. I was born jaundiced and had blood samples taken from my feet every hour for seventy-two hours. The male sitter was doing bodywork on my feet as I wailed uncontrollably . . . "Like a heart with no body to go into." I was paying for the karma of cold medical efficiency, in the flesh.

Saturn's impingement on the peaceful relaxation of BPM IV can also take the form of the *umbilical crisis*. The following is from a holotropic session with Saturn conjunct Uranus in the sky:

> Towards the end, the female sitter did bodywork on my neck and I suddenly went into an experience—which I realized later was the umbilical crisis—of irrevocable separation from my mother. There were strange movements in my neck, like blood flows finding new pathways. I had to survive now, on my own, or die. I related this premature separation to a deep unresolved attachment to my mom—I never let go emotionally. Then I remembered lying in the hospital in a desperately anaesthetized state and a short sequence from my tonsillectomy. My neck become grossly tense and I coughed for a long time.

A final interesting manifestation of the Saturn-Uranus field in the perinatal layer of exploration is rebirth motifs (Uranus) in which the theme of death (Saturn) is explicitly retained. The most common are mandala or quadrangle patterns of happy skeletons or liberated skulls—something like the "grateful dead" archetype. We can see BPM IV elements inflected by Saturn-Uranus in the following holotropic session with Uranus conjunct Saturn, and Saturn opposition Uranus:

> In this relieved atmosphere of birth, I had an image of well-integrated skulls around a beautiful cosmic flame—the flame of Life. Will it ever go out? Maybe. Will consciousness ever end? Matter might end. This whole material universe might be a short passing distraction of the Ultimate Spirit. A sandbox. I am one of the grains of sand. I felt utterly humbled yet connected and surprisingly good with these realizations. I am here for a reason.

Transpersonal Experiences

The range of experience that people encounter in the transpersonal domains under Saturn-Uranus transits is extremely rich and diverse. These might include the lost freedom of various groups through history, transcendent breakthroughs after sustained effort, or the interplay of archetypal opposites.

Identification with the consciousness of animal species can take the form of Oedipal-type encounters in nature, as in this psilocybin mushroom session undertaken with Saturn trine Uranus in the sky:

> The Oedipal feelings deepen into a primal scene. I am a mature gorilla at the moment of killing his father, tearing out the old ape's throat in a surge of aggressive triumph. I feel the primal, revolutionary power of nature! . . . This quickly shifts to the new king's permanent and inescapable fear of his own sons. What a bummer! I realize how important it is for us to confront and transcend the emotional patterns of our animal forebears.

We can see a more resolved form of the same theme in this holotropic experience with Saturn opposition natal Uranus:

> I am an old predator bird dying and being eaten by a younger version of myself. The species archetype stays strong. Animals reach the climax of maturity followed by aging, death, and a new birth. Individual death is no threat to the species. Next, I am an animal in the sea being eaten. It is not actually a problem: death in one place equals birth somewhere else.

Sequences of identification with the *consciousness of inanimate matter*, including man-made objects, may center around the ambivalent effects of modern technology, as in this holotropic session with Uranus conjunct Saturn:

> I identified with the consciousness of a nuclear reactor and felt an ecstatic rush of almost unlimited electric power. Then there was a leak, a malfunction, and I realized I was experiencing the Chernobyl disaster. Deadly, out-of-control energies were breaking loose all over.

Journeyers in holotropic states can also explore various *astronomical phenomena*, such as cosmic energies being sucked into a black hole and then exploding forth in the birth of a new universe somewhere else. In rare instances, they can have a sense of transcending time and causality altogether, in sequences of time travel or time running backwards.

Past life or karmic experiences, during Saturn-Uranus transits, tend to involve the long-term effects and then resolution of karmic problems. Grof observed that past-life experiences seem to evoke healing mechanisms of enormous therapeutic value. Individuals often report that the past conflict they are reliving has direct corollaries with people and situations in their present lives. He observed a number of instances in which people with whom the subject had serious problems in his or her present life, at the exact moment of the therapeutic breakthrough, had a change of heart about the subject or received new information about him or her that changed their feelings in a positive way. The exact, to-the-minute timing of these syn-chronicities precluded any possibility of communication or prior knowl-edge between the individuals involved.[34]

Archetypal and mythological sequences often center on tyrant-rebel polarities such as Zeus and Prometheus, or fathers and kings sacrificing their children, such as Kronos devouring his young or the Massacre of the Innocents from the Bible. Journeyers may also experience an interplay of polarized archetypal principles such as abduction and release or darkness and light, as in this fairytale sequence from a holotropic session with Saturn trine the subject's natal Uranus:

> I realized that I was inside some kind of metaphysical fairytale realm—I was in it, yet all the parts were somehow also a part of my own being. The woods to the right emanated a dark evil force, the realm of a Bad Witch, and a castle to the left, light and happiness, the domain of a good and kind Prince and Princess. I could feel the interplay of these two forces in the fairytale deep within my psyche.

At the deepest layers of discovery, people explore the interplay between *involution* (the Absolute Consciousness' incarnation of parts of itself as the physical universe) and *evolution* (the separate parts beginning to awaken to their true identity). The following report from a supervised and internalized psychedelic session during a world transit of Saturn trine Uranus illustrates how perinatal, death-rebirth elements can open out into the highest transcendent epiphanies:

> I identified with martyrs in the early period of Christianity and, as them, felt overcome with eagerness to be killed, knowing passionately in my being that death is really a birth back into spirit. I couldn't wait: *"Please, kill me!"* I said goodbye to my sitters as my soul went through a black tunnel and died. Moments later I awoke as divine consciousness. I was looking toward human life from this transcendent place. We had made it . . .
>
> I realized that, from the point of view of Absolute Consciousness, there is a completely opposite set of problems. While the psyche's pressing need is to transcend the fear of death and discover its divine identity, for Absolute Con-sciousness, the challenge is how to bury itself into matter in new and interesting ways, in order to entertain itself in the cosmic game.
>
> For the rest of the session I identified more with the part of me that had reached transcendence. Rebirth is not an all-or-nothing project, but an incre-mental one—that resembles ferrying a group of people, one by one, across a river. I had the dual sense of being both emancipated divine awareness, and at the same time, a human being with some remaining material yet to face.

The guiding pattern of holotropic sessions during Saturn-Uranus transits is of dramatically losing an inner battle, then identifying with the winning force and integrating its liberating direction. Journeyers perceive that death in one place leads to birth somewhere else: death equals birth.

The clearly marked, alternating sequences of freedom and constriction that define Saturn-Uranus material can persist until late in the session, and in a lesser form afterward. Because the Saturn archetypal field tends to prolong experiences and delay their full resolution, sitters should, if possible, offer focused bodywork to participants near the end of the day. Sometimes, they may need several rounds of bodywork followed by rest over an extended period.

Saturn-Uranus represents liberation by becoming small and humble. These archetypes require that people learn to accept patiently the universe's timing of their rebirth, but that nothing stays stuck permanently. Through their encounters, they come to realize that, without the Saturnian virtues of persistence and responsibility, the deepest openings would not be possible. In the end, although people often feel thankful when Saturn-Uranus sessions are over, they can be quite impressed by the structure-breaking power of these archetypes. Their basic approach toward the ups and downs of life typically becomes more flowing and trusting:

> In the weeks following the session, I noticed a different attitude toward emotional pain. Instead of avoiding these inevitable moments, I'm beginning to allow, even welcome them when they come up. Saturn's challenges are an integral part of Uranus' liberating force. It seems possible that there is a finite amount of emotional pain in a human lifetime and that the fastest way through it is simply to surrender and experience it fully.

Uranus-Pluto

The rebellion against established structures of all kinds, the intense intellectual adventurousness and restlessness of the era, the radical consciousness transformation, the titanic technological advances in the space age, the general atmosphere of revolution on all fronts—all very much characteristic of the period 1960–72 when Uranus and Pluto were within 15° of exact conjunction.
  Richard Tarnas (Uranus semisquare Pluto 0°35′)
  Prometheus the Awakener, 1995

The history of the world is none other than the progress of the consciousness of freedom.
  G. W. F. Hegel (Uranus trine Pluto, date only, calc. for noon: 0°17′)
  Philosophy of History, 1832

As long as you do not have it, this Die and Become, you are only a dreary guest on the dark earth.
  Johann von Goethe (PL=SU/UR 2°11′)

Uranus-Pluto Transits in Everyday Life

Uranus-Pluto transits correspond to powerful evolutionary and transformative forces in human life, and these are often times of great and sweeping change. The Pluto archetype intensifies Uranus' needs for freedom, innovation, and awakening, while Uranus liberates Pluto's drive toward far-reaching renewal and regeneration. Identifying with the forces of change in the universe, people often feel an electrified impulse to leave the patterns of the past behind, to find untried solutions to old problems and make a better world.

These archetypes support all legitimate efforts toward human progress and reform. In *Cosmos and Psyche*, Tarnas documents the effects in the collective psyche of Uranus-Pluto world transits in the areas of democratic and civil rights breakthroughs, female empowerment, erotic emancipation and liberation of the Dionysian principle, gay rights, ecological awareness, heightened creativity, and scientific quantum leaps. The decades when these planets were aligned through history have corresponded, in a remarkably consistent way, with mass movements and uprisings for freedom and emancipation around the world.

The most recent conjunction of Uranus and Pluto was during the period 1960–1972, which was on many fronts a decade of uniquely profound transformation. We are now experiencing the next major transit in the quadrature cycle—a 90° square—which will be within the operative range of 15° from exact through the year 2020. Widespread alarm about climate change, revolutionary activity in the Middle East, profound feminist uprisings in India, and the sexual revolution in China are just some of the many ways that these archetypes are currently manifesting.

The shadow side of the Uranus-Pluto field emerges when people become carried away in the political arena without adequately owning and taking responsibility for their own shadow qualities. These archetypes can have a wildly manic and fanatical side when they are acted out in the social sphere, inexorably fueling repressive backlashes. However, when the same tumultuous energies are faced internally, they lead to healing expansions of consciousness and perspective that benefit everyone. Emotional healing of any kind puts people in a better position to make a real and lasting contribution in the outer world.

Uranus-Pluto Transits in Deep Self-Exploration

All personal and world transits of Uranus-Pluto offer tremendous opportunities for inner work and are probably the most supportive of all influences for deep self-exploration followed by powerful breakthroughs. These archetypes have an irresistible and exciting quality, putting the releasing process into overdrive and giving emotional discovery a dynamically supercharged feeling. People often become inspired by a kind of sacred inner bonfire that seems to have the potential to burn away their limitations, and make the universe new.

Pluto presses up people's buried inner material, while Uranus works to pull their awareness out the other side into transcendence. These archetypes support profound liberations of repressed vital energies and the lightning strikes of awakening that unite consciousness with its primal divine source. The entire period of Grof's holotropic research in the 1960s and early 1970s, as well as his cofounding of the field of transpersonal psychology with Abraham Maslow and Anthony Sutich in 1968, coincided with the Uranus-Pluto conjunction of 1960–1972. And with another potent alignment in effect now though the 2010s, we are likely to see a dramatic upsurge in the frequency and intensity of holotropic experiences in the wider culture.

Perinatal Experiences

The Uranus-Pluto archetypal field has a general awakening effect, helping people to face their inner material at every stage in the transformational journey. Tarnas found that these archetypes also specifically mediate access to sequences of Grof's BPM III (the Death-Rebirth Struggle) and BPM IV (Rebirth).

In sessions when *Pluto and BPM III* predominate, the Uranus archetypal field will help to liberate the full spectrum of BPM III themes into awareness, dramatically engaging, sustaining, and then suddenly resolving the material. Sequences of *aggressive struggle* may have a titanically unleashed quality. Subjects release enormous amounts of repressed aggression accompanied by images of fiery volcanic eruptions and storms, active attacks in wars and revolutions, mythological battle scenes, or fanatical crowds running amok.

The following is from a supervised and internalized psychedelic session undertaken with Pluto trine natal Uranus, and Jupiter trine Pluto in the sky:

I felt myself becoming a giant, destructive, Shiva-like deity. What was trying to emerge felt like some kind of mythological battle scene portraying the extremes of universal aggression, like the "Clash of the Titans" from Greek mythology, yet I was afraid of its colossal, out-of-control quality. At various points I had feelings of being an absolute loser and failure. Eventually, the material broke through and I identified with a kind of Uranian-Plutonic, perinatal energy that was beyond human control. It/I would have any experience it wanted: I would destroy what I wanted, suffocate when I wanted to, and die when I wanted to. I felt that dying when we want to is the ultimate act of freedom and autonomy—but at the same time, it was clear that this was about ego death rather than biological death.

In the climax of the day, I felt energies from the transpersonal realms pouring up into my body and through my head and ego. I was unable to fully relate to what was happening. There was an extreme experience but "I" wasn't having it—I didn't even exist in those moments. There was no personal reference point for what was taking place. For my ego, it was unimaginable, with only losing and letting go of control. Finally, I saw lava rushing up through the earth and erupting out of a volcano. As my awareness exploded open, I had images of my old friend the octopus from a previous session with his head exploding in transcendent ecstasy. By the end of the day I felt clear, alive, and energized.

This experience changed my relationship with my psyche and the inner divine. I have been able to reach positive transpersonal states in every session, great or small, that I have undertaken since that day.

Sadomasochistic elements under Uranus-Pluto transits also share this unbridled quality. Journeyers can feel strong sexual arousal combined with aggressive, pyrocathartic and other themes, reaching orgiastic levels of intensity. These inner scenes typically include sexual experiences from all possible sides and roles. As the process culminates, the content gradually moves from the physical and biological realms to the spiritual and cosmic. The following is from a psychedelic session with Pluto trine natal Uranus, and Pluto sextile natal Saturn:

> The perinatal experiences took on a cosmic scope as evolutionary energies began to break through all across time and space. I was f***ing the planet Saturn, transcending every barrier of perception and awareness.

Underworld sequences center on the release of demonic patterns of being. People realize that these demonic archetypes, or wrathful deities, were at some point created out of divine consciousness itself—pressed into negative forms during the act of material incarnation—and that this cosmic energy is actually happy to be freed and reunited with the divine source. Uranus-Pluto *scatological themes* include an arousal and then transcendence of feelings of disgust, as conflicts about scatological materials are resolved—for example, in a direct identification with the consciousness of bacteria that happily thrive in scatological conditions. An engaged Uranus-Pluto is also a dramatic influence for healing issues around severe toilet training.

Given the fiery nature of both Uranus and Pluto, it is understandable that these archetypes have a special connection with *pyrocatharsis* or purifying fire. In holotropic states, journeyers can have images of vast conflagrations and explosions, blasting rockets, or fire in a more symbolic form and perceive that it has a magical purifying effect on their souls.

They may also identify with the legendary bird, the Phoenix, who burst into flames, died, and was then reborn from its own ashes.

At the same time, *the effect of the archetypal Pluto on Uranus* (Pluto→Uranus) is to drive Uranus' rebirth-BPM IV impulses toward total manifestation, pushing journeyers "down and through" whatever material is preventing them from full-blown transcendence out the other side. With a deep and systematic approach, all personal and world transits of Uranus-Pluto are a powerful asset for resolution of the entire death-rebirth cycle. Spiritual evolution is often described as a widening or ascending spiral, with each cycle becoming more pronounced in extremes of inner experience, until people reach beyond the dualities of separate identity altogether and attain transpersonal release.

Grof observed that as individuals approach these awakenings, their suffering can begin to reach cosmic dimensions. At the same time, with the presence of the divine and the taste of rebirth coming closer and closer, pain and pleasure fuse and become indistinguishable. Journeyers

Figure 21. Holotropic Breathwork session. "Endgame" John Ablett (Uranus opposition natal Pluto, Pluto square Pluto, and Pluto conjunct Moon). "In a dangerous 'stalemate,' I am choking myself with the umbilical cord, overwhelmed with distress at the death of my twin brother in the womb. My mother dissociates from herself in order to save me, to tell me to hold on, and I emerge, feet first."

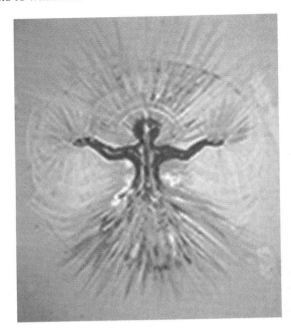

Figure 22. "Energy" An experience of dramatic energetic opening in a Holotropic Breathwork session of a Russian participant, during a world transit of Uranus square Pluto.

experience a merging of all opposites and polarities (pain and pleasure, light and dark, etc.) in an undifferentiated frenzy of driving emotions, which Grof refers to as *Dionysian* or *volcanic* ecstasy. They can also feel powerful currents of cosmic energy flowing through their systems, clearing away the outmoded structures of their body and character armor. Uranus-Pluto represents liberation by facing the archetype *purgatory*, the sense of a finite amount of suffering that has a clear goal and endpoint. Pluto's shattering encounter with death leads to a sudden release from its unconscious hold over people's everyday lives and dramatic healing on many levels.

Finally, *rebirth sequences* tend to be multilayered, with obstetric elements often overlaid with mythological, karmic, and collective themes. The following is from a holotropic session with Pluto square the subject's natal Uranus:

> I saw the dead in an ancient catacombs rise up in a solemn, ecstatic torch procession. I felt spiritually purged and reborn. It was like waking up from a lifetime of slumber, emerging from the birth canal, and coming out the other side of the patriarchal era, all combined.

Transpersonal Experiences

In the transpersonal realms, people may encounter deities representing death and rebirth such as Christ, Osiris, Dionysus, or Persephone—often accompanying perinatal material, as we have seen. Related figures include Inanna, Attis, Mithra, Odin, and Quetzalcoatl. Dionysus was considered the "Zeus of women" and many of the Dionysian rituals and practices around the Mediterranean almost certainly used psychedelic mushrooms (*Amanita muscaria*) and ergot (*Claviceps purpurea*), as depicted in widespread pottery decorations and poetic verses of the period.[35] Many scholars believe that the celebrated *soma* of the ancient Vedic hymns, which had a profound influence on the evolution of Indian as well as Persian culture and spirituality, also refers to the *Amanita muscaria* mushrooms which grow in the Himalayan Mountains.[36]

The fusion of opposites that occurs in the final stage of the perinatal unfolding can also extend into transpersonal layers. The following fairytale sequence from a series of internalized marijuana sessions, of a graduate student, was undertaken with Pluto trine natal Uranus:

> For several years, in session after session, I experienced energies of light and dark twisting in toward each other. The light and dark energy strands confronted each other, integrated, and then rotated out again in a very specific pattern. I realized that this process somehow involved the braided handle of *Little Red Riding Hood*'s basket. As I surrendered to these braiding and twisting sequences, I realized that I was retracing the steps that the Absolute Consciousness takes in order to weave—out of its own substance—strands of archetypal light and dark in order to create the physical universe.
>
> Eventually, the process moved to the end of the basket's handle, where the encounters of light and dark were transcended. I perceived that the basket of treats that Little Red Riding Hood is taking to her Grandmother represents the fully realized experiences of human incarnation—"the full basket" of a lifetime of consciously faced emotional experience. When a person has sufficiently integrated the polarized light and dark energies, they are granted access to the realm of the archetypes—where all energies are actually working together and all contradictions resolvable. I saw that the woodcutter represents the forces of rebirth (the *Hero*) that liberates the feminine soul symbolized by Grandmother (the *Crone*) from the bondage of the Big Bad Wolf (the *Shadow*).
>
> The completion of this fairytale sequence corresponded with many transpersonal experiences in my life, including several identifications with Absolute Consciousness and the Macrocosmic Void.

Perinatal experiences are the bottleneck of powerful evolutionary forces and often open out into profound *meta-historical* themes. Journeyers may experience various archetypal trajectories in human history as being drawn, after a long period of struggle, toward some higher omega point in our species' awakening, the long-awaited, completed birth of humanity.

Figure 23. Shamanic experience of a Ukranian participant in a Holotropic Breathwork workshop, during a world transit of Uranus square Pluto.

Neptune-Pluto

The unconscious is not just evil by nature, it is also the source of the highest good: not only dark but also light, not only bestial, semihuman, and demonic but superhuman, spiritual, and, in the classical sense of the word, "divine."
C. G. Jung (MO=NE/PL 2°11′) *The Practice of Psychotherapy*, 1953

We shall not cease from exploration
And the end of all our exploring
Will be to arrive where we started
And know the place for the first time.
T. S. Eliot (Neptune conjunct Pluto 3°42′) "Little Gidding,"
Four Quartets, 1942

God is a verb.
Buckminster Fuller (Neptune conjunct Pluto 4°39′)
No More Secondhand God, 1963

Neptune-Pluto Transits in Everyday Life

Neptune-Pluto transits combine the powerful drive toward transformation associated with Pluto, with the yearning for cosmic unity associated with Neptune. These archetypes can have a strange and uncanny quality, yet they are some of the most deeply profound and renewing influences that human beings can experience. The Neptune field acting on

Pluto (Neptune→Pluto) opens a higher perspective on Pluto's underworld material, a sacred and soulful context within which people can face their shadow energies through flows of their inner life and imagination. Painting, sculpting, or journaling during these periods can be helpful ways to allow unconscious material to surface and look at it objectively.

People often have more intense dreams. As Hillman writes in his classics *The Dream and the Underworld* and *Re-Visioning Psychology*, the images in dreams are not messages about our external lives which can be decoded in a literal, one-to-one way. They are primarily portraits of the psyche itself, attempts to draw attention down into the archetypal realm beyond the boundaries of individual awareness. According to Hillman, "dreams tell us where we are, not what to do," suggesting to our egos that they are not the center of awareness, but just another image in a multivalent inner universe.[37]

Many dreams are also a reminder of our mortality and an invitation into the world of soul that transcends death. Hillman uses the term "soul-making" to describe the process of feeling, watching, and reworking the imagery in our dreams. For him, it is essential to recognize a different logic when interacting with the psyche—to "see through" the usual literal and naturalistic interpretations of dreams to the archetypal forms behind them. During Neptune-Pluto transits, this process can be unusually effective.

An exercise Hillman recommends is to start with an image in the psyche and then allow it to move in whatever direction it wants to move, without censoring or control, just letting the imaginal movie follow its own direction. He calls this process "pathologizing the myth onward."[38] Though Hillman does not use these terms, people's inner cartoon-play during all Pluto transits often moves in the direction of disowned perinatal elements, especially toward aggressive, sadomasochistic, demonic, scatological, and pyrocathartic themes, which comprise the layer of the psyche Grof terms BPM III. Hillman's active-imagination exercises are thus helpful practice for full surrender into holotropic states.

The effect of the archetypal Pluto on Neptune (Pluto→Neptune) is to forcefully work to clear out any disturbances that impede Neptune's oceanic states of being. If people have unresolved toxic-womb material, the need for this releasing process can announce itself with drastic urges to purify the body, debilitating psychosomatic symptoms, or other strange obsessions. People may become absolutely convinced that their feelings of impurity have an organic basis. Once the toxic-womb material is faced, however, the symptoms disappear.

Learning to recognize the essential harmony between Pluto's obsessive emotional pressure and Neptune's serene mystical union—the instinctual unconscious and the spiritual superconscious—is one of the most important challenges of a human lifetime.

Neptune-Pluto Transits in Deep Self-Exploration

Neptune-Pluto transits are some of the most desirable of all influences for deep self-exploration and, as always, it is recommended that people have a proper support system in place before embarking on their experiences. The archetypal Pluto compels the ascent into Neptune's mystical realms with increased intensity and resolve. At the same time, Neptune de-literalizes people's approach to their darker Plutonic material so that it can be faced as an interesting flow of dreamlike images and vignettes. These archetypes support an easy transition between forms, helping people to feel comfortable surrendering to some of the more strange or repugnant states of being.

One of the themes that journeyers encounter, as we saw, is an integration of the lower Plutonic and higher Neptunian natures in their psyches—the ape and the angel, sinner and saint, pathology and mysticism. People come to realize that facing and taking responsibility for their own shadow terrains opens channels to a more profound spirituality, widening the pathway to the numinous.

Perinatal Experiences

As exploration reaches the perinatal realm, Tarnas found that an engaged Neptune-Pluto field may impel experiences of both Pluto's death-rebirth struggle (BPM III) and Neptune's amniotic paradise (BPM I)—with the other archetype contributing its unique thematic signature. When sessions are dominated by *Pluto and BPM III*, Neptune's passive, yielding nature helps people surrender to Pluto's driving energies, opening a context of higher meaning and soulful inner trust to the healing quest. Individuals are able to consume their material more quickly, by letting the dark feelings completely surround their experiential field.

Aggressive sequences can have a strange or surreal quality, accompanied by strong imagery. Sometimes a period of obsessive feelings in people's lives turns out to have deep roots in BPM III. Full surrender to these forces in internalized sessions can lead to a miraculous release of the symptoms—as Pluto's obsessions fizzle, steam and cool in the sweet waters of the Neptunian divine. *Sexual material* may also include an interplay of primal Plutonic elements and Neptunian mystical union. Journeyers in holotropic states can explore the full range of human sexual manifestations, from sadomasochistic and profane, to soothing, sacred, and oceanic. Ultimately, these archetypes support the release of compulsive forms of arousal based on suffocation, while also increasing the possibility for a deeper spiritual merging after the orgasm.

Similarly, *demonic* or *underworld material* can be faced more smoothly and acceptingly, as a flow of graphic images. People recognize that in order to access states of universal redemption, they have to be willing to surrender to states of universal purgatory. In the inner unfolding, nothing is left out—we cannot repress the shadow side of human nature without also repressing our divine nature. *Scatological sequences* may also have a strangely flowing or mystical quality, as journeyers feel the trauma-based elements of their egos breaking down and decaying into spirit. Imagery of rotting, ruins, and wasting away can deepen into a sense of ultimate ego disposal, as in this session with Pluto conjunct Neptune, and Neptune trine Pluto:

> Near the end of the day, I had an image of utter biological liquidation in some kind of *archetypal shower room*. In a precursor to ego death, I could feel my individuality being completely wiped away. When the last streams of blood are washed down the cosmic drain, nothing remains of the separate self. This session resolved with one of the most blessed and welcome feelings of relief I have ever experienced.

And finally, emerging experiences of loss of reference, corruption, or decrepitude can resolve in healing *pyrocathartic sequences*. Under these transits, Pluto's purifying fire tends to have an exotic and surreal

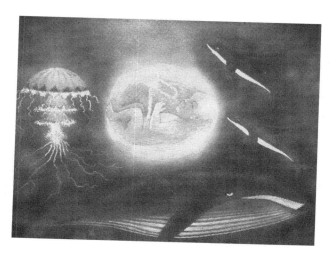

Figure 24. "The Oceanic Womb" Stanislav Grof (Neptune trine natal Pluto). An experience of melted, oceanic ecstasy in a psychedelic session dominated by the first perinatal matrix (BPM I).

Figure 25. "The Amniotic Universe" Stanislav Grof (Neptune trine natal Pluto). Identification with the fetus in a state of blissful union with the entire cosmos.

Neptunian quality, in the form of oriental fire deities or healing fire mandalas. The following is from the resolution phase of a holotropic session, with Pluto sextile the subject's natal Neptune:

> While soaking at the pool later, I returned to the incident where I was impatient with someone in my life and mulled on it painfully for a long, long time. Suddenly, I had an image of purifying fire superimposed on a figure of Buddha. The fire-Buddha was blessedly forgiving me and burning away the agonizing karma.

With all these Plutonic themes, journeyers' sense of the ultimate sacredness underlying the process makes Neptune-Pluto one of the most profound influences for deep inner work.

When sessions center on *Neptune and BPM I*, Pluto adds a powerful impetus for working through toxic-womb material, as we have seen. Nourishing physical contact with trusted sitters can help to replace the rejecting or toxic memories with feelings of connection and belonging. Beyond a certain depth of discovery, something overwhelmingly good and positive takes over, as journeyers fall into the ultimate safety net of Absolute Consciousness.

The following is from an internalized LSD session of a male student with Pluto conjunct natal Neptune:

> For about a month, I had developed an irrational and obsessive fear of feminists at the university I was attending. For some reason, I had a feeling that I

was about to be targeted or punished somehow. These unwarranted emotions emerged out of the blue and then dominated my mind.

The following Saturday, my session began like many others, with vignettes of images from my recent life. Suddenly, a cosmic bell sounded that seemed to announce "bad karma" all around me, then deepened into a sense of guilt, scandal, and ruin. I saw scenes of violent neighbors and feminist lynch mobs coming to get me. It was totally overwhelming. I gradually realized that I was reliving my experience as a fetus in the womb—for the first time in a session—and that the hostile female energy and feelings of bad karma were in the fetal liquid around me. My mother did not want to be pregnant or have children. She suffered from terrible morning sickness and had a strong desire to abort me through the pregnancy. The next Monday, back in class, I noticed that my projections on feminists had completely disappeared.

Finally, Tarnas notes that Neptune-Pluto transits can evoke memories around the end of Neptune's amniotic unity, in which the labor contractions are portrayed in an intense Plutonic way as descent into a giant whirlpool or maelstrom, or of being swallowed by a whale or sea monster. Full surrender to these experiences releases their anxiety-producing effects in people's everyday lives.

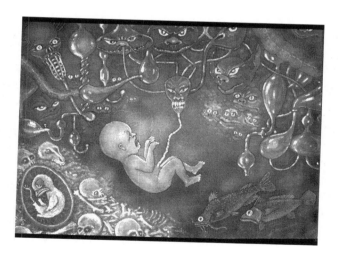

Figure 26. Neptune trine natal Pluto. A "toxic womb" experience in a high-dose psychedelic session. The aggressive immunological forces create a hostile environment which is portrayed as a kind of diabolical laboratory run by insidious demons. Grof found that negative intrauterine experiences of this kind are among important sources of paranoia.

Transpersonal Experiences

As exploration reaches the transpersonal realms, journeyers with Neptune-Pluto transits have an increased potential of entering seamlessly into the consciousness of other people, other life forms, and other modes of being. In holotropic states, they can experience the miracle of separate, individual awareness taking the "Moebius-like leap" into transpersonal awareness. They also discover that being able to identify with other people or groups of people can open up new problem-solving potential and sources of compassion.

Experiences of *animal consciousness* may include fantastic successions of various animals or many at once, such as numerous birds in a dynamic jungle choir. The sounds that people emit can be highly authentic. They may also explore the consciousness of seemingly strange or repellent life forms such as insects. The following is from a holotropic session with Pluto conjunct natal Neptune, and Neptune trine natal Pluto:

> I flashed on the Kafka story about the cockroach. In my altered and fluidly changing state, it seemed conceivable that the universe could create any experience it wanted. If I woke up as a cockroach, I would have no more recourse than when I wake up now as a human being. Letting go means ultimately trusting whatever the universe makes you.

Experiences of *other dimensions or universes* can include shadow elements from different layers of reality protruding into people's awareness, as in this session undergone with Pluto conjunct natal Neptune, and Neptune trine Pluto:

> After some aggressive discharges, out of the blue I experienced a visitation from some kind of weird astral expedition from another dimension. They had distinctly harsh, demonic, and otherworldly features. I don't know why these energy beings suddenly appeared through my psyche into our universe, but I know they didn't hurt me, and I had a sense that my consciousness softened after that short episode.

At the *archetypal level*, people can explore the interplay of nature and divinity, Dionysus and Apollo, or *lingam* and *yoni*. They may confront the blend of savage destructiveness and mystical union contained in a single figure such as Dionysus, Kali, or Shiva. They may also identify with the *ouroboros* or "World Serpent." In what can be seen as the endless self-cannibalism of the world, Mother Nature eternally swallows pieces of herself—as egos, bodies, and entire cultures rise out of, exist for a while, and then dissolve back into the eternal Supracosmic Void.

Journeyers perceive that, although on the level of material forms there is no permanent peace, they can also directly access higher layers of reality where there is only eternal serenity within that ceaseless change. The following supervised and internalized LSD session was undertaken with Pluto conjunct natal Neptune, and a Saturn-conjunct-Uranus world transit:

> Although in my everyday life I would say I support the basic philosophy of the United Nations, for a while in this session, all I could see were images of angry citizens screaming at the U.N. For the rest of the day and for days afterward I had repeated images of the U.N. logo, associated with feelings of anxiety and tension. This seemed to be suggesting in my psyche that the image of perfect peace is, in some ways, a static ideal that neglects human emotional and shadow energies. I saw that the United Nations is a general outgrowth of the faith in reason and rationalism that defined the Enlightenment, and perhaps in the future as the emerging world view reintegrates deep self-exploration into human civilization that a genuine world peace might be more possible.
>
> Gradually the image changed to that of a yin-yang symbol, accompanied by feelings of profound relief. I felt that true peace can only take place when we allow all the diverse energies in our psyches and the collective psyche to safely express themselves and find their own natural equilibrium—symbolized by the eternal balancing of yin and yang.

At these layers of discovery, people explore the relationship between the One and the many—the timeless serenity of the Supracosmic Void within the ceaseless change of the material universes, the sum total of which is sometimes referred to as Absolute Consciousness. This realization is at the heart of the honored Sanskrit chant, *om mani padme hūm:* "The jewel of the Supracosmic Void is inside the lotus of Absolute Consciousness."[39] As the psyche opens to the primal, cyclical and impermanent energies associated with Pluto, it clears a pathway to the eternal and unchanging Divine Mind, symbolized by Neptune. When the shadow is faced emotionally, spiritual ecstasy follows close behind.

Uranus-Neptune

Uranus-Neptune's meaning implies . . . a radical shift or revolution of consciousness, involving the element of transcendence, compared to Uranus-Pluto's greater emphasis, as in the 1960's, on revolution with a more political and elemental component.
  Richard Tarnas (NE=VE/UR 0°03′) *Prometheus the Awakener,* original unpublished version, 1980

As if our birth had at first sundered things, and we had been thrust up through into nature like a wedge, and not till the wound heals and the scar disappears, do we begin to discover where we are, and that nature is one and continuous everywhere.

> Henry David Thoreau (Uranus conjunct Neptune, date only, calc. for noon: 9°49′) *A Week on the Concord and Merrimack Rivers*, 1849

Uranus-Neptune Transits in Everyday Life

Transits of Uranus-Neptune are some of the most magically uplifting and awakening spiritual influences that human beings may access. The archetypes they represent are deeply holotropic, actively working to free awareness beyond the boundaries of the ego and out into connections with higher transpersonal realms. Even those who usually identify with the rational mind and the everyday world can feel hidden doors opening in their beings, alluring them on toward unseen, exotic new adventures and perspectives. These archetypes also unleash people's imaginations, offering the inspiration and subject material for creative work.

People's needs for stimulation may draw them to the mass media, channel surfing, or the internet, portals where they can suspend disbelief and submerge their minds in rapidly shifting fantasy landscapes and alternative realities. Reflecting a hunger for mystical union, some people may also be more prone to substance abuse. Addicts and alcoholics given an opportunity to enter holotropic states will have easier access to the genuine oceanic experiences for which their psyches yearn. On occasion, individuals who are holding on too tightly to the rational, left-brain aspects of awareness may experience these transits as disorienting or confusing, but sooner or later the impulse to let go tends to prevail.

In *Cosmos and Psyche*, Tarnas explores the correlations between Uranus-Neptune *world transits* and events in world history and culture. The resonant themes that he discovered include epochal shifts of cultural perception, utopian social visions, imaginative genius and the flowering of Romanticism, the emergence of new religions, cosmic epiphanies, and revelations of the numinous.[40]

Uranus-Neptune represents liberation from both directions: a strenuous *awakening forward* out of the divine ground of being, and, at the same time, an ecstatic *merging back* into the divine ground of being—the now individuated archetypal hero or heroine returning home. As Tarnas describes the evolutionary arc of the ego of Western civilization, the intellectual and morally autonomous self can now reconnect with the universal matrix that gave birth to it, but on a higher and more conscious level.

Uranus-Neptune Transits in Deep Self-Exploration

The Uranus-Neptune complex is probably the most supportive of all archetypal influences for far-ranging journeys into the higher transpersonal realms, and the decades when these planets align often see widespread spiritual and religious awakenings across world culture. Tarnas notes that while Uranus-*Pluto* alignments symbolize surges of emancipatory forces involving the intense Dionysian, confrontational, and erotic aspects of human nature, associated with Pluto, the Uranus-*Neptune* field seems to offer breakthroughs directly into the serene Apollonian, mystical, and spiritual realms related to Neptune. Some journeyers can largely bypass the more graphic biological and emotional elements of the perinatal matrices altogether for the duration of a Uranus-Neptune transiting cycle.[41]

Responding to these magical influences, greater numbers of people tend to be enthusiastic for adventures in consciousness. The activated Uranus-Neptune field has a general opening effect, helping journeyers to work through material represented by their other transits, as well as specifically drawing their awareness toward transcendence. These archetypes support both a liberation of repressed vital energies and numinous awakenings which have a meta-healing value. Uranus offers quantum leaps to new levels of experience, while Neptune mediates entry to blessed oceanic states.

At times, these archetypes can grant access to the formal pattern and meaning of transpersonal experiences, but without their full emotional depth. The spiritual terrains they open up are authentic—journeyers do transcend the surface of the psyche and access previously unknown inner regions. However, unless powerful Pluto transits are also operating, Uranus-Neptune alignments may, in retrospect, have a milder, somewhat bloodless quality. Yet their awakening glimpses do impart in people a deep faith in their inner healer, helping them to trust and surrender to Plutonic material later on as the process cycles back in to the perinatal matrices. Uranus-Neptune is like a glowing beacon that shines through the fog in a straight line to the Absolute, a pivot of light in the experiential field around which the clearing process can then broaden and expand later.

Although the positive resolutions associated with these archetypes can help to foster a deeper sense of optimism and safety, it is still recommended under all transits to have trusted sitters on hand, in order to maximize the benefits and minimize the risks of psychedelic work.

Perinatal Experiences

As exploration reaches the perinatal layer, Tarnas observed that journeyers will have increased access to both the BPM IV-rebirth experiences associated with Uranus and the BPM I-amniotic unity states associated with Neptune. As noted, these archetypes offer release from several directions. They can help journeyers who are working through Saturn's "no exit" material to melt back into the comforting reunion with Neptune's amniotic paradise. The closest avenue of transcendence for people influenced by BPM II is to return to the blissful union of the womb, from the hellish suffering of BPM II to the serene states of BPM I. On the other hand, those confronting Pluto's driving death-rebirth sequences are granted access to the breakthrough openings of Uranus' rebirth matrix. For them, the closest avenue of transcendence, or way out, is to complete the process and reach states of rebirth—passing from the volcanic catharsis of BPM III to the profound relaxation and satisfaction of BPM IV. Uranus-Neptune transits help journeyers to reach transcendence on either end of the perinatal sequence.

Uranus' rebirth experiences, graced by the archetypal Neptune, will have an especially magical, mythic, and numinous quality. The following is from a psychedelic session undertaken with Uranus trine natal Neptune:

> Listening to Handel's *Messiah* on the headphones, I had the first true understanding of what the Christ is . . . that part of our psyches and the divine that wells up inside to save us from the hell of our emotional pain. I wept and laughed alternately, in a state of spiritual exaltation.

As journeyers rise above the realm of material suffering, they can identify with the ecstasy of martyrs or people who finally die after a long period of pain or torture. The following is from an internalized LSD session during the Jupiter-Uranus-Neptune conjunction of 1996–1997:

> I am a martyr in the Colosseum, seeing my body as just a lovely and seductive morsel calling deliciously out to the lions: *"Come and get it . . ."* I gratefully and ecstatically detach from my feminine, corporeal side as I return home to God.
>
> Later in the session, I was a proud and good king now reduced to a haggard, castoff thing, dying alone in an iron cage hanging from the castle walls. I am relieved that I am about to die, leave the world behind, and return to the source. "Go ahead, take them on! The cares and relationships of this world are too much responsibility—you have them!" As I die, I embrace the Crone in blessed, relieved ecstasy.

In the perinatal unfolding, there is often a threshold moment in sessions when people reach transcendence and then, for the rest of the session, will identify more with divine consciousness than with their separate ego. These moments are accompanied by tremendous feelings of relief and freedom from threat. The following is from a holotropic session with Neptune opposition natal Uranus:

> After this blessed point, I felt the presence of the divine all around and inside me—*as* me—for the rest of the session. All subsequent problems were just clearing out disturbances within the eternal cosmic field.

During perinatal experiences, people may also compassionately identify with their mothers during labor and reach states of loving forgiveness and willingness to be forgiven.

In scenes of *amniotic unity*, the Uranus archetype adds elements of sudden, unexpected awakening into Neptune's oceanic realms. Journeyers can heal toxic-womb memories as they connect with transpersonal themes that share, with the womb, the character of nourishing or cleansing flows of moisture. The following is from an internalized marijuana session with Neptune opposition natal Uranus, and Jupiter trine natal Moon:

> I could feel the replenishing annual floods of the Nile Delta, superimposed over the flow of blood entering my umbilical cord through my mother's uterine artery. This resulted in a dramatic liberation of my toxic-womb feelings. My awareness suddenly moved from an identification with myself as a fetus, up through my mother's blood vessels and into the Feminine transpersonal realms where I have continued to access some degree of oceanic states in every session great or small over many years.

Experiences of rebirth and reconnection with BPM I and nourishing transpersonal states can permanently transform people's awareness and lead to higher functioning in everyday life.

As the Uranus-Neptune field mediates awakenings from the world of biological suffering and out into the universal realms, journeyers can project magical healing qualities onto their sitters. The following holotropic experience was undertaken with Uranus square natal Neptune:

> Freed from projection, I felt myself being carried up into the transpersonal by my sitters. I also knew that I was being delivered by the Great Mother Goddess, blessedly giving birth to a new soul within me.

These alignments can also manifest as blends of the electrifying *Promethean* ecstasy associated with Uranus and the soothing *Apollonian* ecstasy related to Neptune.

Transpersonal Experiences

As exploration continues, people can take far-ranging journeys into the cosmos at large, identifying with the awareness of the entire universe or any subset within that whole. In the endless play of divine forgetting and remembering, Uranus-Neptune represents that part of the cycle where the fountain of spiritual realization pours itself back into the world after a period of drought and despair, the miracle of salvation that follows the dark night of the soul.

Related archetypal themes include the ascension, the magic flight, the world redeemer, and the savior-hero. The sense of a new revelation or

Figure 27. "Kundalini Mother" Katia Soliani (during a world transit of Uranus conjunct Neptune). An experience of profound love for all beings in a session of Holotropic Breathwork.

dispensation can take the form of exceptionally profound archetypal elements, as in this internalized LSD session of a graduate student during the exalted Jupiter-Uranus-Neptune conjunction of 1996–1997:

> I perceived humanity to be a mass of desperate beings dying of thirst, their faces turned expectantly skyward. Above them, the water from a giant reservoir was beginning to flow over some kind of sluice gate toward the mouths below, as the Great Mother Goddess opened the gate. It was that moment when, after five-thousand years of voluntarily receding from the forefront of human awareness, the Mother archetype is now in a position to return and give us what we so deeply need.
>
> I saw that we have been inside the most difficult part of the goddess archetype all along, something like the birth canal of history—manifesting as five thousand years of patriarchal societal structures and unending conflict. In order to have a rebirth there has to have been a loss . . . that incredible moment when the tide shifts and we realize that she was always there, running the whole show. I experienced this returning Feminine archetype as omnipotent,

good and true. It gave me a trust in the higher intentions of history I will never forget.

Journeyers also explore the *holographic* nature of reality, the profound way that every part of the universe contains, in the realm of consciousness, access to the whole. They also have direct experiences of what might be called the emerging *Global Mind*, the sum total of awakening beings on planet Earth who are both appreciative and thankful for the resources they consume, while always being conscious of the effects of those actions on the shared biosphere.

The following series of internalized marijuana sessions, undertaken with Neptune opposition Uranus, and Pluto trine Uranus, suggests the potential for far-ranging exploration of these alignments:

For about three years I felt a compelling need to explore my psyche more deeply. Once a week, late in the evening, I would take two or three inhalations in a soundproof space, turn on some music, lie back and just allow whatever was inside to come up. I used to jokingly refer to this process as "pot-otropic." Each session lasted about four hours and represented a bite-size but substantial piece of inner work.

For the first year, about fifty sessions, I experienced many sequences of vocalizing and discharge of energy through my legs, mainly the release of what felt like perinatal anxiety and compressed vital energies. Then one evening, which at the outset resembled many others, the process suddenly and unexpectedly deepened in a new way. With my attention far out on a stormy mythological ocean, I identified with a ship sinking, something like an *archetypal shipwreck,* and as I went under, merged with the consciousness of the ocean.

This event opened my experiential field in a dramatic way. Over the next few years the process took me through an incredible range of transpersonal territories, including the consciousness of many animal and plant species, material objects and elements, and the interweaving of archetypal energies in the process of cosmogenesis. Some of the most striking were an identification with the sea, with granite, and with the entire Earth. At one point I experienced divine energy flowing into material incarnation in a human womb, then liberated out the other side in spiritual rebirth—the entire cycle—and I was in simultaneous touch with all the parts.

A major threshold was the consciousness of a specific flower which I have not yet identified. It was white, with a long narrow shape and a fluted opening. I directly identified with the awareness of this flower almost continuously for five or six sessions in a row. It was peeling open—endlessly peeling and opening down both sides. As I surrendered, I perceived that, for both human beings and the divine principle, it is more rewarding when we are not in total control of what is happening. The edge of uncontrolled, spontaneous energy flow is where life is most interesting and exciting. The resistances of my head were overcome by sheets of experience.

Then suddenly my consciousness was taken down through the flower's stem into the Earth itself. From then on, I was able to identify with individual awareness and the divine simultaneously—represented by the flower and the Earth. The process then moved over many sessions to the awareness of outer space, to the archetype Shiva, and then culminated in brief experiences of Absolute Consciousness and the Macrocosmic Void. The identification with Absolute Consciousness came on as unexpectedly as every other part of this process. In the middle of a typical session, my mind suddenly began to telescope outward with the question: "But what's beyond that? . . . And what's beyond that? . . . And what's beyond that? . . ."— quickly reaching out to include every conceivable part of the known universe and all other universes—*All There Is.* I just lay back, marveling at the utter completeness of the experience. Nothing I had ever lost or could ever lose was left out.

Several weeks later, another session deepened to the seamless, aware space within Absolute Consciousness and inside all things. I recognized it as the *Macrocosmic Void*—supremely conscious, formless and empty, yet containing all forms in a potential way. This sequence lasted for only minutes in clock time, yet it felt like I had touched Eternity. Arriving at this cosmic birthplace and resting place, the ultimate ground of being within all things, has left a lasting feeling of trust inside me. I saw that within all the forms that come and go in the cycles of material incarnation, there is a blissful resting place waiting to receive all consciousness home.

In retrospect, I had just enough of these openings to relieve the pressure inside me for that several-year cycle—as if Absolute Consciousness had been drawing me toward itself. Even if I am never able to awaken fully to the Absolute or the Macrocosmic Void again while I'm alive, the contact with them was so profound that I feel the cup of this lifetime is half full, regardless of whatever else happens. As I grow older and contemplate the certainness of dying, the memory of connection with them is the one accomplishment of my life that has lasting value and consolation—as if part of my being already exists where it will go after death.[42]

The Uranus-Neptune field has a magical ability to resolve emotional passages and reveal the loving transpersonal awareness behind them. It can help to satisfy people's deepest yearnings to open to the Great Mother Goddess, to the numinous, or God. Uranus-Neptune represents the miracle of reconnecting with our cosmic status, the sacred awakening to our true identity. It is the face of the Divine turned fully back toward His/Her human children. These archetypes mediate the magic leap of faith, the velvet revolution in consciousness that redeems the loss of the womb paradise and, in returning it to us, unveils a profound vision of universal redemption.

The following is from a holotropic session during the memorable Uranus-Neptune conjunction of the late-Eighties and Nineties:

I saw several vivid rebirth motifs as I was coming out of the mother and separating from unhelpful attachments and illusions about who I am and what I need for security in my life.

Letting go is always partly a leap of faith. Although it often feels scary, I'll keep letting go and keep staying open because I have no choice—and ultimately nothing else will satisfy me. Transcendence is not about reaching a place where things are always good, but rather an inner place where you always stay open.

*   *   *

The Modifying Alignments

We can now examine the archetypal meanings corresponding to alignments of the inner planets, from those of Sun-Sun, Sun-Moon and so forth, to those of Jupiter-Jupiter. Because these are short, fast-moving transits, the archetypal fields associated with them tend to be much weaker than those associated with the longer, slow-moving influences of Saturn, Uranus, Neptune, and Pluto. Even major Jupiter transits such as Jupiter conjunct Jupiter, or Jupiter conjunct the Sun, do not by themselves usually represent life-changing awakenings to the transpersonal realms.

When choosing periods for experiential work, the alignments in this section are considered secondary and used mainly to fine-tune a choice of days within an already desirable time period. Mars and Jupiter transits can be helpful to select promising weeks, and those of the Sun, Moon, Mercury, and Venus to further refine a choice of positive days. Knowledge of these influences, even more than with the long-term transits, is not essential for conducting effective holotropic sessions. However, for people interested in exploring the full range of archetypal influences in a given period, I hope the following is helpful.

Sun-Sun

Sun-Sun Transits in Everyday Life

People with transits of Sun to their natal Sun often feel a heightened sense of warmth, vitality, and inspiration. More in touch with their natural playfulness, they may also feel positive surges of confidence for initiating projects, engaging in creative work, or being the center of attention in some way. The flowing transits are especially helpful for cooperative efforts with others. People's spirit of generosity and enthusiasm is likely to be much appreciated.

The square and opposition transits sometimes coincide with passing moments of testing, resistance, or competition. In order to avoid pointless ego conflicts, individuals may need to tone down their personas somewhat and seek compromises. The alignments of Sun conjunct Sun occurring around people's birthdays are usually good times to enjoy loving attention from friends and family.

Sun-Sun Transits in Deep Self-Exploration

The Sun-Sun field is a mildly strong but positive influence in self-exploration, increasing feelings of vitality, spirit, and purpose and giving people the basic confidence to let their inner emotional material emerge and express itself.

The sextiles and trines alignments help to foster a sense of flowing synergy and cooperation between journeyers and sitters. The *dynamic* transits can evoke feelings of conscious purpose and intention as well as bring up issues around competition, especially if people's parents acted in adversarial or dominating ways toward them as children. As their material breaks through, they may display what seem to be arrogant, overwrought, or self-centered versions of themselves. Sitters simply allow this material to play itself out, as the authentic archetype of the Self burns through its challenging expressions and opens a pathway to its more positive forms.

Finally people's birthdays, as well as the three days before and after them, are special times for holotropic states. With something like a *Birth-Celebration* archetype already close to the surface, they can more fully accept the warm attention and encouragement of those supporting them.

Sun-Moon

The relationship of the Sun to the Moon can be understood if we regard the Sun as the basic energy of the self, while the Moon is the medium in which that energy operates. For example, the Sun is our basic will, our physical and psychological energy, representing our conscious intentions in life and our basic style of being and acting. The Moon represents the emotional context in which this process takes place, our sense of emotional security, unconscious attitudes, habits and psychological complexes built up during our earliest years.

Robert Hand (Sun semisextile Moon 0°45′) *Planets in Youth*, 1977

Every artist writes his own autobiography.
Havelock Ellis (Sun conjunct Moon 7°30′) *The New Spirit*

Sun-Moon Transits in Everyday Life

Sun-Moon transits help people to maintain a balance between the yin or feminine aspects of their nature and the yang or masculine parts of themselves. The flowing alignments can indicate a natural harmony between these essential life qualities.

The dynamic transits sometimes correspond to minor, passing challenges, as people's psyches bring attention to whichever element has been disowned. Because of the yang and extroverted bias of modern society, for many people this is likely to be their yin, feminine side. Sun-Moon transits are thus good times to spend quality time at home to rest and recharge. Breathing and exhaling deeply will help the emotional and bodily needs associated with the Moon to catch up to the external purpose and will-power represented by the Sun. If the solar archetype has been disowned, these transits might create situations in which people feel compelled to stand up for themselves or take some personal action.

In general, the Sun-Moon field can help people to adopt a more graceful rhythm in their everyday lives between periods of hard work and those of deep rest and relaxation. Short naps in the middle of the day, when possible, can be very balancing and calming.

Sun-Moon Transits in Deep Self-Exploration

Sun-Moon transits are moderately strong in holotropic sessions. Journeyers can shine the light of conscious attention, symbolized by the Sun, on their inner psychological material and let the emotions flow. At the same time, the Moon archetype, embodied in their human conscience and vulnerability, grounds and centers the Sun's dynamic energies.

The major *world transits* of the Sun and Moon are the important phases of the lunar cycle. Tarnas discovered that these transits can be instructive in choosing days for sessions. He found that the few days before a full moon (world transit of Sun opposition Moon) seem to embody the highest level of dynamic cosmic energies in the monthly cycle, heightening feelings of warmth, enthusiasm, and full-bodied vitality in people's emotional lives. The divine Feminine, or *Shakti*, energies are in their most abundant phase, giving sessions a satisfyingly rich and vibrant character.[43]

Based on their mythology, it is probable that the ancient Egyptians avoided inner exploration during the three days around the new moon. I have participated in holotropic sessions and workshops during new moons, and while there is nothing dangerous or inauspicious about these periods, they do seem to represent a decreased energy level in sessions, like turning down the volume. Holotropic experiences can have a somewhat flat, abridged or anticlimactic feeling—ending sooner—although with powerful Uranus or Pluto transits, they may still have a dynamic character. The main issue is that the decreased flow of emotional energy during new moons is an inefficient use of sitters. If access to sitters and session space is infrequent, it might be better to skip the few days around the new moon. However, if the best line-up of logistics and transits occurs at that time, new-moon periods should not be considered a problem. As well, for a series of sessions planned in advance, they may not be worth adjusting the schedule.

In terms of content, the Sun-Moon field can help people to work through issues around the quality of their parents' relationships with each other, or between their own willpower and emotions. In the perinatal realm of discovery, themes center on the interplay between body and spirit, or existence and meaning.

When uncovering work reaches the transpersonal realms, people may explore the interaction between the feminine and masculine faces of divine consciousness. Related themes include the alchemical marriage of *Sol* and *Luna*, the balancing of the kundalini energies of *Ida* and *Pingala*, or the Gnostic marriage of the transcendent divine with Sophia. We can see several Sun-Moon elements in the following session undertaken with Sun trine the subject's natal Moon:

> I have faced the death-rebirth experience and am no longer under the heel of the negative Feminine. I see an image of a mother goddess with her lover/son consort, representing my new relationship with the Feminine. It then transforms into a luminous yin-yang symbol.

As always, the ideal is to have both male and female support. In the integration phase, sitting between two or more close friends can have a sweetly nourishing and healing effect. Sometimes people may alternate between feeling sociable and needing to process their final residual energies.

In sessions undertaken just before or during a full moon, journeyers may experience the world as overflowing with lush, feminine energy. The grandly orange full moon rising majestically above the horizon is a dramatic moment they will never forget.

Sun-Mercury

Knowledge, in truth, is the great sun in the firmament. Life and power are scattered with all its beams.
Daniel Webster (Sun conjunct Mercury, date only, calc. for noon: 8°46′)

I think, therefore I am.
  René Descartes (PL=SU/ME, date only, calc. for noon: 1°47)
  Discourses on Method, 1637

Sun-Mercury Transits in Everyday Life

The Sun-Mercury archetypal field tends to have an energizing effect on people's thinking, speaking, and learning. The flowing transits are helpful for creative writing, enthusiastic communicating, and getting one's point across. People enjoy an unusual clarity of purpose and mind which can be very effective.

During the dynamic transits, however, the pace of their everyday lives may also become more hectic, with what feels like an increased flow of phone calls, paperwork, and emails that need responses. It may be helpful for people to pause every few minutes and take some deep breaths. The solar archetype's tendency toward enthusiastic self-centeredness may also over-heat their thought and speech. If arguments ensue, they may need to step back and think about their essential priorities before attempting a compromise.

Sun-Mercury Transits in Deep Self-Exploration

These archetypes are a mild influence in sessions, although they can increase people's verbal activity. Once underway, breathers have full permission to express whatever comes up. However, it is best if com-ments by the sitters are kept to a minimum, to help keep the process internalized.

Journeyers may also be more talkative at the end of the day. They will have a legitimate and understandable need to be the center of attention.

Sun-Venus

Friendship with oneself is all-important, because without it one cannot be friends with anyone else in the world.
  Eleanor Roosevelt (Sun semisquare Venus 0°05′)
  In *Ladies' Home Journal,* 1944

Instead of dirt and poison we have rather chosen to fill our hives with honey and wax; thus furnishing mankind with the two noblest of things, which are sweetness and light.
  Jonathan Swift (Sun conjunct Venus, date only, calc. for noon: 4°06′)
  The Battle of the Books, 1704

Sun-Venus Transits in Everyday Life

People graced with Sun-Venus transits often feel an exuberant sense of warmth, love, and affection in their everyday lives. They may have strong urges to reach out and connect with their friends, who, responding to both the generous enthusiasm of the archetypal Sun and the loving grace of Venus, will also enjoy their companionship. These are good times to host or attend parties, dances or concerts or to just take it easy relaxing at home. People's impulses toward beauty, harmony, and creativity may also be awakened.

Usually content and happy times, people with the dynamic alignments tend to feel "pleasantly unenterprising," more in the mood for having fun than for doing any kind of hard work. Their urges for gratification could cause minor problems, however, if they are pursued in a selfish way. Finally, the archetypal Sun's tendency toward self-absorption and Venus' sense of beauty and popularity may lead to feelings of vanity or conceit.

Sun-Venus Transits in Deep Self-Exploration

In holotropic sessions, the Sun-Venus field can enhance people's perceptions of divine beauty and play, their appreciation of music, and ability to bond with their friends. On the less helpful side, they may feel some reluctance to leave the cheerful surface and go into darker inner material, but this is usually a minor and passing issue.

In terms of content, people will be more open to remembering happy times with their fathers, receiving support from their male sitters, and accessing the Divine Father archetype. They may also be attuned to the cosmic forms of Aphrodite, Apollo, Ishtar, or Plato's the Beautiful and the Good. During rebirth experiences, they can feel brotherly feelings for all humanity.

Overall, journeyers tend to feel more likeable and deserving of attention. Sun-Venus transits are perfect for a loving gathering of friends and family at the end of the day. As Grof suggests, an interesting and delicious dinner with exotic and colorful food from around the world followed by long walks in nature will be unusually satisfying. These transits correspond to the happy mood of summer. People may feel a special appreciation for sunshine, flowers, rainbows, stained-glass windows, and light-refracting prisms.

World transits of the Sun conjunct Venus, especially when a third planet forms a flowing alignment with them, can enhance feelings of love, warmth, and celebration for everyone involved in the healing experience.

Sun-Mars

It is in vain to say human beings ought to be satisfied with tranquillity: they must have action; and they will make it if they cannot find it.
Charlotte Brontë (Sun sextile Mars 2°47') *Jane Eyre*, 1847

A talent is formed in stillness, a character in the world's torrent.
Johann von Goethe (Sun trine Mars 1°37') *Torquato Tasso*, 1790

Sun-Mars Transits in Everyday Life

These yang archetypes augment people's natural impulses toward action, motion, determination, and accomplishment. While their basic effect is centrifugal, of energy moving outward, the range of these manifestations will depend on many emotional factors. In most cases, people feel a welcome surge of energy and enthusiasm that can find constructive expression in hard work, exercise, or sports.

On the challenging side, the archetypal field associated with the dynamic transits can sometimes take the form of headstrong, obnoxious, or in-your-face behaviors. An urge to be first and belligerently assert themselves into others' space can lead to rash and unnecessary conflicts. At times, other people may seem to display these provocative attitudes. Whatever their apparent source, a helpful response is to withdraw one's aggressive energies from the social world and find effective outlets for them such as hard work or yelling in a soundproof room.

Sun-Mars Transits in Deep Self-Exploration

The Sun-Mars field is strong and generally helpful in sessions, increasing feelings of energy, enthusiasm, courage, and determination. It also supports the active expression of inner material, especially anger.

However, all dynamic Mars transits, both by personal and world transit require some care. It is essential that people deeply feel and express their aggressive energies without acting them out in the external situation through destructive or violent behavior. Male sitters have an important role in these sessions, by supporting the full intensity of aggressive feelings to surface without judgment or interference. This happens, of course, within the strict guidelines of the internalized protocol. The client stays in the reclining position with eyeshades and headphones on, while the sitters allow any material that arises to be expressed, for as long as it takes to reach a calm and resolved state.

The Sun-Mars field can also help people to work through issues around competition, impulsiveness, and self-centered action. As these issues unfold, they may identify with various bold, macho, headstrong, or aggressive individuals, groups or animals. These might include athletes and warriors, Vikings and pirates, Homeric heroes engaged in deadly combat, or predators in nature. Related figures include Achilles, Hotspur, Hercules, Little John, Atalanta, and the Amazons. Sun-Mars transits also support the release of blocked sexual energies.

The following session with Mars opposition natal Sun, and a world transit of Mars square Saturn, illustrates several important qualities of this archetypal field:

> After a long release of energy, I began to see images of pirates and explorers, figures who embody a dangerous and unsocial, warrior-maverick type of energy. This *Confused Ram* archetype is drawn to the furthest reaches of the world.
>
> I saw how this facet of the Mars principle is never really comfortable within the norms of civilized culture, and vice versa. Society has a need to push these martial energies away and outward, aiming them at external pursuits where they cannot harm anyone inside the society. In modern times, war and sports have been some of the main avenues; formerly it was hunting. But I could see that holotropic states and rites of passage would be much better. I felt on a precarious razor's edge with the emerging feelings and the utmost importance of keeping the session on track.

The final hours of Sun-Mars sessions also tend to be energetic. If people feel unresolved tensions that were not there beforehand, sitters can offer focused bodywork. Physical activities such as walking in nature, swimming in lakes, dancing, or drumming can also help to smooth out the final energies of the day. After well-integrated experiences, breathers will enjoy a sense of health, vitality, and a grandly rewarded courage.

Sun-Jupiter

Oh, what a beautiful mornin'
Oh, what a beautiful day.
I got a beautiful feelin'
Everything's going my way.
    Oscar Hammerstein II (Sun conjunct Jupiter, date only, calc. for noon: 1°35′) "Oh, What a Beautiful Mornin,'" from *Oklahoma!*, 1943

For man, as for flower and beast and bird, the supreme triumph is to be most vividly, most perfectly alive.
    D. H. Lawrence (Sun conjunct Jupiter 1°53′) *Apocalypse*, 1931

Sun-Jupiter Transits in Everyday Life

People enjoying these sunny influences often feel a sense of warmth, expansiveness, and optimism. Flush with inspiration and even joy, the archetypal Sun seems to radiate through their psyches, beaming its generous rays on the world around them. Their spirits may be lifted in new feelings of enthusiasm and vitality. These are great times to breathe deeply, celebrate in nature, and appreciate what is working in one's life.

People can also turn their attention to Jupiter's religious and philosophical explorations, travel plans, and educational goals. They feel a magnanimity of spirit which draws them out to embrace broader realms of experience. As long as individuals retain some balance, these can be good times to expand projects, take courses, or explore new approaches to healing.

The self-righteousness of the Jupiter archetype combined with the self-centeredness of the Sun can also manifest as arrogant, grandiose, or inflated postures. A feeling of entitlement may also lead people into various ethical blind spots or excesses. And finally, a tendency toward unfounded optimism could result in over-borrowing or taking on too many projects.

Sun-Jupiter Transits in Deep Self-Exploration

Sun-Jupiter transits are highly supportive for emotional work and their effects will be greatly enhanced if Uranus, Neptune, or Pluto is part of the alignment. These archetypes have a warming effect on people's awareness, increasing the sense of epic drama in holotropic experiences like turning up the cosmic stage lights. Attuned to the archetypal, mythic nature of their unfolding process, people can more deeply and trustingly surrender to it. In an atmosphere of warmth, optimism, and positive intentions, they connect with the basic goodness in the universe. Logistical resources seem to flow more generously under Sun-Jupiter.

In terms of content, journeyers can work through issues around pride, privileges, and self-centered importance, seeing through the archetypal Sun's blind spots and connecting with its authentic higher nature. Facing Jupiter's shadow qualities is also beneficial and lessens their hold over people's everyday behavior. Sitters simply allow whatever is emerging, including stylized sequences of arrogance, inflation, or grandiosity.

The Sun-Jupiter field can also help people in healing their father issues. They may discover higher contexts around these problems, such as personally accessing traumatic episodes in their father's lives that led to their angry or dysfunctional behavior. Journeyers are more likely to

Figure 28. Holotropic Breathwork session. "Tree of Life" Alejandra Scigliano (Sun trine natal Jupiter, Pluto trine Uranus, and a world transit of Jupiter conjunct Neptune). "Immediately, I could feel my energy raising upward and opening my crown chakra and chest, with rhythmic movements reaching a state of ecstasy. At the same time, all that tremendous energy was rooting passionately rooting downward into the earth. This experience inspired me with the strength and determination to realize a long-held professional dream."

experience their male sitters as supportive and trustworthy, as well as project onto them admirable and life-giving qualities of the positive masculine archetypes.

Transpersonal themes include visions of the golden, sun-warmed beaches of Zeus' mythic Greece, scenes of classical homosexuality with its glorification of the masculine principle, and identification with great-hearted epic heroes. People may also apprehend the virtues of Apollo or Plato's Ideals of the Good and the True. The sense of being the egoic center of the universe can deepen into perceptions of the Sun archetype itself, celebrated in many cultures through history as a representation of the central Godhead. People come to see that their egos are a kind of borrowed facsimile of the divine solar principle, and that they can connect more deeply with that central archetype by staying centered in their own consciousness, whatever it may bring.

The following session undertaken with Jupiter trine natal Sun illustrates classic features of this archetypal complex:

> As I worked through the feelings of hypocrisy, I perceived that I was transcending qualities of arrogance and self-centeredness of my WASP ego structure. I could see images of self-important Englishmen of previous centuries who seemed to represent earlier, racial-karmic versions of myself. I

realized that they were compensating for their own perinatal repressions and blockages and that I might now be able to evolve past these patterns of character armor and defense. Throughout the session, I reflected on the sometimes obnoxious and dominating nature of Sun energy in general, and mine especially. When I finally removed my eyeshades and looked up, the radiating ceiling beams of the studio resembled a giant cosmic sun, and I marvelled at the synchronicity with my transits.

Later while walking through a golden autumn field, I suddenly discerned the archetype of the *Divine Sun* overseeing my entire session. It was beaming through my psyche, illuminating the dark and repressed aspects of my being. I saw images of myself in relation to my father's overpowering solar persona and recognized that there could be no prevailing against or outshining his energy. The answer was to let go and allow my own vitality and spirit to emerge fully from the center of my psyche, in its own way. As this happened, my father's and my own energy lightened, in a complementary way, all the space within my being. Ultimately, I perceived this light as being an expression of the Divine Sun, the symbol of All-Being or what the Hindus refer to as *Brahman*. The individual self is a manifestation of the Universal Self, atman=Brahman.

Sun-Jupiter sessions are the inner emotional equivalent of the Sun shining brightly on a warm summer day. In the evening, walking in nature, enjoying a sunset, or just basking outdoors will have an unusually renewing effect.

Moon-Moon

Moon-Moon Transits in Everyday Life

Transits of Moon to the natal Moon represent brief periods of deeper emotionality in people's daily experience. These feelings can be either pleasant or challenging depending on the emotions that are emerging. Sometimes the moodiness of others, or various external stimuli, can help to bring these feelings to the surface where they may be consciously processed.

During these times, people often yearn for the peaceful serenity of their private home space. The conjunctions and flowing transits are especially sweet for tender emotional bonding with partners and family. All Moon-Moon transits are good times to go inward, rest, and reflect.

Moon-Moon Transits in Deep Self-Exploration

Moon-to-Moon transits are highly conducive to self-exploration. By bringing attention to the inner life, they put people more in the mood to lie down and let their emotions flow. The lunar principle also supports the emergence of mother issues, and female sitters can play an important role by offering physical contact to clients suffering from rejecting womb experiences or unmet needs in infancy.

In the integration phase, Moon-Moon alignments also represent a more yin and passive mood, helping people to connect emotionally with their family and friends.

Moon-Mercury

That is the happiest conversation where there is no competition, no vanity, but a calm quiet interchange of sentiments.
Samuel Johnson (Moon sextile Mercury 1°32′)
From James Boswell, *Life of Johnson*, 1791

Moon-Mercury Transits in Everyday Life

Moon-Mercury transits represent a meeting of the Moon's subjective feelings and responses with Mercury's thought, speech, and writing. The Mercury principle acting on the Moon can help people to articulate their deeper emotions as well as keep some objective perspective on them. Sympathetic listening and responding, as well as honest, sincere communication are favored by these influences. The effect of the Moon archetype on Mercury is to bring more heart and soul to people's thought and speech. They understand that how things are said is just as important as what is being said.

Challenges may ensue if the Moon and Mercury parts of the psyche are out of balance with each other. If the lunar principle dominates, people may become totally submerged in their emotions, unable to think straight or hear what others say. Conversely, if Mercury dictates, their awareness may become overly dry and intellectual and they may have trouble relating to their own or others' deeper feelings.

Moon-Mercury Transits in Deep Self-Exploration

The Moon-Mercury field can encourage people to discuss any trust issues or concerns before their sessions. Breathers with the dynamic transits may struggle briefly with preconceptions or prejudices about their experiences, until the material itself breaks through and surprises them. They may also have a greater need to speak and verbally share what is going on inside. The sitters' role is to quietly accept whatever sounds or utterances people may make, however unusual or out of the ordinary.

Journeyers may also be more talkative in the evening. Even though they may seem to have returned to ordinary reality, they might still be highly vulnerable. It is best if friends and family take their communication cues from the breather and preferably avoid wordy discussions about political trends and current events.

As always, a short debriefing meeting later in the evening or the next morning will help to resolve any residual issues and integrate the experience.

Moon-Venus

Come live with me, and be my love;
And we will all the pleasures prove
That valleys, groves, hills, and fields,
Woods or steepy mountain yields.
   Christopher Marlowe (Moon square Venus 4°39′)
   "The Passionate Shepherd to his Love" c. 1589

Happiness is a warm puppy.
   Charles M. Schulz (Moon square Venus, date only, calc. for noon: 6°53′;
   Moon square Venus-Sun)

Moon-Venus Transits in Everyday Life

These gentle influences enhance feelings of love, tenderness, and devotion in people's daily experience, and they may feel more drawn to cooking, eating, and bonding in sweet and cozy ways at home. Yearning for human connection, they may also enjoy going to parties and spending time with close friends. People tend to have "heightened emotional responses to beauty" and these can be helpful energies for making their homes more pleasant and comfortable.

If for whatever reason people are not taking in love and affection, they may feel a strong craving for sugar. They may also be prone to various emotional excesses or indulgences.

Moon-Venus Transits in Deep Self-Exploration

Mergings of the Moon and Venus principles are an added comfort in emotional exploration. They have a softening influence, opening people's hearts and allowing them to take in deeper layers of nurture. At the outset, they may remember tender moments of nursing, happy times in the family, satisfying romantic relationships, or feelings of first love. Related natural images include milk and honey, fragrant blossoms, lush orchards, and adorable newborn animals.

Archetypal themes center on the love of Mother and Child, the gratitude of Absolute Consciousness for his or her creation, and the spiritual devotion of humanity. People may also resonate with youthful figures such as Tinkerbell or Adonis. The following internalized LSD session of a young male subject with deprivation issues from childhood was undertaken with Venus trine natal Moon:

> At about the four-hour point in the session, in a deeply regressed state, I cuddled up with my female sitter and felt I was safe with mommy. I didn't want dad around. I had images of breastfeeding and experienced, maybe for the first time in my life, that my mom really did love me. Later, I experienced a warm connection with my male sitter and had sweet feelings toward my cousins, who had been my best friends when we were children. I felt the presence of the Great Mother archetype reassuring me that everything was okay, and the way it was meant to be.
>
> Later while soaking in a warm bubble bath, I slowly savored a big glass of milk which tasted amazing. Then we all had dinner of multigrain pasta and tomato sauce made with herbs from the hostess' garden, fresh salad and avocado, and warm garlic toast.

As always, journeyers will benefit from the emotional warmth of a special dinner, gathering, or circle. A cozy and comfortable studio space close to nature with fluffy pillows, soft blankets, colorful art, and beautiful flowers is the ideal setting for these kinds of sacred rebirth experiences.

Moon-Mars

Man is only truly great when he acts from the passions.
Benjamin Disraeli (Moon conjunct Mars 8°50') *Coningsby*, 1844

I am woman, hear me roar.
Helen Reddy (Moon square Mars 5°32') "I am Woman"

Moon-Mars Transits in Everyday Life

During these feisty transits, the Mars archetype stimulates people's home and emotional worlds, represented by the Moon, while the Moon brings inner conviction and passion to their assertive drives, related to Mars. These transits are conducive for cleaning, working, and making improvements around the house. People often feel strong surges of emotional energy to get things accomplished.

The Moon-Mars field can also help people to get in touch with their true feelings, a process which may be either gentle or confronting at different times. If anger emerges, it may be helpful to find effective outlets for these natural energies such as yelling into pillows, in a parked car, or other soundproof space. Raising one's voice at others is one of the worst responses. It is especially important not to direct anger at children.

Moon-Mars Transits in Deep Self-Exploration

The reactive character of the Moon-Mars field is completely turned around to become an asset in holotropic exploration. Given a soundproof space and trusted sitters, the ego's project is changed from how to suppress the contents of the psyche in order to avoid distressing outbursts, to how to most effectively discharge them. Breathers can now let go and give the energies an outlet.

Under Moon-Mars transits, people can focus in on their emotions with less resistance. Sitters should feel comfortable with the full range of material that may emerge in sessions, from powerful physical and emotional catharsis to vulnerable needs for reassuring maternal contact. The supportive enthusiasm of the sitters can inspire a feeling of dynamic, shared adventure.

Moon-Jupiter

The more people have studied different methods of bringing up children the more they have come to the conclusion that what good mothers and fathers instinctively feel like doing for their babies is the best after all.
  Dr. Benjamin Spock (Moon trine Jupiter 1°57′)
  The Common Sense Book of Baby and Child Care, 1946

A moral choice in its basic terms appears to be a choice that favors survival: a choice made in favor of life.
  Ursula K. Le Guin (Moon conjunct Jupiter 1°21′)
  Dancing at the Edge of the World, 1989

Moon-Jupiter Transits in Everyday Life

The gentle kindness of the Moon archetype combined with the generous abundance of Jupiter tends to have an enriching effect on people's home and emotional worlds. They may feel more open and honest about expressing their true needs and feelings. A warmhearted yearning for human companionship may also make these rewarding times to celebrate with their friends, family, and the larger community and reconnect with their roots.

Moon-Jupiter transits are also enjoyable for cooking and eating large meals together, although some people might overeat rich and fatty foods.

They are also helpful for hosting groups with an educational or awareness-raising focus. Finally, people may feel more earthy and grounded, enjoying getting their hands in the soil and appreciating their local animals, plants, birds, and natural bodies of water.

The influence of the Moon archetype on Jupiter is to grace people's religious and ethical ideals with human compassion, bringing them down to earth. People see that real kindness and practical support are more important than abstract ideologies or beliefs. The measure of any belief system is its capacity to support and sustain actual life.

If people are being driven by a sense of inadequacy and do not have access to inner sources of satisfaction, they may be drawn to unrewarding substitutes such as status, prestige, or conspicuous consumption.

Moon-Jupiter Transits in Deep Self-Exploration

Moon-Jupiter transits are highly positive and beneficial in holotropic states. Like turning up the inner volume, people's emotions tend to pour out of their psyches with expansive force and conviction. In an atmosphere of celebration and goodwill, logistical plans also seem to flow more abundantly. Journeyers are more likely to experience their female sitters and the archetypal feminine in general as being nurturing, kind, and life-giving. They may also remember happy periods in their families, satisfying emotional relationships, and connections with good Mother Nature. The following is from a holotropic session with Moon conjunct natal Jupiter:

> I felt like I was failing and losing, alternating with being a newborn and craving contact with mom and dad. I was having the bonding experiences I didn't get as an infant and could feel deeply that my unfilled needs were finally being met. God, what a relief. . . . Every ounce of care was registering permanently on a cellular level.

Facing their mortality in holotropic sessions, journeyers can feel that even dying is not so bad when we have other human beings around us. In these moments, kindness looms as the most important value of all, a meta-ethic in human life. They may also remember periods of tender breast-feeding, perceiving the female body in a sacred way as the source of all life. This can deepen into numinous encounters with the Great Mother Goddess archetype or Rubenesque fertility goddesses of the Paleolithic.

Journeyers may also have direct emotional access to the experiences of their mothers, for example, feeling how the painful deliveries of her children were just another layer in a series of traumas leading back to her own birth. This can lead to permanent feelings of forgiveness and understanding.

As exploration continues in the transpersonal realms, journeyers will feel a deep emotional bond with all living things. They gain a new appreciation for traditions of social harmony and respect such as Confucianism, or for the honor given to the maternal role in matriarchal societies. They can take rich experiential journeyers through the mythology of various racial groups and cultures. They may also relive memories from the collective psyche celebrating periods of abundance, security, and happiness in human history.

Related experiences include the Horn of Plenty cornucopia and provident Mother Earth. People may also encounter the archetype of the Good and Understanding Leader such as "Honest Abe" or the grand Zeus-Rebirth archetype, a warm and benefic island scene with playful celebration on an idealized Mediterranean beach.

Journeyers with Moon-Jupiter transits will benefit from loving social contact at the end of the day and depressed clients have a better chance of reaching a positive resolution and happy feelings. A special shared feast with a variety of tasty and colorful food from around the world can enrich their reentry experiences. These archetypes support a shifting of security needs from an excessive attachment to material things and onto warm emotional connections with other human beings.

Mercury-Mercury

Mercury-Mercury Transits in Everyday Life

Alignments of Mercury to Mercury have a tendency to spark people's mental and verbal activity, and often it seems that they have to deal with a swell of conversations, phone calls, paperwork, and emails that need attention. These transits may also imply more errands, short trips, and running around town. The archetypal fields associated with the flowing transits can help all these tasks to flow more smoothly, whereas those represented by the squares and oppositions may add feelings of hectic pressure.

If the pace of mental activity becomes uncomfortable, it may be necessary for people to slow down and take some deep, slow breaths. They can also release nervous tension by sitting down and moving their wrists and fingers around, while making any sounds that want to emerge. The dynamic transits may also represent differences of opinion. These are good times to lay out one's point of view, receive feedback, and then step back and wait for a positive resolution to present itself.

Mercury-Mercury Transits in Deep Self-Exploration

Mercury-to-Mercury transits are not a strong influence in holotropic sessions, although they can help people to discuss any trust issues or concerns beforehand. Once underway, people may also be more expressive and talkative. As long as journeyers stay lying down, sitters can just sit back and allow the flow of material to emerge on its own, trusting that surface layers will lead automatically to deeper feelings.

Mercury-Venus

Ideas themselves draw the human intelligence towards them with the force of Divine Eros, Ideas both in the sense of intellectual concepts and in the sense of archetypal Figures. One falls in love with a true Idea, is gripped by it with a passion, suffused by its meaning; the brain itself becomes an erogenous zone.
  Richard Tarnas (Mercury conjunct Venus 5°19′) *Prometheus the Awakener*, original unpublished version, 1980

His laughter tinkled among the teacups.
  T. S. Eliot (Mercury conjunct Venus 1°56′) "Mr. Apollinax" 1917

Mercury-Venus Transits in Everyday Life

The Mercury-Venus field enhances the quality of people's thinking and speaking, gracing it with a sense of beauty, harmony, and consideration. With their thoughts turned more toward relationships and aesthetic interests, these can be good times to enjoy easy repartee about love, friendship, movies, music, or art. Individuals may feel a special regard for love songs and romantic themes. Their pleasant routines of morning coffee and the internet, lunch dates with favorite friends, or dinner with a movie and conversation are all rewarding ways to enjoy these lighthearted influences.

Speaking in a more kind and thoughtful way, people will also be able to find compromises and see common ground with others, as Robert Hand describes, more interested in emotionally connecting than in scoring points.[44] These are generally good times to share feelings of affection or appreciation for someone. Finally, Mercury's sense of form and narrative combined with Venus's beauty and harmony make these alignments helpful for creative work.

Mercury-Venus Transits in Deep Self-Exploration

Mercury-Venus combinations are not a strong influence in holotropic sessions, although their pleasant social energies will mildly register. People may speak more gently with their sitters, as well as take in reassuring comments from them. They may also enjoy easy and lighthearted conversations with friends later in the evening.

Finally, Mercury-Venus tends to enhance people's appreciation of the music in their sessions. In the evening, they may resonate with popular music or favorite love songs.

Mercury-Mars

We are most likely to get angry and excited in our opposition to some idea when we ourselves are not quite certain of our own position, and are inwardly tempted to take the other side.
Thomas Mann (Mercury opposition Mars 6°34′) *Buddenbrooks*, 1903

Mercury-Mars Transits in Everyday Life

The Mars archetype acting on Mercury tends to dynamically engage, stimulate, and, at times, provoke people's thought processes. These transits are helpful for decisive communication and hard mental work. Individuals can put more energy into their speaking, writing, and studying—prosecuting matters forward and getting things done. They may also display a quick and snappy sense of humor.

The shadow side of the Mercury-Mars field includes rash and heated speech. People's anger may emerge in the form of sharp comments, outbursts, or sarcasm. They might also be more likely to jump to conclusions or to interpret others' words as mocking or confrontational.

Mercury's influence on Mars is to bring more objectivity and perspective to anger issues, with each transit an opportunity to step back and think about the consequences of acting out before doing so.

Mercury-Mars Transits in Deep Self-Exploration

These transits are moderately strong but supportive markers in holotropic states, with a pronounced tendency to increase the loudness of people's verbal expression. Journeyers should feel free to make any sound at any volume until they feel relief. As the Grof's write:

In Holotropic Breathwork, one has to give full expression to whatever the music is bringing out, whether it is loud screaming or laughing, baby talk, animal noises, shamanic chanting, or talking in tongues. It is also important not to control any physical impulses, such as bizarre grimacing, sensual movements of the pelvis, violent shaking, or intense contortions of the entire body. Naturally, there are exceptions to this rule: destructive behavior directed toward oneself, others, and the physical environment is not permissible.[45]

The Mercury-Mars complex may also bring up memories of being insulted, reprimanded, or yelled at. As always, sitters need to take great care with every word they offer. Journeyers who are facing threatening material may briefly project, interpreting real or imagined words by the sitters, or even silence, as critical putdowns. Despite their headphones playing loud music, they may believe they can hear the sitters making loud, sarcastic, or even ridiculing comments, until the emotions driving these projections break through and are consciously experienced. In order to reduce the chance for these projections, however, it is best if sitters offer comments only when people explicitly ask for support—or on the basis of obvious nonverbal cues. Short, clear, positive statements such as "You're doing great" "We're both here for you" and "You've got lots of time" can be very reassuring.

Journeyers are also more likely to perceive sharp or discordant sounds around them. As challenging perinatal and archetypal themes begin to emerge, they may interpret the music—even serene ocean waves, soothing new-age divas, or Gregorian chants—as harsh, jarring or oppressive. In individual sessions, sitters can accommodate journeyers' requests for a change in the music a few times, and then if they are still uncomfortable with several selections in a row, it probably indicates that emotionally charged material is surfacing rather than a problem with the sound. Usually a short reminder of this possibility will spark recognition in the client.

Finally, dynamic Mercury-Mars transits sometimes coincide with hectic logistical arrangements. Plenty of time should be allowed for travel connections around the event, to avoid the unnecessary stress of fast driving. Before the often alarmingly anxious days before a major session, every support should be given to journeyers to minimize their pressure.

Mercury-Jupiter

And this gray spirit yearning in desire
To follow knowledge, like a sinking star
Beyond the utmost bound of human thought.
Alfred Lord Tennyson (Mercury square Jupiter 0°22′) "Ulysses" 1842

Training is everything. The peach was once a bitter almond; cauliflower is nothing but cabbage with a college education.
Mark Twain (Mercury trine Jupiter 4°02′) *Pudd'nhead Wilson*, 1894

Mercury-Jupiter Transits in Everyday Life

During transits of Jupiter-Mercury, the Jupiter archetypal field has a tendency to broaden people's understanding, inviting them to think in bigger, more integral, and holistic ways. Enhancing both the optimism and idealism of the Jupiter complex, and the attention to detail and practical abilities of Mercury, these transits are generally good times to make plans or expand projects. Individuals may access a remarkable farsightedness. Astute buying and selling are also favored, although perhaps of equal help, they may come up with inventive ways to solve problems or meet their needs without spending money unnecessarily.

The effect of the archetypal Mercury on Jupiter is to awaken people's natural curiosity and interest in higher learning, philosophy, and world culture. These are good times to take courses, read about self-exploration, or travel somewhere inspirational and uplifting. People often become more interested in the big picture and how different things fit together.

On the challenging side, the dynamic alignments, especially when inflated by other Jupiter transits, can heighten any tendencies individuals may have toward overoptimism and excess. They may get carried away by their own grandiose thoughts—exaggerating their potential, promising more than they can deliver, or overextending themselves.

Mercury-Jupiter Transits in Deep Self-Exploration

Mercury-Jupiter combinations are mild but encouraging influences in self-exploration. They seem to help travel arrangements and logistics to flow more smoothly. A feeling of intellectual adventure and optimism will also tend to permeate people's experiences. Finally, they may speak and share more through their sessions.

People with a history of verbal suppression in childhood can sometimes imagine that the sounds they are making are too big or dramatic, and sitters should offer repeated assurances that everything is okay. Although it is normal for journeyers in deeply regressed, vulnerable states to ask for frequent reassurance, they may also realize at certain points that allowing the inner material to fully manifest—filling the perceptual and imaginative space around them—is the quickest way to consume the threatening material.

Specific themes include archetypal good news such as Persephone's father crying out exultantly to the world: "I've brought her home!" Journeyers may also identify with articulate or smooth-tongued characters such as Odysseus, Woden, or Thersites. Another interesting motif is images of spinning newspapers, bringing more and more continuous news, representing the everyday mind's preoccupation with trivia—images which seem to appear as people are in the process of overcoming this tendency. Finally, holotropic exploration can provide insights for solving problems in people's current relationship and work lives—this sometimes centers on the value of feeling more and speaking less.

The optimistic and expansive mindset associated with Mercury-Jupiter transits will help sessions to end on a positive note. However, as always, people should wait at least a week before making any major life decisions.

Venus-Venus

It is impossible to live pleasurably without living wisely, well, and justly, and impossible to live wisely, well, and justly without living pleasurably.
Diogenes

Venus-Venus Transits in Everyday Life

Enhancing natural feelings of love, harmony, and friendship, these are some of the most pleasant of transits. Relationship problems can melt away in the bonds of human kindness and goodwill. A feeling of open-hearted grace also make these rewarding influences for enjoying parties and social events, spending quality time with partners, or appreciating beauty in all its forms. People can sit back, relax, and thoroughly enjoy themselves.

Individuals with the dynamic Venus-Venus transits may not feel much like undertaking any hard work. These are generally better times to take a break or do something fun. They may also find themselves with more than one social opportunity such as getting invitations to several parties and having to choose. Finally a feeling of popularity might lead to moments of vanity or conceit.

Venus-Venus Transits in Deep Self-Exploration

These alignments are moderately strong but desirable in healing sessions. The Venus principle awakens warm and loving feelings that will help people to connect with their friends and take in the support offered to them. Everyone will seem to emanate a good-natured, likeable energy. At the biographical layer of discovery, journeyers may relive conflicts between two people, both of whom they loved—such as their parents during a divorce, or between a parent and a grandparent.

As exploration deepens, journeyers facing the dynamic stage of labor (BPM III) under any transit can, at certain points, develop a tremendous fear of losing control, throwing up, urinating or defecating, and making a mess. Sitters need to reassure them that their healing is more important than any material object or surface. Venus transits also support people in working through memories of sexual abuse or the enforced sexual arousal of birth. At best, they may feel an archetype of Higher Love overseeing their experiences session, creating a trusting field within which they can heal and overcome the wounded places in their psyches.

Venus alignments also support the integration phase of sessions. With people's social energies resonating together, these are wonderful times for a loving circle of friends and family. A feeling of harmony and kindness will tend to permeate the evening. Finally, journeyers enjoying these easy influences may feel a special resonance with beautiful music, gorgeous sunsets, and pristine natural scenes.

Occasionally, when dynamic Venus-to-Venus transits are intensified by stressful transits from Saturn, Neptune, or Pluto, people may experience some lingering boundary issues. Appropriate role modeling of warm and supportive yet non-sexual support by the sitters is essential.

Venus-Mars

In astrology, the concepts of masculinity and femininity have nothing to do with men and women per se, but refer to the active and passive principles that operate throughout the cosmos. Every man and every woman is an amalgam of active and passive forces in varying degrees of tension and interplay, with the tension, or disequilibrium, providing the basis for human sexual motivation.
John Townley (VE=MA/PL 1°06′) *Planets in Love,* 1978

The words "Kiss Kiss Bang Bang" which I saw on an Italian movie poster, are perhaps the briefest statement imaginable of the basic appeal of movies.
Pauline Kael (Venus sextile Mars 4°57′) *Kiss Kiss Bang Bang,* 1968

Man is a social animal.
Baruch Spinoza (Venus conjunct Mars 5°27′) *Ethics,* 1677

Venus-Mars Transits in Everyday Life

These hot-blooded transits combine the receptive, passive, and loving nature of the Venus archetype with the yang, dynamic, and sometimes selfish nature of Mars. The Mars principle acting on Venus (Mars→Venus) can energize people's desires to connect and have fun. These are engaging transits for dancing, music, or sexuality, with Mars adding the passionate urges for gratification and Venus the emotional impulses to merge and enjoy. At best, Venus acting on Mars (Venus→Mars) will bring more grace and heart to people's assertive drives, softening them with human kindness and tenderness. These archetypes also support dynamic creative work.

If individuals are either very yang and masculine, or yin and feminine in their approach to life, embodying one of these modalities to excess, Venus-Mars transits can help to bring them into balance. Habitually yin people may seem to attract Mars' energies from the outside, possibly hurting their feelings and forcing them to stand up for themselves and get in touch with their own strength. Typically yang individuals may, through the good-heartedness and vulnerability of others, experience a softening of their own selfish urges. Finally, the erotic nature of these archetypes can sometimes create tension in non-sexual friendships.

Venus-Mars Transits in Deep Self-Exploration

Venus-Mars combinations are moderately strong but helpful in deep self-exploration. As Tarnas describes, Mars energizes Venus' sensibilities, warming up the cosmic birth canal and getting "the juices flowing." People are likely to feel a more passionate and interactive relationship with the divine principle as their emotions unfold through the session. The Venus archetype will also help them to express their Mars energies in more flowing ways, feeling them deeply with less impedance.

Both Tarnas and Stelzner have noted the evocative nature of music in Venus-Mars sessions. Music has a dramatic opening effect on the psyche, a dynamic carrying wave into which people can surrender and allow their inner material to fully surface. Usually music without words or in a language unknown to the participant is preferred. However, experienced journeyers doing mini-sessions can have worthwhile inner adventures even listening to popular rock music.

Though they support uncovering work at any layer of the psyche, Venus-Mars transits have a special engaging influence on sexually charged memories. When exploration reaches the perinatal realm, they can help to facilitate the sadomasochistic material of BPM III. We can see perinatal-sexual elements in this holotropic session of a male subject with Mars square natal Venus, and a world transit of Venus trine Pluto:

> I felt threatening sexual energies seeming to come at me, alternating with a fear that the female sitter was threatened by my own sexuality. I had a deep fear of being seduced which seemed to encompass the emotions of every

sexually vulnerable person in the world. I could feel the terrible wounding of rape, so deeply in my soul. Then I emotionally identified with the consciousness of rapists, acting out their aggressive energies in the world, at such cost.

As sessions reach the transpersonal strata, journeyers examine the power of Eros-Cupid's erotic impulses in human society. They may explore the polarities of yang and yin in the universe, represented as Shiva and Shakti, Ares and Aphrodite, or lingam and yoni. They may also connect with the *primal androgyne*, an archetypal figure with both sexes in one body.

Dynamic music, dancing, or drumming later in the evening may help people to integrate their experiences.

Venus-Jupiter

To know of someone here and there whom we accord with, who is living on with us, even in silence—this makes our earthly ball a peopled garden.
    Johann von Goethe (Venus opposition Jupiter 0°26′)
    Wilhelm Meisters Apprenticeship, 1796

A very merry, dancing, drinking,
Laughing, quaffing, and unthinking time.
    John Dryden (JU=VE/NE 1°49′) "The Secular Masque" 1700

I didn't get dressed like this to go unnoticed.
    Liberace (Venus conjunct Jupiter 8°36′) Attributed.

Venus-Jupiter Transits in Everyday Life

The union of Venus' friendly loving nature and Jupiter's expansive, abundant character makes these some of the most enjoyable of all transits. With Jupiter enhancing people's urges to socialize and connect, these are great times to host or attend parties, take relaxing vacations, or just celebrate at home. Individuals may be drawn to rich, delicious dinners, exotic world-music dances, and sentimental or dramatic forms of entertainment.

Although people tend to feel more like taking it easy and less interested in exerting themselves, these transits can be helpful for creative work. Their tastes tend toward the full-bodied, sweet and fruity, ranging from the ornately colorful and decorative, to the garish, maudlin and saccharine. With values of grace and beauty heightened in their minds, they may also feel drawn to comfortable and harmonious surroundings, and more sensitive to what they feel is dingy or crass.

The Venus archetype acting on Jupiter (Venus→Jupiter) will help to bring aesthetic considerations to people's philosophical sensibilities. They may feel a special appreciation for spiritual art, music, and architecture such as grand inspiring cathedrals, stained-glass murals, ennobling statues, or lavish polyphonic harmonies. People's relationships will also, at best, embody both the loving warmth of Venus and the higher idealism of Jupiter.

The shadow side of the Venus-Jupiter field occurs when a veneration of beauty and manners above substance leads to shallow or affected behavior. People may adhere to the charming surface of their social worlds and be unwilling to face the deeper or darker currents within themselves or their relationships. They may also display an attitude of entitlement, taking more than they need and feeling reluctant to do their share.

Venus-Jupiter Transits in Deep Self-Exploration

These archetypal forms are mildly strong yet beneficial in holotropic states with one small disadvantage. On the positive side, they help to create a warm and friendly atmosphere in the periods before and after sessions. Venus-Jupiter world transits also enhance a sense of shared fun and adventure which can take isolating pressure off the client. A feeling of rich aesthetic abundance will tend to permeate the day. People appreciate the healing majesty of nature and the extra luxuries that seem to be available such as beautiful surroundings, high-quality music, and uplifting art. The minor drawback is that journeyers' pleasantly passive mood may leave them less enthusiastic about facing their pain. This is not a serious problem, but they may need some encouragement to leave the social world behind and enter the deeper healing zone. Reminders of the even-more-positive places they will be in afterward can be helpful.

In the early phase of exploration, breathers can work through issues around fakeness or shallowness, something like a "snob COEX." They may revisit times when they used prestige or appearances as a kind of social armor to try to raise themselves above others. In regressed states, they may become consumed with feelings of unbearable phoniness, confronting images of themselves as a grotesquely spoiled and conceited pretender. They may also face issues around using the sitters or buying their support. This is a deeply vulnerable admission and should be recognized as a healing opportunity.

It is the sitters' responsibility to be clear, beforehand, about what tangible or intangible compensations they are expecting from the client, so that their own process does not get triggered as the client's feelings of insincerity and fakeness begin to pour out. The following internalized LSD session of a male subject with Venus square natal Jupiter, and Venus trine Pluto in the sky, illustrates several facets of the Venus-Jupiter field:

Overcome with feelings of phoniness which I could neither stop nor hide, I began to feel alarmed that I might lose control and pee on the foamy, terrified of being abandoned by my sitters. In those unbearable minutes that seemed to last an eternity, they could have sold me down the river for the price of a mattress. I felt utterly cheap, without the slightest shred of worth or value.

As this was happening, I identified with a scene which seemed completely authentic in real time: A sad teenaged girl on a small boat somewhere in the outer Amazon, was being sold by her father for the price of a bottle of whiskey.

By supporting journeyers through these vulnerable passages, sitters can help them to move beyond their surface personas and reach places of deeper connection within themselves.

The issue of making a mess is a very important threshold for some people. It is ultimately resolved as they see that their unconscious material is already working to make messes in their lives, and that it is better to expel it now from their systems. If necessary, sitters can gently remind them that their healing is more important than the furniture or the decor, surfaces which can be easily washed or replaced. As these issues resolve, journeyers may then be rewarded with scenes of sumptuous cosmic beauty, dazzling Middle-Eastern goddesses, or Plato's Forms of the Beautiful and the True.

These transits are unusually supportive for a grand lavish feast, loving rebirthday party, or dancing with friends and family, and journeyers have a greater chance of feeling happy and sociable by the end of the day. The following is from a holotropic session with Jupiter opposition Venus, and a world transit of Jupiter trine Venus:

Just as the gorgeous full moon made a trine to my natal Sun, my girlfriend and mom phoned unexpectedly from California. It was sweet timing, in an evening that just overflowed with a loving feminine energy. My girlfriend's voice sounded so beautiful, so incredibly beautiful. I laughed and laughed, feeling jubilation and elation to the highest degree.

Mars-Mars

Mars-Mars Transits in Everyday Life

Mars-Mars transits tend to accentuate people's natural impulses toward action, passion, and assertiveness. These are generally good times to pursue manual work, enlivening exercise, or demanding physical adventure, provided that people remember due caution and do not take unnecessary risks. The trines and sextiles can also help with projects in which their dynamic, yang impulses need to work in harmony with those of others. Finally, the flowing alignments can enhance feelings of passionate synergy in romantic relationships.

On the challenging side, the *dynamic transits* may also indicate moments of anger, competition, or conflict. It is important to be sensitive to other people's feelings, and not casually provoke or cross their boundaries. Sometimes the obnoxious Mars impulses seem to be coming from the outside, through the actions of others. Whatever their apparent source, it is often helpful to reduce aggression from the system by yelling into pillows or in a soundproof space.

Mars-Mars Transits in Deep Self-Exploration

Transits of Mars to Mars correspond to higher levels of energy, enthusiasm, and determination in holotropic sessions. The trines and sextiles are moderately strong, highly valuable influences for any kind of releasing work. The oppositions and squares are also beneficial with a responsible set and setting. The most important is to see these states as an opportunity to work through powerful unconscious emotions in a safe and supported way. As always, it is best to conduct experiences in a soundproof space where full expression can be encouraged for as long as needed—when these criteria are met, the dynamic Mars-Mars transits become a major asset for deep release. The conjunctions may display a mixture of dynamic and flowing attributes.

In general, the double-activated Mars brings a more pointed, yang energy to healing sessions, giving people the courage and determination to face their emotions, get behind and really express them. Sitters function in a quiet support role, allowing the participant's own inner healer to select the material for that day and do the work. It is important that they come into journeyers' space gently, making offers of help rather than demands. As the Grofs suggest: "The basic rule of working with aggressive individuals is not to become identified as the target of the breathers' rage, but be perceived as a friend offering them help in expressing their violent feelings."[46] As always, the sitters' comfortableness with the emerging material and ability to stay calm is an important factor.

As exploration reaches the perinatal realm, journeyers with Mars-to-Mars transits may feel brief activations of the "fight or flight" impulse, a natural response of the fetus in the birth canal subject to prolonged threats to its survival. As people face these emotions and the breakthroughs that follow, they learn to overcome this urge. They begin to withdraw any hostile energies they are projecting into the social world, mobilizing them fully and aiming them at transcendence. In sessions dominated by Pluto and BPM III, Mars to Mars will add tremendous power to the cathartic cycle and expert sitters will welcome these dynamic influences.

Grof found that although most of the unhelpful or *malignant* type of aggression in the psyche is rooted in the perinatal layer, people encounter additional sources when their explorations reach the transpersonal realms. As noted, these include the reliving of embryonic crises, traumatic ancestral, racial or collective memories, identification with hunting or fighting animal species, and various mythological scenes. As their repository of aggression is reduced, people discover a natural impulse to live in more harmonious ways with other human beings and other forms of life.

At the end of sessions, sitters may offer releasing bodywork, a process which can be highly effective under Mars transits. This involves applying steady pressure to specific points of tension identified by the breather, while encouraging full vocal and motor expression. During the square and opposition transits, however, they need to exercise special care, making it clear through their gentle actions that everyone is working together, toward the same goal.

Mars-Jupiter

One hour of life, crowded to the full with glorious action, and filled with noble risks, is worth whole years of those mean observances of paltry decorum.
    Walter Scott (Mars trine Jupiter, date only, calc. for noon: 5°05′)
    Count Robert of Paris, 1832

Latins are tenderly enthusiastic. In Brazil they throw flowers at you. In Argentina they throw themselves.
    Marlene Dietrich (Mars conjunct Jupiter 5°32′) In *Newsweek*, 1959

Mars-Jupiter Transits in Everyday Life

Mars-Jupiter transits combine the expansive idealism, high spirits, and sometimes self-righteousness of the Jupiter archetype, with the dynamic enthusiasm, eager courage, and willful determination of Mars. These are generally good times to put one's ideals into practice, to take action in positive and constructive ways. The German cosmobiologist Reinhold Ebertin describes Mars-Jupiter as "fortunate action."[47] As long as people plan ahead and keep some balance, these archetypes are unusually helpful for beginning new projects—supplying dynamic bursts of enthusiasm to get things going. People often enjoy a good sense of timing, accessing both the energy and the optimism to follow through and ensure that things turn out in a positive way. Mars-Jupiter transits are also supportive for many kinds of adventure or exploration.

The shadow qualities emerge when Jupiter's righteous certainty combines in various obnoxious ways with Mars' headstrong militancy. Whatever particular cause, philosophy, or clannish group people identify with, they may act as if they have a mandate to push their agenda into the space of others. Many fundamentalist ideologies are simply justifications to act out the negative human emotions of aggression and need to feel superior.

Mars-Jupiter Transits in Deep Self-Exploration

Mars-Jupiter transits are extremely strong and positive markers in holotropic states. The archetypal field engaged during these alignments is one of the most desirable for a first holotropic experience or for any healing event when a single date must be chosen. Breathwork workshops conducted under Mars-Jupiter world transits may also embody a more enthusiastic and high-spirited atmosphere.

Tarnas found that the beneficial side of these archetypes resembles a kind of magic bullet, an irrepressible spiritual antidote against people's usual fear and inertia—greatly accentuating feelings of courage, optimism, and adventure in all deep work. Supercharged by the Jupiter principle, Mars' biological energies become a dynamic healing wave carrying people through their emerging material with powerful expressive force.

As exploration reaches the perinatal realm, the Mars-Jupiter field is especially beneficial for working through the dynamic energies of *BPM III*, providing a decisive boost toward full mobilization and release of the material. As these sequences unfold, journeyers may encounter scenes of military pomp and parades, displays of nationalistic aggression, and because of Mars' sexual nature, sequences of phallus or yoni worship. When *BPM IV* themes predominate, the Mars-Jupiter field can heighten feelings of cosmic triumph and success. At any point, journeyers may also deal with issues around self-glorification and self-aggrandizement.

The following psilocybin session undertaken with Jupiter opposition the subject's natal Mars, and Jupiter sextile Uranus, illustrates a BPM IV experience inflected by Mars-Jupiter:

> In the jubilant atmosphere of rebirth, my awareness suddenly opened outward and I was back in another time and place. I was a Roman soldier surrounded on a victorious field of battle by his many friends and cousins in the legion. We had prevailed!
>
> "Brothers!!" I cried out exultantly. I instinctively performed the Roman salute with closed fist to my chest. I somehow recognized this scene as a kind

of transpersonal overlay of my own birth—sharing with birth the emotions of major success after sustained, active effort. Feelings of profound relief, proud bonding, and renewed chances for peace and safety are natural human responses to both the end of a war and a successful delivery.

As uncovering work continues, people may further explore themes of patriotic aggression in collective and racial memories, identify with various deities of war, or participate in grand mythological adventures. The following *racial memory* occurred with Jupiter sextile the subject's natal Mars, and Saturn opposition Sun:

I explored the coats of arms of important English families from about the 15th to the 19th centuries, and the family ego consciousness behind them. I could feel waves of aggressive and righteous emotions—a centrifugal, conquering pride which was not especially pleasant or life-supporting. Despite the worldly power of these family structures, the emotional impact on individual lifetimes was obviously very repressive and constricting. I saw previous racial versions of myself in the Anglo-Saxon bloodline, people who were totally immersed in acting out the shadow qualities that I am trying to transcend.

The guiding character of the above session was dominated by Saturn opposition Sun, and thus the Mars-Jupiter complex manifests in a tightly controlled and defined, as well as sustained form. In the following *collective memory*, occurring with Mars square Jupiter, and Pluto square Uranus, we can see a more Plutonic and unleashed overall effect:

The onslaught of aggressive feelings continued for a long time without any images. Then suddenly I was inside of what felt like the collective German psyche. I perceived the karmic intensity of being German in the first half of the twentieth century, spanning the cataclysmic events of the world wars and the Holocaust.

My entire existence was dominated by a kind of hyper-Wagnerian skyscape—a dark and stormy metaphysical field which was intensely oppressive and berserk-making. As I deeply surrendered to this archetypal realm, I felt that karmic burdening for the present generation of Germans was synchronistically being lifted.

Journeyers may also identify with the awareness of animals that embody feelings of great strength and freedom such as that of horses. Finally, they can discover an appreciation for yogic postures or asanas, as in this ceremonial ayahuasca session of a female writer with Mars conjunct her natal Jupiter:

I had a sense of the supreme value in the conscious use of physical movements and postures (i.e., *asanas*) as a way of opening up energy currents and ensuring that one's *chi* remains in a continual state of dynamic flow.

The robust and decisive character of Mars-Jupiter sessions often continues through the later stages of the day. Journeyers may feel that they have participated in a grandly successful adventure. And with their inner material pouring out so exuberantly, they are more likely to reach early resolutions and well-earned feelings of peace and satisfaction. Bodywork maneuvers also tend to be unusually effective. The one minor concern is that, in their enthusiasm, people may jump back too quickly into everyday routines and projects.

Jupiter-Jupiter

Prosperity tries the souls of even the wise.
Sallust

To go beyond is as wrong as to fall short.
Confucius

Jupiter-Jupiter Transits in Everyday Life

People with the positive and expansive nature of the Jupiter archetype doubly impelled in their psyches tend to feel a greater sense of wholeness, abundance, well-being, and connection. They may enjoy a kind of grandly ennobled perspective, a feeling of being uplifted or elevated in some way. Though these alignments will be outweighed by those of Saturn or Pluto, they generally support an awareness of plentiful resources, expansive opportunities, or at least in the case of hard times, mitigating circumstances.

People often have impulses to reach out and embrace the larger world by going back to school, traveling long distances, enjoying other cultures, and broadening their minds. Jupiter transits can also help people to expand businesses and projects, provided that they show some restraint and do not overextend themselves, which is a real possibility during these transits,

The shadow qualities of Jupiter-Jupiter transits are pronounced and can undo many of their positive effects. Bearings of arrogance, superiority, or entitlement are possible. Individuals may also be prone to immoderate borrowing, spending, or wasting shared resources. It is important to aim some of Jupiter's expansive feelings at widening the pathway to universal consciousness, rather than getting carried away with worldly excesses which have no deep or lasting value.

Jupiter-Jupiter Transits in Deep Self-Exploration

The archetypal field associated with Jupiter-Jupiter transits is moderately strong and highly beneficial in emotional release work. Its positive nature increases exponentially, however, if either Uranus, Neptune, or Pluto is also part of the alignment. Enhancing qualities of optimism, enthusiasm, and confidence, these archetypes help to create a benevolent and high-spirited feeling in holotropic states. They can encourage people to overcome their fears and do a first session, or support anyone moving into deeper layers.

People enjoying major Jupiter transits are more likely to sense that they have an adequate supply of time, support and provisions, everything they need for a healing experience. The following is from a holotropic session with Jupiter trine the subject's natal Jupiter:

> Although my level of trust with the sitters remained high, I had doubts about the timing of the transits right up to the last minute. Although some part of my mind continued sending up negative thoughts, on another level, I saw that this was just emerging fear. It turned out to be a fantastic day. The enthusiasm and cooperation between my friends and sitters were very reassuring after all I've been through over the years. They were taking care of things. The whole experience just flowed along grandly from beginning to end.

Sessions are often permeated with a feeling of high drama and full-bodied emergence of the inner material. Journeyers may have a sense of cosmic auspiciousness, expansive visions, or encouraging insights.

People can also face issues around status, prestige, and conspicuous consumption and how a single-minded pursuit of these things may be adding complication to their lives without providing much satisfaction. These deflating insights can take the form of seeing puffed up, caricatured images of themselves. The following is from an internalized LSD session with Jupiter square natal Jupiter:

> I saw grotesque Jupiterian versions of myself in caricatured forms. Every figure was excessive and puffed up—fleshy centrifugal shadows devoid of substance. I perceived these characters as clinging to phony status and prestige, the material fluff of the world. I could also see personas of myself as a fake aristocrat wannabe and projected that my sitter was an inferior servant, waiting on my every need.
>
> Below these images I began to have sinking feelings of nausea, inadequacy, and fear. Finally I just ended up in a kind of metaphysical, karmic sewer: HYPOCRISY. I realized that, ultimately, a state of hypocrisy results not only from particular bad actions, but from all life strategies that deny the deeper material in the psyche and prevent direct connections with the numinous.

As these Jupiterian themes resolve, people develop strong urges to live in greater harmony with universal laws and natural cycles.

By the end of the day, journeyers may enjoy profound feelings of wholeness as they connect with the exuberance and plenitude of divine energy flows. They see that credit is shared and that their own break-throughs are a win-win opportunity which can benefit others as well. The only drawback is that, in a spirit of generosity, they may overspend on food or comforts in an effort to give back to their friends. These transits support a feeling of celebration which is ideal for a special rebirthday gathering, multicultural feast, or grand, lavish breakfast the next day. The following is from an internalized holotropic experience undertaken with Jupiter con-junct natal Jupiter, and Uranus sextile natal Moon:

> In the morning, we all had a big scrambled-egg, pancake, and maple-syrup breakfast together, laughing and toasting our cups to human brotherhood, sisterhood, and community. It was the best I've ever felt the morning after a session despite not sleeping that night, and I was able to go back to work rested and relaxed two days later. In many sequences of suffering and vulner-ability, my sitters quietly let me have the experiences without judging or abandoning me. Incredible! . . . there were many cherished moments in a day of amazing layers of unfolding emotion.
>
> So many things are working in my life now, especially my close friend-ships and great job. As I reflect on the rest of my time on Earth, whatever may come, it all seems easier now and I know that I will be able to find ways to enjoy every part of the journey. I feel more loving and lovable. My deepest value system underwent some restructuring during the suffering phase of the session. Our time here is transitory and we will all make the awakening jour-ney merging back into Absolute Consciousness which is our true home, but in the meantime, loving human relationships are what are most important in life. This recognition brings tears to my eyes. I wish all my friends and family every happiness.

CHAPTER 7

Putting It All Together: Scenarios in Self-Exploration

A knowledge of astrological alignments is not essential in order to conduct effective holotropic therapy or self-exploration. The most important factors leading to successful outcomes are the presence of trusted sitters, the adoption of a therapeutic set, and the availability of a soundproof space. When these, and some basic medical and psychiatric criteria are met, it is safer than most people realize to undergo holotropic exploration under any planetary alignment. An experienced sitting team will be prepared for every possible manifestation, at any intensity and for any duration.

Under these conditions, the insights from holotropic astrology would be mainly interesting after the fact, as a way to validate synchronicities between the macrocosm of the heavens and the microcosm of inner experience. It is for people who do not have access to ideal conditions that the next section will be most useful, to help them prepare for upcoming energies by planning ahead. The examples below are intended to provide useful information for journeyers in making wise, informed decisions as they grow from a more recreational or haphazard approach to inner journeys to a more supported and internalized approach. The following scenarios are also meant to summarize the ideas introduced in this book in a holistic way, applied to plausible situations in real life. One of the challenges of astrology is in knowing the relative strength of the many factors, recognizing what is more important and less important.

Birth dates and places for the hypothetical subjects below were chosen at random. I have chosen this format in order to cover and illustrate as many issues in the field as possible.

1. A Grieving Elderly Lady Needs Emotional Comfort and Relief

An elderly lady, "Allie" (Chart A), has lost her husband and is feeling waves of grief and despair, crying every day and facing dramatic swings

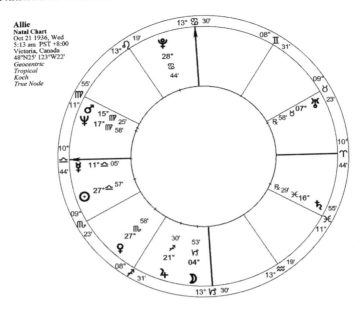

Chart A. Birth Chart "Allie".

of emotion. Allie's daughter and an old friend take turns staying with her, offering as much comfort as they can while allowing her to go through her experiences. She also has a therapist, Jean, who observes that Allie's powerful outbursts are understandable both from her recent loss and as the result of some intense astrological transits: Pluto is conjunct Allie's natal Moon, and Uranus is in square with her natal Moon. (Note that both Pluto and Uranus are within the operative orb for personal transits of 5° past exact.) As well as providing verbal counselling, the therapist suggests that a session of Holotropic Breathwork might be valuable to help Allie through the grieving process and begin to reach some comfort. She agrees to accompany Allie to the workshop and act as her sitter, since they have already developed a supportive relationship with a high level of trust.

With the releasing channels already open, Jean feels that some loving feminine energies would be especially helpful for Allie's first session. On the date they have chosen (Chart B), we can see a dynamic T-square of Venus-Jupiter, the Moon, and Neptune in the sky, suggesting that the gently nourishing mystical impulses of the Moon-Venus-Neptune field are being broadened and expanded by Jupiter. The dynamic T-square alignment will only heighten the emergence of these loving energies, pressing them fully into Allie's awareness. The Moon is also in trine with Allie's

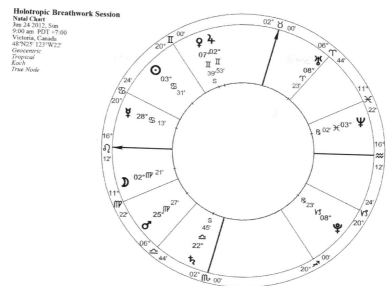

Chart B. Holotropic Breathwork Session.

natal Moon, which is likely to enhance feelings of emotional support and harmony with the people around her.

With the cathartic intensity of Uranus-Pluto on Allie's Moon, and the spiritually soothing Moon-Venus-Jupiter-Neptune world transit, Allie is in a good situation to work through some of her reservoir of painful emotions and reach an experience of the blessed Divine Feminine on the other side.

2. An Organizer of Intentional Dance Events Wants to Add an Increased Level of Safety for His Participants

An organizer of intentional dance events, "Hans," is planning a special celebration and wants to know more about the archetypal energies that will be in effect that evening. A friend points out to him that for the first half of that year (2014), the driving Uranus-square-Pluto world transit of 2006–2020 will be accentuated by both Mars and Jupiter—forming a Mars-Jupiter-Uranus-Pluto grand cross in the sky (Chart C). A grand cross is created by four planets at 90° intervals from each other.

With the proper set and setting, these are powerfully liberating energies, suggesting that the evolutionary wave represented by the Uranus-Pluto square will be expanded by Jupiter while given explosive energetic

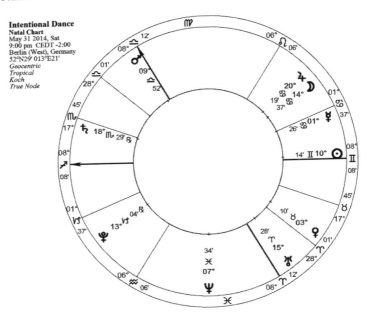

Intentional Dance
Natal Chart
May 31 2014, Sat
9:00 pm CEDT -2:00
Berlin (West), Germany
52°N29 013°E21'
Geocentric
Tropical
Koch
True Node

Chart C. Intentional Dance Event.

outlets by Mars. They are not gentle influences by any means, however. Transits like these can press out buried emotions with intense expressive force. Even in everyday life, dynamic energies will seem to be breaking out all over.

Hans decides that under these energetic conditions it would be wise to add an additional feature to his event, something like a *processing room*. This would be a cozy enclosed room somewhere in the event filled with yoga mats, fluffy pillows, and inspiring art. He organizes a team of three experienced sitters, two females and one male, all of whom will be on shift and sober that evening. The processing room will be available to all participants—who in the course of the night feel that their emerging material is beyond their comfort zone—to come in, lie down and give their process full vocal and physical expression. A short talk by the sitters at the outset of the evening offers people a chance to meet and ask questions.

Under these supportive conditions, the explosive energies associated with a Mars-Jupiter-Uranus-Pluto grand cross would be transformed into a powerful healing asset, and it is likely that a number of participants will have some of the most powerful breakthrough experiences of their lives.

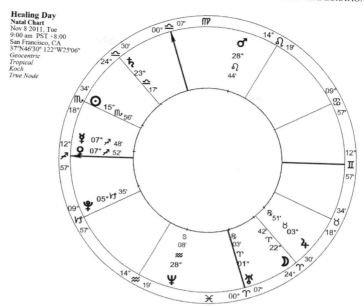

Chart D. Healing Day.

3. Three Spiritual Friends Support Each Other in Healing Sessions with Psilocybin Mushrooms

Three female spiritual friends have been doing psilocybin mushroom healing sessions together once a month. On two previous occasions, they had good experiences with a moderate amount of emotional and energetic release. They are considering doing another healing day in an upcoming period (Chart D).

Looking at this chart with the compelling world transit of Uranus square Pluto and the titanic power of the Mars-Jupiter-Pluto grand trine, it is clear that dramatic upsurges of energy are very possible. Even experienced journeyers can never know in principle when deeper and more intense material than usual might surface—although transits like these are certainly a possible indicator. The fact that these friends have already had rewarding experiences together is no guarantee that their next session will follow the same pattern.

There is always a possibility that people undergoing sessions at the same time might resonate in a disharmonious way, setting off a feedback loop of negative reactions. For example, one person might, while in a regressed infantile state, have a deep craving for bonding and nurture, while someone else is feeling waves of aggressive rebellion and cathartic release.

The Moon opposition Saturn in the sky that day, although a minor subset of the overall influences, could indicate feelings of emotional deprivation or omission issues surfacing in someone's process. Another factor is that one person's aggressive or even sexual feelings might lead them into inappropriate or dangerous acting out in the external environment, which would force the other two to completely abandon their own process to deal with the situation. The Mars-opposition-Neptune world transit, although not usually a problem, can sometimes symbolize strange or unclear boundary issues.

On reflection, they decide that only *two* of them will do sessions, while one remains in normal mode as a sitter. This is a wise and responsible decision, greatly increasing the safety and thus potential depth of their sessions. I have heard of scenarios just like this one, where a group of friends got into a situation where their individual emotional processes had a discordant effect on each other—setting off a negative feedback loop and derailing the healing experience.

The next level of safety would be for only *one* person to enter a holotropic state, while two remain in straight mode as sitters. When journeyers begin to use eyeshades and headphones, the vastly increased level of safety and intensity of their sessions will be well worth the care and effort of the people supporting them. The overall depth of experience that these women could have when only one of them is journeying at a time—i.e., every third session—would far exceed the sum total of healing experiences that they could have when all three are doing sessions every time with the more haphazard set.

4. A Member of the Clergy Seeks a Direct Experience of the Numinous Principle

A member of the clergy, "Father Michael" (Chart E), has been reading about the shamanic practices of non-Western cultures and feels a strong yearning to have a direct emotional experience of the divine or numinous principle for himself. Michael has been feeling an upsurge of primal energies through his inner life and feels that now is the time to let go. He has had a thorough physical and cardiac exam and his doctor has given him a green light for strenuous exertion.

Father Michael is attracted to the structured setting of the Santo Daime Church, which uses medicine from the ayahuasca vine (*Banisteriopsis caapi*) and the plant *Psychotria viridis* in a syncretistic approach combining elements of indigenous plant ceremony and Christianity. His one concern, however, is that the intensity of his process may be outside the level of expression generally accepted in Santo Daime rituals, which often

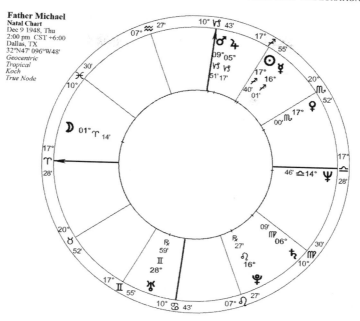

Chart E. Birth Chart "Father Michael".

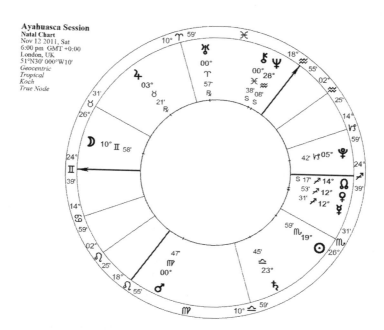

Chart F. Ayahuasca Session.

involve sitting up in chairs or dancing in a circle—though the best of the Santo Daime churches include a special healing area where individuals in deep process can really let go and give their emotional energies full expression. This varies from congregation to congregation, and people interested in having an experience with this well-established institution should check with their local branches.

Michael also hears about a Peruvian shaman who will be conducting an ayahuasca ceremony the same weekend. He decides to meet with one of the shaman's assistants to discuss his concerns. She assures Michael that the shaman is comfortable with any level of emotional intensity, including full vocal expression. The ratio of facilitators to journeyers will also be quite high—one to every three—and journeyers are free to either lie down or sit up. The one guideline is that they stay in their own part of the room and do not physically encroach into the space of other people.

Michael chooses to do his ayahuasca experience with the shaman because of concerns about making too much sound. Looking at his transits, we can confirm the volatility of his emerging process and the wisdom of choosing a setting with no sound constraints. On the date of the session (Chart F), Pluto is forming an opposition to Michael's natal Mars-Jupiter conjunction, and a square to his natal Moon, essentially lighting up his Mars-Jupiter, Moon, Uranus T-square. These transits are highly supportive for deep emotional work. The archetypal field engaged by Pluto square Moon will help to push up buried feelings for processing, while Pluto opposition Mars drives unhelpful energies out of the psyche with enormous releasing force. At the same time, Pluto opposition Jupiter often gives people the sense of a benevolent Higher Power directing the process toward spiritual transcendence.

In addition to these influences, Uranus is conjunct Michael's natal Moon, and in square with both his Mars-Jupiter conjunction and his Uranus. (Note that while the retrograde Uranus is outside of the five degree orb of his natal Mars, it has previously moved within orb, and thus the transit stays continuously in effect). These transits support dramatic emotional awakenings (Moon-Uranus), explosive liberations of energy (Mars-Uranus), and overall quantum leaps in awareness (Uranus-Jupiter and Uranus-Uranus). The grand trine in the sky of Mars-Jupiter-Pluto gives him a double experience of Jupiter-Pluto. As well, Jupiter in trine with natal Jupiter will tend to increase a sense of adequate logistics, emotional support, and cosmic expansiveness, while Mars in trine with natal Jupiter suggests even more decisive courage and breakthrough enthusiasm.

In addition to these influences, Neptune is in trine with Michael's Uranus, often adding to sessions a magical uplifting and awakening quality. Uranus-Neptune will help him to surrender to the darker Plutonic material as well as break through into melted oceanic states. Sessions during any

Uranus-Neptune transit are more likely to resolve in a positive place, and increase the chance that Michael will attain his lifetime hope of gaining direct access to the numinous, the cosmic creative principle, or God.

There are no major Saturn transits and Father Michael feels as he approaches the day that his foot has finally come off the brakes. With these powerful transits and the experienced support of the shaman and assistants, we can expect strong releases of energy and emotion. Under any Pluto transit, this might include discharges of aggression, purging, shaking and crying, profuse sweating, and hypersalivation. The cathartic direction suggested by these transits is likely to offer continued opportunities for healing, and Michael may choose to seek more avenues for holotropic states in the future, including, possibly, individual sessions.

5. A Team of Therapists Conducting Psychedelic Sessions in a Healthcare-Funded Program Consults the Transits of Their Patients

A team of therapists in a healthcare-funded program is conducting a series of voluntary LSD sessions with several highly motivated patients, with each patient doing a session every three weeks. As long-time students of Grof and Jung, they recognize the value of consulting their patients' astrological transits.

They notice that, during an upcoming seven-to-eight-week period, a world transit of Saturn square Neptune will be punctuated by Mars, as Mars forms a conjunction with Saturn and a square with Neptune (centered around the period of Chart G). Upon reflection, they decide to skip two sessions in each patient's series, taking a breather in order to let Mars grind through these challenging transits as peacefully as possible. The time in question would extend from when Mars first reaches 10–15° before exact to either Saturn or Neptune (i.e., applying), to when it makes its last transit of 10–15° past exact to either planet (separating).

Several of their patients are okay with taking a break, but one feels a strong need to keep processing, so they decide to go ahead with one session during the period but with a lower dosage (50–100 mcgs). Another option for patients during dynamic Mars-Saturn-Neptune transits would be to offer sessions with shorter-duration catalysts such as MDMA.

6. A Breathwork Practitioner Looks at the World Transits Before Scheduling a Workshop

During the same period as Chart G, a breathwork practitioner in another city is deciding whether to schedule a workshop. After looking at the

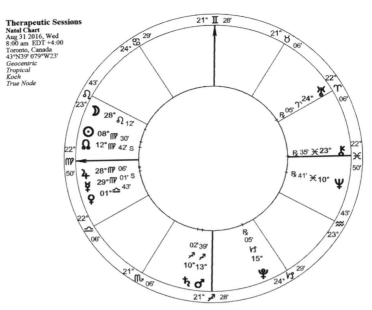

Chart G. Therapeutic Sessions.

world transits, she decides to wait until Mars has moved out of orb of the Saturn-Neptune square. These are not considered dangerous energies, but they can be very discouraging at times, especially for individuals with pre-existing tendencies toward depression or suicide. In general, people are more likely to enjoy a reasonable value of healing breakthroughs under other transits.

7. A Married Couple Considers Sitting for Each Other in Internalized Psychedelic Sessions

"Bill" and "Susan," a fairly happily married couple, have talked about sitting for each other in internalized LSD sessions. They are also considering the period from Chart G above. In the spirit of clearing the air and being completely open and trusting, and because of a fear of it coming out in the session, Bill reveals that he had an affair with someone in the first year of their relationship. After talking about it and processing at length, Susan says she forgives Bill and they decide that he will go ahead with the first session, with her as the sitter. This is a situation where a small amount of knowledge could have a very beneficial effect. It would probably be better if they did not go ahead with their plans to sit for each other.

Small trust issues can become extremely magnified in psychedelic states. It is important that there are no underlying resentments, unacknowledged expectations, or damaging secrets between people. Even under ideal conditions, people in psychedelic states may encounter deeply loaded emotional material, which is why having experienced sitters is so crucial. To begin with, it would probably be best for Bill and Susan to wait until Mars moves away from the Saturn-Neptune square and then re-evaluate their situation. These unusually discouraging archetypes are not especially supportive for entering into new or uncertain emotional states. The ideal at that point would be for them to make arrangements with an outside male-female team to come in and sit for them individually, on different days. The reentry phase later in the evening is the perfect time for a spouse or partner to come into the session room. However, even then it would be preferable to have a spiritual friend or friends also present, to ensure that Bill and Susan's energies are resonating in harmony and that any negative dynamics between them do not impinge on the vulnerable healing time. Partners need to be especially sensitive. Their kindness and understanding during these tender moments can have a miraculous healing effect on their relationships.

8. A Graduate Student Organizes a Psychedelic Healing Session for Himself

A graduate student immersed in transpersonal psychology, "David" (Chart H), is trying to organize a psychedelic healing session for himself. He has participated in several breathwork workshops and sees the value in the internalized way of processing, i.e., with sober sitters, evocative music, eyeshades and headphones, and without any sound constraints or time limit.

On his student budget, David's resources are scarce and he can only afford to undertake one session during or before the fall term. He will be flying in and paying an experienced sitter, as well as feeding her and two close friends to come and assist him. David narrows his choices to two possible dates a few days apart, then consults an astrologer friend for help in fine-tuning the decision.

His friend starts by looking at the long-term world transits that will be in effect on both days (Charts I and J). The Uranus-square-Pluto alignment is still well within the 15° orb for outer-planet world transits, giving all sessions in the decade a dramatic surge of evolutionary healing potential. As well, Pluto is almost exactly conjunct David's Uranus-Neptune conjunction. Pluto conjunct his Uranus represents another strong measure of the liberating and releasing Uranus-Pluto archetypal field, while Pluto

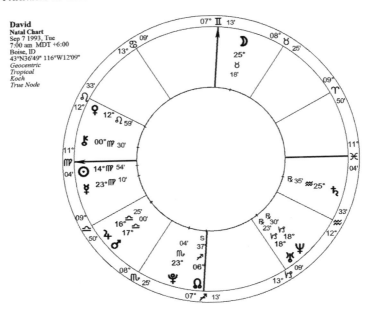

Chart H. Birth Chart "David".

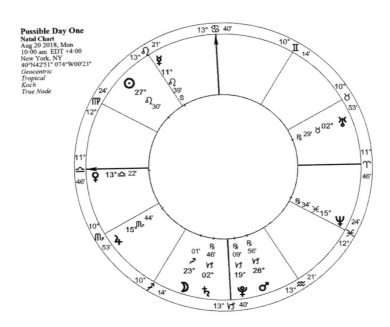

Chart I. Possible Day One.

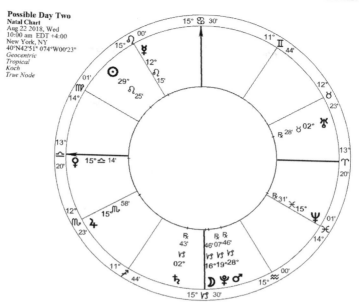

Chart J. Possible Day Two.

conjunct Neptune may help him to surrender and experience his emerging process as just a flow of universal energies. He will have a deep understanding of how facing Pluto's darker shadow material can open and cleanse the pathway to Neptune's serene oceanic states.

These transits represent, essentially, the Uranus-Pluto square of the 2010s lighting up the Uranus-Neptune conjunction of the 1990s and late 80s. The deep spiritual potential symbolized by the Uranus-conjunct-Neptune of David's generation—people born in the 1990s and late 1980s—is being compelled into manifestation by the profoundly evolutionary Uranus-Pluto square of the 2010s.

To add to these tremendously supportive alignments, Pluto is also in square with David's Mars-Jupiter conjunction. Pluto square Mars suggests dynamic surges of Plutonic material pushed up into awareness and eliminated from his psyche, while Pluto square Jupiter can indicate a feeling of Higher Power directing the process, in a kind of cosmic overdrive. Pluto is also still in trine with his natal Sun, offering a further boost of regenerating potential. It is hard to imagine a more potent combination of breakthrough archetypal energies.

David has enough understanding of his process and his transits to plan ahead and set up a proper support system in a soundproof space. It would be, at best, a major waste of the healing opportunity of transits like this to take a powerful psychedelic and then try to function in a social setting. By organizing a safe space ahead of time, David is being both socially responsible and kind to himself.

On the Neptunian side, Neptune is in opposition with David's Sun and sextile his Uranus-Neptune. The activated Sun-Neptune suggests that this may be one of the most mystical periods of his life, as the Neptune archetype dissolves away some of the old, unnecessary boundaries around his solar ego structures, allowing the Divine Sun archetype to shine its truer meaning through his psyche. Neptune is also trine Jupiter in the sky, symbolizing an even more abundant outpouring of higher meaning and connection.

Transiting Mars is not forming stressful transits to either David's Saturn or his Neptune, and is in an evocative trine with his natal Moon. Mars-Moon will help David to effect a balance between forcefully discharging his emotional energies (Mars) while also lying back and taking in nourishment (Moon) from the sitters and the transpersonal realms. There are also a number of helpful sextile transits, of course, but we have touched on the major factors.

About the only minor drawback for deep work is that David has Venus-Jupiter aligned both ways, with Jupiter squaring his natal Venus, and Venus conjoining his natal Jupiter. The passively content feelings that often emerge during Venus-Jupiter transits may make him briefly reluctant to enter into his darker inner material—he muses at the last minute that he already feels good enough so why do a session—but the dynamic impetus of the Uranus and Pluto transits will far outweigh this factor. On the positive side, with the Venus-Jupiter field so highly engaged he may feel very sociable, enhancing a more fun and celebratory mood around the experience. These transits are ideal for a special shared meal or "rebirthday" party later in the evening with favorite friends, by which time David is likely to be in a happy and even ecstatic state of mind.

With his astrologer confirming the positive transits for the entire month, she then looks at the shorter-term transits that will be different between the two possible days. On Possible Day *One* (Chart I), the Moon is conjunct Saturn in the sky, whereas on Possible Day *Two* (Chart J), the Moon is conjunct both Pluto and Mars, and sitting on his Uranus-Neptune conjunction. An activated Moon-Saturn can help people to get serious and face their pain, while Moon-Uranus-Neptune is conducive for breakthroughs into oceanic states. The Moon squaring his natal Mars-Jupiter on Day Two is also a dynamic marker, increasing the level of emotional expansiveness and energetic discharge in holotropic work.

The other factor that changes is that on Day One, the Sun is only two degrees past an exact opposition with David's natal Saturn, whereas by Day Two, it has moved to four degrees past exact, almost out of orb. Essentially, on Day Two, the Moon-Pluto in the sky conjoining his natal Uranus-Neptune is an archetypal field lighting up another archetypal field, synergistically heightening their effects. If resources are scarce and a choice has to be made of only one day, in my opinion, Day Two is a slightly better choice.

This kind of fine-tuning is mainly useful when, because of scarce resources, people only get one opportunity for a positive experience over a long period of time. In contrast, therapists conducting sessions with clients at set intervals, such as one session every two-to-four weeks, will find that fine-tuning of days is unnecessary. The clients' own inner healers will present over time all the contents of the personal psyche, and so there is no point in trying to avoid certain types of experiences—everyone faces everything sooner or later. Even heavy Saturn transits are a subset of a wider healing trajectory, working ingeniously toward the transcendent goals represented by the outer planets. Grof used to say that he looked forward to doing sessions under difficult transits because he felt that he could work through more karma from the collective unconscious.

In the above example, if a client's regular rotation fell on Day One, it would be better not to adjust the schedule but just trust the process. The major transits during the time period encompassing Days One and Two are so spectacularly positive that, in the end, it wouldn't really matter which day David did his session provided that he has adequate support. The only exception would be for the first session in a series—especially with patients suffering from severe depression—in which case, it might be better to minimize heavy transits of Saturn as much as possible for the first experience. However, many people are drawn to self-exploration by a state of suffering—i.e., influenced by the archetypal Saturn—so waiting for better transits is not always possible or desirable. In these situations, it would probably be better to proceed as soon as possible.

9. A Military Veteran Suffering from PTSD Begins a Course of MDMA Psychotherapy

A military veteran, "Brian," has returned home from fighting overseas but is now suffering from acute Post-Traumatic Stress Disorder. Experiencing at times severe nightmares, he is also feeling depressed and withdrawn with outbursts of anger directed at his family. His veteran's support association has been given a licence by the state health authority to begin a course of voluntary MDMA psychotherapy with a group of selected veterans.

Brian has read some of the clinical literature and believes that this approach could help him so he applies for the program. The therapists overseeing the program are considering his application. Their main hesitation is that Brian served in a combat unit and received training in hand-to-hand combat. They feel that this training as well as his tendencies toward anger could pose a threat, or the fear of a threat, to the therapeutic staff if Brian should become confused and begin to act out his aggression in the outer space of the session room.

Even normally peaceful individuals can, during perinatal sequences, come under the influence of powerful aggressive energies. During this releasing process, it is essential that they stay in the reclining position while allowing the energies to fully express themselves from their systems. Although the expert supervision of the sitters and the level of trust the client has with them are the most important factors in a successful outcome, there should also be a guaranteed level of safety in everyone's minds. Grof found that if the client becomes alarmed and begins to project his or her feeling of danger on the external situation, the calmness of the sitters and their trust in the process will buy time, during which the client can recognize his or her projections and the importance of returning to the internalized state with eyeshades and headphones, and facing the material directly.

I would like to offer a suggestion for work with military veterans in this kind of scenario. Two or more veterans in the same therapeutic program could take turns helping each other as extra sitters. The presence of another person who has shared some of the same intense life experiences would add an extra level of support during the releasing phase of sessions. Additionally, the physical strength of another veteran would create a higher level of safety and trust for the therapeutic team in general. The ideal would be for soldiers who served in the same military unit to help each other. Combat experiences have a powerful bonding effect and these bonds of friendship and respect could then be used to support the healing process.

10. A Young Meditator Experiences Kundalini and Spiritual Emergency

A young meditator, "John" (Chart K) on a day like many others (Chart L), begins to experience *kundalini* energy moving through his body accompanied by *kriyas*, dramatic emotional and energetic discharges with images of death and rebirth. Despite its intensity, John perceives that what is happening is a profound spiritual awakening. Several of John's friends also recognize his experiences as classic manifestations of what Christina Grof termed "spiritual emergency," and gather in his home to discuss how best to support him. They invite a Holotropic Breathwork-trained therapist familiar with kundalini and spiritual emergency, and a family friend who is an archetypal astrologer.

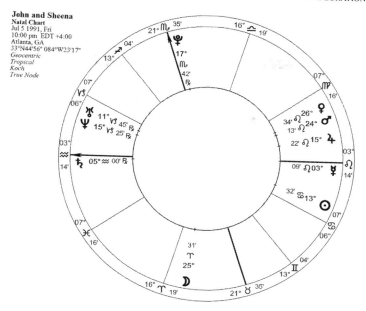

Chart K. Birth Charts "John" and "Sheena".

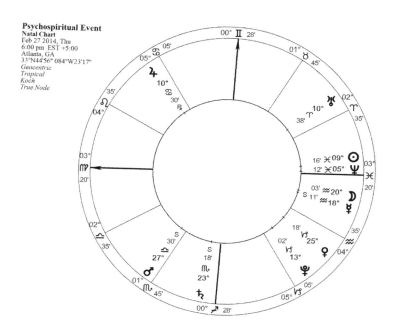

Chart L. Psychospiritual Opening.

Looking at his chart, the astrologer confirms that John is facing some intense and potentially very liberating transits. These include a dynamic T-square of Jupiter, Uranus, and Pluto in the sky, lining up on his natal Sun opposition Uranus-Neptune. As well, Mars, although it has passed out of orb of the T-square, is about to station (i.e., appear to stop) and go retrograde back into alignment, and thus it has remained in effect. (Tarnas demonstrates that a transiting planet forms a transit more-or-less continuously from the first time it comes within applying orb, until it has moved beyond separating orb for the final time). Thus, there is actually a dynamic Mars-Jupiter-Uranus-Pluto *grand cross* alignment. These energies come on swiftly and decisively. They can be an indicator of quick positive outcomes and healing resolutions, provided that journeyers have the support to let the driving energies play themselves out.

The astrologer points out that transiting Saturn is also in square with John's Venus-Mars. Although not without some challenges, these Saturn transits represent a weak subset of a much more inevitable liberating force. People under the influence of Mars-Saturn can feel a tension between the assertive and expressive energies of their inner Mars and the suppressive, constricting force of their Saturn. These pressures can be effectively worked through, however, with dynamic-tension exercises such as firmly pushing the palms together and growling, squeezing a rolled-up towel and coughing, or making fists and shaking. And with transiting Saturn also squaring John's natal Venus, the people around him need to take great care to offer unconditional support rather than any kind of judgment or time limits on his process.

Encouraged, the group decides to transform a room in John's house into a twenty-four-hour processing space, to which he enthusiastically agrees. They put up mattresses against the windows, both for soundproofing and for extra safety, and set up a schedule with a male-female team on hand for four-hour shifts around the clock. The primary purpose of the sitters is to give nondirective encouragement, to provide nourishing contact if John requests it, and to keep him from hurting himself. With his Saturn-square-Mars transit, they need to ensure that he doesn't attempt any dangerous maneuvers that might injure his neck or back. They should also be aware of the potential for sequences of suffocation and breakthrough coughing from birth which, if allowed to surface, could be very healing. During any spiritual-emergency situation, sitters also need to remind people to eat grounding food and take in vitamins so that they don't become dangerously thin—although some weight loss is inevitable. Finally, the therapist offers to conduct a group breathwork session for any of John's team who, during this demanding period, feel a need to do some of their own emotional work.

Most of the time, John perceives that his process has an end-point, which is a defining feature of Plutonic-BPM III experiences. He feels that he just needs the time and permission to work through the material piece by piece. In this almost-ideal situation, we might expect a fairly rapid resolution of John's process, perhaps one-to-three weeks, as his psyche presents the material shaken loose by the kundalini. There is a very high likelihood that he will reach a more healthy and integrated state than he was in before the kundalini awakening began.

11. A Young Woman Diagnosed with Bipolar Disorder Wants to Stop Taking Lithium

A young woman, "Sheena," born the same day as John above (Chart K), wants to stop taking her lithium and is looking at doing it during the same period as John's kundalini experience (Chart L). Sheena was diagnosed with bipolar disorder in her late teens, after some euphoric spiritual experiences accompanied by dangerous acting out at high speed in automobiles, which endangered both herself and others. Several times, she also seriously considered testing a thought that she might be able to fly above the earth, by harnessing the energy of passing trains.

As well as a difficult birth, the contributing factors in Sheena's problems were a long period of being swaddled as an infant—demonstrated as a factor in the onset of manic depression—and a demanding work ethic in her family which valued material achievement and future success over present happiness and peace of mind.[1] The several previous occasions when Sheena tried to go off her lithium met with disaster. Facing an acute resurgence of manic feelings, she began to dangerously act out and had to be forcibly hospitalized by the authorities. Now severely depressed, she has also been prescribed Prozac by her family doctor.

Sheena has been reading about transpersonal psychology and feels that her process has been mistakenly labelled in the existing medical model as a chemical imbalance. She believes that her unfolding spiritual journey has been suppressed by the chemical straitjackets of the lithium and Prozac, and that she now has the perspective to face her unconscious contents without projections and acting out. Sheena is considering renting a cabin in the woods for ten days, which is all she can afford, and has six close friends who have agreed to assist her while she stops taking her medication. However, her family, influenced by a mixture of both fundamentalist religious and traditional scientific backgrounds, as well as legitimate care for her well being, do not understand this approach, and Sheena knows that if she has any run-ins with the authorities she will be recommitted without support.

This is a very painful state of affairs with no satisfactory response. On the promising side, Sheena has a fairly deep mental understanding of her process and a new awareness of the importance of facing her process internally. On the more cautionary side, she does not have the support of her family. She already has several precedents of dangerous acting out in which she forced the involvement of both the police and the psychiatric establishment. She has a file. Most knowledgeable professionals including breathwork practitioners would be reluctant to work with her on, for starters, legal grounds, because of her past history. There is a real possibility that any problems she could ever have in the future might be attributed to their intervention.

The bigger and most important question, however, is: what are the chances that Sheena could weather the storm of manic emotions and grandiose ideation that emerged during her previous attempts to quit her medication and reach a workably calm state—in the ten-day period of time that she has the cabin and the promised support of her friends. Unfortunately, the track record of manic individuals is not encouraging in this regard. The possibility that she could reach a balanced equilibrium in this short of a time period is small though not zero. As well, however loving and devoted her friends are, they may not realize the intensity of the process they are about to become involved in. Six people's support spread out over a series of long twenty-four-hour days is almost certainly not enough to keep Sheena from harm if she reverts to her well-worn pattern of attempting to aggressively escape from all limits and containment—which are, at root, her projections of the murderous birth canal and her need to free herself from it and reach a state of rebirth. Even with the best of intentions, this is not a promising recipe for success.

Sheena's intellectual understanding of her process is what makes this situation so poignant. If she had access to a twenty-four-hour inpatient facility under the care of therapists practicing a psychodynamic approach, there is a good chance that she could work through enough of her personal material, or all of it, and attain her goal of discarding the repressive medication and reaching a genuine spiritual breakthrough. Psychiatrists conducting psychedelic therapy have had good results with this category of patient.[2] However, without the full support of either her family or the medical community, Sheena faces a difficult challenge, and she may live out the rest of her life with a sense of lost dreams and diminished potential. The absence of this support at the present time can only be considered a preventable, cultural tragedy.

Epilogue

Just four-hundred generations ago, our ancestors lived as nomadic hunter-gatherers in small family groups scattered around the world. Only a few millennia later, spread across the face of the Earth, we can now grow vast mountains of food, heal many of our most feared diseases, and speak with people anywhere in the new global village. Modern technology has given us extraordinary power to solve problems, and at one time it seemed that we stood on the edge of a hopeful future. Yet to many, witnessing the flood of irrational and heartbreaking events in the daily news, it seems clear that humanity's emotional development has not kept pace with this technology. In many ways we have ignored our exploration of the inner subjective world.

This problem is deeply rooted in an important decision by the fathers of modern science. In the turmoil of seventeenth-century Europe, Galileo Galilei, René Descartes, and their peers were struggling to find a higher value system that could improve the living conditions of humanity. To this end, Galileo and then Descartes proposed a focus on *objective* qualities in the physical world that could be measured in a quantitative way (such as number, shape, gravity, duration, and position), rather than on subjective beliefs or perceptions, qualities which only seemed to divide people. As the religious wars of the Reformation plunged Europe into chaos, the following generations of scientists took up Descartes' challenge and fulfilled it with an almost religious dedication of their own.

Four centuries later, modern science has given to humanity tremendous influence over nature and changes in the standard of living. In most parts of the world, life spans have been extended and, in many places, people enjoy an increased level of material comfort. Yet our industrial civilization has come with a great price and many unintended consequences. Along with problems of alienation and depression, we now face many serious external challenges, including the threat of climate change and global warming, continuing wars and genocides, the persistence of treatable diseases, and the ongoing despoilment of our air, water and soil.

The fact that we have the technologies to adopt a more ecologically sustainable economy but continue to rely on harmful sources of energy may be grieved by our descendants as irrational and suicidal behavior. We have the means to solve these problems, and yet it sometimes seems as if there are forces in the psyche that prevent us from acting in our own best interests. Despite advances in intelligence, the human mind is still unconsciously driven by many of the same destructive and self-destructive emotions that governed it thousands of years ago in the Stone Age: these emotional forces have not gone away but sit unhappily working against us below the pavement of our modernity. As every depth psychologist understands, whatever we are unconscious of, inside us, runs our lives.

Grof used to say that when someone is landing a jet at the O'Hare airport in Chicago, he or she needs to be in the *hylotropic*, "moving toward matter" mode of awareness—to find higher meaning in life, many cultures have found that we need to periodically enter holotropic or "moving toward wholeness" states. Over the millennia, a number of effective methods have been developed for entering these territories. As well as emerging through the traditions of shamanism, the ancient mystery religions, aboriginal healing rituals, and rites of passage, procedures for entering holotropic states have been introduced through the different schools of yoga and Buddhism, through Taoism, Sufism, and mystical Christianity. Grof notes that while Western culture encountered holotropic states on a mass scale during the psychedelic revolution of the 1960s, the enormous positive value of these experiences was obscured by the often irresponsible and chaotic nature of the youth movement.

Almost half a century later, I believe it is time for our culture to reconsider this earlier assessment and take another look at the responsible, therapeutic use of holotropic states. We can maintain the important benefits that science has given to us, while restoring the lost avenues for healing and transformation that were left behind in our rapid scientific advance. In many ways, humanity is being forced to undergo this adjustment. Fundamental aspects of the global crisis, including insatiable greed, aggression, and self-destructive tendencies, clearly have deep emotional roots which can only be resolved on an inner, psychological level.

The processing of unconscious material thus has important implications that reach beyond the healing of emotional and psychosomatic disorders for the individuals who do the inner work. Grof's research demonstrates that this transformation includes a reduction of aggression and the development of ideological, racial, gender, and cultural tolerance, ecological sensitivity, compassion, and sense of planetary citizenship. These changes are beneficial not only for the individuals involved in the process, but for society at large.

An unprecedented transformation seems to be underway in human understanding, a collective spiritual birth labor that will have long-term consequences for humanity as well as for many other life forms. We now find ourselves in a race against time and as the ancients knew, holotropic states of consciousness provide the crucial missing element that may, I believe, help us to make this transition. If the observed healing and renewal in values could occur on a large enough scale, they might increase humanity's chances of overcoming its serious challenges and making the evolutionary leap to a more peaceful and sustainable future.

Endnotes

Chapter 1: The Birth of a New World View

1. Wasson, Ruck, and Hoffman, *Road to Eleusis*.

2. "Cycles and Symbols Conference" (1990), San Francisco, California.

3. See Hand, *Horoscope Symbols and Essays on Astrology*.

4. Tarnas, *Cosmos and Psyche*. Tarnas suggests that the fundamental component in a cultural or scientific paradigm is its cosmology. The cosmology of a world view refers to the actual physical place, the context within which that world view exists, and, more deeply, to its metaphysical and cosmic dimensions. With *Cosmos and Psyche*, I believe that the emerging holotropic world view finally has its missing component: an essentially Platonic-Pythagorean universe which is intelligibly ordered by archetypal patterns of meaning and experience, and in which the macrocosm of the solar system mirrors archetypal processes in the microcosm of human life.

In this world view the highest and most treasured capacities of human reason and cognition are ultimately recognized as expressions of the universe's own intelligence. But, integrating the modern development of an autonomous self, the human being is also recognized as having both freedom and responsibility for consciously and creatively enacting these powerful forces in the most life-enhancing forms possible.

5. See Capra, *Tao of Physics*; Herbert, *Mind Science*; Bohm, *Wholeness and the Implicate Order*; Wolf, *Taking the Quantum Leap*; Goswami, *The Self-Aware Universe*; Pribram, *Languages of the Brain*; Sheldrake, *A New Science of Life*; Prigogine, *From Being to Becoming*; Gleick, *Chaos*; Bateson, *Mind and Nature*; Barrow and Tipler, *The Anthropic Cosmological Principle*.

6. Wilber, *Atman Project*, *Spectrum of Consciousness*, and *Up From Eden*; Laszlo, *Creative Cosmos*, *Science and the Akashic Field*, and *Subtle Connections: Psi, Grof, Jung, and the Quantum Vacuum*.

7. Le Grice's inauguration, with co-editor Rod O'Neal and assistant editor Bill Streett, of the influential journal *Archai: The Journal of Archetypal Cosmology* in 2009 is another encouraging development. This annual journal publishes articles by scholars in the field of archetypal cosmology with solid academic and professional criteria. Some of the new generation of archetypal astrological scholars contributing to this journal include Rod O'Neal, Grant Maxwell, Chad Harris, Sean M. Kelly, Becca Tarnas, Bill Streett, and Clara Lindstrom.

I would also mention the series of illuminating online articles by Bill Streett, the best monthly columns I have seen that integrate Tarnas' archetypal approach and methodology.

8. See also Grof's overviews on the convergence of consciousness research with modern science in *Beyond the Brain* and *Healing Our Deepest Wounds*, and von Franz's *Number and Time: Reflections Leading Toward a Unification of Depth Psychology and Physics*.

9. The first material in this field to be published, that I am aware of, was by Grof in a chapter of his book *When the Impossible Happens* (2006) entitled "Psyche and Cosmos: What the Planets Can Reveal About Consciousness." He followed this in 2009 with an article in *Archai*, Issue 1 (*The Birth of a New Discipline*) called "Holotropic Research and Archetypal Astrology."

Matthew Stelzner, a doctoral student of Tarnas and Grof at the California Institute of Integral Studies, is also highly experienced in the practice of archetypal and holotropic astrology, and his podcasts with guests such as Tarnas are a rich source of insight into cultural trends, current events, and famous personalities. See correlationspodcast.blogspot.com as well as his informative lectures on Ustream www.ustream.tv/search?q=matthew+stelzner.

Chapter 2: Transpersonal Psychology and
Archetypal Astrology

1. Ring, *Life and Death: A Scientific Investigation of the Near-Death Experience*; Ring and Cooper, *Mindsight: Near-Death and Out-of-Body Experiences in the Blind*; Ring and Valarino, *Lessons from the Light: What We Can Learn from the Near-Death Experiences*; Jung, "Synchronicity: An Acausal Connecting Principle" in *Collected Works of Carl Gustav Jung*; Tarnas, *Cosmos and Psyche*; Moody, *Life After Life*; Stevenson, *Children Who Remember Previous Lives, Reincarnation and Biology*, and *Twenty Cases Suggestive of Reincarnation*; and Bache, *Lifecycles: Reincarnation and the Web of Life*.

2. See, for example Kuhn's *The Structure of Scientific Revolutions*, Capra's *The Turning Point*, and Grof's *Beyond the Brain* and *Healing Our Deepest Wounds: The Holotropic Paradigm Shift*.

3. Grof observed that BPM I experiences are also often accompanied by post-natal memories that share with the womb a feeling of undisturbed unity and connection. These include memories in which important needs were satisfied, such as harmonious periods in the family, good mothering, play with peers, or fulfilling love. Related memories are of nature experienced at its best, as "Mother Nature," including vacations in beautiful natural settings or swimming in the ocean and clear lakes.

Reaching Neptunian states of melted or oceanic type of ecstasy is a breakthrough threshold in psychotherapy and self-exploration. Grof found that subjects who reach these states experience a dramatic disappearance of symptoms, increase in positive feelings, and a new appreciation of all aspects of life. They can also become spontaneously interested in the great mystical traditions and philosophies of world culture, including the various schools of yoga, Taoism, Kashmir Shaivism, Zen, Kabbalah (the mystical form of Judaism), Gnosticism (the mystical form of Christianity), and Sufism (the mystical form of Islam).

4. Associated memories from postnatal life during BPM II experiences include situations that posed a threat to survival or bodily integrity such as war experiences, painful diseases, near drowning and episodes of suffocation, or serious accidents, injuries, and operations. Equally common are memories of imprisonment, brainwashing, and abuse. In this context, individuals can also work through severe emotional traumatizations, including an oppressive family atmosphere, threatening situations, deprivation, rejection, or humiliation.

The early stage of birth thus forms a powerful template for feelings of loss and suffering in human life. The pain of delivery becomes a prototype for the formation of the separate ego later in childhood. However, from a deeper perspective, the difficult stages of birth can also be seen as an essential interface or "step-down transformer," where aspects of the universal consciousness or "karma" can enter an individual lifetime to be experienced and worked through.

As difficult as this aspect of labor might be, it is a crucial stage in emotional development. By passing from the suffering in the birth canal to the liberation of delivery, people develop a lasting faith that they can face challenging situations and survive them.

5. Grof, *Beyond the Brain.*

6. Grof, *Beyond the Brain, LSD Psychotherapy*, and *Psychology of the Future.* See in particular his chapter: "Varieties of Sexual Experience: Dysfunctions, Deviations, and Transpersonal Forms of Eros" in *Beyond the Brain*, pp. 200–231.

7. Grof, *Realms of the Human Unconscious* and *LSD Psychotherapy.*

8. Grof and Grof, *Holotropic Breathwork.*

9. Observations in holotropic states suggest that the event of birth, which may only take hours in clock time, is for the fetus experienced as an eternity. Most people realize that a child's subjective awareness is much more open than that of an adult. Every day is an epic drama filled with a flood of intense emotional experiences.

Grof's research suggests that the fetus's consciousness is significantly more open than that of a child. Every nuance of the birth process and the mother's body is experienced with strong positive and negative emotions and sensations approaching archetypal dimensions. The sequences of crushing pressure, life-threatening suffocation, and activation of biological energies during birth are registered on a level of intensity usually unsurpassed by any other event in the lifetime, except possibly for some people, dying. Conversely, the feelings of cosmic unity in the womb and triumphant ecstasy of the completed birth form the prototypes of happiness, security, and success in later life. See *Realms of the Human Unconscious, The Adventure of Self-Discovery*, and *Psychology of the Future.*

10. Grof, *Beyond the Brain* and *Psychology of the Future.* Biographical memories associated with BPM III include struggles, fights, and adventurous activities such as active attacks in battles and revolutions, experiences in military service, rough airplane flights, cruises on a stormy ocean, or hazardous car driving. People can relive, in fast sequence, highly sensual memories of carnivals, amusement parks and nightclubs, or wild parties. Other memories include experiences of seduction or sexual abuse, and in females, the delivery of their own children.

Although the BPM III energies are universally present in humans as a potential source of psychopathology, whether this part of the psyche reaches consciousness to cause problems in a given individual will depend not only on the intensity and duration of the birth but on many post-natal factors. These include the quality of parenting, the level of emotional safety in childhood, and the presence of trauma or abuse that can create pathways for the negative perinatal material to reach present awareness. Grof observed that good mothering and lack of significant problems in the early life will serve to encapsulate the traumatic aspects of birth within a buffer of positive memories. Conversely, painful events in childhood and later life facilitate the emergence of the difficult perinatal themes into people's ongoing experience of the world.

11. Grof, *Beyond the Brain*, *The Adventure of Self-Discovery*, and *Psychology of the Future*.

12. These breakthrough sequences are not a one-time experience. People's psyches will tend to present their unresolved emotional material in different ways and from different directions, until the process is completed.

Biographical memories associated with BPM IV include escapes from dangerous situations, the end of wars, survival of accidents, or overcoming of severe obstacles by active effort. Recalled scenes of nature include the beginning of spring, the end of an ocean storm, and sunrise.

13. Although in 2006 Pluto was recategorized by the International Astronomical Union as a dwarf planet, its observed correspondence with a set of archetypal characteristics—including powerful experiences of psychological death and rebirth and long-term evolutionary processes—seems to have not been affected. For the sake of ease of writing, I will continue to technically refer to Pluto as a planet.

14. Tarnas, "An Introduction to Archetypal Astrology." www.cosmosandpsyche.com/ PDF/CosmosAndPsyche/IntroductiontoAstrology.pdf (accessed February 6, 2013).

15. Observations from archetypal astrology suggest that other alignments such as the semisextile 30°, semisquare 45°, quintile 72°, sesquiquadrate 135°, biquintile 144°, and quincunx 150° are significant but less powerful than the major aspects described above, especially when they occur by transit. Although these somewhat more minor aspects will often register at some point in a holotropic session, the archetypal fields associated with them do not usually dominate the emotional character of sessions in the same way that conjunctions, oppositions, squares and, to a lesser extent, trines typically do.

In general, the 60° sextile alignments are considered to be of medium strength in potency, falling somewhere between the major and minor aspects as transiting influences in deep work. For the most part, sextiles are not included in my description of the archetypal combinations in this book. However, their mildly supportive influences are always an asset, helping journeyers to face and complete the material represented by their other major transits.

16. Tarnas, *Cosmos and Psyche*.

17. These are basic correlations, however. The unfolding of people's emotional and spiritual lives will always be subject to individual variability and inflections, rather than following an exact, predictable formula.

18. The paradox in everyday life is that when we are emotionally stuck, we are stuck halfway between feeling uncomfortable and descending far enough into our leftover pain to release it. The protective ego prevents us from suffering deeply enough to work through the inner material. The original human problem to be faced in self-exploration, then, is the wound of birth

and our consequent fear of death and dying. The bigger problem, however, is our ongoing repression of that wound, a repression that can gradually impoverish the entirety of life.

19. The ultimate experience of rebirth occurs after facing and working through the full range of dynamic BPM III material described above. In Greek mythology, this pattern of active struggle followed by liberation is depicted by the long, arduous labors of Hercules. Eventually Hercules kills the vulture that has been tormenting Prometheus—representing the gnawing power that unconscious perinatal energies have over human life—and sets Prometheus free.

20. Uranus' shadow qualities can be understood as forms of mania or "incomplete rebirth." Grof discovered that manic depression has deep roots in the perinatal layer of the psyche, involving an interplay between elements of BPM III (the Death-Rebirth Struggle) and BPM IV (Rebirth and Separation from the Mother). Essentially, the manic individual has experienced a taste of inner freedom (BPM IV), but it is exaggerated, distorted and threatened by their remaining BPM III material, especially by the intense aggressive and depressive emotions leftover from birth. In his or her manic phase, the individual's free-spirited mood comes across as hyper, caricatured, and driven.

   The depressive phase of the cycle occurs when the underlying reservoir of Plutonic-BPM III energies once again breaks through into awareness, depressing the person's emotional state. In order to access the integrated rebirth experience, he or she must be willing to face and work through the challenging perinatal sequences that precede the completed birth. See Grof's clinical explorations of manic depression and other psychological disorders in *Psychology of the Future*, *LSD Psychotherapy*, and *Beyond the Brain*.

21. Personal communication, 2009.

Chapter 3: Issues in Psychedelic Therapy and Self-Exploration

1. Grof, *LSD Psychotherapy*.

2. Stan and Christina Grof coined the term *spiritual emergency* to describe situations where the contents of a person's psyche begin to spontaneously emerge into awareness. The precipitating factors might include intense spiritual practices such as mental concentration, meditation, or dream work, or emotional stresses such as personal loss, the end of a relationship, or death in the family. See Grof and Grof, *The Stormy Search for the Self: A Guide to Personal Growth through Transformational Crisis* and, as editors, *Spiritual Emergency: When Personal Transformation Becomes a Crisis*.

3. It should be noted that a person's partner or spouse is not the best choice for a sitter. The possibility of counter-projections is very real, even for experienced sitters. In order to clear out the deepest layers in the personal psyche—material which is overwhelmingly emotional and pre-verbal—sessions need to be focused solely on the process of the journeyer rather than on issues around the relationship, i.e., only one person processing at a time. The ideal is for a person's partner or spouse to come in at the end of a session, to help relieve the primary sitters and create a smooth and loving transition back to ordinary reality.

4. Grof, *The Ultimate Journey*.

5. Grof, *LSD Psychotherapy*.

6. Grof, *ibid*.

7. Wikipedia article, "MDMA" (accessed May 14, 2010).

8. Grof, *Realms of the Human Unconscious*, *LSD Psychotherapy*, and *Psychology of the Future*.

Chapter 4: The Astrological Archetypes

1. Grof, *LSD Psychotherapy*, *Beyond the Brain*, and *Psychology of the Future*. Grof discovered that individuals can heal problems related to the Moon archetype, in holotropic states, by finally receiving the nurture they missed in infancy and childhood. His research suggests that children who were unwanted in utero, isolated after birth, or starved for warm human contact are left with a vacuum in their psyches. They will retain a deep, unconscious hunger for maternal nurture and may spend their whole lives looking for substitutes.

However, nothing that people might accomplish or receive in everyday reality can satisfy the unmet inner needs. Because the problems occurred in people's childhoods, they can only be resolved by emotionally returning to the original state of vulnerability and then receiving the nourishing contact they missed at that time. This therapeutic process is referred to in different therapeutic modalities as "emotional-corrective experiences," "reparenting" or "fusion therapy."

2. Hand, *Horoscope Symbols*.

3. Grof and Grof, *Holotropic Breathwork*. The Grofs write that Aldous Huxley, after his experiences of psychedelic states with mescaline and LSD-25, similarly came to the conclusion that "our brain cannot possibly be the source of these experiences. He [Huxley] suggested that it functions more like a reducing valve that shields us from an infinitely larger cosmic input. The concepts such as 'memory without a material substrate' (von Foerster 1965), Sheldrake's 'morphogenetic fields' (Sheldrake 1981), and Laszlo's 'psi or Akashic field' (Laszlo 1993, 2004) bring important support for Huxley's idea and make it increasingly plausible."

4. Hillman, *Re-Visioning Psychology*.

5. Casey, *Making the Gods Work for You*.

6. Grof, *Beyond the Brain*.

7. Hand, *Horoscope Symbols*.

8. Wilber, *The Atman Project*.

9. Summarizing these insights, Grof writes in *The Cosmic Game* that: "The overall scheme of the cosmic drama involves a dynamic interplay of two fundamental forces, one of which is centrifugal (hylotropic or matter-oriented) and the other centripetal (holotropic or aiming for wholeness) in relation to the creative principle. The undifferentiated Cosmic Consciousness shows an elemental tendency to create worlds of plurality that contain countless separate beings. . . . And conversely, the individualized units of consciousness experience their separation and alienation as painful and manifest a strong need to return to the source and reunite with it. . . . One part of us, the holotropic one, wishes to transcend the identification with the body-ego and experience dissolution and union with a larger whole. The other part, the hylotropic one, is driven by the fear of death and by the self-preservation instinct to hold onto our separate identity."

This transcendentalist, idealist, or holotropic understanding of reality, explored by Grof in *The Cosmic Game*, underlies my approach to astrology and the one presented in this book.

10. Personal communication, 2013. Tarnas also presents systematic evidence for this understanding in *Prometheus the Awakener: An Essay on the Archetypal Meaning of the Planet Uranus*.

11. Grof, *LSD Psychotherapy*.

12. Letter from C. G. Jung to Bill Wilson, January 30, 1961.

Chapter 5: The Transit Cycles of Neptune-Neptune, Saturn-Saturn, Pluto-Pluto, and Uranus-Uranus

1. For example, Tarnas was experiencing his exact Uranus-opposition-Uranus transit in 1989, when after ten years of intensive writing and research, he completed *The Passion of the Western Mind* and delivered the epilogue as a contribution to the "Philosophy and the Human Future" conference at Cambridge University, England in August of that year.

2. Jung was undergoing his Uranus return during the period 1957–1960 when he wrote the highly honored summary of his life's work, *Memories, Dreams, Reflections*. Grof, at eighty-one years of age now experiencing his Uranus return, has published his fourth new book in seven years, has seen the inauguration of an annual Global Holotropic Breathwork Day with participants from all over the world, and has been graced to see his dream come true of the rebirth of psychedelic research in clinical psychiatry, including promising work in the treatment of post-traumatic stress disorder in military veterans.

Chapter 6: The Archetypal Pairs

1. After the title quotes in each chapter, I have included the author's name, his or her relevant natal aspect, and the number of degees that the aspect is away from exact. For example, "C. G. Jung (Sun square Neptune 0°16')" indicates that the pioneering psychiatrist was

born with the Sun in a 90° square with Neptune—0 degrees and 16 minutes from the exact angle. The term *minutes* in geometry signifies 60ths of a degree.

2. The descriptions in these chapters apply to all transit combinations that involve the two planets or luminaries being discussed. For example, the chapter "Transits of Sun-Neptune" can be used to illuminate the meaning of: a) transits of Neptune to the natal Sun; b) transits of Sun to natal Neptune; c) Sun-Neptune world transits; and d) transits that activate a Sun-Neptune natal aspect. The disadvantage with these kinds of general descriptions is of course the differences in duration and intensity. Sun-to-Neptune transits are operative for six to ten days and represent brief openings to numinous and creative feelings. In contrast, transits of Neptune to the natal Sun are in effect from three to four years and correspond to profound mystical, spiritual, and creative awakenings that can permanently change people's relationships with their inner lives.

3. Tarnas, *Cosmos and Psyche*.

4. Grof, *Realms of the Human Unconscious* and *Psychology of the Future*.

5. Though I have not discussed transits to the Ascendant and Midheaven in this book, they are fairly important influences in holotropic astrology. One of the problems with using them, however, is that they are contingent on very precise times of birth and many people do not have an accurate natal time. Therefore, any reference to these transits in people's charts needs to be presented in a careful and tentative way.

Essentially, transits to the Ascendant and Midheaven, especially by conjunction, opposition, or square, will accentuate the archetypal qualities associated with the transiting planet. For example, Saturn aligning with the Ascendant or Midheaven may correspond to a heightened emergence of Saturnian and possibly BPM II (no-exit) themes in people's holotropic experiences. Uranus lighting up the Ascendant or Midheaven can help to facilitate experiences of BPM IV (rebirth and awakening).

6. Grof, *LSD Psychotherapy*.

7. Campbell, *Hero With a Thousand Faces*.

8. Grof, *Realms of the Human Unconscious*, *LSD Psychotherapy*, *Beyond the Brain*, and *Psychology of the Future*.

9. Grof, LSD Psychotherapy.

10. Tarnas, *Cycles and Symbols Conference*, 1997.

11. Although the aggressive energies in the perinatal layer of the psyche are extreme, they are a natural part of the birth cycle. Grof suggests that nature may have intended this process so that our early ancestors would gain the courage to face adversity and persevere in challenging environments, because they had already been through the prototype of intense struggle followed by breakthrough during the sequence of birth. The natural pattern of delivery imparts in human beings a deep courage that they can endure difficult situations and survive them, that things will eventually get better. The powerful emotions of birth may have been necessary for our early survival and evolution.

12. Grof, *Beyond the Brain* and *Psychology of the Future*.

13. Grof, *Beyond the Brain*.

14. All short Tarnas quotes, unless otherwise noted, are from personal communications.

15. Tarnas, *Prometheus the Awakener*, original unpublished version, 1980.

16. Grof, *LSD Psychotherapy*.

17. Ebertin, *Combination of Stellar Influences*.

18. Grof and Grof, *Holotropic Breathwork*.

19. The Grofs write that in contrast with the astonishing diversity of competing psychological theories with their widely different strategies and approaches, holotropic experiences function as an *integral approach* to self-exploration and therapy. In these states, the psyche's own "inner healer" selects the most relevant material and brings it up into awareness for processing. The sitters function as trained co-adventurers, intelligently supporting what is already trying to happen.

They note that the basic *allopathic* strategies of traditional psychotherapy, with their focus on suppressive medications, routinely suppress symptoms without treating their underlying causes, which is like a mechanic disconnecting the warning light in someone's car and then telling them that it is okay to go back out on the road. In contrast, holotropic states function as a kind of universal *homeopathic* remedy. Symptoms are recognized as the emergence of a spontaneous healing process that is attempting to complete itself. Facilitators support the direction that the psyche itself is trying to move, which is observed to be intrinsically healing. See Grof and Grof, *Holotropic Breathwork* and Martin Boroson, "Radar to the Infinite: Holotropic Breathwork and the Integral Vision" in *Exploring Holotropic Breathwork™: Selected Articles from a Decade of* The Inner Door.

20. Grof and Grof, *Holotropic Breathwork*, "Therapeutic Mechanisms," pp. 150–151.

21. Grof, *Ultimate Journey*; and Wasson, Ruck, and Hoffman, *Road to Eleusis*.

22. Interestingly, the same subject had an experience of eagle and raptor consciousness many years later, this time with Saturn trine natal Mars. In that session, the focus was on the definition and edges of the birds' sharp beaks and talons, rather than on their transcendent character.

These different experiences under different transits, while involving the same basic subject (hawks and eagles), illustrate an important tenet in archetypal astrology. Planetary alignments do not correspond in an unvarying, one-to-one way with concrete particulars— for example, Mars-Uranus with the consciousness of eagles—but on *essential qualities*. All the archetypal qualities are spread through the entire material universe, present to some degree of manifestation in all concrete particulars. For example, there is the potential for some beauty in an ugly cat and for ugly behavior in a beautiful person. It is also possible for challenging experiences to have some positive results in people's lives and for too much success to have some negative ones.

23. Tarnas was experiencing both Uranus square his natal Jupiter, and a Jupiter-square-Uranus world transit, during the watershed period in the late-1970s when he discovered the planet-BPM correlations and the association of the planet Uranus with the archetypal figure of Prometheus, initiating the field of archetypal cosmology.

24. Sakoian and Acker, *The Astrologer's Handbook.*

25. Grof, *LSD Psychotherapy.*

26. Grof, *Psychology of the Future* and *Beyond the Brain.*

27. I consider Tarnas' publication of *Cosmos and Psyche* in 2006 to be the defining moment in the shift in cultural world views currently underway; I also have a special regard for Grof's *The Cosmic Game.* Tarnas' work presents systematic and compelling evidence for a higher Universal Mind, while Grof's book suggests and explores the nature of that intelligence.

28. Grof, *Beyond the Brain*, pp. 305–306.

29. The above brief description does not even begin to do justice to Tarnas' comprehensive research in this area. Interested readers are encouraged to see his chapters in *Cosmos and Psyche* on Saturn-Pluto world transits: pp. 207–288.
   Drawing on the research of Lloyd deMause in the field of *psychohistory*, Grof further suggests that many of humanity's most destructive behaviors—such as those that routinely manifest in pronounced forms during Saturn-Pluto world transits—are the result of negative perinatal and archetypal material surfacing in the collective psyche. See his epilogue in *Beyond the Brain*: "The Current Global Crisis and the Future of Consciousness Evolution."

30. Tarnas, *Prometheus the Awakener*, original unpublished version, 1980.

31. The Italian diplomat Niccolo Machiavelli, exponent of the political ideologies of realism and pragmatism—including the claimed benefits of ruling by brutality, fear, and deception—was born with Saturn trine Pluto. The British philosopher Thomas Hobbes who wrote that life in the state of nature is "solitary, poor, nasty, brutish, and short" was born with SU/MA=SA/PL. The British philosopher and sociologist Herbert Spencer who coined the term "survival of the fittest" was born with Saturn conjunct Pluto.

32. The French theologian John Calvin, known for his alarming and fiery sermons on the threat of absolute damnation, was born with Saturn square Pluto.

33. Grof, *Beyond the Brain.*

34. Grof, *Adventure of Self-Discovery.*

35. Wasson, Ruck, and Hoffman, *Road to Eleusis.*

36. Sessa, *Psychedelic Renaissance*, pp. 83–84.

37. Hillman, *Dream and the Underworld.*

38. Hillman, *Re-Visioning Psychology*

39. Grof, *Cosmic Game.*

40. Tarnas, *Cosmos and Psyche*, pp. 353–452.

41. See Christopher Bache's classic of the Uranus-Neptune era, *Dark Night, Early Dawn.* In a series of powerful internalized sessions, Bache gained access to some of the most transcendent realms of human experience, including Absolute Consciousness. He also experienced the basic patterning and transpersonal elements of the perinatal matrices.

42. The process of systematic, internalized marijuana sessions has several unique qualities which we can now briefly review. When smoked, marijuana is fast-acting and has a relatively short duration. People can set up their space, ingest the substance, and be processing within a few minutes. The above experiences convince me that with a systematic approach, journeyers can, over time, traverse vast areas of inner ground.

  The key element here is *internalized.* Just smoking pot, per se, is not necessarily liberating and can be just another way of numbing oneself. To work through unconscious material, journeyers need to lie down in a space where they are free to make a reasonable amount of sound, let their bodies move, and be willing to follow their emotional process wherever it takes them. Internalized marijuana sessions might be considered an option when people feel a need for regular processing, but do not have access to expert sitters or a fully adequate processing space. Individuals undergoing these types of mini-sessions may still feel some amount of fear before every experience—like dropping down into the unknown over and over—but these emotions will be far less intense than what people often feel as they approach high-dose psychedelic sessions. Of course, the same medical and psychiatric cautions would apply to people considering these kinds of mini-sessions as to those undergoing breathwork or psychedelic experiences.

  Journeyers doing marijuana sessions, who have serious emotional-deprivation issues from childhood, may still want to have a sitter on hand for at least a part of every session and a partner or spiritual friend to bond with at the end. On the other hand, people who are relatively emotionally healthy, and without serious deprivation issues or a history of acting out, may be able to access transpersonal layers of nourishment directly in their experiences. However, it is still advisable to have a sitter on hand for at least a part of every few sessions.

43. Tarnas, personal communication, 1980.

44. Hand, *Planets in Transit.*

45. Grof and Grof, *Holotropic Breathwork.*

46. *ibid.*

47. Ebertin, *Combination of Stellar Influences.*

Chapter 7: Putting It All Together: Scenarios in
Self-Exploration

1. Grof, *Psychology of the Future* and *Beyond the Brain.*

2. For more clinical explorations of the architecture of emotional and psychosomatic disorders, see Grof's *LSD Psychotherapy*, *Beyond the Brain*, and *Psychology of the Future*.

Bibliography and Suggested Reading

Addey, John M., compiler. *Harmonics in Astrology: An Introductory Text-book to the New Understanding of an Old Science.* Green Bay, WI: Cambridge Circle, 1976.

Arroyo, Stephen. *Astrology, Karma and Transformation: The Inner Dimensions of the Birth Chart.* Sebastopol, CA: CRCS, 1978.

Arroyo, Stephen. *Astrology, Psychology, and the Four Elements.* Davis, CA: CRCS Publications, 1975.

Assagiolo, Roberto. *Psychosynthesis.* New York, NY: Penguin Books, 1976.

Aurobindo, Sri. *The Life Divine.* Pondicherry, India: Sri Aurobindo Ashram, Publication Department, 1977.

Bache, Christopher M. *Dark Night, Early Dawn: Steps to a Deep Ecology of Mind.* Albany: State University of New York Press, 2000.

Bache, Christopher M. *Lifecycles: Reincarnation and the Web of Life.* New York: Paragon House, 1980.

Barrow, John D., and Frank J. Tipler. *The Anthropic Cosmological Principle.* Repr. Oxford: Oxford University Press, 1986/1996.

Bateson, Gregory. *Mind and Nature: A Necessary Unity.* New York: Dutton, 1979.

Bateson, Gregory. *Steps to an Ecology of Mind: Collected Essays in Anthropology, Psychiatry, Evolution and Epistemology.* Repr. Chicago: University of Chicago Press, 1972/2000.

Bible, *The Authorized King James Version.* Wheaton, Ill: Tyndale House, 1981.

Bohm, David. *The Essential David Bohm.* Edited by Lee Nichol. London: Routledge, 2003.

Bohm, David. *Wholeness and the Implicate Order.* London: Routledge and Kegan Paul, 1980.

Bohr, Niels. *Atomic Physics and the Description of Nature.* Cambridge: Cambridge University Press, 1934.

Bolen, Jean S. *Goddesses in Everywoman: A New Psychology of Women.* San Francisco: Harper & Row, 1984.

Bolen, Jean S. *Gods in Everyman: A New Psychology of Men's Lives and Loves.* San Francisco: Harper & Row, 1989.

Bonny, Helen, and Louis M. Savary. *Music and Your Mind.* New York: Harper & Row, 1973.

Boroson, Martin. "Radar to the Infinite: Holotropic Breathwork and the Integral Vision" In *Exploring Holotropic Breathwork™: Selected Articles from a Decade of* The Inner Door. Santa Cruz, CA: Hanford Mead Publishers, 2003.

Campbell, Joseph. *The Hero with a Thousand Faces.* 2nd ed. Princeton: Princeton University Press, 1968.

Campbell, Joseph. *The Masks of God, Volume 3: Occidental Mythology.* New York: Viking, 1964.

Campbell, Joseph. *Myths to Live By.* New York: Bantam, 1972.

Campbell, Joseph and Bill Moyers. *Joseph Campbell and the Power of Myth with Bill Moyers.* New York: Mystic Fire Video, 1988.

Capra, Fritjof. *The Tao of Physics.* Berkeley, CA: Shambhala Publications, 1975.

Capra, Fritjof. *The Turning Point: Science, Society, and the Rising Culture.* New York: Simon and Schuster, 1982.

Casey, Caroline W. *Making the Gods Work for You: The Astrological Language of the Psyche.* New York: Three Rivers Press, 1998.

deMause, Lloyd. "The Independence of Psychohistory." In *The New Psychohistory.* New York: The Psychohistory Press, 1975.

Des Pres, Terrence. *The Survivor: An Anatomy of Life in the Death Camps.* New York: Oxford University Press, 1976.

Ebertin, Reinhold. *The Combination of Stellar Influences.* Translated by Alfred Roosedale and Linda Kratzsch. Aalen, Germany: Ebertin-erlag, 1972.

Eliade, Mircea. *Cosmos and History: The Myth of the Eternal Return.* New York: Harper & Row, 1959.

Elgin, Duane. *Voluntary Simplicity.* New York: William Morrow & Co., 1981.

Engelsman, Joan Chamberlain. *The Feminine Dimension of the Divine.* Wilmette, IL: Chiron, 1987.

English, Jane Butterfield. *Different Doorway: Adventures of a Caesarean Born.* Mt. Shasta, CA: Earth Heart Publishing, 1985.

Ferrer, Jorge. *The Participatory Turn: Spirituality, Mysticism, Religious Studies.* Albany, NY: State University of New York Press, 2009.

Ferrer, Jorge. *Revisioning Transpersonal Theory: A Participatory Vision of Human Spirituality.* Albany NY: State University of New York Press, 2002.

Feyerabend, Paul. *Against Method: Outline of an Anarchistic Theory of Knowledge.* Rev. ed. London: Verso, 1988.

Fodor, Nandor. *The Search for the Beloved: A Clinical Investigation of the Trauma of Birth and Prenatal Conditioning.* New Hyde Park, NY: University Books, 1949.

Forte, Robert, ed. *Entheogens and the Future of Religion.* San Francisco, CA: Council on Spiritual Practices, 1997.

Freud, Sigmund. *Civilization and Its Discontents.* Standard Edition, vol. 21. London: The Hogarth Press, 1961.

Freud, Sigmund. *The Interpretation of Dreams.* Standard Edition, vols. 4 and 5. London: The Hogarth Press, 1953.

Freud, Sigmund. *Jokes and Their Relation to the Unconscious.* London: The Hogarth Press and the Institute of Psycho-Analysis, Vol. VIII, 1960.

Fromm, Erich. *The Anatomy of Human Destructiveness.* New York, NY: Holt Rinehart & Winston, 1973.

Gauquelin, Michel. *The Cosmic Clocks: From Astrology to a Modern Science.* Chicago: Regnery, 1967.

Gauquelin, Michel. *Cosmic Influences on Human Behavior.* Translated by Joyce E. Clemow. New York: Stein and Day, 1973.

Gilligan, Carol. *In a Different Voice: Psychological Theory and Women's Development.* Cambridge: Harvard University Press, 1982.

Gimbutas, Marija. *The Goddesses and Gods of Old Europe,* 6500-3500 B.C.: *Myths and Cult Images.* Rev. ed. Berkeley: University of California Press, 1982.

Gimbutas, Marija. *The Language of the Goddess: Unearthing the Hidden Symbols of Western Civilization.* San Francisco: Harper & Row, 1989.

Gleick, James. *Chaos: Making a New Science.* New York: Viking, 1988.

Goleman, Daniel. *Emotional Intelligence.* New York, NY: Bantam Books, 1996.

Goswami, Amit. *The Self-Aware Universe: How Consciousness Creates the Material World.* Los Angeles, CA: J. P. Tarcher, 1995.

Greene, Liz. *Relating: An Astrological Guide to Living with Others on a Small Planet.* York Beach, ME: Samuel Weiser, 1978.

Greene, Liz. *Saturn: A New Look at an Old Devil*. York Beach, ME: Samuel Weiser, 1976.

Greyson, Bruce, and C. P. Flynn, eds. *The Near-Death Experience: Problems, Prospects, Perspectives*. Springfield, IL: Charles C. Thomas, 1984.

Grof, Christina. *The Thirst for Wholeness: Attachment, Addiction, and the Spiritual Path*. San Francisco, CA: Harper, 1993.

Grof, Christina, and Stanislav Grof. *The Stormy Search for the Self: A Guide to Personal Growth through Transformational Crisis*. Los Angeles: J. P. Tarcher, 1991.

Grof, Stanislav. *The Adventure of Self-Discovery*. Albany: State University of New York Press, 1988.

Grof, Stanislav. *Beyond the Brain: Birth, Death, and Transcendence in Psychotherapy*. Albany: State University of New York Press, 1985.

Grof, Stanislav. *Books of the Dead: Manuals for Living and Dying*. London: Thames and Hudson, 1993.

Grof, Stanislav. *The Cosmic Game: Explorations of the Frontiers of Human Consciousness*. Albany: State University of New York Press, 1998.

Grof, Stanislav. *Healing Our Deepest Wounds: The Holotropic Paradigm Shift*. Newcastle, WA: Stream of Experience Productions, 2012.

Grof, Stanislav. "Holotropic Research and Archetypal Astrology," *Archai: The Journal of Archetypal Cosmology*, Volume 1, Number 1 (Summer 2009). Edited by Keiron Le Grice and Rod O'Neal. San Francisco: Archai Press, 2011.

Grof, Stanislav. *LSD Psychotherapy*. Pomona, CA: Hunter House, 1980. (Republished in 2001 by The Multidisciplinary Association for Psychedelic Studies (MAPS) Publications in Sarasota, Florida).

Grof, Stanislav. *Psychology of the Future: Lessons from Modern Consciousness Research*. Albany, NY: State University of New York Press, 2000.

Grof, Stanislav. *Realms of the Human Unconscious: Observations from LSD Research*. New York: Viking Press, 1975. (Republished in 2009 as *LSD: Doorway to the Numinous: The Ground-Breaking Psychedelic Research into Realms of the Human Unconscious*. Rochester, VT: Inner Traditions).

Grof, Stanislav. *The Ultimate Journey: Consciousness and the Mystery of Death*. Sarasota, FL: MAPS Publications, 2006.

Grof, Stanislav. *When the Impossible Happens: Adventures in Non-Ordinary Realities*. Boulder, CO: Sounds True, 2006.

Grof, Stanislav, and Christina Grof. *Holotropic Breathwork: A New Approach to Therapy and Self-Exploration*. Albany: State University of New York Press, 2012.

Grof, Stanislav and Christina Grof, eds. *Spiritual Emergency: When Personal Transformation Becomes a Crisis*. Los Angeles: J. P. Tarcher, 1989.

Grof, Stanislav, and Joan Halifax. *The Human Encounter with Death*. New York: E. P. Dutton, 1977.

Hand, Robert. *Essays on Astrology*. Atglen, PA: Schiffer Publishing, 1982.

Hand, Robert. *Horoscope Symbols*. Gloucester, MA: Para Research, 1981.

Hand, Robert. *Planets in Transit: Life Cycles for Living*. Rockport, MA: Para Research, 1976.

Hand, Robert. *Planets in Youth*. Rockport, MA: Para Research, 1977.

Harner, Michael. *The Way of the Shaman: A Guide to Power and Healing*. New York, NY: Harper & Row, 1980.

Herbert, Nick. *Mind Science: A Physics of Consciousness Primer*. Boulder Creek, CA: C-Life Institute, 1979.

Heisenberg, Werner. *Physics and Philosophy: The Revolution in Modern Science*. Repr. New York: Prometheus Books, 1958/1999.

Hillman, James. *The Dream and the Underworld*. New York: Harper & Row, 1979.

Hillman, James. *Re-Visioning Psychology*. New York: Harper & Row, 1975.

Hines, Brian. *God's Whisper, Creation's Thunder: Echoes of Ultimate Reality in the New Physics*. Brattleboro, VT: Threshold Books, 1996.

Homer. *The Odyssey*. Trans. E. V. Rieu. Revised Edition. London: Penguin Classics, 2003.

Huxley, Aldous. *Perennial Philosophy*. New York and London: Harper and Brothers, 1945.

Jacobson, Bertil, et al. "Perinatal Origin of Adult Self-Destructive Behavior." *Acta Psychiat. Scand.* 76:364–371, 1987.

James, William. *A Pluralistic Universe*. Cambridge: Harvard University Press, 1977.

James, William. *The Varieties of Religious Experience*. New York, NY: Collier, 1961.

Jung, Carl G. *Collected Works of Carl Gustav Jung*. 20 vols. Translated by R. F. C. Hull. Edited by H. Read, M. Fordham, G. Adler, and W. McGuire. Bollingen Series XX. Princeton: Princeton University Press, 1953–79.

Jung, Carl G. *Memories, Dreams, Reflections*. New York: Pantheon Books, 1961.

Jung, Carl G. *The Red Book*. New York: W. W. Norton and Company, 2009.

Jung, Carl G. et. al. *Man and His Symbols*. New York: Dell Publishing, 1968.

Keller, Evelyn Fox. *Reflections on Gender and Science.* New Haven: Yale University Press, 1985.

Kellogg, Joan. *Mandala: The Path of Beauty.* Baltimore, MD: Mandala Assessment and Research Institute, 1978.

Kelly, Sean. *Individuation and the Absolute.* New York: Paulist Press, 1993.

Kelly, Sean, and Donald Rothberg, eds. *Ken Wilber in Dialogue: Conversations with Leading Transpersonal Thinkers.* Wheaton, IL: Quest Books, 1998.

Kuhn, Thomas S. *The Copernican Revolution: Planetary Astronomy and the Development of Western Thought.* Cambridge: Harvard University Press, 1957.

Kuhn, Thomas S. *The Structure of Scientific Revolutions.* Chicago: University of Chicago Press, 1962.

Laing, Ronald D. *The Divided Self.* New York: Penguin, 1965.

Laing, Ronald D. *The Politics of Experience.* Harmondsworth, England: Penguin, 1967.

Lao-tzu. *Tao Te Ching.* Translated by Stephen Mitchell. New York: Harper & Row, 1988.

Laszlo, Ervin. *The Creative Cosmos: A Unified Science of Matter, Life and Mind.* Edinburgh, Scotland: Floris Books, 1993.

Laszlo, Ervin. *Science and the Akashic Field: An Integral Theory of Everything.* Rochester, VT: Inner Traditions, 2004.

Laszlo, Ervin. *Subtle Connections: Psi, Grof, Jung, and the Quantum Vacuum.* The International Society for the Systems Sciences and The Club of Budapest, 1996.

Laszlo, Ervin, Stanislav Grof, and Peter Russell. *The Consciousness Revolution: A Transatlantic Dialogue.* London and Las Vegas, NV: Elf Rock Productions, 2003.

Laszlo, E. and Ralph H. Abraham. *The Connectivity Hypothesis: Foundations of an Integral Science of Quantum, Cosmos, Life, and Consciousness.* Albany, NY: State University of New York (SUNY) Press, 2004.

Le Grice, Keiron. *The Archetypal Cosmos: Rediscovering the Gods in Myth, Science and Astrology.* Edinburgh: Floris Books, 2010.

Le Grice, Keiron. "The Birth of a New Discipline: Archetypal Cosmology in Historical Perspective." In *The Birth of a New Discipline. Archai: The Journal of Archetypal Cosmology*, Issue 1 (summer 2009), edited by Keiron Le Grice and Rod O'Neal. Repr. San Francisco: Archai Press, 2011.

Le Grice, Keiron. "The Dark Spirit in Nature: C. G. Jung and the Spiritual Transformation of Our Time." In *Beyond a Disenchanted Cosmology. Archai: The Journal of Archetypal Cosmology.* Issue 3 (Fall 2011). Edited by Keiron Le Grice, Grant Maxwell, and Bill Streett. San Francisco: Archai Press, 2011.

Le Grice, Keiron. *The Rebirth of the Hero: Mythology as a Guide to Spiritual Transformation.* London: Muswell Hill Press, 2012.

Litt, S. "A Study of Perinatal Complications as a Factor in Criminal Behavior." *Criminology,* Volume 12, Issue 1, 1974.

Lorenz, K. *On Aggression.* New York, NY: Harcourt, Brace & World, 1963.

Lovejoy, Arthur O. *The Great Chain of Being: A Study of the History of an Idea.* Cambridge: Harvard University Press, 1936.

Lovelock, James. *Gaia: A New Look at Life on Earth.* Oxford: Oxford University Press, 1979.

Mansfield, Victor. *Synchronicity, Science, and Soul-Making: Understanding Jungian Synchronicity Through Physics, Buddhism, and Philosophy.* Chicago: Open Court, 1995.

Martin, Joyce. "LSD Analysis," in H. A. Abramson (ed.) *The Use of LSD in Psychotherapy and Alcoholism.* Indianapolis, IN: Bobbs-Merrill, 1967.

Maslow, Abraham. *Religions, Values, and Peak Experiences.* Columbus, OH: Ohio State University, 1964.

Maslow, Abraham. *Toward a Psychology of Being.* Princeton: Van Nostrand, 1962.

Merchant, Carolyn. *The Death of Nature: Women, Ecology, and the Scientific Revolution.* San Francisco: Harper & Row, 1980.

Metzner, Ralph. *The Unfolding Self: Varieties of Transformative Experiences.* Novato, CA: Origin Press, 1998.

Miller, Jean Baker, ed. *Psychoanalysis and Women.* New York: Penguin, 1973.

Moody, Raymond A. *Life After Life.* New York, NY: Bantam, 1975.

Moody, Raymond A. *Reunions: Visionary Encounters with Departed Loved Ones.* New York: Villard Books, 1993.

Mookerjee, Ajit. *Kundalini: The Arousal of the Inner Energy.* New York: Destiny Books, 1982.

Nietzsche, Friedrich. *Thus Spoke Zarathustra.* Trans. Richard Hollingdale. New York: Penguin, 1968.

O'Neal, Rod. "Seasons of Agony and Grace: An Archetypal History of New England Puritanism." PhD diss., California Institute of Integral Studies, 2008.

Pagels, Elaine. *The Gnostic Gospels.* New York: Random House, 1979.

Pahnke, Walter. "Drugs and Mysticism: An Analysis of the Relationship between Psychedelic Drugs and the Mystical Consciousness." Ph.D. Dissertation, Harvard University, 1963.

Pauli, Wolfgang. "The Influence of Archetypal Ideas on the Scientific Theories of Kepler." Translated by P. Silz. In C. G. Jung and W. Pauli, *The Interpretation of Nature and the Psyche*. New York: Pantheon, 1955.

Peat, F. David. *Synchronicity: The Bridge Between Matter and Mind*. New York: Bantam Books, 1987.

Perls, Fritz. *Gestalt Approach and Witness to Therapy*. Palo Alto, CA: Science and Behavior Books, 1973.

Perry, John W. *The Far Side of Madness*. Englewood Cliffs, NJ: Prentice Hall, 1974.

Plato. *The Collected Dialogues*. Edited by E. Hamilton and H. Cairns. Princeton: Princeton University Press, 1961.

Plotinus. *The Enneads*. Translated by S. MacKenna. 3rd rev. ed., by B. S. Page. Introduction by P. Henry. London: Faber and Faber, 1962.

Popper, Karl, R. *Conjectures and Refutations: The Growth of Scientific Knowledge*. New York: Harper Torchbook, 1968.

Pribram, Karl. *Languages of the Brain*. Englewood Cliffs, NJ: Prentice Hall, 1971.

Prigogine, Ilya. *From Being to Becoming: Time and Complexity in the Physical Sciences*. San Francisco: Freeman, 1980.

Prigogine, Ilya, and Isabelle Stengers. *Order out of Chaos: Man's Dialogue with Nature*. New York: Bantam Books, 1984.

Ptolemy. *Tetrabiblos*. Translated by J. M. Ashmand. North Hollywood, CA: Symbols and Signs, 1976.

Rank, Otto. *The Trauma of Birth*. New York: Harcourt Brace, 1929.

Reich, Wilhelm. *The Mass Psychology of Fascism*. New York: Simon and Schuster, 1970.

Ring, Kenneth. *Life and Death: A Scientific Investigation of the Near-Death Experience*. New York: Quill, 1982.

Ring, Kenneth, and Sharon Cooper. *Mindsight: Near-Death and Out-of-Body Experiences in the Blind*. Palo Alto, CA: William James Centre for Consciousness Studies, 1999.

Ring, Kenneth, and Evelyn Elsaesser Valarino. *Lessons from the Light: What We Can Learn from the Near-Death Experiences*. New York: Plenum Press, 1998.

Rogers, Carl. *Client-Centered Therapy: Its Current Practice, Implications and Theory*. Boston: Houghton Mifflin, 1951.

Rothberg, Donald. "Philosophical Foundations of Transpersonal Psychology," *Journal of Transpersonal Psychology*, 18, 1, 1986.

Rudhyar, Dane. *The Astrology of Personality*. Santa Fe, New Mexico: Aurora Press, 1936.

Rudhyar, Dane. *The Astrology of Transformation: A Multilevel Approach*. Wheaton, IL: Quest Books, 1980.

Rudhyar, Dane. *Birth Patterns for a New Humanity: A Study of Astrological Cycles Structuring the Present World Crisis*. Wassenaar, Holland: Servire, 1969.

Ruether, Rosemary Radford, ed. *Religion and Sexism: Images of Woman in the Jewish and Christian Traditions*. New York: Simon & Schuster, 1974.

Sannella, Lee. *The Kundalini Experience: Psychosis or Transcendence?* Lower Lake, CA: Integral Publishing, 1987.

Sessa, Ben. *The Psychedelic Renaissance: Reassessing the Role of Psychedelic Drugs in 21st Century Psychiatry and Society*. London: Muswell Hill Press, 2012.

Sheldrake, Rupert. *Habits of Nature*. Repr. Rochester, VT: Park Street Press, 1995.

Sheldrake, Rupert. *A New Science of Life: The Hypothesis of Formative Causation*. Los Angeles: Tarcher, 1981.

Sheldrake, Rupert. *The Presence of the Past: Morphic Resonance and the Habits of Nature*. New York: Times Books, 1988.

Singer, June. *Boundaries of the Soul: The Practice of Jung's Psychology*. Garden City, NY: Doubleday/Anchor Press, 1972.

Smith, Huston. *Beyond the Post-Modern Mind*. Rev. ed. Wheaton, IL: Quest, 1989.

Smith, Huston. *The Forgotten Truth: The Common Vision of the World's Religions*. San Francisco: Harper & Row, 1976.

Sparks, Tav. *Doing Not Doing: A Facilitator's Guide to Holotropic Breathwork*. Mill Valley, CA: Holotropic Books and Music, 1989.

Sparks, Tav. *The Wide Open Door: The Twelve Steps, Spiritual Tradition, and the New Psychology*. Centre City, MN: Hazelden Education Materials, 1993.

Spretnak, Charlene. *Lost Goddesses of Early Greece*. Boston: Beacon Press, 1984.

Stevenson, Ian. *Children Who Remember Previous Lives*. Charlottesville, VA: University of Virginia Press, 1987.

Stevenson, Ian. *Twenty Cases Suggestive of Reincarnation*. Charlottesville, VA: University of Virginia Press, 1966.

Streett, Bill, and Kishner, Jeffrey, eds. *The Astrology of Film: The Interface of Movies, Myth, and Archetype*. Lincoln, NE: iUniverse, Inc., 2004.

Sutich, Anthony. "The Emergence of the Transpersonal Orientation: A Personal Account." *Journal of Transpersonal Psychology* 8:5–19,1976.

Swimme, Brian. *The Hidden Heart of the Cosmos: Humanity and the New Story.* Maryknoll, NY: Orbis Books, 1996.

Swimme, Brian. *The Powers of the Universe* (DVD). San Francisco, CA: The Center for the Story of the Universe, 2004.

Swimme, Brian, and Thomas Berry. *The Universal Story: From the Primordial Flaring Forth to the Ecozoic Era.* Repr. San Francisco: Harper San Francisco, 1992/1994.

Talbot, Michael. *The Holographic Universe.* San Francisco, CA: Harper Collins, 1991.

Tarnas, Richard. *Cosmos and Psyche: Intimations of a New World View.* New York: Viking Press, 2006.

Tarnas, Richard. "An Introduction to Archetypal Astrology" 1987. http://www.cosmosand-psyche.com/pages/essays/ (accessed February 6, 2013).

Tarnas, Richard. *The Passion of the Western Mind: Understanding the Ideas That Have Shaped Our World View.* NY: Harmony Books, 1991.

Tarnas, Richard. *Prometheus the Awakener: An Essay on the Archetypal Meaning of the Planet Uranus.* Woodstock, CT: Spring Publications, 1995.

Taylor, Kylea. *The Breathwork Experience: Exploration and Healing in Non-Ordinary States of Consciousness.* Santa Cruz, CA: Hanford Mead Publishers, 1994.

Taylor, Kylea. *The Ethics of Caring: Honoring the Web of Life in Our Professional Healing Relationships.* Santa Cruz, CA: Hanford Mead Publishers, 1995.

Taylor, Kylea. *Exploring Holotropic Breathwork™: Selected Articles from a Decade of* The Inner Door. Santa Cruz, CA: Hanford Mead Publishers, 2003.

Taylor, Kylea. *The Holotropic Breathwork Workshop: A Manual for Trained Facilitators.* Santa Cruz, CA: Hanford Mead Publishers, 1991.

Teilhard de Chardin, Pierre. *The Future of Man.* New York: Harper and Row, 1964.

Townley, John. *Planets in Love: Exploring Your Emotional and Sexual Needs.* Rockport, MA: Para Research, 1978.

von Foerster, Heinz. "Memory without Record." In *The Anatomy of Memory.* Edited by D. P. Kimble. Palo Alto, CA: Science and Behavior Books, 1965.

von Franz, Marie-Louise. *Alchemical Active Imagination.* New York: C. G. Jung Foundation Books, 1997.

von Franz, Marie-Louise. *Number and Time: Reflections Leading toward a Unification of Depth Psychology and Physics.* Evanston, IL: Northwestern University Press, 1974.

Wambach, Helen. *Life Before Life*. New York: Bantam, 1979.

Wasson, Gordon, Albert Hoffman, and Carl A. P. Ruck. *The Road to Eleusis: Unveiling the Secret of the Mysteries*. New York, NY: Harcourt, Brace and Jovanovich, 1978.

Watts, Alan. *The Book: On the Taboo Against Knowing Who You Are*. New York: Vintage Books, 1966.

Watts, Alan. *Psychotherapy East and West*. New York: Pantheon, 1961.

Wilber, Ken. *The Atman Project: A Transpersonal View of Human Development*. Wheaton, IL: Theosophical Publishing House, 1980.

Wilber, Ken. *The Spectrum of Consciousness*. Wheaton, IL: Theosophical Publishing House, 1977.

Wolf, Fred Alan. *Taking the Quantum Leap*. San Francisco, CA: Harper & Row, 1981.

Yockey, Hubert P. *Information Theory and Molecular Biology*. Cambridge: Cambridge University Press, 1992.

Zukav, Gary. *The Dancing Wu Li Masters*. New York: W. Morrow, 1979.

Index

Absolute Consciousness, 8, 46, 47–48, 52, 55, 79, 91, 97, 114, 160, 291*n*41
Achilles, 146, 230
Addiction, 53, 181, 216
Adonis, 236
Aggression, 159, 172, 272, 278
  biographical sources of, 133, 186
  and Mars, 24, 43, 118, 120, 229, 250, 252, 253
  passive forms of, 132, 141
  perinatal sources of, 11, 12, 24, 43, 121, 123, 130, 187, 188, 203, 288*n*11
  and Pluto, 23, 56, 129, 151, 188, 265
  and sexuality, 123, 130, 147, 152, 247
  rape and sexual abuse, 7, 13, 116, 123, 188, 245, 283*n*10
  transcendence of, 168, 251, 278
  transpersonal sources of, 131, 146, 149, 251
Alchemy, 154, 226
Alzheimer's, 88
Amazons, 230
Anesthesia, reliving effects of, 162, 163, 198
Anarchism, archetypal impulse behind, 51
Anima mundi (world soul), 3, 96, 98
Animals, consciousness of, 8, 10, 70, 85, 108, 135, 164, 174, 178, 183, 190, 199, 214, 230, 235, 253
Apocalypse, archetype of the, 191
Apollo, 10, 16, 20, 53, 80, 81, 131, 160, 214, 217, 219, 228, 232
  (*see also* Ecstasy)
Archai: The Journal of Archetypal Cosmology, 281*n*7, 282*n*9
Art,
  appreciation of, 78, 90, 168, 248
  artistic breakthroughs, 72–73, 168, 175
  cosmic creative principle as artist, 47
  in session spaces, 64, 236

spiritual, 248
  utilitarian, 115
  (*see also* Beauty, Mandalas)
Archetypal astrology, 4, 15, 16, 26–28, 284*n*14
  as archetypal telescope, 5
  as archetypally predictive, 5, 7, 17, 77, 289*n*22
  in contrast with traditional astrology, 4, 77
  as Rosetta Stone, 3
Arendt, Hannah, 193
Ares, 95, 247
Artemis, 173
Ascendant, transits to the, 113, 288*n*5
Aspects,
  definition of, 17–19
  minor aspects, 284*n*15
  sextiles, 284*n*15
Astronomical phenomena,
  consciousness of, 109, 149, 199
Atman–Brahman unity, 9, 37, 46, 51, 80, 233
Autoerotic asphyxiation, 11
  (*see also* Suffocation, Sadomasochism)
Ayahuasca, 34, 85, 99, 130, 154, 155, 158, 159, 169, 253, 262, 264

Bache, Christopher, 291*n*41
Bacteria, consciousness of, 153, 204
Bankhead, Tallulah, 171
Beauty,
  appreciation of and responses to, 42, 268, 228, 235, 244, 245, 247
  beautiful goddesses, 92, 171
  cosmic beauty, 16, 41, 42, 92, 99, 117, 170, 171, 198, 228, 249
  in the integration phase of sessions, 64, 86, 236, 248, 249
  in nature, 31, 90, 91, 141, 189, 282*n*3

problems around, 92, 116, 117, 141
and vanity, 42, 65, 115, 141, 228,
    244, 248
and Venus, 41, 42, 90, 140, 167, 240
in visions, 86, 169
Beloved, the archetype of the, 41, 57,
    91, 117
Beauvoir, Simone de, 164
Bipolar disorder, 36, 176, 275–276,
    285n20
    (see also Manic feelings)
Birthdays, 224
Blake, William, 49
Basic Perinatal Matrix I, 9–10
    related postnatal memories, 282n3
Basic Perinatal Matrix II, 10
    related postnatal memories, 283n4
Basic Perinatal Matrix III, 11–14
    related postnatal memories, 283n10
Basic Perinatal Matrix IV, 14
    related postnatal memories, 284n12
Breastfeeding, 14, 82, 163, 235, 236
Brontë, Charlotte, 229
Brontë, Emily, 86
Browning, Elizabeth Barrett, 90
Buck, Pearl, 105, 167
Buddhism, 20, 51, 52, 60, 80, 85, 135, 166,
    183, 184, 212, 278

Calvin, John, 290n32
Campbell, Joseph, 41, 45, 53, 75, 128
Carr, Emily, 175
Casey, Caroline W., 23, 41, 44, 90, 101, 175
Causation, 57
Chakras, 80, 128, 166, 171, 178, 232
Chaos theory, 5
Chi energy, 253
Chinese philosophy 127
    (see also Confucianism, the Golden
    Mean, Taoism)
Christ, 13, 20, 70, 80, 148, 155, 160, 177,
    178, 183, 207, 218
    Christianity, 200, 262, 278, 282n3
Christ complex, 160
Churchill, Winston, 118, 137
Circulus diaboli, 181
Clash of the Titans, 146, 203,
Claustrophobia, perinatal roots of, 71, 121
COEX systems (memory systems of

condensed experience), 102, 107,
    133, 194
Confucianism, 51,239, 254
Cornucopia, the, 96, 98, 239
Cosmic creative principle, 2, 10, 24, 28,
    37, 58, 66, 83, 95, 110, 131, 265
    the world as virtual reality, 47–48, 114
Cosmic Game, The (Grof), 46, 47, 180,
    287, 290
Cosmic Shadow, 131, 191
    (see also Evil)
Cosmic unity, feelings of, 20, 51, 78,
    208, 283n9
    yearning for, 87, 89
Cosmogenesis, 221
Cosmology, the birth of a new, 281n4,
    290n23, 290n27
    (see also Tarnas)
Cosmos and Psyche (Tarnas), 4, 26, 27, 175,
    179, 186, 202, 216, 281n4, 290n27
Crone or Hag archetype, 21, 109–110, 117,
    136, 137, 207, 218
Cronos, 21, 104, 184, 200
Crucifixion, 152, 188

De Goya, Francisco, 113
De Musset, Alfred, 193
Death,
    fear of, 48, 62, 70
    transcendence of the fear of, 2, 8, 24, 48
    (see also Ego death)
Deep indigenous tradition, 31, 33
    (see also Ayahuasca)
DeMause, Lloyd, and the field of
    psychohistory, 290n29
Demeter, 14, 21, 85, 164, 183
Demonic experiences,
    in perinatal sessions, 12, 13, 22, 55, 65,
    131, 135, 139, 148, 152, 189, 191,
    196, 204, 208, 211, 214
    in toxic womb experiences, 53, 59
    (see also Evil)
Depression, origins in birth trauma, 26, 48,
    63, 101, 181, 266, 271, 277
    (see also Bipolar disorder)
Deprivation issues, 7, 107, 115–116, 236,
    262, 291n42
    (see also Traumas of omission)
Deus ex machina, 176

Dictators, 123, 126
Dietrich, Marlene, 251
Diogenes, 244
Dionysus, 13, 54, 131, 148, 154, 207, 214
(see also Ecstasy)
Disraeli, Benjamin, 236
Divine Child archetype, 160
Divine Consciousness, 14, 18, 19, 21, 46,
48, 52, 54, 57, 58
the Divine Feminine, 86, 91, 142, 163,
225, 259 (see also Great Mother
Goddess)
the Divine Masculine, 157 (see also God)
human history as a love affair
with, 46, 57
(see also Absolute Consciousness, the
Universal Mind)
Divine Womb, 100
DMT, 35
Dryden, John, 247
Dylan, Bob, 156

Earth Mother, 136
Ecological values and imperatives, 2, 15,
74, 158, 163, 178, 202, 277–278
catastrophe, 189, 191, 277
(see also Mother Nature)
Ecstasy (and ecstatic experiences), 42, 74,
189, 204, 215, 218, 283n9
Apollonian–oceanic, 10, 19, 53, 81, 82,
91, 98, 211, 219, 282n3
Dionysian–volcanic, 11, 13, 70, 147, 206
Promethean–illuminative, 14, 166,
178, 219
(see also MDMA)
Ego, 11, 37, 47, 48, 51, 52, 53, 54, 55, 61
Ego death, 14, 25–50, 68, 71, 204, 211
Einstein, Albert, 9
Electra complex, 182, 197
Eleusis, 2, 33, 166
(see also Mystery religions)
Eliot, George, 111
Eliot, T. S., 46, 208, 240
Ellis, Havelock, 225
Elysian Fields, 51, 80
Encapsulation of traumatic experiences,
39, 284
(see also Trauma)
Energy blocks, 122

Ergot, 2, 207
Evil, 12, 23, 117, 127, 140, 142, 148,
200, 208
(see also Cosmic Shadow, Demonic
experiences)
Evolutionary energies, 23, 33, 54, 55, 132,
150, 155, 200, 202, 204, 205, 207,
216, 259, 267, 269, 279
evolutionary history, 60, 64, 66, 178,
179, 288n11
Extremism, psychological roots of, 51, 194

Fairy tale realms, 117, 127
Fall from paradise, perinatal roots of the,
10, 21, 66, 88, 102, 117, 132, 156,
179, 183, 191, 222
Fate, archetype of, 48, 136, 191
Father, issues with, 37, 80, 88, 102, 105,
116, 138, 154, 157, 159, 231, 233
positive memories of, 79, 80, 157,
159, 228
directly reliving experience of, 158, 231
Father archetype, 61
angry or terrible father archetype, 21,
122, 197, 200
heavenly or supportive father archetype,
21, 79, 80, 151, 159, 160, 163,
197, 228
Fear, 100
perinatal roots of, 121, 142, 148, 177,
183, 187, 213, 221, 284–285n18
and aggression 43, 122
of aging, 65, 117
of change, 51
of death, 2, 8, 62, 287n9
of hubris, 176
of losing bodily control, 196, 245
of making sounds, 105, 113
of rejection or abandonment, 10, 113
and Saturn, 47–48, 101, 119, 192,
194, 195
in sessions, 145, 197, 272
and sexuality, 145, 197, 272
of thoughts, 40
Feminine principle, 14, 21, 38, 80, 84, 85,
92, 107, 136, 143, 148, 161, 164, 168,
169, 184, 219, 220, 226, 238
(see also Divine Feminine, Great Mother
Goddess, individual goddesses)

Ferguson, Marilyn, 132
Flashbacks, 34
Focused bodywork, 124, 145, 149,
     151, 174, 192, 198, 201, 230,
     251, 254
Forgiveness, 15, 63, 74, 75, 94, 158, 178,
     189, 219, 239
Fractal patterns, 166
Freedom,
     inherent in the new cosmology, 281*n*4,
     and Jupiter, 45
     and Saturn, 66, 93, 194
     of thought, 164–165
     and Uranus, 15, 16, 24, 51, 72, 121, 160,
          173, 177, 179, 201, 285*n*20
Frigidity, 147
Frost, Robert, 156
Fuller, Buckminster, 208
Furies, the, 136

Galileo, 3, 277
Gay rights, 202
Generation gap, 193
Genocide, 71, 84, 190
     (*see also* Collective memories)
Gide, André, 49
Global Mind, the, 221
God, 14, 47, 80, 92, 99, 135
     and founders of modern science, 3
     and Neptune, 51–52, 59, 78
     (*see also* Great Mother Goddess, the
          Divine, Absolute Consciousness)
Goethe, Johann von, 128, 201, 229, 247
Golden Mean, the, 127
Goldman, Emma, 161
Good, archetype of the, 96, 128, 153, 212,
     220, 221, 228, 231, 232
     good and evil, 12, 117, 127, 131, 148,
          200, 208
     Great Mother Goddess, 143, 164, 169, 219,
          220, 222, 238
     (*see also* the Divine Feminine,
          Feminine principle, individual
          goddesses)
     Terrible or Devouring Mother archetype,
          10, 21, 109, 136, 147, 184
Greeks, ancient, 16, 33, 127, 166, 176
Greene, Liz, 4, 23, 54, 61
Grim Reaper, archetype of the, 54, 66

Grof, Stanislav, 1–2, 8, 9, 40, 43, 46, 47,
     51, 53
     codeveloper of Holotropic Breathwork, 7
     collaboration with Richard Tarnas, 3–5,
          15–16, 19–25, 30, 48
     discovery of the perinatal matrices, 1, 7,
          9–15, 25
     psychedelic research, 1, 29–35, 55
Grof, Christina,
     codeveloper of Holotropic Breathwork, 7
     introducing the term spiritual
          emergency, 272, 285

Hades, 154, 191
Hammerstein II, Oscar, 230
Hand, Robert, 4, 23, 39, 44, 67, 78, 93,
     224, 240
Harsh Taskmaster, the, 47, 66
Hate and bitterness,working through, 107,
     116, 118, 119, 120, 143, 153, 187, 197
Heart chakra, opening of in rebirth
     experiences, 80, 166, 171
Hercules, 13, 188, 230, 285
Hegel, G. W. F., 201
Hell, 10, 21, 103, 108, 113, 182, 183, 185,
     187, 218
     (*see also* Hades, Underworld
          experiences)
Hero, archetype of the, 13, 14, 75, 158,
     160, 173, 207, 216, 219, 232
     the hero's journey, 128
Hesse, Hermann, 118
Hieros gamos, 154
Higher Power, 53, 181, 264, 269
     (*see also* the Divine, the Great Mother
          Goddess)
Higher sanity, 53, 178
Hillman, James, 40, 209
Hobbes, Thomas, 188, 290
Holmes, Oliver Wendell, 143
Holographic nature of reality, 5, 221
Holotropic astrology, 5, 257, 282
Holotropic Breathwork, 2, 3, 7, 12, 35, 92,
     162, 242, 258, 272, 287*n*2
Holotropic mode of consciousness, 1, 8–9,
     47, 96, 180, 184, 278, 287*n*9
     holotropic experiences as an integral
          approach to healing, 289*n*19 (*see also*
          Inner healer)

contraindications for holotropic and
   psychedelic states, 35–36
Hubris, 176
Hylotropic mode of consciousness, 8, 21,
   47, 96, 180, 184, 278, 287*n*9

Ibogaine, 34, 146
Icarus, 75, 177
Idealism, 3, 78, 87, 96, 152, 243
Impotence, 147
Inanna, 154, 171, 207
   (*see also* Ishtar)
Incarnation, process of, 27, 48, 52, 66, 100,
   109, 160, 180, 184, 193, 200, 204,
   221–222
   (*see also* Involution)
Incest, 142
Indian and Vedic philosophy, 78, 89,
   139, 207
Inflation, psychic, 78, 80, 125
Inner healer, 17, 144, 161, 172, 217, 250,
   271, 289
Inorganic materials, objects, and processes,
   consciousness of, 8, 64–65, 123–124,
   149, 191, 198, 199, 221
Intentional dance events, 31, 32, 259–260
Intrinsic human values, 15, 74
Involution, 21, 66, 200
Ishtar, 92, 171, 228
Isis, 21, 85

James, William, 86
Johnson, Samuel, 234
Judgment,
   Divine, 10, 13, 69, 126, 188
   parental, 102, 107, 116
Jung, Carl Gustav, 208, 287*n*2
   and astrology, 26
   and depth psychology, 4, 5, 8, 27,
      60–61, 70
   discovery of the archetypes, 3, 16, 53,
      54, 78, 132, 161, 208
   and synchronicity, 17
Jupiter (planetary archetype), 44–46

Kabbalah, 98, 282*n*3
Kael, Pauline, 245
Kali, 13, 54, 109, 131, 137, 154, 184,
   191, 214

Kepler, Johannes, 3
Kerouac, Jack, 171
Kübler–Ross, Elisabeth, 100
Kwan Yin, 21, 85, 183

Lakshmi, 14, 164
Languages, resonance with ancient, 89
Lao Tzu, 44, 286*n*3
   (*see also* Taoism)
Laszlo, Ervin, 5
Lawrence, D. H., 230
Le Grice, Keiron, 5, 281*n*7
Le Guin, Ursula K., 237
Liberace, 247
Lingam, 214, 247
Loneliness, 103, 114–116
   of the cosmic creative principle, 47,
      83, 110
Lord of the Rings, 124, 153
Lotus, the, 184, 215
Love, 38, 41–42, 82, 85, 90, 93, 114, 115,
   116, 140, 141, 142, 167, 168, 170,
   220, 228, 235, 244, 245
   Divine, 18, 47, 57, 71, 80, 91, 141, 171,
      236, 245
   feeling unloved, 83, 108
   and hate, 116, 143, 197
   tough love and Saturn–Pluto, 193

M.A.P.S. (The Multidisciplinary
   Association for Psychedelic
   Studies), 29
Machiavelli, Niccolo, 290*n*31
Mandalas and paintings presented in this
   book,
   mystical, oceanic (Neptunian) themes,
      20, 60, 83, 98, 99, 211, 212, 220, 232
   constricted, "no exit" (Saturnian)
      themes, 22, 103, 121
   shadow, death–rebirth struggle
      (Plutonic) themes, 23, 71, 130, 137,
      145, 152, 192
   rebirth, breakthrough (Uranian) themes,
      25, 159, 169, 174, 205, 206
Manic feelings
   at the end of sessions, 160, 167, 179
   fanaticism, 202
   restlessness or hyperactivity, 24, 73,
      161, 165, 202

Manic depression (*see* Bipolar disorder)
Mann, Thomas, 241
Marijuana, 34, 64, 65, 109, 153, 207, 219, 221, 291*n*42
Marlowe, Christopher, 235
Mars (planetary archetype), 42–44
   (*see also* Aggression)
Martyrs, 200, 218
Maslow, Abraham, 203
Massacre of the Innocents, 200
Maya, 66, 114, 184
MDMA (ecstasy), 34, 265, 271
Mead, Margaret, 164
Menopause, 170
Mercury (planetary archetype), 39–41
Midas, 176, 177
Midheaven, transits to the, 288*n*5
Midlife transits, 67, 68, 72, 73
Midpoints, definition of, 18
Mill, John Stuart, 193
Milton, John, 185
Moon (planetary archetype), 38–39
   sessions during full moons, 225, 226, 249
   appreciation of moonlight after sessions, 86, 164
Maternal bloodlines, power of, 136, 164
Mother Teresa, 114
Mother, accessing experiences of in labor, 136, 177, 283*n*10
Mother Goddess, (*see* Great Mother Goddess)
Mother Nature, 82, 91, 148, 184, 214, 238, 282
Mount Olympus, 14, 158
Music, appreciation of, 168, 171, 228, 241, 242, 245, 246, 247, 248
   angelic, 170
   evocative, 63, 70, 168, 190, 241, 246
   serene, 87, 90, 93, 242
   rock, 246
Mystery religions, 2, 166, 278
   (*see also* Eleusis)

Narcissus, 92
Nature, 2, 5, 10, 31, 32, 48, 54, 61, 64
   destruction of, 43, 148, 277–279, 189
   (*see also* Ecological values and imperatives, Mother Nature)
Nazism, 123, 139, 188, 196

Near–death experiences (NDEs), 8
Neptune (planetary archetype), 19–21, 51–54, 58–61
Nietzsche, Friedrich, 128
Nin, Anaïs, 143, 167

Obsessive compulsive disorder, 34
Odysseus, 117, 244
Oedipus, 140
   Oedipal complex, 116, 197, 199, 182
   (*see also* Electra complex)
O'Neal, Rod, 281*n*7
Oppenheimer, Robert, 185
Optimism, archetypal sources of, 44, 96, 166, 217, 231, 243, 244, 252, 255
   overoptimism and inflation, 96, 176, 231, 243
Orbs of transits, 18–19, 179, 258, 264, 267, 274
   increased orbs for Saturn–Saturn transits, 61–62
Osiris, 13, 70, 117, 207
Other dimensions and universes, experience of, 214
Ouranos, 21, 50, 184
Ouroboros, 214
Out–of–body experiences (OOBEs), 8

Pain, 11, 13, 39, 43, 46, 48, 49, 61, 62, 103
   relief from chronic, 12
Paradigm shift, 9, 290*n*27
   anomalous phenomena requiring a, 8–9
   (*see also* Cosmology)
Paradise, existence in, 9, 19, 51, 80, 82, 98
Partners as sitters, 115–116, 120, 266–267, 285*n*3
Parvati, 14, 21, 85, 92, 135, 136, 164, 183
Passion of the Western Mind, The (Tarnas), 4, 61, 149, 287*n*1
Past–life experiences, 8, 159, 164, 199
Patriarchy, 104, 117, 136, 142, 143, 206, 220
   as the "5000–year birth canal of the Great Mother Goddess", 143
Persephone, 13, 70, 92, 148, 154, 163, 178
Pessimism, 112, 113
Phoenix, 205
Physical contact in the healing of deprivation issues, 64, 212, 234
   (*see also* Traumas of omission)

Plants, the consciousness of, 8, 70, 221–222
Plato, 2, 3
  Platonic Forms, 16, 60, 92, 154, 228, 232, 249, 281*n*4
  Neoplatonism, 3
Pluto (planetary archetype), 22–24, 54–56, 66–71
  reclassification as a dwarf planet, 284*n*13
Post–traumatic stress disorder (PTSD), 29, 271–272
Pressures, physical, 62
  (*see also* Pain, Tension)
Pribram, Karl, 5
Prigogine, Ilya, 5
Process room, 32
  (*see also* Intentional dance events)
Projections, psychological, 53, 68, 87, 107, 120, 133–134, 197, 242, 275
  importance of avoiding counter–projections, 181, 285*n*3
  of perinatal pressure or sense of catastrophe, 43, 47, 69, 88, 112, 114, 173, 177, 182, 184, 197, 242, 250, 272, 276
  on female sitters, 80, 110
  on feminists, 213
  on male sitters, 102, 122, 147, 197
  positive projections on sitters, 84, 153, 197, 219, 232
  romantic, 91
  value of Saturn in reducing projections, 106
Prometheus and Promethean impulses, 50, 51, 72, 73, 156, 159, 164, 193, 200, 285*n*19, 290*n*23
  (*see also* Ecstasy)
Prometheus the Awakener (Tarnas), 58, 95, 185, 201, 215, 240
Protectress archetype, 85
Providence, 98
Psilocybin mushrooms, 30, 32, 34, 207, 261
Psychedelic substances, 2, 5, 7, 26, 29–36
  contraindications (*see* Holotropic states)
  dosage of, 33–34
  as non–specific amplifiers of psychological processes, 30
  purity of, 34–35
  (*see also* Grof)

Punishing attitudes, psychological roots of, 106, 119, 120, 122, 186, 187
Purgatory, 13, 206
Pyrocatharsis, 12, 22, 148, 204

Quantum leaps, 175, 176, 178, 202, 217, 264
  (*see also* Science)

Racial and collective memories, and identification with various human groups, 8, 25, 84, 104, 136, 142, 159, 171, 178, 190, 232, 252–253
  phylogenetic memories, 66, 178
Rape, 120, 123, 142, 188, 189
  (*see also* Aggression)
Rebirth experiences, 1, 8, 11, 14–15, 24–25
  correlations with Uranus 15, 16, 24–25, 49–50
  obstetric features of, 12–13, 135, 157, 162–163, 177, 188, 206
  visual motifs in, 14, 169, 198, 223
Reddy, Helen, 236
Religions, emergence of new, 216
Repression, psychological, 50, 72, 174, 233, 285*n*18
Retraumatization, the issue of healing versus, 162
Revolution, 11, 14, 193, 199, 201, 202, 215
Rites of passage, 1, 67, 230, 278
Romanticism, 3, 216
Roosevelt, Eleanor, 100, 124, 227
Rubenesque fertility goddesses, 238
Rudhyar, Dane, 4

Sadomasochism,
  perinatal roots of, 11, 22, 123, 131, 141–142, 147, 152, 177, 188, 189, 204
  self–flagellation in religious sects, 11
Sallust, 254
Samadhi, 9
Samsara, 99
Santo Daime Church, 147, 262, 264
Sarton, May, 140
Saturn (planetary archetype), 21–22, 46–49, 61–66
Scatological experiences, 12, 13, 55, 134, 135, 148
  resolution of, 152–153
Schopenhauer, Arthur, 111

Schulz, Charles M., 235
Science, 3, 4, 5, 8, 40, 58, 277
  anomalous phenomena in, 8
  cosmic creative principle as ultimate
    scientist, 47
  limitations of Newtonian–Cartesian
    model, 8, 53
  quantum leaps in the history of, 175
Scott, Sir Walter, 251
Selfhood, sense of basic, 37, 55, 128, 156
  the archetype of the Self, 224
  Self–realization, 48, 73
  (see also Atman–Brahman unity)
Senex, 66
Set, varieties of in holotropic or
    psychedelic experiences,
  internalized, 31
  mystical, 32
  recreational, 32
  criminal, 32
Seth archetype, 117
Setting, in holotropic experiences, 31
Sexuality, 15, 24, 42, 54, 92–93, 116, 117,
    142, 143, 177, 246
  and aggression, 123, 130 (see also
    Sadomasochism),
  erotic emancipation, 13, 123, 142, 168,
    170, 173–174, 202
  oceanic sex, 92–93
Shakti, 54, 92, 95, 154, 184, 225, 247
Shamanism, 1, 33, 159, 208, 242,
    264–265, 278
Sheldrake, Rupert, 5
Shiva, 13, 54, 55, 68, 92, 95, 131, 135,
    136, 154, 184, 203, 214, 222
Sibling rivalry, 7, 107, 116
Sisyphus, 188
Soma, 207
Soul, 62, 84, 207
  and beauty, 41
  and the Moon, 38, 81–82, 106, 161, 234
  of nature, 86
  and Neptune, 52, 81–82, 87, 91,
    209–210
  soul–making, 209
  (see also Anima mundi, Soul mate)
Soul mate, the longing for a, 90
Spencer, Herbert, 290n31
Sphinx, the, 21, 136, 140
Spinoza, Baruch, 245

Spiritual emergency, 31, 34, 272,
    274, 285n2
Spiritual materialism, 96, 181
Spock, Dr. Benjamin, 237
Star Trek, 124, 191
Stelzner, Matthew, 246, 282n9
Sting, 78
Streett, Bill, 281–282n7
Suffocation and choking, traumatic effects
    of, 7, 35, 43, 102, 121, 123, 130,
    274, 283
  and sexual arousal, 11–12, 123, 130, 211
  (see also Autoerotic asphyxiation)
Sufism, 282n3
Sun (planetary archetype), 37–38
  appreciation of sunlight after sessions,
    81, 160
  the Divine or Cosmic Sun archetype, 21,
    80, 160, 233, 270
  the Sun Hero, 160
Superego, 122
Supracosmic or Metacosmic Void,
    identification or encounters with the,
    8, 52, 214, 215
Sutich, Anthony, 203
Swaddling, as causal factor in manic
    depression, 176, 275
Swift, Jonathan, 227
Synchronicity, 3, 8, 16, 17, 87, 89, 96, 165,
    200, 233

Taoism, 9, 44, 51, 86, 93, 278, 282n3
  (see also Lao Tzu)
Tarnas, Richard, 14
  and archetypal astrology, 4–5, 15–28
  and the birth of a new world view,
    281n4, 290n27
  collaboration with Stanislav Grof, 3–4
  correlation of astrology with the Basic
    Perinatal Matrices, 9–28
Tarot, 98
Tennyson, Alfred Lord, 114, 242
Tensions, physical, 35, 68, 69, 70, 73, 74,
    120, 121, 122, 139, 145, 156, 161,
    172, 177, 194–197, 239, 251
  dynamic tension exercises, 119, 124, 274
  release of nervous tension, 165, 166
  (see also Pain, Pressures)
Tezcatlipoca and Quetzalcoatl, 184
Thor, 146

Thoreau, Henry David, 216
Tinkerbell, 236
Toilet training, 7, 73, 107, 204
Townley, John, 245
Toxic–womb memories, 10, 53, 59, 79, 83, 91, 95, 97, 98, 109, 182, 209, 212, 213, 219
Tragedy, the archetype of, 195
Transits, definition of, 17–19
   (*see also* World transits, Orbs)
Transpersonal psychology, 5, 7–27, 53, 181, 203
Traumas, 7, 12, 13, 20, 39, 48, 63, 64, 70, 74
   of commission, 107, 116 (*see also* Encapsulation, Post–traumatic stress disorder)
   of omission, 107, 116, 262 (*see also* deprivation issues)
Triangle emotional situations, 168, 197
Trickster archetype, the, 27, 50, 167
Trollope, Anthony, 118
Trust and trust issues, 26, 28, 30–31, 33, 39, 42, 51, 53, 65, 88, 91, 97
Truth,
   the archetype of the True, 221, 232, 249
   and Jupiter, 45, 125
   and Neptune, 58, 78, 89
   and Uranus, 164, 166
Twain, Mark, 132, 164, 243

Umbilical crisis, 198
Underworld experiences, 70, 75, 84, 123, 128, 131, 132, 138, 144, 148, 154, 155, 163, 204, 209, 211
Universal Mind, the, 8, 17, 27, 37, 47, 61, 76, 89, 114, 127, 167, 290*n*27
Uranus, (planetary archetype), 24–25, 49–51, 71–76, 285*n*20
   as cosmic midwife, 76, 162

Vagina dentata, 193
Velvet revolution in consciousness, the, 222
Venus (planetary archetype), 41–42
   (*see also* Beauty)
Vicious spoiler archetype, 109, 124, 184
Virgin archetype, 92, 136, 164

Watts, Alan, 114
Webster, Daniel, 226
Wells, H. G., 149
Wharton, Edith, 137
Wilber, Ken, 5, 46
Wilde, Oscar, 180
Wilson, Bill, founder of Alcoholics Anonymous, 53
Winfrey, Oprah, 114
Wise Old Man archetype, 16, 104
Witch archetype, 137, 200
Witches' sabbath, 135
World transits,
   of Jupiter–Uranus, 175
   of Saturn–Pluto, 186
   of Uranus–Neptune, 216
   of Uranus–Pluto, 202

Yahweh, 21, 54, 104, 154
Yang energies, 18, 37, 78, 104, 225, 229, 246, 249–250
Yeats, W. B., 140
Yin energies, 18, 91, 141, 225, 226, 234, 246
Yin–yang balance, 18, 215, 225, 226, 246, 247
Yoga, 52, 95, 144, 278, 282*n*3
Yoni, 214, 247, 252

Zeus, 16, 50, 104, 146, 154, 200, 232, 239

Made in the USA
Lexington, KY
31 December 2015